This is an Amazing Book!

It is a Challenging & Empowering Read!

Would love to talk to you about it in the Fall —

Dr. George Lightning Vitsary

Wealth of Selves

NUMBER FOURTEEN:
Rio Grande/Río Bravo
Borderlands Culture and Traditions
NORMA E. CANTÚ
General Editor

Wealth of Selves

Multiple Identities
Mestiza Consciousness
AND THE
Subject of Politics

Edwina Barvosa

Texas A&M University Press
COLLEGE STATION

This paper meets the requirements
of ANSI/NISO z39.48-1992
(Permanence of Paper).
Binding materials have been chosen
for durability.

Library of Congress Cataloging-in-Publication Data

Barvosa, Edwina.
Wealth of selves : multiple identities, mestiza consciousness,
and the subject of politics / Edwina Barvosa. — 1st ed.
p. cm. — (Rio Grande/Río Bravo ; no. 14)
Includes bibliographical references and index.
ISBN-13: 978-1-60344-069-1 (cloth : alk. paper)
ISBN-10: 1-60344-069-0 (cloth : alk. paper)
1. Pluralism (Social sciences)—Political aspects. 2. Identity
(Philosophical concept)—Political aspects. 3. Pluralism (Social
sciences)—Psychological aspects. 4. Hispanic Americans—Ethnic
identity. I. Title. II. Title: Multiple identities, mestiza
consciousness, and the subject of politics. III. Series.
HM1271.B377 2008
305.868'07301—dc22
2008014709

Contents

Acknowledgments

This book has undergone a half-dozen major iterations over the past ten years, and I am deeply indebted to many people who discussed the idea of multiple identities with me at various times. Comments from others that may have seemed slight to them nonetheless made vital contributions to the twists and turns that this project has taken over the past decade. I am grateful for those insights, without which this project would remain as yet unfinished.

In particular, I would like to thank Seyla Benhabib, who directed this project as my doctoral dissertation at Harvard University and who encouraged me to address issues in contemporary political philosophy, feminism, and moral philosophy. Richard Tuck and John B. Thompson directed me as a graduate student at Jesus College, Cambridge; and later Richard Tuck also supervised this project at Harvard. From these scholars I gained my background in intellectual history, social theory, and political philosophy, as well as a sensibility for the interconnections between these endeavors and for interdisciplinary work in general. Both John and Richard have continued to mentor and support me over the years, and I am deeply indebted to them both.

As an academic border-crosser working in a number of different scholarly fields, I am fortunate to have people to thank in a variety of different academic circles. Thanks to Mala Htun, Jennifer Pitts, and Jill Frank for reading very early chapters of this work before we left Boston for different destinations. Among my colleagues at University of California, Santa Barbara in Chicana/o Studies and other disciplines, I am grateful for insights on this project from Howard Winant, Paul Spickard, Barbara Herr-Harthorn, Jonathan Inda, and Ralph Armbruster-Sandoval. Among the circle of scholars who are working on U.S. Latina/o politics and associated with the Latina/o Caucus of the American Political Science Association, many took the time to talk with me about the racial and ethnic dimensions of multiple identities at different times over the years. Most importantly, they have also given me a community with unwavering support of my research and work as a Latina scholar. Among them I'd especially like to thank John A. Garcia, Luis Fraga, Manny Avalos, John Bretting, Lisa García Bedolla, Cristina Beltran, Anna Sampaio, Michael Jones-Correa, Ron and Rosemary Schmidt, Gary Segura, and Val Martinez-Ebers. I would also like to thank Ray Rocco and Otto

ix

Santa Ana at UCLA for reading the manuscript and for offering me both insightful comments and warm encouragement.

In addition to these many contributors, four scholars in different disciplines and fields gave me feedback or other guidance that redirected this project in fruitful ways when I had reached sticking points. Renaldo Macías refined and informed my thinking on co-construction of self in context. Tracy Strong drew my attention to Amélie Oksenberg Rorty's writings on akrasia and self-deception that now have a pivotal place in this work. Peter Hall helped me to see early on the variations between my account of multiple identities and the one within American pluralist thought. Finally, Howard Giles deepened my sense of the relevance of Social Identity Theory to our understanding of identity. I'm grateful to all four of these men for drawing my attention to ideas that have very much shaped this project.

For financial reasons my toehold in the academy was slight throughout my student years. I owe many thanks to those professors who encouraged me through the most difficult times when I was inclined to leave school and go to work to better support my family. Thanks especially to Martha Andresen, Leo Flynn, and Elizabeth Creighton at Pomona College. Mark Kishlansky at Harvard helped me during a period of homelessness when I certainly would have otherwise left the academy; I thank him for his generous mentorship and for showing me some of the hidden ropes of the academy. Funding agencies also made an enormous difference. The Ford Foundation Minority Fellowship funded my graduate studies at Cambridge as well as my postdoctoral work with Reynaldo Macías at UCLA. Thanks to Chris O'Brien for her many years of encouragement and support. In my time at U.C. Santa Barbara this project was also supported at different times by U.C. Regents' Junior Faculty Fellowship and by grants from the Institute for Social, Behavioral, and Economic Research, the Center for Chicano Studies, and the University of California, Santa Barbara. These grants funded my research assistants who provided me with invaluable support in collecting the materials for this project. Thanks to Francisco Castillo, Megan Albrandt, Fernando Ramirez, Javier Angulo, Karen Castro, Richard Huizar, and Diane Mercado for their work on earlier versions. Warm thanks to Raquel Arreola for her hard work and comments on the next to final version, and very special thanks to Kathleen Maloney for her extremely hard work, as well as her insight and energy in the long final stage of this project. Without Kathleen and the efforts of these students this work could not have been completed.

xi ACKNOWLEDGMENTS

I am extraordinarily blessed with family and friends who have provided me with conversation and encouragement during this project. A first-generation college student, my family—Mexican American on one side and German American on the other—has been incredibly supportive and encouraging of this project over the years. If my kinfolk secretly wondered if I would ever finish this book, they never let on. My parents, Eduardo and Pamela Barvosa, read and critically commented on my doctoral dissertation as well as on three chapters of this last iteration. Hailing from the Texas-Mexico borderlands, my parents' border perspectives have not only formed me, but also been an invaluable resource in this project—I'm especially grateful for our ongoing conversation about the type of self-integration that personal integrity requires. Thanks also to my brother Edward and his family, as well as Ruth Harvey, Elizabeth Montalbano, and Heidi and Jo Jo Garcia for their warm encouragement and support.

In addition to my family, my friends have talked with me about the course of this project and provided both insight and encouragement for many years. Thanks to Toni Taylor and Jana Renner for many hours of conversation and care, and for confirming that ordinary knowledge is much more effective and wise than anything philosophers can produce. Barbara Herr-Harthorn and Natalie Schonfeld talked with me about this project often over the years, and always encouraged me to put my ideas forward when I most needed help. Cheryl-Ann Michael and P. E. Digeser read and reread chapters at various stages, offering both critical commentary and warm encouragement; words can't convey my gratitude for their friendship and spirit in my life. Thanks also to Lara Plattner and Dee Langford for their faith in me, and to my friend and former husband Bill Carter for his enthusiastic support and for many dinner hours spent discussing identity. Thanks as well to my friend Adam D. Hanna and to Juan Vicente Palerm—a friend and far more seasoned writer than I am who wisely counseled me to finally let this project go and to turn my attention to others. Many thanks also to Mary Lenn Dixon for her strong and enthusiastic support of this project; I've learned so much from her. Many thanks to Thom Lemmons for his expert wordcraft. And at last my deepest thanks to Paige Urban, whose loving friendship has inspired so much of this work. I hope that this book does justice to the contributions of all who have played a part. All errors and omissions that the following pages may contain remain my own.

Santa Barbara
November 2008

Wealth of Selves

Introduction

Some say philosophy is the love of wisdom—and that love is erotic. Others say philosophy is like private investigation. It is the search for clues to knowledge about aspects of life that we do not yet fully understand. In *political* philosophy there is truth in both of these descriptions.[1] Consequently, this book is a kind of philosophical mystery tale. It is a passionate search for wisdom about an often-overlooked aspect of our selves that has personal and political consequences for us every day. But thanks to mystery writers like Agatha Christie and Raymond Chandler, private investigation is much more familiar to us than political philosophy. So true is this, that the similarities in the practice of each remain unclear. When Humphrey Bogart portrayed Raymond Chandler's Phillip Marlowe in *The Big Sleep* for example, Marlowe's new client General Sternwood asked Marlow to describe himself. Bogart gamely replied, "There isn't much to tell. I'm 38. I went to college. I can still speak English when my business demands it."[2] As a political philosopher, I am not much different from Marlowe. I'm 38. I went to college. And like other philosophers with degrees from Harvard or Cambridge, I can use the "specialized language" common to our profession. But like Marlowe, I can still speak English when my job demands it. This will be one of those times.

I introduce myself and the mystery at the heart of this book to you directly in the hope of interesting you in exploring the multiple identities that you—that all of us—generally have. Already in one short paragraph, my words may have brought to your mind alternately your sexual identity, your professional identity, and if you have one, your identity as a movie or mystery buff. When reading the words "our" profession you may have felt excluded from this book's intended audience if you are not a professional scholar. You might have felt especially included if you are. You probably oriented yourself to me in terms of your age or education. And you likely estimated me measured in part by whatever age happens to mean to you. Each of these multiple identities—sexual, generational, laboring, subcultural—and others you undoubtedly have, each represent in you a distinct, but also linked, way of thinking and acting in the world that exists as an integral part of you. By awakening and even manipulating these multiple identities as I have, my aim is not to sell or to persuade you. Instead, my goal is to suggest that the clues to the character and political implications of multiple identities already lie in each of us.

The Backstory

For the most part however, we are not used to thinking of ourselves as having multiple identities. This is primarily a function of how prevailing ideas of the self and identity have developed over time. Philosophical notions of the self emerged among the ancient Greeks who understood the self principally in terms of the soul.[3] Throughout the Middle Ages the idea of the self as soul became intertwined with debates over religious questions, such as the soul's potential continuation in an after life. Medieval interest in the self thus tended to focus on the idea of "individuation"—or how one soul could be seen as different and unique from another. As the medieval period morphed into the early modern, philosopher René Descartes argued that evidence for the immaterial soul could be found in conscious thought as consciousness encounters and recognizes the soul as independent of the material body.[4]

Because of this early emphasis on the soul and individuation, the idea of personal identity as we think of it today did not emerge until the seventeenth century. At that time, philosopher John Locke turned his attention away from individuation to the problem of what accounts for "personal identity"—i.e., the continuing sameness of the self over time—despite the self's changeability. Locke's answer to the problem of self-sameness despite change is that consciousness *itself* creates personal identity by being fully self-knowing. For Locke, self-knowing consciousness creates connections among its past and present thoughts and actions and builds from those connections a comprehensive and single *unitary identity* with continuity over time. Locke further argued that such a unitary identity was a *necessary* basis for critical reason and for individual moral and political *agency*—i.e. the capacity to choose—and in turn for legal responsibility.[5] Locke's idea of a unitary personal identity as the essential basis for reason and agency has been enormously influential in the West, where the unitary self is still often associated with individualism and freedom in liberal democracy. As such, the idea of a unitary self continues to have currency today among our common sense notions of the self.

Further still, the Lockean ideal of a unitary self gained additional momentum in the eighteenth century from the quite different but equally influential philosophical work of Immanuel Kant. Unlike Locke, Kant was not solely interested in the empirical, experience-derived dimensions of identity, although he did acknowledge the importance of the empirical self.[6] Instead, Kant was primarily interested in understanding the human capacity for independent thought, thought that could be considered as prior to and independent of the influence of any social experience. Kant called this presocial reasoner a "pure" or "transcendental self." For him, the unity of transcendental self-consciousness is the necessary source of human thought and reason. In one of his later essays, Kant defined Enlightenment as the mature "use of one's own understanding without the guidance of another."[7] Thus, while Locke and Kant were concerned with different dimensions of the self in terms of self-conscious experience, both claimed that a unitary quality of the self was the necessary ground for conscious thought and, in turn, for moral and/or political choice (*agency*), self-guided thought (*autonomy*), and responsible freedom. Kant's account of the self shaped much of Enlightenment thought, which in turn shaped Western modernity, including modernity's legacies of colonialism and empire, scientific progress, rationalism, and individualism. In short, for at least four centuries, Western philosophers have held that a unitary quality of the self is a necessary basis for independent thought, responsible action, and freedom.

Although the Western philosophical tradition has been dominated by the idea of a unitary self, a second less influential tradition also developed in which thinkers regarded the self as characterized by multiplicity. Philosopher David Hume began this secondary tradition of thought in the eighteenth century when he disagreed with Descartes' view that inner thought could reveal the soul. Hume argued that inner consciousness involved only a rapidly flowing multiplicity or "bundle" of disconnected perceptions. Hume contended that although this multiplicity of perceptions is unruly and diffuse, human beings have a natural tendency to ascribe connection and identity to those multiple perceptions. We imagine our disconnected array of perceptions to have a oneness that defines our identity. For Hume our personal identity is thus merely the imagined connections between our multiple—and otherwise radically disconnected—perceptions.[8]

In the late nineteenth and early twentieth centuries, however, the founding psychologist and philosopher William James challenged Hume's bundle theory of the self and offered an alternative account of its multiplicity that explicitly discussed multiple identities. James famously wrote, "[g]enerally speaking, *a man has as many social selves as there are individuals who recognize him. . . .* we may practically say that he has as many different social selves as there are distinct *groups* of persons about whose opinion he cares. He generally shows a different side of himself to these different groups."[9] As will be discussed in chapter four, William James thought much more than our imagination linked our multiple identities. Rather, he argued that our multiple identities are held together by our raw cognitive capacity and complex momentary workings of the mind.

William James's account of the self influenced early pluralist thought in the United States and contributed directly to what would become the first of three waves of liberal pluralism. With James in mind, early political pluralists regarded "the subject of politics"— i.e. the conscious embodied selfhood of the potential participant in democratic politics—as having multiple identities derived from multiple group memberships.[10] Early twentieth century pluralists related these multiple identities to democratic politics by reasoning that in a diverse democracy, a citizen's multiple identities and their associated political commitments were formed by the plurality of politically significant groups to which the subject belonged. As pluralism evolved in the post-War era, second wave pluralists continued to emphasize the multiple identities and group affiliations of political subjects/selves. However, post-War pluralists also began to focus on how multiple identities could confer internal contradictions on subjects, if and when their various group identities and commitments were in tension or contradiction. From this idea that political subjects may have contradictory commitments and identifications, political scientist Robert Dahl formulated the notion of "cross-cutting cleavages," with which he characterized the United States' political terrain as cohesive, as well as fluid and shifting, because a citizen's multiple identities and group memberships could foster that citizen's participation in different issue constituencies at different times. Thus instead of a democracy's diversity producing destabilization and polarization along static factions or "reinforcing cleavages," the political fluidity made possible by multiple and contradictory identities could actually result in greater democratic cohesion.[11]

Yet, as philosophers have noted, while first and second wave pluralism regarded the self as having multiple identities, early pluralists narrowed that multiplicity to a single identity in the actual moment of political choice. Early pluralism channeled political decision making by the multiple subject into institutional mechanisms and constituency formations that could incorporate the influence of only *one* identity perspective at a time, not multiple contradictory perspectives.[12] With only one of many identities contributing to reasoning and choice, multiple identities have little role in political thought and decision-making in first and second wave pluralist accounts. In contrast, later third wave pluralists have better attended to the potential influence of multiple identities on reasoning in democratic politics, but have done so abstractly, without proposing a detailed account of multiple identities and how they may shape political thought.[13]

Finally, also within this second tradition of thought are early Critical Theorists Max Horkheimer and Theodor Adorno, as well as founding psychoanalyst Sigmund Freud. These thinkers endorsed some aspects of Enlightenment thought, but rejected and sought to modify others—especially Kant's account of the transcendental unity of the self. Horkheimer and Adorno argued that the idea of unitary self and Enlightenment reason—typified for them by Kant's philosophy—foisted onto nature and the self a false unitary quality. That false unity privileged a form of "instrumental" reason that, in turn, concealed and rejected the Otherness within the self and among ourselves.[14] For Horkheimer and Adorno, Kant's unitary account of the subject and the hostility toward difference and Otherness at the heart of Enlightenment reason, resulted in the destructive degradation of nature, and the brands of genocidal *unreason* seen in the moral atrocities of European imperialism and later the Holocaust.[15] Wishing to prevent the horrors produced by instrumental reason and the homogenizing biases associated with the unitary subject, Adorno proposed that if the self could be understood as decentered and multiple, Enlightenment reason could be diversified and its destructive tendencies changed. As some critical theorists have pointed out, however, Adorno did not complete this project of rethinking the self as multiple and diversifying its available forms of reason. In particular Adorno did not theorize how the multiplicity of elements within the self might be organized, or how inner contradiction might contribute to or detract from alternative forms of critical thought.[16]

Horkheimer and Adorno regarded their rejection of the unitary subject as akin to Sigmund Freud's psychoanalytic critique of the unitary subject. Freud, like Horkheimer and Adorno, remained committed to various aspects of the Enlightenment project even as he rejected the Kantian conception of a unitary subject.[17] Freud's theory of the Unconscious divided the Self into the Conscious and Unconscious and differentiated the self into the Ego, Id, and Superego. This differentiation rejects the idea that the subject is centered by a single, fully self-conscious, self-transparent, or self-defining identity and ego that had been advocated by Locke, and in a quite different way by Kant. In short, Freud "decentered" the self by theorizing it as fundamentally divided in character.[18]

The Death of the Unitary Subject

Eventually, the differences in these two strands of the Western philosophical tradition[19]—one strand advancing a unitary subject, the other advocating a multiple subject—might have been reconciled in the normal course of philosophical debate.[20] But the chance for that quiet reconciliation vanished rapidly sometime in the 1980s with the widely reported death of the unitary subject. While the assassin remains untraceable, the instrument of death—the philosophical shift known as "the linguistic turn"—is evident. Like other monumental shifts in thinking, this mid-twentieth century turning-to-language was slow in coming, but virtually Copernican in its consequences for how we see the self and social life. Initiated by Ludwig Wittgenstein, the linguistic turn introduced the notion that the meanings of concepts, social practices, and the qualities of human "nature" and identity are not essential, necessary, or unchanging. Rather these dimensions are "socially constructed"—in and through the language-mediated processes of social life. Concepts, practices, and the qualities of the self are produced, reproduced, and/or iteratively transformed through our everyday language and speech, *as well as* through material processes that necessarily involve language in various ways.

Thinkers in different domains of thought have developed our now-prevailing notions of social construction. In ordinary language philosophy, Ludwig Wittgenstein conceived of social life as made up of "language games" that exist on the basis of transformable social convention. Continental philosophers such as Michel Foucault and Jacques Derrida have written of discourses that construct attitudes and desires and the analytical practices that could deconstruct those linguistic constructions. Constructivist anthropologists and sociologists have described how social groups and group identity came to be understood as the products of language, and of linguistic approximations that gather diversity within group boundaries—boundaries that are set and continually reset through symbols and signs.[21]

This turn to language as constitutive of all self and society meant that accounts of the unitary subject that regarded the self, personal identity, and/or some core or unifying dimension of the self as existing independent of social influence were inherently flawed. The unitary self was now dead. But with that self's demise, the notions of self-guided thought, autonomy, freedom, and agency that had been associated with the unitary subject for centuries seemed also given up. Not surprisingly, the magnitude of the academic uproar that followed this sudden shift was proportional to the enormity of perceived loss. As one scholar put it, the peculiar "intensity of rejection" of the death of the subject seemed to be rooted in our difficulty in "resisting the unselfconscious assumption that we are 'selves' . . . beyond the socially constructed personae . . . something 'prelinguistic' finally that makes sense of our very polymorphousness."[22] This writer further proclaimed that politically the new constructivist way of thinking would only produce political paralysis in that the socially constructed subject is "politically enervating. . . . [and] for effecting or even theorizing social *change* it is useless."[23] Thus a new problem of individuation—one slightly different from the medieval version—now emerged. How was the socially constructed subject to be understood as distinct from the language that forged it? How could it choose for itself when its very ways of thinking came from social forces that originated beyond it?[24] How could critical thought ensue without an independent Lockean or Kantian unitary subject?

But destabilized selves are resilient, and philosophers are no different. Before long new books appeared discussing what would emerge from the loss of the unitary subject. Titles included *After Identity* and *Who Comes After the Subject?*[25] Some noted that while the unitary subject had passed, we now seemed to talk about the self, identity, and our multiple identities more than ever. As Ernesto Laclau put it in the later 1990s, "there is today a lot of talk about social, ethnic, national and political identities. The 'death of the subject,' which was proudly proclaimed *urbi et orbi* not so long ago, has been succeeded by a new and widespread interest in the multiple identities that are emerging and proliferating in our contemporary world."[26] Signs that there were multiple identities *within* people as well as *among* them also began to multiply. Some political scientists—particularly those in comparative politics and area studies—began to point to how those living in multilingual and multiethnic political regimes had multiple identities, and how their shifting back and forth among different group identities influenced the politics in various regions including the Caribbean, the former Soviet Republics, Northern Ireland, and sub-Saharan Africa.[27]

In addition, as discussion of multiple identities increased in political science research, bookshelves in the United States became laden with autobiographies of people describing their lives in terms of shifting among their various identities, in ways similar to those discussed by William James. Rebecca Walker—the daughter of famed novelist Alice Walker—for example, writes of her multiple racial identities in *Black, White, and Jewish: Autobiography of a Shifting Self.* Marie Arana, an editor at the *Washington Post,* describes living her multiple ethnic identities in her memoir *American Chica: Two Worlds, One Childhood*. In *My Sense of Silence,* Lennard Davis, who is the hearing son of deaf parents, describes his identities as both hearing and deaf, and his life in both social worlds. In the collection of autobiographical essays entitled *Twice Blessed,* Jewish writers recount their lives as gay and lesbian Jews who have in various ways—sometimes in secrecy—attempted to live their Jewish and gay lives among others who reject their particular combination of sexual and religious identities. And in the historical narrative-cum-memoir *Transgender Warriors,* Leslie Feinberg describes her life as a woman, a man, and a transgender person, who navigates her multiple gender identifications in often-resistant social realms.[28]

As other scholars have noted, the greater visibility of the idea of multiple identities in political and social life has urged researchers to make "a variety of calls, particularly among some political scientists, to recognize and make political provision for the multiple identities that we all have."[29] Within political science and political theory scholarly debates have emerged over the political implications of multiple identities—especially with regard to producing social cohesion in settings of diversity and conflict. Perspectives run the gamut from those who regard multiple identities as a positive factor that will help smooth societal conflicts, to those who take the opposing view that multiple identities will inevitably foster political polarization and undermine stable democracies.

Among those who consider multiple identities likely to have positive effects, some claim that multiple identities can be an important basis for making liberal democracies more inclusive and may be a necessary basis for making individuals capable of democratic citizenship in an age of diversity and globalization.[30] Others have suggested that multiple identities are an important dimension for resisting gender subordination and building progressive political coalitions.[31] Still others see the interconnections—or intersections—among multiple identities as a key to fostering agency and autonomy among subordinated groups, and which may be useful as a basis for progressive labor organizing.[32]

More neutral assessments of the political implications of multiple identities within political science have come in the subfield of American politics, and especially in U.S. racial and ethnic politics, and some political sociology. For example, multiple identities have been regarded as a tool for understanding landmark developments in Latina/o politics in 1970s Chicago, and as a factor in ethnic political mobilization.[33] In law and jurisprudence, multiple identities and theories of how those multiple identities intersect have been pivotal in critical race theory analysis of violence against women of color.[34] Within third wave pluralist democratic theory, multiple identities have been seen as important to understanding new forms of democratic organizing and new possibilities for crafting political decision-making from a variety of perspectives.[35] Multiple identities have also been used to describe the dynamics of Asian American politics, and employed in articulating intersecting forms of Chicano and Latino subordination and feminist responses to that subordination.[36]

On the other side of the spectrum, however, other scholars have considered the political implications of multiple identities to be negative. Some, such as communitarian philosopher Alasdair MacIntyre, see decentered and multiple social identities as undermining moral and political judgment and as potentially conducive to fascist political reasoning.[37] Others—including many who favor rapid monocultural assimilation by immigrants—regard some configurations of multiple identities, especially multiple *national* identities, as leading to nation-state dissolution and potentially to political chaos.[38] Still others, like Samuel Huntington, regard Americans who have multiple *ethnic* identities as contributing to the steady demise of U.S. national identity and to increasing political polarization within the United States.[39]

The State of the Investigation

But to debate the political effects of multiple identities without having a full sense of what multiple identities are, is arguably to get ahead of the question. And herein lies the mystery of this philosophical investigation. For while inquiry and debate have already begun as to the political consequences of multiple identities, with very few exceptions contributors to that debate have depended largely on brief and sketchy accounts of what we mean when we refer to multiple identities. In a typical approach, for example, one political theorist, argues that decentered subjects "have the power to energize their social democracies" by forwarding "claims of justice, fairness, fidelity, and ethicality on behalf of those [to whom] social democratic regimes tend to be deaf"—yet describes decentered subjects in less than a paragraph.[40] As a prior issue then, a mysterious question is still with us: what are the practical and philosophical characteristics of multiple identities? This mystery can be investigated as two interrelated questions. First, how does a multiple, socially constructed, and embodied consciousness bring together divergent and even contradictory senses of self into a cohesive and socially functioning whole? What relationship does that diverse but cohesive whole have to political reason or critical thinking? Second, what relationship does subjectivity with multiple and decentered identities have to political life?

This second question—what relationship does the socially constructed subject have to political life—is an enormous one, however, and one that immediately raises at least two other related questions. First, how, if at all, can the multiple and socially constructed subject be considered capable of free choice? And second, how does the socially constructed subject stand in relationship to the powers of social construction held by political institutions? Both of these questions are themselves worthy of book length investigation, and are far beyond the scope of any project that also seeks to deeply investigate the character of multiple identities. Fortunately, therefore, for this investigation, two other works already address these two intersecting questions.[41]

In her important book *The Subject of Liberty*, Nancy Hirschmann addresses the first related question by presenting a theory of freedom for the socially constructed subject. She applies that framework to issues relevant to contemporary patriarchy as well as intersecting forms of racial, ethnic, class, religious and sexual subordination. Given the scope of her own project, however, Hirschmann reasonably does not offer a sustained account of a decentered and multiple subject. Instead, she explores and theorizes freedom considering the desires that are commonly constructed as parts of female subjectivities, as well as the constructed social barriers within which women make choices. Thus, the task remains to offer a detailed account of multiple subjectivity and to explore how different configurations of multiple identities can foster or inhibit critical thinking. Such an investigation would provide needed theoretical background to the constructivist theory of freedom Hirschmann has proposed.

In addition to the question of freedom, is the second related question of the state's role in shaping the identities of its citizens. Various traditions in political thought have taken different positions on this question. Some have argued that liberal regimes can and should engage in crafting the self. Others have contended that such selfcraft should be avoided on liberal political principles. The socially constructed quality of multiple identities and decentered subjectivity in general brings this question to the foreground. Liberal and illiberal states are clearly among the factors that construct the self, and they may do so with a variety of political means and objectives. How then is the state's role in self-making to be evaluated? P. E. Digeser addresses this second question with regard to liberal democratic states in *Our*

Politics, Our Selves?: Liberalism, Identity, and Harm. In this analysis of the relevant competing perspectives, including constructivist and communitarian critiques of liberalism and the unitary subject Digeser carefully weighs the advantages and harms of each approach and offers a compelling argument that liberal democracies have qualified permission—neither an obligation yet nor a prohibition—to engage in selfcraft for various political ends.[42] What remains is to look at the relationship of selfcraft to political aims—this time not from the perspective of the state, but from the perspective of the subject and how selfcraft may proceed from the subject's own agency. Thus, in the later chapters of this book, I investigate the relationship of selfcraft of multiple identities to politics.

With the philosophical investigations of Hirschmann and Digeser, the two questions that intersect most pressingly with the mystery of multiple identities have already been well addressed. The remaining mystery, then, is how it is possible for the self to be at once diverse and self-contradictory in its identities, and yet also a cohesive whole capable of shifting its social identifications from context to context. In addition, because Digeser and Hirschmann have already incorporated feminist and liberal perspectives at length in this general topic area, I would argue that the contributions of feminists and liberal pluralists have been well considered. However, the perspectives of two other groups of investigators on multiple identities—neoclassic assimilationists and communitarians—could beneficially be considered in additional detail.

As is discussed at length in chapter one, some scholars—who I'll refer to as neoclassic assimilationists—have revived the classic assimilationist arguments of the 1950s and 1960s, united them with more current insights into identity formation, and then applied these outlooks to contemporary political circumstances. In considering U.S. democracy through such a framework, Samuel Huntington contends that multiple identities divide the self and one's loyalties and commitments and may consequently destabilize U.S. democracy. Huntington's proposed solution is that political subjects must toss out—i.e. sublimate—all identities that are not compatible and consistent with a single unitary identity as an "American." On this view, whatever multiple identities are, they cannot be productively sustained in collective political life and must be reformed into a unitary self more fit for politics.

A second approach comes from communitarian philosophers such as Charles Taylor and Alasdair MacIntyre, both of whom have acknowledged that multiple identities exist within most selves. In different ways, however, both contend that unifying self-narratives can and should bring an ordered and a more or less *re*centered quality to that multiplicity. On this communitarian view the diverse identities of the self can be politically and personally detrimental unless they are rendered mutually consistent and compatible. Thus, for the benefit of self and politics, self-narratives can and should bring a stable order to the multiplicity of the self.[43]

Neither neoclassic assimilationists nor communitarians have systematically explored the character of multiple identities however. In contrast, in the investigation that follows I offer a detailed theoretical account of multiple identities. Moreover, unlike the approaches of communitarians and neoclassic assimilationists, this account of multiple identities does not lead to the conclusion that all contradictory elements within the self must be banished or that the multiplicity of the self must be somehow recentered. Rather, this investigation leads directly to forms of self-integration that can accommodate contradiction and inconsistency in ways that are potentially politically fruitful.

Methods and Aims

Any investigator who tackles a mystery—philosophical or otherwise—must decide where to begin and how to proceed. When Lauren Bacall confronts Humphrey Bogart's Marlowe in *The Big Sleep*, interrogating him as to what his first step will be, he sidesteps her veiled intrusion with the quip, "Oh, the usual one." When she retorts "I didn't know there was a usual one," he evades her probing again with the wisecrack, "Oh, sure there is. It comes complete with diagrams on page 47 of 'How to be a Detective in Ten Easy Lessons'—correspondence school textbook, and uh, your father offered me a drink . . . "[44] Of course there is no such textbook, and neither private investigation, nor the passionate pursuit of wisdom are simple or formulaic in their methods and means. Marlowe's catch-as-catch-can approach includes scholarly research, impersonating a nerdy bibliophile, chasing ultimately false leads, suffering defeats, and hailing breakthroughs, all in the pursuit of information. In the end, some parts of Marlowe's mystery remain unsolved. But in the process he pieces together enough information to give as plausible an explanation to his mystery as he can.

The similarities between my method and Marlowe's are more similar than it may be wise to admit. Moreover, the mystery undertaken here is centuries old. I do not claim to have solved every aspect of it—rather my aim is simply to offer for discussion as plausible an explanation as I can. To do so, I've approached the mystery of the character and consequences of multiple identities as a *problem-driven interdisciplinary study*. Why an interdisciplinary investigation? As Wendy Brown has argued, some scholarly problems in political philosophy—particularly problems with practical political implications—require an interdisciplinary approach.[45] In my view, the problem of the philosophical character and political implications of multiple identities falls into this category.

Simply put, no single disciplinary approach has had all of the clues needed to solve the mystery of how the multiply constructed self can be at once diverse, decentered, and changing, as well as cohesive and whole. In social psychology, for example, Social Identity Theory has developed a working framework of multiple identities that regards identity contradiction as something that is present but which goes largely unfelt by individuals, thus rendering those identity contradictions insignificant. In contrast, in borderland studies, racial and ethnic studies, and postcolonial studies, emphasis has been placed on identity contradiction, its felt effects, and how the source of felt identity contradiction is often political conflict. What relationship potentially exits between these diametrically opposed approaches? Could they each offer clues to understanding different aspects of multiple identities? Feminist thought, for instance, has consistently emphasized the embodied quality of the subject. Yet, feminists have seldom connected the character of embodiment to biosocial processes of interpretation as neurobiologists have done. Philosophers have theorized self-integration and stressed the risks of dissociated identities, but have not sought out the character of dissociative disorders as clinical psychologists have in order to develop an informed contrast and comparison between integrated, fragmented, and dissociated identities.[46] Postcolonial theory has offered useful accounts of identity hybridity, but seldom grounded that theoretical work in detailed studies of the construction of ethnic group identities such as those found in anthropology, sociology, or cross-cultural psychology.[47]

In short, while many different disciplines have developed important clues to the character of multiple identities, none have amassed enough clues to fully solve the puzzle of how a decentered and multiple subjectivity can unite fluid multiplicity and contradiction with cohesion and similarity over time. This investigation has thus required turning to many different disciplines for insight, including political science and political theory, philosophy, racial and ethnic studies, borderland studies, psychoanalysis, anthropology, sociology, postcolonial theory, feminist theory, and within psychology broadly, social psychology—especially Social Identity Theory—clinical psychology, neuropsychology, and cross-cultural psychology.[48]

While this inquiry has been strongly influenced by works in psychology—especially by the work of William James and the Social Identity Theory originated by Henry Tajfel—every interdisciplinary investigation must also have some knowledge base upon which it fundamentally relies. Thus, while this interdisciplinary inquiry draws clues from many sources, it is principally grounded in major disciplinary influences within political and social theory. The first of these influences is the work by Gloria Anzaldúa, Jane Flax, and Amélie Oksenberg Rorty. For various reasons, I consider all three of these thinkers as engaged in political theory, but also in *borderlands thought*. All three thinkers grapple with the issue of inner diversity and inner contradiction—the borderlands within us—in relationship to critical thought, choice, and action. In addition, like other "border dwellers," Anzaldúa and Flax both bring multiple personal and/or professional perspectives to their philosophical writing. Moreover, both Anzaldúa and Flax look to political life and its social borders and boundaries as the source of multiple identities. Both see identity contradictions as having positive possibilities alongside their negative aspects and their sometimes unruly quality. The influence of these three women thinkers on this project has been profound, and can be felt throughout the following pages. Secondly, this investigation takes its general cues and general approach from the concerns and possibilities raised by the early Critical Theory of the Frankfurt School and its critiques of the Enlightenment subject, especially Adorno's claim that the hazards of instrumental reason might be reduced by reconceiving the subject as multiple rather than unitary.

In the chapters that follow, I investigate the mystery of multiple identities, focusing primarily on the character of multiple identities. In the course of that inquiry, I piece together a number of different clues to build a theoretical framework of multiple identities—how they are formed, manifest, and are interrelated. This theory of multiple identities can be seen more broadly as a philosophical account of the decentered and multiple subject. In the course of sketching this account of multiple identities from many disciplinary sources, I also offer a number of component concepts, categories, and typologies that can potentially forward our understanding of multiple identities. These include an expanded theoretical account of intersectionality—i.e. the interconnections among different identities—and a theory of how identity contradictions relate to the fragmentation or integration of multiple identities and to critical reasoning. I also include a two-tiered account of embodied personal identity that builds on William James's approach, by adding insights from the linguistic turn that took place after William James's death. With this account of personal identity in mind, the following investigation also offers a typology of identity contradiction, explores the links between identity contradictions, self-fragmentation, self-integration and political life, and proposes a three-part conception of selfcraft and self-integration. Finally, the investigation offers concepts that underscore the significance of multiple identities for racial, ethnic and other group conflicts in contemporary regimes, and thereby also generates conclusions about how multiple identities relate to democratic politics.

While this philosophical work aims to accomplish this list of tasks, as a piece of scholarly inquiry it also has its limitations. First among these limits is that this book *does not delve* exhaustively into the debates regarding the self and subjectivity in any one academic discipline, including political philosophy. By its nature, problem-driven interdisciplinary research does not seek to engage in the standing debates in any discipline, but instead seeks to draw upon the resources of many disciplines to address a mystery of pan-disciplinary concern. Tackling a problem from diverse scholarly perspectives requires choosing to engage with only those disciplinary materials that are most relevant to addressing the problem at hand. The drawback to this is that interdisciplinary work of this kind will seldom satisfy a taste for canvassing the debates *within* individual disciplines.

Thus, the interdisciplinary method adopted in this inquiry has both advantages and disadvantages. The disadvantages arise not only from the limitations of its necessarily broad scope, but also from the fact that interdisciplinary study remains something of a scholarly stepchild. As scholars we welcome interdisciplinarity in principle, but when faced with its reality, warming to it can be a challenge. This is understandable. By virtue of their ends interdisciplinary studies take off into realms of scholarship beyond our formal training, presenting immediate challenges to accessibility and easy assessment. If the jargon that operates among the subfields of a single discipline can hinder scholarly communication, then the difference in terms and jargon *across* disciplinary divides can make reading scholarship out of one's field an onerous task. Moreover, while some scholars have rightly argued that interdisciplinary research is necessary for problem-driven research in political philosophy, academic standards and practices for interdisciplinary inquiry are not yet fully established. Interdisciplinary studies are still relatively unfamiliar, and those that exist are often difficult to categorize. Moreover, because such studies cut across disciplines they cannot be fairly judged by disciplinary standards—by which they will always be found to be lacking—because they do not engage with disciplinary debates in exhaustive detail. Yet, as Wendy Brown has argued in favor of the need for interdisciplinary work in political theory: "[i]f we do not make these crossings, we literally make ourselves stupid . . . about the world and the knowledges that will incisively apprehend and criticize it."[49] In this crossing, my aim is to bring the wisdom of many disciplines to bear on my study of multiple identities.

While interdisciplinary studies have potential drawbacks—especially of inaccessibility and disciplinary limits—*if* they can be made accessible, interdisciplinary studies such as this also have the advantage of potentially contributing to ongoing discussions in a variety of disciplines, and to address questions of broader multi-disciplinary—or general—concern. In the case of the following investigation, for example, while this study does not take the details of disciplinary debates as its focus, dimensions of the following work do potentially contribute to discussions in at least four different disciplines.

In racial and ethnic studies, borderland studies, and in the area of American politics this work offers an account of how multiple identities may have helped sustain systems of racial hierarchy and subordination in the post–civil rights era even while there has simultaneously emerged a post–civil rights consensus on the value of anti-racism.

In Chicana/o and Latina/o studies and borderland studies, this work offers an extension and application of Gloria Anzaldúa's concept of *mestiza consciousness* into mainstream philosophical questions of the subject, agency, and post-Enlightenment reason.

In political science, this work contributes in varying degrees to all four subfields of the discipline. In American politics it contributes to an understanding of how concerns with the divided political loyalties of immigrants who maintain multiple ethnic identities are rooted in faulty understandings of the potential to integrate both multiple ethnic identities and strong commitment to a single nation state.

In comparative politics and area studies this investigation adds insight to the growing number of works that examine how multiple identities influence politics in different regions and nation states as a function of immigration, regime change, linguistic or cultural diversity, the rise of regional political units, and other factors.

In international relations, as well as the other subfields of political science, this inquiry contributes to our understanding of how group identity commitments emerge from group conflicts and may, in turn, either sustain or undermine the continuation of those group conflicts.

In political theory, this book contributes an exploration of the decentered multiple subject that both critiques the prevailing conception of a narrative self and offers an alternative framework of self-integration that incorporates identity contradiction, ambivalence, and inconsistency. It also offers an application of Latina feminist thought—especially the work of Gloria Anzaldúa—to the questions of subjectivity, agency, and reason since the linguistic turn.

In addition to contributing to debates in philosophy, political philosophy, political science, and racial and ethnic studies, this inquiry may also be of interest to scholars in other domains of study. In Social Identity Theory, social identity theorists may take an interest in the exploration of identity contradiction as a *felt* experience, which departs from established Social Identity Theory. Feminist scholars may take an interest in the account of embodiment of a decentered and multiple subject as well in the discussion of intersectionality. Critical race theorists may also be interested in the further development of the concept of intersectionality and its role in the integration of the self, as well as in negotiating intersecting systems of subordination. Scholars in gay, lesbian, transgender and queer studies may also be interested in the concept of gender akrasia discussed in chapter four, and in the readings and theorization of writings by lesbian scholars, Minnie Bruce Pratt and Gloria Anzaldúa, especially in chapter six.

To make these potential contributions actual, however, requires that the disadvantage of the potential inaccessibility of interdisciplinary investigations is somehow overcome. In an attempt to do this, I have taken three steps in the hope of fostering interdisciplinary exchange. First, each chapter is as jargon-free as possible. In each, I seek to at once assume little or no background knowledge of the topic while nonetheless entering into an advanced theoretical exploration. Much of this balance is struck through substantive notes that are designed to meet the needs both of political philosophers who would like additional disciplinary specifics and references to ongoing debates in the field, and the needs of readers who are reading out of their field and would like explanatory background in plain English.

Second, even in plain English prose, the mysterious questions under investigation are complex and challenging for the initiated and uninitiated alike. If they were not, their mysteries would have been solved centuries ago. To make the questions at hand readily accessible, however, all of the chapters that follow make liberal use of metaphors and imagery drawn from familiar sources in order to illustrate potentially unfamiliar philosophical points. These include readings of films such as *Casablanca,* and the use of autobiographies, scenarios and characters, as the mystery unfolds.

Finally, in addition to these measures toward interdisciplinary exchange, each chapter is also written to be read independently and/ or out of order should doing so meet the needs of the reader. While each chapter builds on the previous chapters, each chapter also pieces together clues on particular questions in which readers may have particular disciplinary-based interests. Readers interested in multiple identities with regard to immigration and classic assimilationism, for example, may focus primarily on chapter one. Those interested in the contributing role of identity contradiction to critical reasoning may have more initial interest in chapter three, and so on. As the concluding chapter hopefully shows, this work is more than the sum of its parts. But I also hope that its parts are accessible to those with focused interests for turning to interdisciplinary inquiry on this topic.

The Chapters

The chapters that follow investigate the character of multiple identities, and offer a broad account of their political implications. In chapter one, I begin by looking into the known characteristics of multiple identities from sources in political science. In particular I turn to Samuel Huntington's recent work on American national identity and the threat posed to it by the maintenance of multiple ethnic identities. While Huntington finds multiple identities among immigrants—particularly Latinos—to pose a threat to U.S. democracy, there is much to agree with in his basic account of multiple identities. From it, I identify eight mutually agreed upon characteristics of multiple identities and two characteristics—of identity formation and boundary setting—for which I contest Huntington's definitions and offer alternatives based on sources in constructivist anthropology and sociology. With these ten characteristics in mind, I critically engage with Huntington's claim that multiple ethnic identities among Latinos rules out their having robust national identities with the United States. I argue instead, that a better understanding of the character of multiple identities indicates that there is no reason to believe that ethnic immigrants cannot at once maintain heritage ethnicities at the same time that they gain American ethnic and national identities.

In chapter two, I turn from descriptions of multiple identities among Latinas/os to sketch a theory of multiple identities. This theory has a number of components including a five-part model of embodied subjectivity, descriptions of the complex process of self identification, variations in the way the multiple identities are ready as frames of reference for thought and action, and an expanded theory of the interconnections between multiple identities both within social life and within ourselves—or what feminist scholars of color have called *intersectionality*. Although this chapter is largely devoted to outlining a theoretical framework, that framework is illustrated with a variety of empirical examples drawn from research in anthropology, sociology, political science, and cultural studies. Resources for this theory are found in Chicana studies, borderland studies, and Social Identity Theory.

The chapter two investigation—and especially the examples used to illustrate intersectionality—yields the hunch that understanding identity contradiction is an important factor for interpreting the overall character of multiple identities. Thus in chapter three, I investigate the question of what role identity contradiction plays in how people engage in critical thought. Some philosophers, such as Alasdair MacIntyre, have argued that multiple identities are not, in and of themselves, sufficient to sustain critical thinking and that some other factor of the self—a factor separate from those identities—is necessary for critical thought to take place. For MacIntyre, the inability to engage in critical thought on the basis of multiple identities can be politically dangerous—a point that he illustrates with the example of a train engineer who unwittingly collaborates with the Nazis in transporting Jewish peoples to concentration camps. In contrast, Gloria Anzaldúa has argued that the contradictions among multiple identities provide all the resources necessary for critical and creative thought.

In chapter three, I juxtapose the approaches of Anzaldúa and MacIntyre to identity contradiction. I find that these thinkers share much more in their accounts of identity contradictions and reasoning than their opposing conclusions would suggest. As with the discussion of Huntington's approach in chapter one, small differences in the understanding of specific aspects of identity can make a big difference in how the character of multiple identities is perceived. In this case, MacIntyre's failure to account for the intersection among multiple identities makes a great deal of difference in various understandings of the character and effects of multiple identities. With the character of *intersecting* multiple identities in mind, it becomes clear that multiple identities and especially *the contradictions among them* offer not only sufficient but also much needed intellectual resources for critical thought.

Having discovered that identity contradictions can provide a necessary resource for critical and creative thought, the fact remains that identity contradictions—while useful—may nonetheless fragment the self by dividing the identities within our psyches. Chapter four, therefore, investigates how it is possible for a decentered and multiple subjectivity to bring an array of multiple identities, variations, and contradictions together into a whole—that is at once cohesive enough to hang together and also loosely organized and decentered enough to allow for fluid shifts in identification from one context to the next.

To investigate this, I turn again to William James's work and to his account of thought-in-the–moment, which he illustrates with the metaphor of a herdsman. Uniting James's account with social constructivism and Social Identity Theory, a two-tier account of personal identity emerges that offers an explanation of how one may have a sense of self-sameness that is combined with multiplicity, fluid identification, and identity contradiction both in and over time. In this two-tier model, the self is held together as a cohesive whole in two ways—first as a complex self-system, and second by the optional processes of self-integration.

Within this second tier of personal identity the cohesiveness of the self permits degrees of cohesion from a bare and highly fragmented minimum to highly self-integrated identities. These varying degrees of self-integration are, in many cases, highly influenced by how individuals cope with identity contradictions. I turn to the work of Amélie Oksenberg Rorty to explore how some responses to identity contradiction can be self-fragmenting in ways that have political consequences. In closing I offer a five-part typology of identity contradiction.

If identity contradiction can be fragmentary in negative ways as well as positively productive for creative and critical thought, then it becomes important to determine more specifically how identity contradictions can be integrated. In chapter five, I explore three possibilities: first, that identity contradictions should be eliminated via ranked guiding preferences; second, that identity contradictions can be unified through coherent and comprehensive narratives of the self and its priorities; and third, that ambivalence, ambiguity and flexibility toward identity contradictions can also be a means to self-integration at times. Harry Frankfurt adopts the first of these approaches; the second is endorsed by Alasdair MacIntyre and Charles Taylor; and the third is advocated in various works by Gloria Anzaldúa, Jane Flax, and Amélie Oksenberg Rorty.

In chapter five, I place the perspectives of Anzaldúa, Flax and Rorty in dialogue with those of Frankfurt, MacIntyre, and Taylor and I find reason to believe that ambivalence, ambiguity, and inconsistency can be self-integrative of multiple identities in politically significant ways. From the commonalities and variations in these various approaches to self-integration I offer an alternative basis for self-integration refered to as *integrative life projects.* This approach is an alterative to narrative identity and rank-ordered endorsements that nevertheless draws some of the aspects and benefits from those models while—unlike those models—also allowing for contradiction, ambivalence and inconsistency to be part of self-integrative processes. This alternative model is illustrated through a reading of *Casablanca,* including a response to Umberto Eco's reading of the film.

Finally, in chapter six, I explore in greater detail the optional processes by which individuals may seek to self-integrate their multiple identities. For this I turn again to Gloria Anzaldúa's work and to her account of the "Mestiza Way" of selfcraft. I expand her account into a three-part practice of selfcraft and illustrate that process through a reading of autobiographical writings by Minnie Bruce Pratt. Analysis of Pratt's work also yields clues as to the limits of narrative to unify the self—limits that are potentially avoided with the model of integrative selfcraft begun in chapter five.

In the concluding chapter, I draw together clues from the preceding chapters to give an accounting of the basic political implications of multiple identities.

CHAPTER ONE

Multiple Identities
and Immigrant Political Loyalty
Replies to the Query *Who Are We?*

Each one of us has multiple identities and multiple sites for action;
Worker and workplace are but one type. . . . Community, household,
cultural practices, our bodies—these are all sites for identity and for
action.
SASKIA SASSEN, Foreword in *Latino Metropolis*

No country, and certainly no democracy. . . . benefits from large scale
immigration of those with multiple loyalties and attachments.
STANLEY RENSHON, "Dual Citizenship + Multiple Loyalties =
One America?"

The political significance of multiple identities arises from more than
their sheer multiplicity. Other characteristics include their group-
based formation, their contextual expression, and their potential for
varying presentation. Failure to consider these and other aspects of
multiple identities can generate false conclusions regarding their political implications and cause unfounded misapprehensions regarding
their potential risks and disadvantages. Thus partial understandings
of multiple identities can distort public political debates—including
those on immigration, national identity, and political cohesion in
diverse democracies. In many Western nations, for example, immigrants face identity-related challenges based on the widespread view
that retaining a heritage ethnic identity is necessarily incompatible
with strong identification with one's adopted nation. Therefore, when
immigrants, or their native-born descendants, express their heritage
ethnic, religious, or subcultural identities in everyday life, the association of those identities with foreign lands leads some of their fellow
countrymen to regard them as perpetual foreigners.[1]

In the United States, this viewpoint has its origins in classic assimilationist thought, which holds that immigrants must shed the
cultures of their heritage lands of origin and replace that heritage
cultural identity with one identity—an identity with the United
States mainstream, understood by many assimilationists as racially
white, Anglo-Saxon, Protestant, and monolingual English-speaking.[2]
However, classic assimilationism has been discredited by scholars on
a variety of grounds for decades, and has been succeeded by neo-

assimilationist perspectives.[3] Neo-assimilation finds that although immigrant assimilation inevitably takes place over several generations, there are significant personal, social, and familial advantages to slow-paced *acculturation,* in which immigrants cultivate *both* American English language and culture *and* their heritage ethnicities and languages. Studies show that the advantages of slow acculturation over rapid assimilation are so great that the prospects for upward mobility and social and political incorporation for immigrants are now considered to be improved not by rapid assimilation, but by holding onto multiple ethnic identities.[4]

Despite shifts in scholarly understandings, however, classic assimilationism still seems to hold sway in the U.S. popular imagination.[5] Consequently, claims to U.S. national identity by ethnic immigrants are still subject to challenge or rejection by those who presume that *any* expression of immigrant ethnic identities signifies a rejection of the United States and an unwillingness to be American. This assumption about the impossibility of multiple cultural identities typically results in pressure in U.S. society for immigrants to choose to identify only with the U.S. cultural mainstream. This pressure has sometimes risen to hostility, as it did, for example, in the aftermath of the September 11, 2001 terrorist attacks, when Americans appearing to have Arab, Muslim, or Middle Eastern identities were suspected by some—including some members of law enforcement—to be potential enemies of the United States in sympathy with its terrorist attackers. This assimilationist logic was also applied to the internment of Japanese Americans during World War II.[6] In both cases, the political result has been contributions to lasting social divisions—scars that damage the cohesion of all Americans as commonly recognized members of a diverse democracy. For some Middle Eastern and Japanese Americans, however, the consequences of misunderstanding an immigrant's potential to have multiple identities have been deadly.

In part one of this chapter, I explore the complex attributes of multiple identities through a consideration of Samuel Huntington's recent claim that the multiple ethnic identities of U.S. Latinos are a threat to U.S. national identity and to the stability of democracy in the United States. While Huntington describes the complex characteristics of multiple identities accurately in many ways, he makes one very basic false assumption about identity and identity formation that undermines his argument regarding Latinos. In investigating Huntington's account, I locate eight characteristics of multiple identities that are widely descriptive of their basic character. Having found these important clues to the character of multiple identities in Huntington's work, in opposition to Huntington, I argue that by taking into account group identity formation, the intersections among multiple identities, and their varying expressions and intensity, it is clear that immigrant ethnic cultural assimilation is *not* necessary to foster and maintain national identity and political cohesion. On the contrary, there is reason to believe that welcoming the positive maintenance of robust immigrant ethnic identities in immigrant communities can help to foster stronger and more productive immigrant identification with the United States and its major political and social institutions.[7]

In part two of the chapter, I consider the specific loyalties and commitments of different categories of Latina/o immigrants, including first generation immigrants, native born children of immigrants, and Latina/o transmigrants. I argue on theoretical grounds that among these groups, Latinos are likely to have multiple ethnic identities but typically only one, or at least one primary, national identity—an identity with the United States, the nation of their birth or adopted nation of long-term residence. Only transmigrant Latinos and recent immigrants who have not been long in the U.S. are likely to have strong national identities with other regimes with which they must balance new national loyalties. Yet, considered in light of modern conceptions of distributed loyalty, the activities and commitments of even transmigrant Latinos suggest that they have strong loyalty to the United States as their place of permanent or long-term residence. Finally, I further contend, contrary to Huntington, that the Latina/o cultural inheritance of both native-born and immigrant bicultural Latinos—while different from the mainstream culture—is compatible with and constitutive of that culture in so many ways as to render untenable the view that Latina/o biculturalism threatens U.S. democracy or the United States' general way of life.

Characterizing the Multiple Identities in the Lives of Latino Immigrants

Shadowed by assimilationism, many find it difficult to assess the political implications of the multiple ethnic identities—i.e. the biculturalism—of U.S. Latinos. U.S. Latinos are a highly diverse, pan-ethnic group comprised of U. S. residents with heritage in any of the cultures or nation states of the Americas that exist south of the United States. U.S. Latinos include both immigrants and native-born citizens.[8] Families of native-born Latinos may have been resident for one generation or many, and some native-born Latinos can trace family residence in the U.S. Southwest to before U.S. acquisition. Culturally, many Latinos retain and cultivate ethnic identification with their cultures of familial origin—their heritage cultures—as well as identification with U.S. mainstream ethnic culture. For native-born Latinos raised in the United States gaining an ethnic identification with the U.S. cultural mainstream is an inevitable and unavoidable consequence of growing up in the United States.

Among foreign-born immigrants who arrive as adults, or those who immigrate as children (the 1.5 immigrant generation), however, ethnic identification with the U.S. mainstream is acquired through acculturation over time as a result of continued residence in the country. With long-term residence, Latina/o immigrants inevitably become socialized in and eventually identified with the U.S. cultural mainstream to a greater or lesser degree. Linguistically, English mastery is a major priority. Ninety percent of Puerto Rican Americans, Cuban Americans, and Mexican Americans agree that *every* U.S. resident should learn English. Accordingly, major studies find that 98 percent of all children of immigrants know English well or very well and that their preference for and rate of English usage consistently rises over their lifetime.[9] Given time and opportunity, Latina/o immigrants learn and use English at overwhelming rates. At the same time, many retain competency in Spanish, indigenous or other heritage languages as part of their ethnic identities.

While Latinos, as a rapidly growing demographic group, exhibit no reluctance to learn and speak English, their multiple ethnic identities still render them suspect to some of their fellow countrymen. Political scientist and Harvard University professor Samuel Huntington, for example, considers Latina/o biculturalism a threat to U.S. national identity and ultimately to the stability of U.S. democracy itself. In his recent book *Who Are We?: The Challenges to America's National Identity*, Huntington argues that Mexican immigration in particular is producing a "demographic *reconquista*" of the United States that is "blurring the border between Mexico and the United States, introducing a very different culture," and in some areas "promoting the emergence of . . . blended society and culture, half-American and half-Mexican."[10] For Huntington, this increasing hybridization has initiated what he calls a "cultural bifurcation" now underway in which Latina/o culture(s) could potentially shift the historical dominance of Anglo-Protestant culture in the United States. For Huntington, this shift would destabilize U.S. democracy by eroding its necessary cultural basis—a cultural basis without which he considers U.S. national identity to be in crisis.[11]

In terms of the political implications of multiple identities,

Huntington argues that the multiple—or what he calls "ampersand identities"—of Latinos are a source of particular risk. As long as Latinos refuse to identify primarily with the U.S. mainstream and choose instead to maintain two languages, two cultures, and possibly two loyalties to different nation states, their multiple identities are, in his view, potentially politically destructive to multicultural democracy.[12] Uniting assimilationist claims with reference to diversity, Huntington contends that multiple identities are destructive because U.S. society has been and must continue to be a "multiethnic, multiracial society *with an Anglo-Protestant mainstream culture* encompassing many subcultures with a common political creed *rooted in that [Anglo-Protestant] culture.*"[13] Without this core culture, Huntington contends, our capacity for democratic self-governance is at risk. Thus, he argues that if Latinos continue to maintain their own ethnic cultures alongside Anglo-Protestant culture, and that culture is decentered as the U.S. mainstream, the American public will lose its capacity to self-govern collectively based on a common set of political principles.

In Huntington's widely discussed and influential consideration of the political significance of multiple identities, he rightly notes that increasingly multiple identities are the product of mass migration, contemporary diasporas, and transnational communities, factors that are also contributing to more widespread and liberal dual citizenship laws in various nations.[14] In addition Huntington not only acknowledges the human capacity to have multiple identities, he succinctly enumerates eight of the most complex and important characteristics of multiple identities.

The eight well-rendered elements of Huntington's account of multiple identities are as follows. He rightly identifies that, 1) identities are predominantly socially constructed, and that 2) individuals with multiple group identities can shift among their different identities from one context to another depending on which of their identities they deem relevant in each context. He further recognizes 3) that our multiple identities may contradict, and 4) they also may be interrelated in complex ways. In regard to contradiction, he specifies, for example, that different identities may place competing demands on those who have them. (In addition to this competing demand contradiction, I specify four other types of identity contradiction in chapter four.) Among the various possible relationships between multiple identities, some identities may be constructed as compatible and/or nested, while others are mutually exclusive. Still other identities may be constructed as hierarchically ordered and in that ranking seen as compatible or zero-sum. Moreover, using the example of military units Huntington notes that when smaller less inclusive groups are a nested part of larger group they can either reinforce larger group cohesion, or undermine it.

Huntington also states 5) that different members of one social group may identify themselves with the group by using different social markers from the totality of markers commonly seen as signaling group membership. Huntington describes this with reference to different individual nations in a group of nations. While all nations in the group have citizens, the definition of citizenship and the path to citizenship chosen by each can vary widely. Yet those varied choices still allow them to legitimately claim their identities as nations and be recognized as such by other nations.[15] This potential—called "selective identification,"—is a function of the social construction of identities. Selective identification makes it possible for members of a social group to vary their expressions of that identity from other members without forfeiting their claim to group identity.

Likewise, 6) Huntington rightly acknowledges that those subscribing to a particular group identity may identify with that group with varying degrees of intensity. Some members of a faith community, for example, will be more highly identified with their religious identity than others group members. While Huntington does not state it, it follows logically that the intensity with which a person identifies with a specific group identity can also alter over time.

In addition, 7) drawing from social identity theory, Huntington dwells on the concept of "salience" as important to understanding how the different identities within a person's subjectivity are activated in some relevant contexts but remain inactive in others. In the opening pages of his book, *Who Are We?*, Huntington points out for example, that the terrorist attacks on the U.S. on September 11, 2001, made U.S. national identity "salient" for Americans in a way that it generally is not. Because the nature of the attack was one upon the United States and Americans *as such*—the context of the attack made salient for all residents of the United States their identities as Americans. Further describing identity salience, Huntington gestures to the fact that when we make determinations regarding which identities are salient for us in a given context, we do so based on two factors: (a) the nature of the situation, and (b) the way in which we would like to categorize or present ourselves in that situation.[16] He also notes correctly that in our choices of self-categorization, people with multiple identities tend to seek a balance between claims to similarity to others and differences from them.

Finally, and perhaps most importantly, 8) Huntington recognizes that in regard to presenting ourselves in our chosen identities in specific contexts, our identity enactments are inevitably subject to what might be called "co-construction" by those we encounter in those contexts. Simply put, unless others help to co-construct our identities by recognizing us as having the identities that we claim for ourselves, it becomes difficult, if not impossible, for us to identify ourselves as we wish.[17] While Huntington spends relatively little time developing these points or citing his sources for them, they are entirely in keeping with contemporary approaches to identity that can be found in a wide variety of scholarly domains, including Chicana Studies (especially the work of Gloria Anzaldúa), postcolonial studies, and social psychology, particularly Social Identity Theory originating in the work of Henri Tajfel (for discussion of these and other sources, see chapter 2).[18]

Given Huntington's sophisticated and up-to-date account of the more complex and detailed characteristics of multiple identities, it is surprising that he fails to correctly describe the most basic concept of multiple identities–the definition of identity itself. Huntington defines identity as "an individual's or a group's sense of self . . . a product of self-consciousness, that I or we posses *distinct qualities* as an entity that differentiates me from you and us from them."[19] Yet to claim that identities are socially constructed and that our identity presentations are co-constructed by others in context, rules out the far too simple notion that identities are just the "distinct qualities" that distinguish us from others. Huntington compounds this oversimplification by making the counter-intuitive claim that while individual identities can be altered quite easily, group identities are largely static and cannot generally change. Both of these claims contradict the way he otherwise characterizes identities and multiple identities.

Alternately, a more accurate and full definition of identity— and one more consistent with Huntington's account of multiple identities—may be found in Social Identity Theory, a body of scholarship to which he sometimes refers. Social Identity Theory utilizes a well-known definition of identity in which all identities can be divided into *social identities* and *personal identities*. Social identities are collective identities that each of us has by virtue of internalizing and engaging in the ways of life of the social groups and roles of which we are members. Social identities include all possible social groups, including social role identities (e.g. professional identities), or broad social category identities such as gender identity—any collective identity derived from identification with the socially constructed "lifeworld" of specific social roles, groups, and categories. Personal identities, in contrast, are the identities we have by virtue of our unique relationships to specific others—sister to Eugenia, co-worker to Sal, mother to Paul.

As Huntington acknowledges, all identities are socially constructed. In the category of personal identities, for example, Bill as husband to Sue, and Sue as wife to Bill construct their personal identities as husband and wife to each other within their specific and unique relationship as a married couple. Others who recognize their personal identities as husband and wife can acknowledge those identifications in their interactions with each spouse.[20] Social identities, however, are constructed in a Wittgensteinian sense, from the materials—the sets of meanings, values, and practices—contested through convention as definitive of those group identities in a given time and place. As Huntington notes in his example of the nations with opposing approaches to citizenship—different group members can be recognized as group members based on quite different, even contradictory "distinct qualities." What distinguishes them as group members then cannot be their "distinct qualities" but rather how the various qualities they do exhibit are understood by themselves and others in relationship to a group boundary. That group boundary is cast and recast in everyday interactions in which individuals categorize themselves and others as either within or outside of specific group boundaries.

Anthropologist Fredrick Barth made this last point regarding group boundaries in his classic 1969 work *Ethnic Groups and Boundaries*. In it Barth demonstrates that ethnic groups are not defined by inherent or primordial qualities, but by the ongoing process of boundary setting in everyday contexts. Thus, the cultural practices and values of an ethnic group may change significantly over time as group norms and preferences shift and as group members come and go. However, as long as members exist who claim that the refashioned practices are part of what defines their ethnic lifeworld, then the ethnic group persists.[21] Likewise, social anthropologist Anthony Cohen described boundary setting as the basis of group formation in the social construction of communities and groups in general. Cohen argues, for example, that in a diverse nation such as Britain, national identity is crafted through various symbols and "approximation myths" by which diverse people can identify themselves in different ways with the same national community.[22]

By adopting a too simple definition of identity that is out of sync with his otherwise complex account of multiple identities, Huntington denies the collectivity and boundary-based formation of all social identities. This error, in turn, underpins Huntington's highly unusual claim that *ethnic identities are not cultural identities.* Rather he claims that ethnic identities are defined by the immutable characteristic of family lineage—that is, one's ethnic identity is quintessentially signified by the ethnic identity of one's grandfather—that ethnic identities are not cultural identities is pivotal in Huntington's overall argument. For if it is true that ethnic identity is not a cultural identity, then Huntington may insist—as he does—that a core Anglo-Protestant *culture* is necessary to the stability of U.S. democracy without having technically adopted the position of ethnic nationalism, and falling prey to the widely accepted criticisms of that perspective.[23]

Unfortunately for the soundness of Huntington's argument, his claim that ethnic identities are not cultural identities is both idiosyncratic and untenable. In the vast scholarly literature on ethnicity in political science and throughout the social sciences, such a definition of ethnic identity is almost unheard of. The nearest argument would be that of scholars who regard ethnicity as a primordial, even ineffable, affective bond of kinship among co-ethnics.[24] But even primordialist definitions typically regard ethnicity as a bond within a kinship *community*—not family lineage alone—and as an affective tie to the ways of life of that collective, a collective life scholars conventionally refer to as "culture." Aside from primordialists, the great majority of scholars have long regarded ethnic group identity to be a cultural identity. Max Weber, for example, (who Huntington repeatedly invokes through his references to the Protestant work ethic), regarded ethnicity as a cultural identity that could be built on no empirical basis at all, but only on the subjective belief in common descent of ethnic group members.[25]

By choosing an oversimplified and unsound definition of identity and thereby ignoring the cultural and boundary-oriented basis of ethnic identity, Huntington does, despite his intentions to the contrary, link one ethnic identity—i.e. Anglo-American ethnic identity—with U.S. national identity in the manner of ethnic nationalism. In so doing, he defines other ethnic identities as mutually exclusive with U.S. national identity. For Huntington, ethnic identities may be tolerated as long as they are lived as "subordinate cultures" to the Anglo-Protestant core culture that he believes must ground U.S. national identity.[26] While Huntington advocates Anglo-centered national identity with the aim of preserving democratic stability, as he himself notes, scholars generally agree that equating a national identity with a single ethnicity in a diverse society is likely to foster division and *destabilize* democracy, not sustain it.[27]

Latina and Latino Multiple Identities and U.S. Democracy

Because democracy is better served by understanding national identity as a commitment to the political principles of the nation—not as a common ethnic culture as Huntington contends—then assessing national unity in the context of Latina/o immigration and biculturalism depends in part on knowing what configurations of ethnic and national identities Latinas and Latinos tend to have.[28] Therefore, specifying ethnicities and national identities as different kinds of social identities is important. Ethnic group identity can be understood in general, in terms of a group member's knowledge, commitment to, and practice of at least some defining aspects of ethnic group life. National identities—particularly in democratic multicultural societies—are best defined in terms of knowledge and a commitment to the political principles and laws that define the nation's political system of governance. While ethnic identities can become politicized and may intersect with national, religious, or other social identities, they are *not* in general principally defined by commitment to the political principles or practices of any given nation. This distinction is highly relevant to the task of assessing the political implications of multiple identities of Latinos. Latina/o biculturalism represents the multiple *ethnic*—that is cultural—identities of Latinos. Consequently, *Latina/o biculturalism does not necessarily indicate that Latinos have multiple national identities,* defined as a commitment to the political system of other regimes.

Because it is the possibility of multiple *national* identities that generates anxieties about the presumed disloyalty of immigrants to their adopted nation, three questions remain to be answered if a reasonable assessment of the political effects of multiple Latina/o identities is to be reached: 1) does biculturalism—e.g. multiple ethnic identities—benefit or detract from the capacity of Latinos to be productive members of the United States?, 2) do Latina/o biculturals have multiple *national* identities in addition to their multiple ethnic identities?, and 3) if they do, how do those multiple national identities shape their sense of loyalty to the United States as a political regime or their support for its way of life?

All three of these questions are ultimately empirical questions, yet there is relatively little large-scale, longitudinal data available to address these questions.[29] Settling these questions would require a systematic large-scale inquiry directed at Latinos themselves.[30] And even were such data available, the reliability of answers would depend greatly on how well the research methods used could accommodate the possibility of fluid identification and shifting identity salience including shifts induced by the study itself. Yet, even without extensive empirical data it is possible to make informed assessments about the national identities and loyalties *most likely* to exist among bicultural Latinos based on the most common settings in which their multiple identities were formed. To make an assessment based on the character of multiple identity formation, it is helpful to divide U.S. Latinos into subcategories based on their nativity, place of childhood, and adult residence. This division will become especially important when answering the second of the three questions at hand on the political effects of Latina/o biculturalism on national identification.

Regarding the first question, however, of whether bicultural identity hinders the capacity to become American, it is clear from available research on biculturalism in general that biculturalism is an asset not a detriment to the incorporation of immigrant groups into receiving states. A significant change has taken place in scholarly assessments of the value of biculturalism. Once regarded as damaging, biculturalism is now regarded as generally beneficial, not only for individual biculturals and their families, but also for important societal processes such as upward mobility of immigrant groups. While the earliest research on biculturalism viewed identification with and participation in two or more cultures as psychologically damaging, by the 1940s scholars of biculturalism began to reach very different conclusions.[31] By then, the bicultural identities of "marginal men" were demonstrated to be adaptive, and to foster secure group and community membership, successful participation in prevailing social practices, and to provide a basis for community building.[32] Based on these positive findings the initial valorization of assimilation in research on biculturalism increasingly gave way to the endorsement of *acculturation* in which immigrants and their offspring retain and cultivate their heritage cultures while *also* cultivating competence in and identification with the dominant culture(s) of their adopted nations.[33] In this view, biculturalism is not a temporary phase but rather a valuable end in itself that offers many advantages.

Specifically, there are numerous advantages to biculturalism for both individuals and the societies in which they live. The advantages to the individual include better cognitive functioning and superior mental health and well-being relative to monoculturals or assimilated former biculturals.[34] Studies have also shown biculturalism to be directly correlated to positive behavioral and psychological adjustment among youth, and to serve as a buffer against stress, alienation and loneliness among college age biculturals.[35] Other studies demonstrate biculturalism's role in adjustment within family life and across different social contexts, and also indicate that biculturalism is correlated to high global self-worth.[36] In related research on the benefits of bilingualism, studies have shown bilingualism (a common marker of biculturalism) to be associated with heightened cognitive and affective abilities, and can be linked to "higher self-esteem, higher educational and occupational expectations, and higher academic achievement."[37] Moreover, studies in cross-cultural psychology indicate that when contradictions exist between cultural identities, biculturals tend to develop skills to cope with those conflicts. Those skills produce another distinct advantage, namely the potential for more complex thought regarding everyday problems, as those with multiple cultural identities use their multiple cultural frames of reference to assess the problems at hand. One study of bicultural competence, for example, found that bicultural Mexican American mothers were more able to interpret child development in terms of multiple determinants than their monocultural Mexican or Anglo counterparts.[38] The potential political implications of this advantage are explored in chapters three, four, and six below.

In terms of the societal and national advantages of biculturalism, studies of biculturalism and immigrant incorporation find that gradual acculturation is far superior to rapid assimilation for the positive incorporation and long-term success of immigrants in a number of ways. Rapid assimilation—especially in second generation children of immigrant parents who are less fluent than their children in the dominant culture—can destabilize family cohesion, eroding the possibility of intergenerational communication on complex topics and reversing child-parent dependencies in ways that often "undercuts parental authority and places children at risk" of downward mobility.[39] A slower paced acculturation process, in contrast, provides a more stable basis for parental guidance and mutual intergenerational support. In addition, research shows that the support of co-ethnic social networks (e.g. family, friends) and ethnic communities can often provide a supportive environment for the acquisition of new cultural and language knowledge that are essential to social, economic, and political incorporation. Likewise, the subeconomies of ethnic enclaves can provide important access to economic incorporation of immigrants to the United States. Finally, as studies cited above show, immigrant biculturalism and immigrant community membership can enhance immigrant resilience to entrenched patterns of racial and ethnic dis-

crimination potentially enhancing the prospects for national identification and incorporation among racialized immigrants.

This final point regarding the benefits to immigrant incorporation of lasting immigrant identity—while it may seem counterintui-
tive from an assimilationist perspective—can be illustrated with sociological data on West Indian immigrants. Sociologist Mary Waters,
for example, finds that among highly ethnically identified immigrant
youth, many "specifically see their ethnic identities as keys to upward
social mobility, stressing, for instance, that their parents' immigrant
values of hard work and strictness will give them the opportunity to
succeed." For them, their immigrant ethnic identity is very much an
U.S.-based identity—"it is in the context of U.S. social life that the
youngsters base their assumptions of what it means to be Jamaican or
Trinidadian."[40] Hence, for some immigrants *it is through strong ethnic identity that some racialized immigrants become most highly identified with the United States,* its ways of life, and its major political
and social institutions. This is an intersectionality-based possibility
in multiple identity formation that is consistent with a point made
by Samuel Huntington, with reference to the military, namely, that
small group cohesion can often reinforce larger group unity. Overall
then, in terms of the first question of whether Latina/o biculturalism benefits or detracts from the capacity of Latinos to be productive
members of the nation, the evidence is strong that having multiple
cultural identities has benefits that far exceed monoculturalism and
enhances the potential for productive membership in the nation
among Latinos and other immigrants.[41]

The second important question in assessing the impact of the
multiple identities of Latina/o biculturals on U.S. national cohesion
is whether or not Latina/o biculturals have multiple *national* identities in addition to their multiple ethnic identities. The answer to this
question depends on the socialization that bicultural Latinos have received. As Huntington accepts, all identities are socially constructed.
Thus multiple *national* identities can only be gained when individuals
are significantly socialized to them. Despite misperception however,
U.S. Latinos, have *not* categorically been socialized to multiple *national* identities. Rather, based on their immigrant trajectories, only
some subsets of Latinos are likely to have socialization to a national
identity other than U.S. national identity. Moreover, as discussed
below, even those Latinos that have multiple national identities may
still choose to identify with the U.S. over other nations.

Given the variations in Latina/o experience, arguments such as
Huntington's homogenize Latinos, ignoring that Latinos have dif-

ferent configurations of multiple identities, relatively few of which incorporate commitment to more that one political regime. In order to correct this faulty approach, I would suggest that there are at least three categories of U.S. Latinos that are relevant to determining whether bicultural Latinos identify significantly with nations other than the United States to degrees or in ways that are damaging to U.S. national identity or societal cohesion. These categories are 1) native-born Latinos, 2) foreign-born Latina/o immigrants who are U.S. citizens or long-term residents, authorized or unauthorized, and 3) recent foreign-born Latina/o immigrants, foreign born sojourners, and active transmigrants including dual citizens, dual nationals, and active but unauthorized transmigrants. This is a complicated category. Here transmigrants are defined as those who engage significantly and in an ongoing basis in social and political life in the United States *as well as in* one or more specific locations in another nation-state. But because transmigrant status is defined by the activity of cross-border life practices, it is technically a designation in which native-born and long established immigrants could also participate. However, the research data discussed below suggests that with some exceptions, transnational activity is undertaken primarily by recent foreign-born immigrants and is less prevalent among native-born and long-term Latina/o residents.

This distribution of transnational activity, however, is an empirical question on which I would contend current research data is inconclusive. As shown by research data discussed below, studies of recent immigrants and their activities in the U.S. often do not quantify the degree of transnational activity in which new immigrants are engaged, which could vary from none to a lot. Similarly, studies of transmigrant activity do not always identify which immigrant "cohort" to which participants belong. Thus the distribution and scope of actual transnational identification and activity is difficult to assess empirically at present. My analysis is a theoretical one, however, and my arguments are based on the character of multiple identity formation. Thus, for this purpose, I will provisionally assume that transmigrants exist primarily among recent immigrants and will discuss commitment patterns of recent immigrants as indicative of transmigrant commitments as well.

Considering first the category of native-born Latinos, such native-born Latinos—i.e. second generation immigrants—are the *least likely* to have the socialization necessary to have gained a political identification with the nation-state from which their forebears immigrated. Born and raised in the U.S., their most sustained experience of a political nation state is of the United States. Given this primary socialization, native-born Latinos—like any other person—would need significant and sustained experience to have a thorough knowledge of and substantive identification with the domestic politics of another state. While the rates of such socialization are an empirical question, it is reasonable to anticipate that relatively few native-born Latinos have sustained transnational experience sufficient to substantively identify with the domestic *politics* of the nation-state from which their forebearers immigrated. Moreover, anecdotally at least, even those foreign-born Latina/o parents who take their U.S.-born children to visit sending locations do so with the understanding that it will result in *cultural* knowledge and cultural identification with the cultural heritage found in local lands, but not in *political* identification with the sending state. When asked about the emerging identities of his U.S.-born sons, for example, one Salvadoran immigrant parent permanently settled in the U.S. but engaged in transnational activity in his childhood village described the likely impact of having his son visit his father's birthplace. "My children" he said, "*they will become Americans,* but I took the elder on my last trip so that he would learn about his roots and take pride in them. This, I think, will help him along."[42]

Given their primary socialization in the United States as the nation-state of their birth and long-term residency, it is most likely that native-born immigrants will have internalized no other national identity, and consequently will identify themselves *nationally* only as Americans. Critics may ask nonetheless, why then do Latinos often refer to themselves with reference to other nation-states? Again this is an empirical question regarding the meaning of terms and symbols in specific ethnic group vocabularies. But terms and symbols may convey different meanings in different contexts. Thus, for such native-born immigrants, to say that they are "Mexican," "Chicano," "Latino," "Guatemalan," or "Oaxacan" potentially expresses an *ethnic* identitification not a national one. It is likely to express familial history, an inherited past—real or imagined—through which native-born immigrants construct their heritage identities and claim belonging in specific ethnic communities. Moreover, because icons too may have various meanings among users, even expressions of identity conveyed using foreign flags, may still generally express *ethnic* identity—an identification with a culture that has its origins in other lands and locations—not national identities with political systems and domestic interests of sending states.[43]

The second relevant category of Latinos includes immigrants

who are permanent or long-term residents of the United States (authorized or unauthorized), or recent immigrants who already intend to reside in the U.S. permanently. Based on theoretical understandings of identity formation, for Latinos in this category, a long period of socialization in the United States will allow them the time needed to internalize as a new identity scheme a sense of the U.S. political system, its laws and principles, and to chose to identify with the U.S. as a nation-state with a particular political system. Latinos in this category may or may not have once had national identifications with the sending state as a political regime. If they are 1.5 generation immigrants and came to the U.S as children before the age of thirteen, they may have had relatively little sense of the sending state as a political entity. My father and my aunts, for example, were born in Mexico, but grew up in southwest Texas along the U.S.-Mexican border near Eagle Pass. While my father and his sisters refer to themselves and our family as "Mexican," doing so refers to *ethnic* identity. In terms of a *national* identity however, they each regard the United States as the only home they have ever known.

If, however, Latina/o immigrants emigrated as adults and had a national identification with their nation of origin, they may come to have multiple national identities—one with the U.S., and one with the state of origin—after a period of socialization in the Unites States. As Huntington points out, however, individuals may identify to varying degrees with their different social identities. As will be discussed in chapter two, the identities that are most frequently activated and salient for us in everyday life are likely to become over time the identities to which we are more highly identified. Those identities that draw from us an affective bond, ones to which we feel a strong attachment for various reasons, will become those with which we are most highly identified. The immigrant experience of my father, for example, is not far removed from that of many other immigrants from Mexico who have grown to love the United States as the nation to which they are solely or primarily identified. A decorated WWII veteran, naturalized on his way to the Normandy invasion, my father is among the many Mexican Americans who have historically given strong support to U.S. war efforts abroad.[44] Many Mexican Americans believed that wartime service would demonstrate their loyalty to the U.S. and settle question of divided loyalty. That hope, however, was largely disappointed by the continuation of ethnic subordination in the segregated post-war U.S.[45]

If the names of nations are used by Latinos to refer to their immigrant ethnicity, what does this theoretical analysis say about the propensities of foreign-born U.S. Latinos to support U.S. causes in instances when loyalty is relevant, such as in foreign policy? Although there is much research on the effects of long-term socialization on levels of identification (see chapter two) there is virtually no existing survey data that focuses on the specific configurations of multiple identities among foreign-born Latinos and the relationship of those multiple identifications to their viewpoints on U.S. foreign policy. This is perhaps largely because in general—with the exception of participation in the military—native-born and foreign-born U.S. Latinos have not been significantly involved in U.S. foreign policy. Instead Latinos have largely chosen to concentrate on domestic civil rights issues in which their *ethnic* identities, rather than their national identities, are likely to be salient. Yet, there is evidence that were Latina/o political elites to be more involved in international affairs that their international perspectives would not undermine national interests.[46] A recent survey shows that the majority of Latina and Latino elites believe that ethnic group interests either should not subvert U.S. foreign policy interests or should forward those U. S. interests abroad (67 percent). Only a minority of those surveyed (26 percent) believed that Latina/o leaders should pursue ethnic group goals without reference to U.S. national interests. The same priorities are revealed in broader Latina/o public opinion polls. In a 1990 survey, a majority of three of the largest Latina/o ethnic sub-groups indicated that they were more positive about the United States than they were about their familial countries of origin. Moreover, the Latinos surveyed indicated that they felt more positively toward Great Britain than toward those Latin American nations in which they claimed no heritage.[47]

Yet, those Latinas and Latinos who have been directly involved in policy-making report having been challenged in their public service by colleagues who hold classic assimilationist assumptions. A recent survey of Latino Foreign Service officers, for example, revealed that based on their ethnicity, Latinos were frequently charged with having divided political loyalties by colleagues who presumed they would privilege the interests of Latin American states against those of the United States.[48] In these interpersonal level conflicts, political loyalty is understood to be exclusive, and anyone with more than one *ethnic* identity is presumed to have loyalties so divided as to preclude full membership, commitment, and identification with the *nation* in which they reside. Such an outlook however fails to take into account that having multiple social identities presents a wide range of possibilities in which multiple *ethnic* identities are compatible with robust national identity and loyalty.

The third category of Latinos that is significant for assessing the political significance of Latina/o biculturalism is the category of recent immigrants, sojourners, and transmigrants. It is among Latinos in this category that there is the greatest possibility of Latinos having robust multiple national identities. As a consequence of the history of imperialism and empire, globalization, and other factors, global migration patterns have produced patterns of transnational migration that crisscross the globe.[49] In the Americas, as elsewhere, some transnational communities have emerged in which transmigrants develop and sustain life, cultural identities, familial relationships and responsibilities, economic and civic commitments, and attachments across national borders.[50] By living transnationally, transmigrants not only come to hold multiple identities but to practice and refresh them on a routine basis in their everyday lives.[51] Recent Latina/o immigrants may not engage in transnational activity, but because their time in the U.S. has been relatively brief, they may not as yet have enough sustained socialization to have gained a robust identification with the U.S. political system. The time it takes for such a national identity to form may vary from person to person. Sojourners, who expect to return to their sending regime permanently, may be unwilling and/or less likely to actively internalize meanings, values, and practices associated with the U.S. political system, and to be less likely to identify highly with those meanings that they do internalize.

Thus it is only among recent Latina/o immigrants, transmigrants, and sojourners that there is a strong possibility that Latinos will have multiple *national* identities or strong identifications with sending states. The question remains, however, what influence are those multiple national identities likely to have on the propensity of U.S. Latina/o transmigrants to have political loyalty to the United States as a political regime? Do multiple national identities influence the willingness of transmigrant Latinos to affirm U.S. ways of life? How might this question be assessed if Latina/o transmigrants are considered to have multiple identities? Once again, definitive research findings that might settle this point are not available. However, as I will argue in the remainder of this chapter, it is possible to assess the *likely loyalties* of Latina/o transmigrants and recent immigrants by taking a closer look at the life choices of those Latinos, and by considering the nature of loyalty in the context of contemporary multiple identities. For this purpose however, available research data seldom distinguishes those recent immigrants who are engaged in transnational activity from those who are not. However, because cash remittances to sending states are so large, and because the initial aim of many Latina/o immigrants is to gain resources to help family in their states of origin, in the discussion below I will assume that recent Latina/o immigrants are also transmigrants, although this may not always be the case.

Distributed Loyalty and Citizenship as (Re)Marriage: Reinterpreting the National Commitments of Latino Transmigrants Through the Marriage Metaphor

Of the three categories of U.S. Latinos then, only recent immigrants, sojourners, and transmigrants are likely to have socialization and configurations of identitiy that potentially include strong commitments of a political kind to another nation-state. Because Latinos in this category retain and act upon transnational ties, Latina/o transmigrants might be considered the worst offenders against Huntington's ideal vision of Latinos who are solely identified with the Unites States and its mainstream culture. For by Huntington's measure of ampersand identities, transmigrant Latinos seem to be too engaged abroad to be seriously committed to membership in and loyalty to the U.S. polity.

Yet, the question of whether or not the multiple national identities of Latina/o transmigrants poses an obstacle to their strong identification and political loyalty to the U.S. as their nation of new and primary residence depends to a large extent on how loyalty is defined. The "divided loyalty thesis" that so often accompanies assimilationist reasoning, defines political loyalty as indivisible. Loyalty is categorical and any other loyalty dilutes it. Yet this view of loyalty not only ignores our capacity to maintain multiple identities and the loyalties that those identities may involve, it also rests on an anachronistic account of loyalty that many regard as out of sync with the shape of contemporary societies. Alan Wolfe is among those who have explored and reconsidered the modern character of loyalty. He points out that in premodern cultures, especially medieval societies, the "outlets for loyalty" were limited in number as a consequence of the social order. That limitation made it clear exactly to what or to whom the subject was expected to be unswerving loyal.[52]

In contrast, modern segmented societies—especially those characterized by liberal capitalism—are diverse and complex with many outlets for loyalty and many incentives to shift or remake our loyalties. Wolfe argues that in contemporary societies, traditional conceptions of loyalty must be "recast in terms compatible with liberal or capitalist values."[53] Drawing from Josiah Royce's analysis, Wolfe argues that loyalty should center on the act of having loyalty—of being loyal to something. This approach leads to an updated conception of loyalty in which loyalty is something that people spread among a number of different objects of loyalty. Loyalty, in this modern sense, is not simply about choosing which things to which to be loyal, for example, our friends or our country. Rather, as Wolfe states "most of us feel the ties of both friendship and patriotism. The question is how we balance them, not how we choose between them."[54] In this view, loyalty should be understood as shared or "distributed loyalty," in which people allocate their loyalty among a variety of objects of loyalty, such as our families, friends, localities, countries, selves, and various social groups.

In relationship to multiple national identities, this notion of distributed loyalty suggests that, in the case of having multiple national identities, individuals could distribute their loyalties among different states in ways that would honor their membership in each. In so doing, they would make commitments to accept and prioritize various meanings, values, and practices as guiding dimensions of their lives. The execution of those commitments would mark the articulation of their loyalties and would provide the measure by which their loyalty is distributed among many objects. Changes in commitments over time would likewise mark how their loyalty commitments are made and remade. Moreover, it is by those commitments that conflicts of desire, commitment, and loyalty are resolved or balanced. Further, like multiple identities themselves, different loyalties would be exercised only in their appropriate places and times.[55]

If loyalty is seen as a commitment that is distributed and balanced, then transmigrants may potentially distribute their loyalty among different nations in a full and meaningful manner. In the case of transmigrant U.S. Latinos, it remains to be considered how Latina/o distributions of loyalty are to be understood based on the commitments that they routinely exhibit—assuming that such commitments express their national memberships and identities.[56] To consider questions regarding degrees of commitment to a nation, scholars often turn to metaphors to think about national membership—which is typically referred to as citizenship. Although not all transmigrant Latinos are citizens or authorized residents of the United States, we may still look to such common metaphors of citizenship to consider the degree of loyalty to a nation-state that is indicated by the choices, activities, and commitments of residents, regardless of their legal status.

Among the metaphors most widely used to consider questions of loyalty and commitment to a nation, the *marriage metaphor* is arguably among the most useful. Moreover as will be discussed below, the marriage metaphor as a family-based metaphor is particularly apt to the circumstancs of immigrant and transmigrant Latinos. On one face-value reading of the marriage metaphor of citizenship, the cross-border commitments of transmigrant Latinos and the multiple national identities that they often have do seem to betray a sacred political trust. After all, bigamy—a marriage in which a person has more than one spouse—offends our prevailing notions of marriage, and thus justifiably offends our law. If citizenship is analogous to marriage, then having multiple national identities and memberships is perhaps at odds with loyalty to the U.S.—as a marriage to two *political* spouses.[57]

But, on the other hand, if having multiple national identities is less analogous to bigamy and more akin to divorce and *re*marriage, then perhaps we should view the multiple loyalties and commitments of transmigrants somewhat differently.[58] The life choices of most Latina/o transmigrants clearly seem to display sustained commitment to taking part in the fabric of U.S. society, including commitments to living and working in the United States, commitments to raising children and caring for family members here in the U.S., and commitment to taking part in the daily lives of their local communities and the U.S. economy as a whole. Assuming that the marriage metaphor is an appropriate one for considering the question at hand, it may be that the metaphor sheds light on several reasons why the political commitments and loyalties of U.S. Latinos within multiple nation-states may be considered not only possible, but also acceptable *as expressions of loyalty to the political principles that define the United States.*[59]

First, in the case of marriage, it is reasonable and customary in the U.S. for *some* elements of the marriage bond to be exclusive while others are not. These "exclusive" activities typically include sexual activity and procreation, and leave open the possibility of other opposite gender (or same-sex) relationships that do not include sex or childbearing. In the case of dual citizenship and national identity, this might be analogous to restrictions on holding high political office, that leave open the possibility of other lower levels of participation.

Second, marriage allows for a whole variety of non-marital loyalties and allegiances. In most marriages there is room for spouses to have a range of non-marital relationships and to retain loyalties and commitments to other relationships. To some extent, we even judge the health of a married relationship by the hospitableness with which it incorporates pre-existing or new extra-marital relationships. In the era of widespread divorce and blended families (a shift from the nuclear to the globalized family, if you will) this also extends to cordial and more-or-less complex ongoing relationships with former spouses. For example, it is often necessary for spouses to retain bonds of joint financial responsibility with former husbands and wives and to share homemaking-related responsibilities as joint custodial parents legally and morally bound in the care of minor children.

In cases of divorce and separation therefore, we look for and expect continuing bonds between former spouses in the form of legal, emotional, social, and economic ties and practices that endure even when spouses have divorced and remarried shifting a primary commitment to a new life partner. It is *especially* when spouses have moved on to new marriages that we honor as morally right the continuation of certain life projects and commitments to support the emotional, financial, and general well-being of those "left behind." Those who do not do so are rightly labeled as dead-beat moms and dads, whose lack of loyalty to their past commitments, and to the present consequences of those commitments, are seen as morally bankrupt. Retaining such bonds does not prevent a spouse's integration into a new life partnership, but on the contrary, exhibits their moral and social fitness for doing so.

Reading the marriage metaphor with special attention to extra-marital bonds and loyalties can provide insight into whether the multiple national identities of transmigrants and recent Latina/o immigrants can include the kinds of commitments necessary for meaningful loyalty to the United States. Here, the marriage metaphor can be almost literally extended to many (though not all) of the circumstances of those Latina/o immigrants and transmigrants in the U.S. who maintain significant identification with their nation of origin. Granting that some kind of positive identification with the U.S. among transmigrants is desirable, a closer examination of the character of the life activities of most Latina/o transmigrants suggests that their transnational commitments do not detract from, and in many cases partly drive, their commitment to the U.S. as their primary place of residence. Rather, those relationships, taken as a whole, seem to resemble the kinds of continued familial bonds and commitments that we would expect from divorced and separated families. On such a reading, living in the U.S. and the commitments made in doing so represent for Latina/o transmigrants a political remarriage in which the relationship of transmigrants to the U.S. and to their families in sending states is one of *national-political* divorce and remarriage.

From this perspective, the commitments of transmigrant Latinas/os to the U.S. as a new marriage appear numerous and include first and foremost the uprooting of their lives elsewhere to immigrate to the U.S., and uprooting that is often expensive and now increasingly dangerous. For example, Mexican, Central American, and Caribbean Latina/o immigrants have often come to the United States as economic and/or political migrants. For political and economic reasons generally beyond their control, they have become unable to feed and protect their families at home (sometimes as a consequence of U.S. involvement in their countries of origin).[60] Consequently they have migrated (often without formal authorization) to the United States in search of work that will enable them to support the family members that they have left behind. Current estimates indicate that there are now over 10.3 million U.S. Latina/o unauthorized residents living in the U.S., including 6.4 million households.[61]

The commitment made by recent Latina/o immigrants (a group that I presume here to include the bulk of transmigrants) to live and work in the United States over time has deeply integrated Latina/o immigrants as part—although an often exploited and socially and politically subordinated part—of the overall U.S. economic, social, and political landscape.[62] For many recent immigrant Latinos, the work that they find in the U.S. is typically low paid and labor intensive. When Latina/o immigrants lack legal status, they are especially vulnerable to economic exploitation, and are often paid below the legal minimum wage. The average income for unauthorized immigrant Latina/o families "is more than 40% below the average income of either legal immigrant or native [Latino] families."[63] Low incomes create poor living conditions for many recent immigrants. Rents and living costs are commonly high and many immigrants live together in houses and apartments (and sometimes outdoors), working multiple low-wage jobs just to survive and to save.

Despite some earlier trends and current stereotypes to the contrary, however, many unauthorized Latina/o immigrants to the U.S. are married and/or heads of family households. Of the estimated 10.3 million unauthorized Latina/o immigrants in the U.S. 54 percent of men are married or in some kind of committed household. Only one in five unauthorized Latinas are single.[64]

Yet, the contribution of Latina/o immigrants to the United States is enormous, particularly in economic terms. Setting aside momentarily the issue of labor exploitation, U.S. Latina/o transmigrants meet U.S. demands for low-wage labor in many sectors of the U.S. economy. In the service, agriculture, and light manufacturing sectors the disproportionately low wages of immigrant laborers keeps production and productivity high and consumer costs low. Thus the commitment of immigrant Latinos—including unauthorized and transmigrant Latinos to come to the U.S. to work—contributes enormously to the well-being of the U.S. domestic economy. One sign of commitment to life in the U.S. among recent Latina/o immigrants may be seen in the rates of home ownership among unauthorized immigrants, which have been rising as mortgage lenders are increasingly seeking out the business of unauthorized Latinos.[65]

Moreover, the commitment to work among Latinos is statistically unsurpassed. For the *six decades* between 1940 and 2000, Latino men in California, for example, have had the highest rates of labor force participation. Their participation rates have exceeded those of whites, African Americans, and Asian Americans, and this despite their low incomes vis-à-vis other racial and ethnic groups. Moreover, the labor participation rate was higher among Latino *immigrants* than among U.S.-born Latinos.[66] Additionally, despite widespread (and frequently politicized) assumptions to the contrary, unauthorized Latina/o immigrants working in the U.S. contribute billions of tax dollars and social security payments to the U.S. economy and to public coffers annually. Those tax dollars, in turn, support public expenditures and social services from which Latinos benefit comparatively little. Despite popular misconceptions, Latinos, *especially* unauthorized Latina/o immigrants, have some of the lowest levels of welfare use among all ethnic and racial groups. For example a study commissioned by Los Angeles County revealed that for every dollar of county-funded social services that undocumented Latinos received, they contributed $4.56 in state and federal taxes. As one scholar has commented, "[s]tudies in state after state show that immigrants pay their fair share of taxes. Even the undocumented pay into social security through false numbers."[67]

There are also other signs that recent Latina/o immigrants and transmigrants have significant commitments to living in the U.S. that also contribute significantly to the well-being of U.S. polity. In addition to impressive Latina/o commitments to labor in the U.S. economy (despite receiving short shrift in it), Latina/o immigrants are becoming increasingly geographically dispersed across the country. Not only in the six states with the largest Latina/o populations (California, New York, Texas, Florida, Illinois, and New Jersey), but also across the country new Latina/o immigrants have been forming an increasingly large, visible, and productive part of urban and many rural U.S. populations. Geographical diversification of Latinos, has included commitment to living in the Midwest, especially in rural areas. In many cases, the arrival and settlement of Latina/o immigrants in the Midwest is helping to rebuild economic and civic stability, and to reinvigorate cities and towns that suffered from the decline of heavy industry at the end of twentieth century. For example, meatpacking—a generally dangerous occupation—has become an increasingly common type of employment among many Latinos in the U.S. Midwest.[68]

As a consequence of their labor contributions and commitments to the U.S. economy, Latinos also constitute a large and growing commercial market.[69] As consumers of domestic goods and services, U.S. Latinos, as a whole, spend billions of dollars annually. With at least 10 million unauthorized Latina/o immigrants in the U.S., many domestic firms are increasingly catering to their specific needs. Some financial institutions have increasingly accepted the consular issued *matrícula* identification cards to open bank accounts and to obtain credit, including mortgages. At present, 6 percent of the bank accounts open at Wells Fargo are held by unauthorized Latinos.[70] As immigrant Latinos invest themselves in the U.S., domestic retailers, manufacturers, and other businesses have begun to meet the tastes, interests, and needs of immigrant Latinos in their production and marketing plans. As they do so, domestic businesses confer legitimacy on unauthorized Latina/o immigrants as active members of the society whose lives are more and more deeply woven into the fabric of U.S. life.

Perhaps a still more compelling display of the "remarriage" among many Latina/o immigrants to a life in the U.S. is their decision to bear and raise children in the United States. Many children of Latina/o immigrants are U.S. citizens by birth. Of the estimated 4.7 million Latina/o children who have unauthorized parents, 3.1 million are native-born citizens.[71] The decision to raise children in the U.S. means that from early in life, the children of Latina/o immigrants will live within, and be socialized by, institutions that continue to privilege Anglo-American culture (e.g. public schools, mainstream media).[72] While those children grow up with the influence of their Latino families, local community organizations, and churches, as stressed above, the vast majority of those children will inevitably regard the United States as their land of origin. The identification of native-born Latina/o children with the U.S. may also foster commitments to the U.S. as a nation-state among immigrant and transmigrant parents who experience deepening commitment to the place where they raise their children.[73]

In addition to these commitments to work and family life in the U.S., however, many U.S. Latina/o immigrants—as (potentially) also transmigrants—also maintain various social, economic, and civic commitments in their lands of origin. Many Latina/o transmigrants save and collectively send billions of dollars in remittances back to their families and communities of origin year after year. In 2005 alone, Mexican immigrants in the United States returned 20 billion dollars to family members in Mexico; Guatamalans that year remitted 2.9 billion.[74] Many transmigrants visit the lands of their origin when they can, perhaps once or twice per year (although this practice is hindered for many by increasingly strict border controls). However, even in their absence, the hard-earned dollars of transmigrants feed, clothe, and educate the transmigrant's families abroad. Furthermore, their remittances are often used to build better homes, churches, and roads in rural areas and to build badly needed water and sanitation infrastructure. On the social and cultural side, transmigrant remittances also often help pay for religious celebrations and fiestas in their native villages and towns.[75]

As Huntington notes, engaging in transnational forms of civic engagement in this way has become an increasingly extensive and sophisticated enterprise among many U.S. Latinos. Many Latina/o transmigrants, for example, are members of "hometown associations" which are civic groups of U.S. Latina/o transmigrants from particular villages or states in Mexico or other sending nations. Based in the United States, these associations raise and pool resources for civic and social activities here in the U.S. and in their "hometowns" abroad. Some hometown associations have used their economic clout to negotiate with national and state governments, including successful efforts to obtain federal matching funds from the Mexican government for public works projects carried out in rural Mexico.[76]

Such expressions of transnational civic commitment, however, need not be seen as disloyalty or disengagement with the U.S. political system but, on the contrary may also be seen as a committed expression and extension of U.S. political principles of democratic civic engagement abroad. From their permanent base in the United States, transmigrant civic associations have borrowed political techniques from U.S. political practice and hybridized them in ways best-suited to enable them to pursue transnational political and civic goals. Their activities produce democratic "political remittances" that have, in some instances, compelled governments, such as the Mexican government, to better live up to their own domestic political and economic responsibilities. In their transnational commitments, transmigrant Latinos do not ignore U.S. political principles but export democratizing practices and principles of accountability and civic initiative to other regimes many of which have less robust democratic traditions.[77]

With this brief sketch in mind, it is useful to ask again whether the kinds of domestic and transnational activities often engaged in by Latina/o transmigrants are the political and moral equivalent of remarriage. Should we conclude that the motives and practices of Latina/o transmigrants are politically and morally repulsive and diametrically opposed to "American" national identity, as Samuel Huntington suggests? At first glance, it may seem that Latinos with strong multiple national identities are not putting their emotional, social, and economic investments into the United States as much as they are in Mexico or other sending states. Yet, if we step further back and look at the totality of the loyalties and commitments of Latina/o transmigrants, and regard their loyalties as *distributed loyalties* structured in part by the "divorces" imposed by migrant life, the picture looks quite different. For many, their financially-driven commitment to live their adult lives in the U.S. often extends to social and societal bonds and commitments involved in raising their children in the United States. Their commitments to the U.S. are thus subsequently transferred to the generations of U.S.-born Latinos that follow. In this sense, the commitment of Latina/o transnationals to the United States and the loyalty that commitment implies seems clearly present and enduring in character as a multigenerational legacy.

In addition, while there are variations—and generalization always obscures real diversity—it would appear that Latina/o cultural norms, on the whole, lay heavy emphasis on family commitment and responsibility, frequently encompassing both immediate and extended family. Many Latinos embrace these cultural norms, taking familial responsibilities seriously and often prioritizing them above all others; it is financial responsibility to one's family that typically motivates Latina/o migration. Once relocated, some Latinos continue to maintain their responsibilities to family members abroad as the billions of dollars in annual remittances amply demonstrate. The effort to build homes, infrastructure, and needed facilities "back home" may be both an effort to meet familial and community needs *and* to maintain the affective ties of family, friendship, and community in their place of origin. Such robust commitment to one's family is not generally considered anathema to U.S. national identity even in a narrow definition such as Huntington's.

Even so, for many Latina/o transmigrants, the commitments that they have to their land of origin are perhaps necessarily limited to financial and civic contributions and continued emotional bonds maintained through long distance communication and periodic visits. Many, if not most, Latina/o transmigrants do not return to Mexico or other lands of origin to reside, and those who do eventually leave the U.S. may have invested their adult lives in it, devoting many of the most productive years as laborers in the U.S. economy.[78] The U.S. thus becomes their de facto home—the place where they live on a daily basis, the place that their children consider home, and the place where their everyday community and work life is centered. Like members of the Jewish diaspora, however, Latina/o transmigrants and Latinos may retain affective and cultural ties and identifications to their land of origin at the same time that they are firmly committed to residence in the U.S.

Moreover, even when transmigrant Latinos practice their affective ties and cultural identifications with people and places in their lands of origin through concrete economic, familial, cultural, and civic activities in the sending states, such practical expressions of a Latina/o's transnational identities *do not rule out* or undermine ongoing identification with the United States. On the contrary, such community-oriented activities abroad may punctuate and enrich, rather than displace or detract from Latina/o lives in the United States.[79] Like a strongly Jewish-identified New Yorker who engages in political activity in Israel, the Mexican or Guatemalan transnational who continues to be engaged in civic activities in his place of origin is simply maintaining the bonds of kinship and sense of belonging and personal origins that most of us wish to cultivate in some way or another as we live in the United States.

Given the enormous commitment, sacrifices, and contributions that Latina/o transmigrants make to the well-being of the U.S., should we begrudge Latinos or members of other diasporas their affective ties to their heritage communities and to the families that still reside there? Through the marriage metaphor for citizenship, these affective ties and commitments appear to be no more and no less than equivalent to the continued maintenance of extra-marital relationships and responsibilities to family members and children who have been dispersed by the dissolution of a marriage. Since we applaud those parents who maintain responsibilities to dependents separated from them by divorce, there is little reason to withhold that approval in cases where transmigrants retain ties and responsibilities to those separated from them by (often forced) migration.

In terms of multiple identities, acceptance of transnational commitments and activities is especially warranted when loyalty to one nation does not prevent loyal identification with another. Only in rare instances, such as in the case of war between two countries with which a person is identified, would this require making a choice between such loyalties (e.g. American Germans during WWII). On the contrary, the kinds of life activities common among Latina/o transmigrants seem not to detract from, but rather to *reinforce and contribute fine examples* of the values and principles supposedly central to "American identity." Ironically, while Huntington regards the invading hordes of Latinos as having little in common culturally with the U.S. mainstream, the kinds of commitments and activities most commonly and strongly displayed among Latina/o transmigrants demonstrate the kind of hard work, civic, and familial commitments that Huntington regards as the foundational constructs of U.S. political identity. Huntington emphasizes, in particular, the propensity of Americans to work longer and harder than members of other nations—a quality he attributes to Anglo-Protestant culture. Yet, as demographer David Hayes-Batista has demonstrated compellingly with reference to California Latinos, "Since 1940, Latino males in California have demonstrated the highest labor-force participation, the longest work week, the greatest involvement in the wealth-generating private sector, the lowest use of public assistance, and the greatest propensity to form intact families."[80] Latinos may be neither English in origin nor predominantly Protestant in faith, but they clearly exemplify the commitment to work that Huntington valorizes as quintessentially American.

Thus Huntington fails to recognize the apparent convergence in social and moral values between the dominant Anglo-American ethnic culture and Latino cultures. Indeed, as mentioned above, Huntington attempts to persuade his readers that the moral and political values of Latinos and Anglos are so widely divergent that together they cannot sustain common politics. Consequently, he contends that as Latinos grow in numbers and remain bicultural, cultural bifurcation and U.S. political disintegration becomes inevitable. Yet, to support this important claim, Huntington offers only the evidence of quotations from a few Latina/o conservatives, a Mexican novelist, and a Mexican politician rather than turn to readily available new scholarship or longitudinal demographic data on U.S. Latinos such as that cited here.[81]

Among his few sources, Huntington turns to businessman Lionel Sosa to prove the radical incompatibility between Anglo and Latina/o moral values. Huntington quotes Sosa as saying that Latina/o "values remain quite different from an Anglo's."[82] Yet in *The Americano Dream,* from which Huntington is quoting, Sosa's next sentence—which Huntington does not quote—goes on to describe this vast difference in values between Latinos and Anglos. He writes, Latinos "still put family first, still make room in their lives for activities other than business, are more religious and more community-oriented. [And] [p]erhaps because their own parents spent so much time guiding them, they will set aside time for their own children."[83] Huntington does not explain how these particular alarming tendencies constitute a national threat.

Therefore if we grant to Huntington that Sosa is authoritative on Latina/o culture, it seems that there is by no means an unbridgeable gap between the Latina/o core cultural values and those of mainstream Anglo society. On the contrary, although Huntington dramatically asserts that there are irreconcilable differences in moral and political priorities, it is fairly easy to imagine building common political cause from the values and priorities invoked by both Latinos and Euroamericans. Both are concerned, to varying degrees with family life, work life, and economic security including such issues as education. Contrary to what Huntington suggests, there seem to be significant points of value convergence among Latinos and other U.S. residents. Chapter five discusses this further.

On the whole then, the multiple national identities of Latinos, *including* those of highly identified transmigrant Latinos, do not pose a theoretical or practical threat to Latinos in developing and maintaining U.S. national identity and loyal commitment to the U.S. as a political regime. Transmigrant values (e.g. work ethic, family commitments, economic independence) are as much in keeping with U.S. identity as those of most native-born Euroamericans. In most cases, Latina/o transmigrant immigrants are only doing what, in a globalized world, the bonds of family and marriage—even a dissolved marriage—bind us to do. It seems strangely inconsistent to mourn the lack of civic pride, civic organization, and community-based familial commitment among native-born Euroamericans and yet deride and reject the expression—however transnational—of those same values and practices when they are exhibited by Latina/o immigrants and transmigrants living and working in the U.S.[84] Practices common among many working poor Latina/o immigrants display practical commitments to what are already generally considered to be core U.S. values. Rather than render them unfit for U.S. citizenship, and a threat to U.S. national identity as Huntington argues, I would contend that their particular configurations of multiple identities and the practical endorsements and commitments associated with them make transmigrant Latinos well-oriented for U.S. national identity and for whatever robust forms of political integration the U.S. is willing to make possible.[85]

If the multiple ethnic and national identities of Latinos are fully consistent with U.S. identity and loyalty to the United States as a political entity, then there is still a lesson to be learned from Huntington's critique regarding the general implications of multiple ethnic identities for U.S. national identity. As Huntington points out in his brief description of multiple identities, identity expressions depend on the cooperation and recognition of others in the co-construction of our identities in contexts. In the absence of that recognition and co-construction it becomes impossible to claim the identities that we wish to claim. In a very real sense then, it is not that immigrants who retain ethnic identities do not wish also to be Americans. Rather, it is that the narrow, assimilationist, constructions of U.S. national identity do not allow them to meaningfully do so. When Huntington and others contribute to public political discourses that define immigrant ethnic and ethno-religious identities as mutually exclusive with U.S. national identity, they ignore that people may retain multiple identities that make it possible for them to be American as well as culturally Korean or Indian, Buddhist and secularist, and so on and to distribute and balance loyalties among the social groups and ways of life to which they are committed.

Moreover, this practical possibility is not something to simply tolerate, but something to embrace and capitalize upon. As Huntington himself acknowledges, multiple social identities can be related to each other in many different ways. Quoting Edmund Burke, he notes that smaller group identities that are nested within other larger group identities can either undermine or *reinforce* the cohesion of the larger group depending on how they are constructed. In his military example, the army that welcomes and fosters group attachment and cohesion of the "little platoon" promotes commitment and love of the larger army and fosters its cohesion and success.[86] Likewise, a nation that fosters group attachment and welcomes it among ethnic groups, and finds ways to construct and define that attachment as reinforcing the cohesion of the whole, may find ethnic group identities an asset rather than a challenge to its ability to bring disparate people together as a nation.

Thus, it is not the multiple ethnic identities of Latinos that are likely to undermine U.S. identity and national cohesion. Rather it is divisive assimilationist discourses such as Huntington's that identify ethnic identity as mutually exclusive with national identity. In so doing, Huntington and others refuse to construct U.S. identity in ways that incorporate the multiple cultural identities of its citizens— thus denying that the benefits of biculturalism are an asset to the nation because immigrant ethnic identity can often support the path to national identity. Such a posture would allow those Americans with multiple ethnic identities to better embrace U.S. national identity as their own. In this sense, understanding the fluid relationships among multiple identities is crucial to understanding their political implications. In the chapters that follow, I investigate the character of the relationships among multiple identities.

CHAPTER TWO

Mestiza Consciousness and Intersectionality
Toward an Interdisciplinary Framework
of Multiple Identities

[W]e may practically say that [a man] has as many different social selves as there are distinct groups of persons about whose opinion he cares. He generally shows a different side of himself to each of these different groups.... From this there results what practically is a division of the man into several selves; and this may be a discordant splitting, as where one is afraid to let one set of his acquaintance know him as he is elsewhere; or it may be a perfectly harmonious division of labor, as where one tender to his children is stern to the soldiers or prisoners under his command.
WILLIAM JAMES, *Principles of Psychology*

The self is "a series of clusters ... the geography of selves made up of the different communities [that] you inhabit."
GLORIA ANZALDÚA, *Interviews/Entrevistas*

Mestiza consciousness also provides for new understanding. It models a tolerance for ambiguity, a transgression of rigid boundaries, of borders set up by dominant groups to distinguish 'us' from 'them.' It is a consciousness that lives on the borders—lives in neither place and both. Mestiza consciousness raises questions and suggests new thinking about locatedness and its relation to identity.
SARAH HOAGLAND and MARILYN FRYE, "Feminist Philosophy"

The previous chapter's discussion of the multiple identities of U.S. Latinos suggests that a thorough understanding of the *political* implications of multiple identities requires a more detailed and rigorous account of multiple identities than is presently available. While multiple identities are being discussed more and more in political science, it is not yet entirely clear in theoretical or practical terms what we mean when we use the term multiple identities. What is needed then, is a framework of multiple identities and decentered subjectivity that can be used as a basis for exploring the political implications of multiple identities. In this chapter, I turn to Gloria Anzaldúa's concept of *mestiza consciousness* as a starting point from which to build a basic interdisciplinary account of multiple identities that will be further developed and used as a basis for further inquiry into the character of multiple identities and their political implications in later chapters.

Gloria Anzaldúa's account of mestiza consciousness offers an important critique of the unitary subject.[1] As such, it is a contribution that has been influential in a variety of scholarly domains including history, ethnic studies, feminist thought and women's studies, and political philosophy.[2] Anzaldúa's influence has grown as other influential feminist thinkers such as María Lugones and Chela Sandoval have interpreted her work.[3] Anzaldúa's first detailed account of mestiza consciousness appears in her 1987 book *Borderlands/La Frontera: The New Mestiza*. As discussed below, in *Borderlands* Anzaldúa explores the formation of multiple identities in areas of cultural overlap and mixture that she refers to as the "borderlands."

As a mixed-genre meditation on cultural *mestizaje* and decentered subjectivity, however, *Borderlands* was written to *evoke* theoretical ideas rather than exhaustively explore and develop those ideas analytically. As such, Anzaldúa creatively gestures toward new concepts and highlights novel interconnections by bringing together a diversity of perspectives and outlooks. Of her method she writes, "I try to . . . find language for my ideas and concepts that comes from the indigenous part of myself rather than from the European part . . . [and so I produce] this little nugget of knowledge [that] is both indigenous and western. It's a hybridity, a mixture, because *I live* in this liminal state between worlds, between realities, between systems of knowledge, between symbology systems."[4] In this sense, Anzaldúa's work in *Borderlands* is itself an expression of the kind of mestiza consciousness that she was describing and is an expression of Anzaldúa's own *mestizaje*.

With this method Anzaldúa's does "provide for new understanding" through her concept of mestiza consciousness just as Sarah Hoagland and Marilyn Frye suggest in the epigraph above. However, Anzaldúa does so by offering nuggets of novel hybrid knowledge upon which further understanding of multiple identities can be built. Thus, Anzaldúa's work in *Borderlands* is not—and was not intended to be—a detailed and rigorous account of decentered subjectivity or multiple identities. Nonetheless, Anzaldúa's conception of mestiza consciousness is an exceptional starting point for a detailed theoretical account of multiple identities because it has numerous commonalities with other important discussions of multiplicity, and combines these elements with novel insights that warrant further investigation and elaboration.

Specifically, Anzaldúa's conception of multiple identities shares dimensions with work by other scholars who have considered subjectivity and politics. Like William James and researchers in Social Identity Theory for example, Anzaldúa recognizes that multiple social identities are the aspects of self through which individuals interact effectively with very different groups of people. Like W. E. B. Du Bois in his concept of double consciousness, Anzaldúa contends that social hierarchies of race and ethnicity can structure multiple identities and render some combinations of identities so contradictory that they are painful to live and experience. Like pluralists such as Robert Dahl, Anzaldúa recognizes that when members of a society have multiple identities, this multiplicity may simultaneously unite and divide them in various ways. This, in turn, can foster overall cohesion among a disparate people by constantly unsettling group divisions.

While Anzaldúa's work has significant aspects in common with work by other thinkers, Anzaldúa also offers unique insights and illuminating combinations of elements that make her conception of mestiza consciousness groundbreaking and more useful than other conceptualizations as a starting place for understanding the political implications of multiple identities. For example, while Robert Dahl and Gloria Anzaldúa both emphasize the political significance of multiple identities for the connections they can create among disparate peoples, Dahl only describes the effects of multiple identities on the spontaneous remaking of groups and alliances within political contexts from the perspective of the broader democratic society itself. In contrast, Anzaldúa's work also offers a sense of what the politically important shifts among different multiple identities are like from the perspective of individual citizens and she gives an account of what that dynamic is like on an everyday basis. Moreover, unlike Dahl, Anzaldúa theorizes the critical political thought processes of citizens with multiple identities, which she argues involve a syncretic amalgamation of the best of contrasting perspectives, rather than simple alternation among different perspectives when different policy issues arise.[5]

In addition, while Anzaldúa's work has much in common with Social Identity Theory (SIT), in contrast to it Anzaldúa emphasizes not only that contradictions are possible among multiple identities, but that those contradictions are in some cases intensely *felt* by individuals. Most importantly, she argues that while identity contradictions can potentially be painful, they can provide the intellectual and affective basis for creative thought and analysis. In turn, she suggests that the creative impetus provided by identity contradiction can help individuals produce hybridized practices and approaches to political problems through which they can change prevailing norms and work to transform political problems rooted in those norms. Thus in contrast to Dahl's pluralist approach, Social Identity Theory and other approaches, Anzaldúa's account of multiple identities uniquely emphasizes identity contradictions and highlights how identity contradictions can become a source of political critique and social transformation.

Although Anzaldúa's conception of mestiza consciousness is an excellent starting point for investigating the character and political implications of multiple identities, it is sketchy at best as a framework for describing multiple identities in detail. Consequently, it is useful to unite Anzaldúa's approach with insights drawn from other domains of scholarly study. As discussed in the introduction, working towards an interdisciplinary account is warranted because it makes it possible to benefit from the most useful research available. Thus, while taking an interdisciplinary approach is clearly important, like other forms of *mestizaje*, scholarly work that is produced betwixt and between disciplinary spheres has rewards but also hazards. In particular, and as stressed in the introduction, interdisciplinary studies of this kind run the risk of disappointing the disciplinary expectations of readers. Some readers may consider some of the material surveyed here to be overly familiar, while others may find its new terminology inadequately explained. Some will find fault in this approach for giving short shrift to disciplinary debates and subtleties, while others will fault it for canvassing too much material. In short, the need for interdisciplinary work is not always matched with a given reader's pleasure at its departure from familiar disciplinary norms.

In this chapter, I acknowledge the challenges of reading interdisciplinary work through disciplinary expectations by using many subheads to label different topics so that readers may direct their attention to aspects of multiple identities of most interest to them. In part one, I situate the concept of mestiza consciousness within a broader concept of embodied subjectivity that draws from both philosophy and social psychology. In part two, I further supplement the definition of identity introduced in chapter one with the notion of identity schemes and by highlighting the variety of elements other than identities that are also common aspects of subjectivity. I follow this with an extended account of identity salience, identity formation and the relationship of mutually exclusive multiple identities to social and political conflict. In part three, I further illuminate the social construction of the self in relation to selective identification, identity enactments and self-presentation, and the way that levels of identification can produce shifts in levels of identification over time. The chapter closes with an initial look at the significance of identity contradictions for the political implications of multiple identities— an inquiry that is continued in chapter three.

Mestiza Consciousness and Decentered Subjectivity

In her writings, Gloria Anzaldúa articulates the idea that the self is formed by a complex intersection of different cultural groups and contexts that construct the self in multiple ways, analogous to the borderlands itself. In her influential book, *Borderlands/la Frontera: The New Mestiza,* Anzaldúa names this borderland self *la mestiza.* *La mestiza's* consciousness is a mixture of different and contradictory identities that Anzaldúa calls *mestiza consciousness.*[6] The multiplicity of competing identities that mingle and collide in the self may contradict each other and stand in relations of conflict and mutual influence.

Specifically, *la mestiza* may be socialized in different sets of cross-cutting social relations including class, ethnicity, race, gender, sexuality, nationality, religion, region, language community, and subculture. Living embedded in a multitude of conflicting social relations of culture, class, and sexuality, the *mestiza* gains a multiple or "dual identity" in which the subject straddles multiple lifeworlds. For Chicanos/as in particular, for example, Anzaldúa points out that Mexican Americans often identify partly, but not completely, with both Mexican and Anglo-American cultures. These multiple dimensions of social embeddedness and construction give the subject a composite identity that is a "synergy of two cultures with various degrees of Mexicanness or Angloness."[7] As such, mestiza consciousness is a specific form of decentered subjectivity that is produced through immersion in a complex web of social relations including various relations of subordination and privilege.

Constructed with different intersecting identities, *la mestiza* maintains these competing identities and lives them in everyday life. Living different identities requires *la mestiza* to continually engage the different sets of meaning, value, and practice that make up each of her different identities. In Anzaldúa's words, "[c]radled in one culture, sandwiched between two cultures, straddling all three cultures and their value systems, *la mestiza* undergoes . . . a struggle of flesh, a struggle of borders."[8] This struggle is the struggle to juggle and negotiate competing value systems and sets of meaning and practice conferred by competing cultural frames of reference.[9]

Anzaldúa's understanding of multiple identities is abstract. For it to serve as a basis for understanding the political implications of multiple identities, it is helpful to situate it within a broader conception of decentered subjectivity—but one that incorporates the idea of multiple identities. Such accounts of the subject are common in many domains of psychology and social psychology. There are many other examples of work that take a similar approach. Psychologist Richard Ryan notes, for instance, that "a growing number of paradigms view personality not as a self-unifying system, but rather as a collection of selves that operate independently in different contexts."[10] Looking for metaphors to describe subjectivity, some psychologists have conceptualized it as similar to a "'handbag,' a portable repository for various identity schemas that are cued up by differing social contexts."[11]

Psychologist Jefferson Singer, for example, has described the self as containing a variety of different identities. In his view:

> we do not possess just one unchanging image of self with clearly defined content. We see ourselves as multiple Me-Selves, each Me-Self differing depending upon the context and role dictated by that context. Each Me-Self contains cognitive, affective and motivational information relevant to its particular context.[12]

Singer's account echoes the words of William James and Gloria Anzaldúa quoted in the epigraphs above. All three thinkers regard subjectivity as composed of various identities related to different communities with which a person is identified. The self is *decentered,* in that no single identity is considered *a priori,* to be central or the most important identity of the collection within.

Further, within social psychology as a whole, "the realization that the self-concept can no longer be explored as if it were a unitary and monolithic entity" has led social psychologists to conceptualize subjectivity as containing a wide variety of elements.[13] These include pieces of internalized knowledge that are a "set or collection of images, schemas, conceptions, prototypes, theories, goals or tasks."[14] These pieces of self-constituting knowledge or "self-knowledge" include identities, but also other elements such as partial identities, identity fragments and other non-identity elements such as isolated beliefs, fears, traits, attitudes, and so on. As the idea that subjectivity is a collection of diverse pieces of self-knowledge spread throughout social psychology and to other disciplines such as sociology, it has become "commonplace to refer to the multiplicity of identity" and for each identity itself to be understood as involving a wide variety of elements including identity-specific cognitive, affective, and motivational knowledge, and knowledge of specific social roles and statuses.[15]

Thus identity can be defined as it exists within subjectivity as an *identity scheme*—a system of internalized pieces of knowledge made up of the cognitive, affective, and motivational elements related to understanding and enacting a particular identity.[16] In this, an identity scheme is made up of different identity-specific pieces of knowledge (also called self-constructs) including systems of *meanings* (i.e. the categories and definitions involved in the cognitive processing of information), schemes of *values* (which inform and structure affective evaluation), and sets of *practices* (that suggest a range of possible actions as motivational elements). These aspects of identity schemes are encoded in memory and are linked together in a single identity scheme as retrievable pieces of interrelated, identity-associated knowledge. *Ecphory* is the process by which humans activate and retrieve encoded memories. Information that is encoded in memory can be retrieved again only if it is activated by a specific retrieval cue. This retrieval cue must in some way match or "reinstate" the original encoding. Thus, identity schemes can be seen as sets of deeply encoded episodic, semantic, and procedural memories. Each identity frame has associated sets of memories, and as the subject enters different social contexts, aspects of those contexts are recognized through cognition as fitting patterns that, in turn, serve as retrieval cues for specific memories and, potentially, the identity schemes of which those memories are a part.[17] In addition, different identity schemes are potentially linked to each other through the overlapping or sharing of particular cognitive or affective elements (e.g. specific memories, ideas). The result is a subjectivity made up of complex webs of interrelated self-knowledge in which different identity schemes may intersect. The political implications of identity intersections are explored in detail in chapters three and four.

Subjectivity in general is not comprised of identities alone. Rather *subjectivity* refers to the self as a thinking, feeling, and embodied psychophysiological entity. As such, subjectivity can be understood to be comprised of five capacities—or subsystems of subjectivity—through which the subject negotiates the experience of physical stimuli (stimuli grasped through the senses) and internal stimuli (self-mediated thoughts and feelings) and the competing demands that those two types of stimuli can place upon human attention.[18] These capacities include three cognitive faculties and two physiological faculties that link the cognitive and the physical body. The cognitive faculties are traditionally divided into *cognition, affect,* and *motivation,* better known perhaps as *thought, feeling,* and *will.* These three elements are widely recognized in psychology as well as other fields. Philosophically, and specifically in Kantian terms, they may be thought of generally as pure reason, judgment, and practical reason.

Of these three subsystems of subjectivity, *cognition* (thought) includes processes of categorization and pattern recognition that involve perception, concept formation, and memory. Through cognition, the subject identifies and organizes information across different levels of abstraction. *Affect* (feeling or judgment) involves the evaluation of cognitively organized information in a given time and place. Affective evaluation often operates in a hierarchical manner through the production of a rank order of feelings or preferences in a given moment. However, the specific affective evaluations that humans generate from context to context are dynamic in character. Thus, a subject's "evaluative hierarchies are not fixed and will shift with situational cues."[19] *Motivation* involves the ordering and execution of actions to achieve a given goal. Together, the processes of cognition, affect, and motivation, are informed and structured by various meanings, values, and practices, socially constructed elements that are learned, internalized, and performed, and that are drawn from specific social discourses, structures and social groups that construct the subject over time.[20]

In addition to cognition, affect, and motivation, two other organizational systems form the interface between the cognitive systems of the self, the material world, and the body. The first is the *behavioral system* in which motoric actions are performed with minimal conscious thought based in response to cues from the physical world and/or our bodies—e.g. speech, riding a bike. These motoric subroutines can include complex behaviors that rely on the "overlearning" of complex actions. Once overlearned in this way, they become automatic and can take place with minimal attention. This "allows attention to be directed to more voluntary and complicated behavioral choices" such as what to say or where to ride.[21]

Finally, a fifth system (following Jefferson Singer) is the *psychophysiological system,* which involves those structures within the body that control physiological responses to stimuli by regulating homeostatic functions such as breathing, heart rate, and other involuntary processes and responses. This system ensures, for example, that it is not normally necessary to consciously think about breathing in order to inhale, or to consciously will one's heart to beat for it to do so. Yet, because the cognitive and physical systems are interconnected via this psychophysiological subsystem, some conscious cognitive functions can influence these "involuntary" bodily functions.

In this five-part system of subjectivity, there is interpenetration between the cognitive systems and the physical body. That is, while each of the five faculties of subjectivity works independently, these systems are complex, interconnected, and overlapping. For example, bodily dynamics can influence cognitive processes since physical cues, such as pain, can be categorized cognitively, evaluated affectively, and can inform motivation and intentional action. Conversely, cognitive processes can have physical manifestations. For example, a person may experience an involuntary flush in response to a comment made by her co-worker. Yet, the supposedly "involuntary" physiological response–one that regulates bodily functions—is triggered by embarrassment (an affective evaluation) that, in turn, depends on interpretation of the co-worker's comment (cognitive categorization).[22] Because the psychophysiological, and other subsystems can function at a conscious or at an unconscious level, these combined subsystems encompass both the conscious and the unconscious subjectivity.

Together, these subsystems unite with all internalized pieces of knowledge to form embodied subjectivity as a whole. Together these combined capabilities enable the subject to make the interpretations and distinctions needed to negotiate the competing internal and external demands of daily living. What then is the relationship of identities to this system of subjectivity? To use a common metaphor, the elements of stored self-knowledge that make up a person's subjectivity (e.g. identity schemas, identity fragments, isolated beliefs, etc.) are to the subsystems of subjectivity as computer data files are to a computer's operating system. Cognitive capacity is the bare *ability* to categorize; however, the meanings that are stored as self-knowledge of specific social categories are the raw material through which that bare capacity is utilized. Thus, stored self-knowledge of the descriptive elements that define the social categories of woman, man, or Latino, are *cognitive self-constructs* (i.e. systems of meaning) the subject uses to cognitively perceive themselves and others. Similarly, values and standards of assessment associated with different self-constructs, such as different aesthetic sensibilities, emotional responses, or feelings of social belonging are *affective self-constructs*. And practices, patterns of conduct, and drives for action or inaction that represent internalized knowledge are *motivational self-constructs*.

In this sense, identity schemes are different frames of reference in and through which the subject thinks, feels, judges, and acts in the world. Different identity schemes are made up of "self-constructs" (a term from social psychology) that refers here to discrete pieces of internalized knowledge. For example, knowledge of how to operate a drill or how to perform a formal introduction are internalized practical or social skills. Likewise, a fearful aversion to snakes, and a sense of calm in response to the smell of rain are affective and esthetic sensibilities that are internalized as socialized pieces of knowledge that, in turn, become part of the self. In these examples, the first two pieces of self-knowledge might be associated with different social identities, whereas the third and forth might exist as isolated fears and pleasures. Whatever way they are configured within subjectivity, however, all of these self-constructs are socially constructed and internalized either as parts of specific identity schemes, or as parts of identity fragments or other attitudinal schemes, or as relatively independent elements of subjectivity. Given the specifics of socialization and internalization, different identity schemes may become linked by shared pieces of self-knowledge. The significance of such identity intersections is addressed at length in chapters three and four.[23]

Salience as the Activation of Identities

The interdisciplinary framework of subjectivity just described incorporates a constructivist understanding of identity as well as key concepts from philosophy and psychology. It has two notable advantages over traditional unitary accounts of the subject. First, unlike most traditional philosophical accounts of subjectivity, this acount amply highlights how subjectivity is *embodied*. It identifies the specific elements of interconnection between cognitive and physical capacities of the body and mind as intertwined aspects of subjectivity. Second, this framework also places feelings, emotion, and aesthetic judgments—referred to collectively as affect—on a structural par with cognitive functions, including pattern recognition and analytical functions associated with logical reasoning. This is important given the historical tendency in Western thought to subordinate emotion and affect to "reason" as definitive of rationality. In the context of European imperialism this subordination of affect, in turn, became instrumental in justifying the subordination of women, non-European peoples, and others, whose political voices were strategically defined as dominated by emotion and hence invalid.

As it stands, however, this interdisciplinary framework of decentered subjectivity does not yet account for how specific internalized identities or other self-constructs become activated or "salient" from one context to another even as other identity schemes remain inactive. Nor does Gloria Anzaldúa's account of mestiza consciousness explain the elements of identity activation or "salience" that were discussed with reference to ethnic and racial identity in chapter one. Anzaldúa does, however, dwell on the fact that mestiza consciousness involves having and living different identities in different social contexts and relationships. She refers to the ability of *la mestiza* to switch among her multiple identities, and to thereby think and act differently in different social contexts. Feminist philosopher and interpreter of Anzaldúa, María Lugones, has influentially referred to this capacity to shift among different identities from one situation to another as "world traveling."[24] Yet, neither Anzaldúa, Lugones, nor the framework of subjectivity sketched above fully explains how this shifting takes place.

Fortunately, the specific processes of identity activation are explained and analyzed in Social Identity Theory (SIT), and in the empirical research and self-categorization theory that has emerged from SIT. For this aspect of subjectivity, it is helpful to turn again, and in greater depth than in chapter one, to SIT. Social Identity Theory is an influential body of research in social psychology that originates in the research of Henri Tajfel (1919–1982). Tajfel's influence and that of SIT, in general, can be seen today in the work of many scholars and various schools of thought, not only in social psychology, but also in other disciplines such as communication.[25] While other schools of thought in social psychology also address the issue of identity salience, I consider SIT most useful for three reasons.

First, SIT focuses, not only on the social construction of identity and the resulting diversity of the self, but it also attends to the role of judgment and choice within the complex processes that are involved in the social construction of the subject. In this, SIT regards the decentered and multiple subject as both constructed and *constructing* with regard to identity and identity enactment. With this dual focus, SIT acknowledges the enormous influence of social construction without concluding that the will and voluntary actions of the subject are dominated or determined by the dynamics of language-mediated social constructions that exceed them. As becomes evident in the chapters to come, keeping the constructed and constructing aspects of the decentered and multiple subject continually in mind is important to understanding the political implications and possibilities that can arise from multiple identities.

Second, SIT offers an extended and detailed explanation of the processes of identity enactment, and its co-construction in context. As demonstrated in chapter one, this collective aspect of identity formation can have significant political importance. Social Identity Theory—like Anzaldúa's account of mestiza consciousness—thus gives attention to the social adaptation and flexibility that multiple identity enactments often involve. In this, SIT moves away from approaches to personality that continue to regard specific aspects of the self—especially traits and some group identities such as racial and gender identities—as personal and interior, rather than as social group related and flexibly co-constructed and manifest in context.[26]

Finally, SIT emphasizes the *collective* character of social group identities as a basis for collective *action*. In so doing, the identity-related concepts that are central to SIT comprise—as Tajfel intended—an important tool for analyzing social group dynamics including intergroup and societal conflicts, prejudice, forms of social subordination, political polarization, and other group political dynamics. In this, SIT examines issues of group subordination and social exclusion that are also addressed in Gloria Anzaldúa's account of mestiza consciousness. As will become clear in later chapters, these issues are also central to the political implications of multiple identities, and are thus central concerns of this book.

Social Identity Theory (including self-categorization theory) explains the processes by which multiple identities become activated. It begins with the fact—borne out in empirical studies—that among all of the identities and other self-constructs stored within a given subjectivity, only a small portion of these identities are activated as consciousness at any given time. The subset of self-constructs that is activated as the interpretive-feeling-acting outlook in a given moment is commonly called the *working-self* or *working self-concept*.[27] The identities that are activated in a given moment as the working self are considered to be "salient" in that moment, and the specific dynamics of how a given identity becomes activated in a particular context is referred to as *salience*. When a specific identity scheme or other self-construct is "salient" as the working-self it is actively in use in the cognitive, affective, and motivational processes of the subject in a given time and place.[28]

In general, SIT posits that a given social identity (or other nonidentity self-construct) will become "salient" (i.e. activated as the working-self) when it best fits the relational dimensions of a context based on the subject's perception and interpretation of the information that he or she considers relevant to the immediate situation and their goals and aims within it. Particular identities will thus "fit"— that is, will be cognitively, affectively, and/or motivationally associated with a particular social context or personal relationship. Determinations of "fit" may be conscious or unconscious, and are generally arrived at, in part, through socially constructed and interpreted cues that are part of each social context or interpersonal interaction.

Specifically, social cues bring to mind an association between a given setting or interactions and specific identity schemes or other self-constructs. Internalized identity schemes are learned in association with particular social contexts and relationships. They are encoded in memory and retrieved from memory in part through those constructed and internalized associations. Thus, different identity schemes come to be thought of as relevant to and to be performed in specific social contexts or social interactions.[29] Self-constructs associated with particular social identities are associated with group life and its composite meanings, values, and practices. Self-constructs associated with specific personal identities are internalized in connection with the unique and idiosyncratic relationships that we have with individual parents, lovers, co-workers, etc. In the context of group life, or interaction with a specific person with whom we are identified, the identities that "fit" or are associated with those group or personal relationships become salient.

In addition to interpretations of and responses to social cues, identity salience is also (as mentioned in chapter one) a function of active—but also constrained—acts of self-presentation. Not only do subjects interpret social cues, they also make judgments regarding how they wish to identify and categorize themselves with reference to those social cues *within the constraints that condition each social context* (constraints of identity co-construction are discussed further below). In any given context, all subjects with multiple identities will make conscious or unconscious judgments as to identities they feel best fit the setting and how they wish to identify and present themselves in the context at hand. Judgments of fitness for a particular identity in any given instance will be influenced by 1) the subject's "past experiences, present expectations and current motives, values, goals and needs," 2) by the self's degree of identification with that identity, 3) how frequently or how recently that identity has been salient, and 4) how important and valued that identity is in relation to other identities within a person's stored self-concept.[30] In any given instance in which a shift in identity salience takes place, subjects will be more or less ready to have different identities among their multiple identities become salient, based on their interpretation of the cues and context at hand.[31]

On the whole, passive (cue) and active (self-presentation) salience dynamics are constantly in motion. Whenever a subject enters a new situation—or the situation that they are in changes in significant ways—aspects of that context will cue particular identities by bringing to mind the internalized elements associated with that cue. This, in turn, initiates within subjectivity—at a conscious or unconscious level—the cognitive and affective processes informed by the specific subset of internalized identities or other self-constructs that have become salient. Identity salience is thus a function of how the subject understands and wishes to engage their various identities *and* the perceived limitations placed on identification in an immediate situation. This complex process involves not only categorizing oneself, but also categorizing those we encounter, in order to relate ourselves to them as we identify ourselves. Consequently, salience and identification are greatly influenced in each given situation by the words and actions of others as well as by the agency of the subject.[32]

Identification and the Contextual Co-Construction of Identity[33]

The complexity of identity salience suggests that *identification* can and should be understood in at least two ways. First, to have an identification—i.e. identification as a noun—means to have internalized an identity scheme comprised of sets of meanings, values, and practices that are specific to a given identity scheme. Any such identification is an internalized collection of self-knowledge. Second, when understood as a verb, identification refers to the *process* of self-identification as the act of claiming an identity or multiple identities for oneself to and before others. This act of self-identification involves placing oneself into various identity categories. Consequently, self-identification to and before others also includes two further subprocesses.[34]

The first subprocess of self-identification involves how persons conceive of and prioritize their own identities and other self-concepts. In this sense, identification refers to the degree of commitment or bonding—the emotional or affective attachment—that a subject has toward an internalized identification, including a personal identity with a given individual or a social identity with membership in a particular social group. One can hold an identity dear and regard it as very important among one's range of self-concepts, while regarding other identities as relatively unimportant. For example, in her study of West Indian immigrants to the U.S., sociologist Mary Waters finds that the patterns of self-identification among U.S.-born children of West Indian immigrants vary significantly and are shaped by patterns of racialization associated with the U.S. color line. Unlike the complex systems of color spectrum and caste that prevail in the Caribbean and throughout Latin America, the U.S. color line divides all Americans into two mutually exclusive racial categories of Black or white. Thus, while West Indian immigrants might not be regarded as Black in their lands of origin, West Indian immigrants to the U.S. are generally regarded as racially Black as if they are non-immigrant Blacks. In the face of this racial categorization however, some West

Indian immigrants become highly identified with their immigrant ethnicity—as Jamaican, Haitian, Trinidadian and so on—and have much less identification with their racial identity as Blacks. In contrast, others become highly identified racially as Black Americans, and have very little, if any, immigrant ethnic identification.[35]

Moreover, Waters finds that not only are there differences in the degrees of ethnic and racial identification among West Indians, but that those degrees often shift over time as individuals revise their self-understandings. Waters writes: ". . . identities are fluid and change over time and in different social contexts. There are cases we found of people who describe being very Black American-identified when they were younger who become more immigrant-identified, when they began high school and found a large immigrant community" with which they wished to be identified.[36] Waters' findings are similar to those of other studies of second generation immigrants. In the Children of Immigrants Longitudinal Study, for example, over half of the second and third generation immigrant youth responding indicated a significant change in their ethnic self-identifications in a four year timespan.[37]

The second subprocess of self-identification involves those processes by which individuals lay claim to particular identities *in specific contexts,* and thereby locate themselves in the system of social categories present or relevant within a given social setting. The identity or identities that an individual claims can vary from context to context. A person with an identification as a lesbian (i.e. an internalized identity scheme as a lesbian) may actively represent or identify herself to others as a lesbian in one context, yet choose not to actively represent herself as a lesbian in another setting. Thus, practices of self-identification with a given identity can vary from one context to the next while the identification itself (i.e. as an internalized identity scheme) remains part of the individual's subjectivity.[38] As I will argue in chapters five and six below, the flexibility and potential inconsistency of self-identification can play a significant and useful role in actively self-integrating multiple identities in subjectivity as a whole.

By combining SIT's account of fit and identity salience with Anzaldúa's account of multiple identities within social conflict, it is possible to begin to theorize further how multiple identities are experienced in the midst of social and political rifts. As seen in chapter one with regard to Latina/o ethnic identity for example, all of the dimensions of identification that subjects may undertake are constrained by various social and political factors including group conflicts. That is, self-identification is not simply voluntary or wholly personal, but is conditioned and constrained by what I will call here "contextual co-construction" in which individuals in the midst of identifying and presenting themselves to others in social contexts will encounter either acceptance or rejection of their identity claims by others. Identities—both social and personal—are *relational* in that *claims to group identities require the acceptance of those claims by others within social interaction to be successful.* Such mutual or relational processes of identification thus introduce the interpretations and views of others into the processes of self-identification as co-constructors of our identities. In the politicized context of some group conflicts and/or established group hierarchies, encountered co-constructions may or may not reinforce one's own momentary identity claims.

When the co-constructions of others are out of sync with one's own self-understanding, those opposing messages can produce emotional pain or confusion in social encounters.[39] Moreover, when those co-constructions involve rejections of identity claims, they can place strong limitations on the self-identification options available, or at least unassailable, to a person in a given setting or settings. In Mary Waters' study, for example, immigrant youth frequently describe the challenges and difficulties of identifying as they would like when encountering the identity-related expectations of others. One seventeen year-old Haitian woman, whom I will call Claudia, described her multiple identifications this way:

> When I'm at school and I sit with my black friends and sometimes *I'm ashamed to say this,* but my accent changes. I learn all the words. I switch. Well, when I'm with my friends, my black friends, I say I'm black, black American. When I'm with my Haitian American friends, I say I'm Haitian. Well, my being black, I guess that puts me when I'm with black Americans, it makes people think that I'm lower class . . . Then if I'm talking like this [regular voice] with my friends at school, they call me white.[40]

As she notes in the passage, Claudia's identity enactments are shaped by much more than her sense of self or her desire to retain her friendships. As she describes them, her acts of self-identification are informed and constrained by the projection of class and racial hierarchies that her peers accept and reiterate. As Claudia struggles to develop methods for presenting her identities as a Black woman *and* as a Haitian woman in different contexts, she is acutely aware of the costs in stigmatization and rejection by friends and others that she will incur if she presents her multiple identifications in unwelcome ways in different settings. In some cases, presenting her Black identity will lead to stigmatization as those she encounters will regard her as "lower class" in association with her Black racial identity. In yet other settings, her black peers will use ridicule and denial to check any showing of ethnic identity in the form of ethnic vocabulary or intonations that do not conform to prevailing racial group expectation. In this, Claudia's identifications are co-constructed by others in that she is faced with the need to gauge and structure or "negotiate" her moment-to-moment identifications and identity claims in relation to the constraining expectations of others in various settings. Those constraining expectations are, in turn, shaped by longstanding political conflicts involving racial divisions and racialized political divides.

Negotiating Multiple Identities in Context

In my reading of it, the example of Claudia's shifting among her multiple identities reveals two further dimensions about the character of multiple identities. First, Claudia's self-description indicates that it is possible to be consciously aware—even at a fairly young age—of the process of shifting among multiple identity schemes from one setting to another and to be self-critical of how one goes about that process. In this instance, Claudia describes herself, sadly, as ashamed that she has developed ways to present her multiple racial and ethnic identities through linguistic code switching of accents and speech patterns. She is aware of her use of vocabulary, intonation, and other speech elements to reflect and claim her identities in contexts in which they are expected and accepted by those she values. In this sense, her experience is consistent with the psychological account of multiple identities advanced by William James in the early twentieth century in which James famously argued that we have as many different social selves as we have people or groups of people for whom we care. James's account of the multiplicity of the self is central in my account of the political implications of multiple identities and his analysis is considered in detail in chapter four.[41]

Second, the example of Claudia from Waters's work also demonstrates how living multiple identities may involve "negotiating" those identities in the sense that individuals may encounter a number of obstacles or limitations to their self-identification in the daily course of self-identification. In some contexts, evading or surmounting those hindrances may require them to modify or adapt their self-identifications, forego some identifications temporarily, or suffer denial or rejection on the basis of their self-identifications. Such awareness of the limits imposed on self-identification in various social terrains is not new. Many, if not most, social settings involve social expectations that impose constraints on self-expression and identification in the form of immediate critiques that may range from stares or stigmatization to jeers and harassments. There are few settings, for example, in which it is socially expected and accepted to present oneself in relatively uncommon identities, such as a nudist or a full-dress Trekkie. Those who are highly identified in these ways and present those identities often anticipate, and do receive, some negative social sanction for doing so.[42]

Yet, the example of Claudia in Waters's study suggests that the constraints on self-identification may be equally great, or sometimes greater, when a person's multiple identities include common identifications that are socially constructed as mutually exclusive—particularly when those constructions are a function of ongoing group conflicts, political contestation, or hierarchical social relations such as patriarchy, racism, or heterosexism. Identifying with groups on both sides of mutually exclusive social categories such as white/Black, native/foreign, rich/poor, Jewish/gentile, male/female, hearing/deaf, or Eastern/Western conditions self-identification in ways that force those with multiple identities to make choices regarding how they will present themselves and what identities they will assert in specific contexts.[43] In Claudia's case, racial Black and ethnic Haitian identities are constructed as mutually exclusive by her peer groups. Because she identifies and routinely claims both of these identities however, she must balance the risks of racial and class stigmatization on the one hand, with the risk of the denial of her Black identity by peers on the basis of her ethnicity on the other. In this situation, class is associated with racial identity and ethnic identity in a cross-cutting manner that I will discuss further below.

In sum, the complexities of identification require the subject with multiple identities to "negotiate" their multiple identities in various contexts. Such negotiation involves grappling with and acting in response to the sometimes cross-cutting demands of co-constructed expectations and self-identification in specific social contexts. For some individuals—such as those whose identities are more or less nested and compatible and who cross few contested borders—these negotiations may be so easy and untroubled as to make the process of negotiating multiple identities itself invisible or unfelt. For others—especially those with identities that are socially constructed as mutually exclusive on the basis of social or political conflict—those negotiations will be complicated and potentially fraught with challenges, anxiety, and sometimes pain. It is this latter kind of person—the person whose configuration of multiple identities includes highly contradictory or mutually exclusive identities—that Gloria Anzaldúa is principally referring to in *Borderlands*.[44]

For Claudia this "negotiating" of her multiple racial and ethnic identities contextually through language code-switching is one way to manage the minefield of contradictory expectations that her identifications excite in others (another would be to withdraw from one or both). Given her specific configuration of multiple identities, the particular challenges to her identity claims that Claudia faces are a function of the social and political group conflicts in the broader society that *relate and divide* two of the social groups with which she identifies and feels herself to belong—Haitians and American blacks. In this negotiation, I would contend that Claudia's membership and belonging are genuine in that they are rooted in her socialization and conscious identity claims. Yet for Claudia, as a border-crosser among groups in conflict, her belonging is never final or complete. This is because—once again—all claims to social group identity, membership, and belonging depend, in part, on the acceptance and acknowledgement or rejection by others of those identity claims. In Claudia's case, in neither sphere in which she lives and identifies is she accepted entirely for *all* of her multiple identifications. Each sphere accepts only a subset of her identities. Thus, by having multiple identities and choosing to live as a border-crosser between divided or conflicting groups, Claudia's prospects for gaining acceptance of her identity claims are always troubled by the palpable risk of rejection based on her multiplicity of identities. Those rejections are ultimately rooted in the ongoing conflicts between the multiple social groups with which she identifies.

But if negotiating multiple identities in contexts is also negotiating the grassroots terrain of group political conflict, how do border-crossers negotiate their multiple identities? While Anzaldúa supplies almost no detail on this question, social identity theorists have given significant attention to this process of identity shifting in which perceivers understand themselves—as Claudia does—to have consciously initiated a shift in their salient identities in relation to contextual factors. Social identity theorists argue that when identity salience shifts are conscious decisions—*and it is vital to note that in many cases they are not conscious decisions or even readily perceptible to us*—subjects may initiate them on the basis of a wide range of possible elements.[45] Specifically, self-categorization theory conceives identity salience as a function of not only the "fit" between an identity scheme and a social situation (as discussed above) but also of the "perceiver's readiness" to employ a particular identity (personal or social) as the relevant identity for a given circumstance based on past experience and current motives, expectations, and needs.[46] Considering both fit and perceiver readiness, John Turner describes conscious salience shifts as the "active selectivity of the perceiver in being ready to use categories which are relevant, useful and likely to be confirmed by the evidence of reality."[47]

In light of this definition, identity salience shifts in the negotiation of multiple identities are potentially politically relevant because they can involve a conscious evaluation—from the identity scheme(s) presently salient—of how a person wishes to identify themselves in their current context. In contexts of political or social conflict, those choices may be strategic and politically charged, as well as potentially emotionally confusing or painful. African American lawyer and scholar Kimberlé Crenshaw describes a moment after her first-year exams at Harvard Law School when she and a black male colleague are invited by a third black male colleague to celebrate with a drink at an elite men's club in which he was one of the few black members. Upon approaching the club door Crenshaw and her friend are stopped suddenly by the club member who recalls sheepishly—after an awkward pause in which Crenshaw bristles with expectation of racial exclusion—that Crenshaw must enter through the back door of the club because she is female.

In that moment, Crenshaw, who becomes angry at the insult, must decide how to present herself as a Black person and a woman with two black men in an elite white male setting. Of the choice she writes:

> I entertained the idea of making a scene to dramatize the fact that my humiliation as a female was no less painful and my exclusion no more excusable than had we been sent to the back door because we were Black. But, sensing no general assent to this proposition, and also being of the mind that due to our race a scene would in some way jeopardize all of us, I failed to stand my ground. After all, the club was about to entertain its first Black guests—even though one would have to enter through the back door.[48]

Readiness to identify in certain ways and judgments of identity fit are not the whole story however. For although all self-constructs stored in memory are, in principle, *available* as frames of reference for thought and action, they are not all equally *accessible* as being readily or easily available for activation. Some multiple identity schemes and constructs are more readily accessible for use than others, and varying levels of accessibility are a consequence of: 1) the self's level of identification with a given identity scheme, 2) how frequently that identity scheme is salient, and 3) how recently an identity was activated. Of these three factors, the level of identification is the most important one in determining accessibility.[49] The most accessible identity schemes are those with which the subject is most highly identified, followed by the most often activated, and then most recently activated. All three of these influences shape the readiness and ease with which an identity can become salient. In Claudia's case, because she is highly identified with both black and Haitian identity, they are also likely to be her most frequently salient identities as well.[50]

Variations in accessibility can play a significant role in which multiple identities are most likely to shape our daily thoughts and actions. The salience of little used, and thus less accessible, identities will generally give way to the salience of more frequently used and/ or highly identified identity schemes. Those more accessible identity schemes are, in turn, more likely to serve as frames of reference for thought and action. This is illustrated in empirical studies in social psychology called sequential priming studies in which a person is given numerous cues to make a particular identity highly accessible to them. If they are then shown a different cue and asked to perform a cognitive task, such as a sorting evaluation, their initial sorting will conform to the most recent cue, but after a short time, they will then revert to the more accessible frequently cued scheme.[51]

This accessibility preference is an important clue for understanding the political relevance of multiple identities. It suggests that identity salience—*and thus individual perceptions and responses*—can be manipulated over various timeframes to different and potentially politically relevant effects. On one hand, it is possible for political actors to intentionally manipulate identity scheme accessibility through frequently repeated political messages. I discuss this possibility in the concluding chapter.[52] On the other hand, individuals may also self-manipulate identity accessibility as a part of selfcraft. This process of manipulating identity accessibility is central to self-integration of multiple identities, and is theorized in detail in chapter six.

While identity accessibility—and thus the readiness of particular outlooks—can be manipulated, I would suggest that the self-manipulation of identity scheme accessibility is not completely open. Rather, like self-identification, identity accessibility in context is also constrained by co-constructions of various kinds over various time frames.[53] Consequently, it is possible for identity accessibility and salience to be shaped by social and political circumstances. For example, Japanese American anthropologist Dorinne Kondo describes a slow but significant reduction in the accessibility of her American ethnic identity in favor of her Japanese ethnic identity during several months immersed in fieldwork in Japan.[54] Having been engaged in participant-observation and living full-time with a Japanese host family, Kondo had no interactions with co-ethnic Americans, and had not identified herself as an American to others for many months. One afternoon, Kondo suddenly catches her reflection in a shop window and is stopped short by this unexpected self-encounter. She is shocked to see that she is visibly indistinguishable from a Japanese housewife. Kondo realizes that her daily research context has demanded that her Japanese identity be almost constantly salient while her identity as a Western anthropologist and American has been activated only rarely. As a consequence of disuse, her American ethnic identity had become relatively less accessible to the degree that it had become difficult for Kondo to remember how thinking and acting as an American would feel.

While Kondo was initially unconscious of the slow shift in the relative accessibility of her different identities, once made aware of it, she acted quickly to increase the accessibility of her American identity. She returned to the United States and immersed herself in scholarly and cultural settings that would bring her American identity back into frequent daily use.[55] When she returned to Japan, she rented an apartment next door to her host family in which her identities as an American and scholar could be salient in privacy each day without negatively influencing her research. As a scholar with the resources to relocate quickly internationally, Kondo was relatively free in this case to act to reshape the relative accessibility of her Japanese and American identities.

In other cases however, political conflicts or other circumstances may present co-constructions that constrain one's ability to shape the regular salience and accessibility of certain identities. For example, due to ongoing political conflict between the U.S. and Cuba and the travel restrictions associated with them, Cuban American political scientist Maria de los Angeles Torres—who is highly identified as both Cuban and American—is much less able than Kondo to move freely and without consequence between international sites that are important to her. The political conflict between Cuba and the U.S. results in co-constructions that constrain Torres' self-identifications. Based on the long-standing conflict, some perceive her Cuban and American identities to be mutually exclusive and project onto Torres a contradiction among her Cuban and American identities. Island Cubans reject Torres' claims to Cuban identity because of her life in the United States. Conversely, Cuban Americans reject her claims to Cuban and American identity as a consequence of her willingness to return to Cuba and work for normalized relations with the Castro regime.

While struggling within the constraints of political conflict, Torres seeks to reject these mutually exclusive constructions of her multiple identities as Cuban and American. She states, "[e]ach time I return across time and space, each time I move between cultures and economic systems, I am more convinced that I do not want or need to accept the either/or conception of my identity that demands that I choose sides." In reaching this conclusion, Torres wishes to link her Cuban and American identities into an integrated whole of co-equal ethnic identities. She writes, "[m]y search for coherence and voice has been my politics. For years I felt that I had to neatly put away the pieces of my identity in different parts of the world, but more recently I have come to understand that I need not accept the categories that divide who I am. Instead, I must construct new categories, new political and emotional spaces, in which my multiple identities can be one."[56] Nonetheless, for Torres, lasting political conflict and the ostracism of multiple communities continue to place practical limitations on her ability to identify with her multiple identities as she would wish in specific contexts.

On the whole, political conflict is an important constraining condition on how Torres and others in similar "liminal" spaces may live their multiple identities. Group political conflict precludes the kinds of interconnections between her diverse identities and communities that Torres would seek to realize were Cuba-U.S. conflict not present. Frustrated, she writes, "every time we seem closer to a reconciliation the Cuban government pulls a stunt that pushes us away," leaving Torres and many others in the Cuban exile community in the U.S. to grapple with the contradictions among the identities to which they are most strongly identified.[57] This example, like that of Claudia, underscores how conflict-induced intersections, contradictions, and fragmentations can exist among multiple identities and shape identity-based motivations and experience. Consequently, intersectionality is also a central characteristic of multiple identities, and a key aspect of their relevance to politics.

Intersectionality and Multiple Identities

In recent decades, intersectionality has become an important concept through which scholars have described the diversity of identity, as well as sought to understand and investigate the experiences of groups and individuals who are marginalized in society. The concept originated in the civil rights era with women of color who were marginalized as women in the black and Chicano civil rights movements and also as racial and ethnic minorities in the feminist movement.[58] These women of color argued that their experiences differed from those of white women and black men or Chicanos because of the compound effects of multiple subordinations of race/ethnicity, gender, and class that shaped their lives and subjectivities. African American feminist thinkers Kimberlé Crenshaw and Patricia Hill Collins, in particular, theorized intersectionality as a way to understand the multiplicity of identity, and as a heuristic device for studying social subordination and conflict.[59] In Collins's account, intersectionality is the view that "systems of race, economic class, gender, sexuality, ethnicity, nation, and age form mutually constructing features of social organiza-tion."[60] Crenshaw presents a similar account of intersectionality and further argues that attending to intersectionality has legal, political, and policy implications in that various legal doctrines—such as an-tidiscrimination doctrine—fails to protect women of color because they cannot account for the compound social burdens associated with multiple social group identities.[61]

Intersectionality as described by Crenshaw and Collins can be illustrated by the example of Claudia, who describes an intersection between her racial and class identities when she states, "Well, my be-ing black, I guess that puts me when I'm with Black Americans, it makes people think that I'm lower class . . . "[62] In her social contexts, race intersects with class in a compound manner such that race is presumed to be an indicator of class status in the hierarchical social order. For Claudia, these *additive intersections* mean that when she is recognized as black she is not only stigmatized racially but *also* stig-matized in terms of class.

Because Crenshaw and Collins seek to specify the experiences of women of color and others who sustain *multiple* subordinations, they advance a conception of intersectionality that tends to empha-size this additive type of intersectionality. Both use intersectionality in which related social constructions converge. Given their focus on the compound subordination of women of color, both Crenshaw and Collins use the concept of intersectionality to distinguish between those with multiple compound subordinations as part of their iden-tity configurations such as poor women of color, and those whose identity configurations include the cross-cutting effects of combined privilege *and* subordination—such as black men who have gender privilege but racial disadvantage, or middle-class white women who suffer patriarchy, but have class and racial privilege.[63] Crenshaw argues, for example, that as a function of their privileges, black men and white women are better protected by anti-discrimination doctrine, because it defines and measures racial and gender subordination against the experiences of cross-cutting group privileges that women of color simply do not have.[64]

If however, the concept of intersectionality is conceived more broadly, it could be used to describe the specificities of all of these various kinds of multiple identity configurations—including those with *and* without compound disadvantage. If so, it could be a useful tool for taking into account important variations in levels of privilege and subordination as well as elements of commonality among diverse individuals and groups. It follows from this possibility that we may wish to build on what Crenshaw, Collins and other women scholars of color have established by further specifying other dimensions of intersectionality. Toward that goal, I suggest that intersectionality could be characterized as involving three *separate moments or modes of intersectionality*. Each of these three modes varies in its constructive effects on the lives of individuals.

The first mode is the one emphasized by Crenshaw and Collins in which multiple identities and social relations produce compound or additive meanings or influence on individual experience, group relations, or social outcomes.

The second moment is one in which multiple social identities generate alternative or cross-cutting meaning or influence. In Claudia's case, her Haitian ethnic identification is read (by some) as conferring increased social status—a shift significant enough to deny her black community membership and identity in the minds of some of her black friends. Here ethnic and racial identities are constructed as mutually exclusive and are thought to influence social status in opposing ways. A still more striking example of this cross-cutting effect of ethnic and racial identity on class advantage will be discussed below.

The third mode of constructive effects of intersectionality occurs when social identities and relations are overlapping in their content such that they share group specific meanings, values, or practices. In Claudia's cases, for example, she states "Then if I'm talking like this [regular voice] with my friends at school, they call me white."[65] The implication of her closing sentence is that Haitian ethnic identity and mainstream white identity groups share a common vernacular speech, such that her locutions in "regular voice" could signify *either* Haitian ethnic or mainstream identity. In this case intersecting—

that is overlapping—linguistic practices present an opportunity for those who wished to check Claudia's ethnic expression to denigrate them by categorizing her as white in a manner unwelcome to her.

In addition to these three constructive moments of intersectionality, we might also further the framework of intersectionality offered by Crenshaw and Collins by seeing intersectionality not only as compound social constructions, but as specific associations and/or overlaps *in the mind* between different social identity schemes and group relations. This intrapsychic or *internal intersectionality* includes both 1) the association between identity schemes we inherit and internalize in various social spheres, and 2) those associations or overlaps that we may craft for ourselves (see chapter six). In the case of Claudia, for example, the intersection between race and class in her social interactions link race and class in her subjectivity and self-understanding. Moreover, the association of race and class in her mind is not neutral, but rather negatively valenced with reference to her ethnic identities—that is Black identity is associated in her mind with subordinated racial *and* lower class status in a manner that crosscuts the presumed class privilege of her Haitian ethnic identity.

The complexity of these intersections and their connection to shifting identity salience can be seen in another example from Water's study in which a twenty year-old Jamaican immigrant describes the cross-cutting associations between her ethnic, class, and racial identities. Her comments bear quoting at length.

> At my workplace I was hired because I was Jamaican. They fired all the black Americans, and the lady, I asked her how come she hired me, and she said, well, because you are different, you are Jamaican . . . I am the only black person who works there, and one time we went out [after work] and this girl [I work with] was having a fight with her boyfriend, and she said to come here, and he said, "what do you think I am a nigger?" And one of the other girls turned around to me and said, "Oh, don't get offended, you are not black anyway." I was so upset. I was upset because I was like, I'll just be caught in between. I was like, what am I? Purple, green, yellow? Even though I don't like to be labeled just being black, I am black. I don't know.[66]

In this example, this Jamaican woman's ethnic and racial identity are framed by her white co-workers as mutually exclusive. Her immigrant ethnic identity is distinguished from American Black identity and confers on her economic opportunities and interracial social inclusion that are denied to American Blacks. The bewildering cost of those privileges, in this instance, is the face-to-face denial of black identity to a self-identified black woman by a white woman, for the purposes of preempting her potential resistance to racial stereotyping.

The significance of *internal* intersectionality here is two-fold. First, identity intersections from additive or cross-cutting influences reflect the practical terrain of social and political identity group conflicts in which the self is immersed and/or has been socialized. In this example, the color line, new ethnic hierarchies, and longstanding class ranks all shape the practices of daily self-identification and self-understanding. Yet, there is a disjuncture between these social influence intersections and the intrapsychic intersections that are expected as part of one's self-understanding. In short, political influence and constrained personal self-understandings that shape thought and action may be quite different and shape identification patterns in ways that defy present social norms. Those alternative self-understandings may be inherited as social constructions from marginal sources or selfcrafted.

The second important dimension of intersectionality is that intersecting identity schemes have a potential to become simultaneously salient as frames of reference even if they are regarded as socially contradictory (although that potential is lowered or eliminated for fragmented identity schemes; for discussion, see chapter four). In other words, identity schemes and other self-constructs that intersect within subjectivity in *any* of the three modes just outlined— additive or cross-cutting social influence, shared content, or internal intersection—can be connected in subjectivity as a whole, and thus *may* become salient together as intersecting frameworks for thought and action even if they are regarded *socially* as contradictory or have contradictory content. In contrast, identity schemes that are disconnected in the mind (i.e. non-internally intersecting) are unlikely to do so.[67]

For example, in the case of the Jamaican woman described above, her economic opportunities and work life link her ethnic and class identities in a positive association of upward mobility based on the racial and class subordination of blacks. Yet while this intersection of ethnicity and class construction of black and Jamaican identity is mutually exclusive, the young woman has not embraced that societal fragmentation and regards herself as *both* black and ethnically Jamaican. As such, her black racial and ethnic identities intersect in her embodied psychophysiology as co-present identity schemes. Moreover, and as a consequence of the internal intersection of her racial and ethnic identity schemes, both her racial *and* ethnic identity come to mind for her as a basis for interpreting the racial slur she witnesses and the denial of her black identity that follows. The pain of contradiction that she feels is a product not of a contradiction in her own self-understanding—but rather arises from the contradiction between what identities *she* understands herself to have, and what identities she is allowed to claim without objection by those around her. As Anzaldúa notes, those objections are often a source of deeply felt frustration and pain.

It is this experience of *felt* identity contradiction that Anzaldúa's account of mestiza consciousness has theorized so well. In contrast, however, SIT has taken a related, but also opposing position toward identity contradiction. In general, social identity theorists have held that while a person's subjectivity as a whole may include identity schemes that are contradictory or have incompatible self accounts, those identity contradictions typically go *unfelt* because only a consistent subset of multiple identity schemes are salient in a given time. In this SIT view, contradictory identity schemes cannot become salient at the same time and all simultaneously salient self-constructs and identities must be congruent and consistent with each other. As one team of researchers put it, while "contradictory or conflicting constructs can be simultaneously possessed by an individual; *they simply cannot simultaneously guide cognition.*"[68] This approach to contradiction is also found in other strands of social psychology. An extended account of the concept of "the self" in social psychology describes a self in which ". . . only the phenomenal self [i.e. the working self] would be under pressure to be internally consistent; the person could otherwise hold widely discrepant and even contradictory views about self. As long as these did not become activated simultaneously, the person might never notice the contradiction."[69] On the whole then— in contrast to Anzaldúa's approach—SIT and social psychology regard internal identity contradictions as possible, but generally unfelt and insignificant for daily or political thought and action.

This latter approach to identity contradiction is also largely consistent with what has emerged in Anglo-American philosophy. Western philosophers have generally held that identity contradictions and all other internal contradictions fragment the self and should be resolved in the interest of effective agency and self-integration. This view—adopted in different ways by philosophers such as Alasdair MacIntyre and Harry Frankfurt—suggests that contradictions among identities are unproductive, and those that are felt should be excised before they disable agency and effective thought and action. This philosophical approach differs significantly from that of philosophers such as Jane Flax and Amélie Rorty, who, like Gloria Anzaldúa, regard the presence of identity contradictions—both felt and unfelt—as having both productive and damaging potential that is realized primarily through how individuals handle their identity contradictions.

Given these various approaches to identity contradiction, much of the character and political significance of multiple identities seems to lie in the character and significance of identity contradiction. Rhetorically we might ask, how can and should the young Jamaican woman quoted above handle the identity contradiction that comes to her when others reject her claims to black identity based on prevailing social hierarchies and ongoing racial, class, and political conflicts?

The next four chapters investigate and evaluate the relative validity of the three approaches to the contradictions among multiple identities: namely 1) that identity contradictions exist but go unfelt in SIT, 2) the philosophy that identity contradictions are felt and must be resolved (MacIntyre, Frankfurt), and 3) the philosophy that the productive or destructive quality of identity contradictions often lies in how effectively those contradictions are recognized and handled (Anzaldúa, Flax, Rorty). Through the following investigation it becomes clear that there are some important insights to be gained from all three approaches to multiplicity and identity. The integrating of multiple identities ultimately involves seeking to identify and manage identity contradictions that we may not feel and/or our willingness to utilize and maintain some contradictions as a source of creative tension that can provide us a critical distance on our own identities. I begin this further investigation in the next chapter by considering the critical and creative value of inner contradiction as it is understood in the work of Alasdair MacIntyre and Gloria Anzaldúa.

CHAPTER THREE

Identity Contradiction in Creative and Critical Thought
The Case of Nazi J

Resemblance among the parts of a continuum of feelings (especially bodily feelings) experienced along with things widely different in all other regards, *thus constitutes the real and verifiable 'personal identity' which we feel.* There is no other identity than this in the 'stream' of subjective consciousness.
WILLIAM JAMES, *Principles of Psychology*

It is a peculiar sensation, this double-consciousness, this sense of always looking at one's self through the eyes of others ... One ever feels his twoness—an American, a Negro; two souls, two thoughts, two unreconciled strivings; two warring ideals in one dark body, whose dogged strength alone keeps it from being torn asunder.
W. E. B. DU BOIS, *Souls of Black Folk*

The previous chapter began to build upon Gloria Anzaldúa's account of mestiza consciousness to construct a theoretical framework of multiple identities. Within this framework identity schemes operate as composite components within a decentered and embodied subjectivity. Different identity schemes and other pieces of internalized self-knowledge are activated as frames of reference for thought and action in different contexts. In this process of identity shifts, the priorities and judgments of individuals themselves shape their interpretations and constrained responses to socially constructed contextual cues. As yet however, this framework does not specify how, if at all, individual judgments and critical thought generally spring from the multiple identities that make up a decentered subject.

In this chapter, I investigate the potential for multiple identities to play a pivotal role in critical thought. This inquiry is important for understanding the political implications of multiple identities for two reasons. First, because critical thought and choice by citizens is fundamental to political life, the relationship between multiple identities and critical thought is necessary to assessing the implications—positive or negative—of multiple identities for political life. To the extent that multiple identities might either foster or inhibit critical ability, multiple identities could either support or undermine an individual's capacity for meaningful participation in political decision-making and action.

Second, as discussed in this book's introduction, the idea of a modern decentered subject that is entirely socially constructed *and* made up of identities practiced in different social contexts is sometimes regarded as lacking the attributes necessary for critical thought. Various philosophers have expressed this concern. Communitarian critics of liberalism Alasdair MacIntyre and Charles Taylor, for example, have argued that modern liberal societies segment social life in ways that produce subjects who live "betwixt and between" the different communities and lifeworlds with which they identify. For Alasdair MacIntyre, in particular, this fragmentation of society and identities disables the human capacity for critical thought by eroding the *identity-independent* worldviews and moral standpoints upon which critical thought depends.[1]

Conversely, in her account of mestiza consciousness, Gloria Anzaldúa contends that it is exactly in living betwixt and between multiple lifeworlds and identities that human beings gain a heightened capacity for critical thought. For Anzaldúa, multiple identities not only give people the varying knowledges of different lifeworlds, but also increase their cognitive skill and potential for complex thought, suited to both critique and creativity. To Anzaldúa, multiple identities are a necessary resource for critical thought, not a hindrance to it. In the writings published before her death, however, Anzaldúa had not yet fully specified the dimensions of mestiza consciousness that account for critical and creative thought.

Building once again on Anzaldúa's account of mestiza consciousness, and adding to the framework of multiple identities begun in chapter two, I find from further analysis that it is the *contradictions in the content* of different identity schemes and the *socially constructed intersections* among multiple identities that are the two specific aspects of multiple identities that facilitate critical thought. I contend that MacIntyre's analysis of modern decentered and multiple subjectivity overlooks the potential intersections among multiple identities— especially mutually exclusive ones—within individual subjectivity and within the group or community life in which those identities are constructed, internalized, and enacted. This "intersectionality" at once mitigates identity fragmentation and links contradictory identities both within subjectivity and—as alluded to by W. E. B. Du Bois above—within the flow of consciousness that creates the feeling of personal continuity and selfhood in time.[2] I argue that when linked by specific intersections, identity contradictions provide distanced vantage points and substantive alternatives that are the necessary basis for critical thought. Contrary to MacIntyre, I claim, these aspects of multiple identities can form the sufficient basis for critical thought without recourse to identity-independent frames of reference.

To systematically explore the relationship between multiple identities and critical thought, this chapter is divided into three parts. In the first part, I juxtapose the approaches of Anzaldúa and MacIntyre regarding critical thought, and explore through examples how intersecting multiple identities can serve as a basis for critical thinking. In part two, I illustrate the political-moral relevance of this dimension of multiple identities by rereading several examples of moral lapse introduced by MacIntyre in his critique of fragmented societies and selves. In part three, I consider the influence of intersecting and contradictory multiple identities on moral judgment in the face of moral atrocity through a rereading of MacIntyre's example of the unwitting Nazi collaborator "J." I contend, contrary to MacIntyre, that in this case, J's failure to engage in critical moral thought was not a function of his fragmented multiple identities but rather of a lack of identity contradiction and diverse internalized moral outlooks within his subjectivity. From this analysis, I conclude that a lack of deep diversity among multiple identities within a given subjectivity may hinder the capacity for critical judgment in contexts—including politicized contexts—that require critical thought.[3]

Locating the Identity Sources of Critical Thought

In his 1984 book *After Virtue,* communitarian philosopher Alasdair MacIntyre bemoaned the loss of traditional modes of communal society and identity in which "it [was] through his or her membership of a variety of social groups that the individual identifies himself or herself and is identified by others." In premodern societies, MacIntyre argued, personal connections and group memberships—memberships in families, belongings as a "member of this household, that village, this tribe" constituted for each of us "part of [our] substance." These various memberships defined "partially at least and sometimes wholly" the obligations and duties, and commitments and connections that individuals lived by as their guiding principles.[4] In this "individuals inherit *a particular space* within an interlocking set of social relationships; lacking that space they are nobody, or at best a stranger or an outcast." But, for MacIntyre, within that "particular space," the subject has a social identity—a broader social belonging—that places him or her "on a journey *with set goals.*" The social identity we have been given by membership in a community is devoted to trying to make progress "toward a *given end.*"[5]

As modern societies have given up the idea of teleological ends, balked against the constraints of community, and valorized the freedoms of liberal individualism, MacIntyre argues, "the self is now thought of as lacking any necessary social identity, because the kind of social identity that it once enjoyed is no longer available."[6] Referring to accounts of the self by Erving Goffmann and Jean Paul Sartre, MacIntyre argues that modern subjects instead assume a range of social roles that are not truly substantive or definitive of the self.[7] In his 1999 essay entitled, "Social Structures and their Threats to Moral Agency," MacIntyre extends his previous claim in a manner that warrants detailed consideration for its clues to the character of multiple identities and critical thought. In his later argument, MacIntyre stressed that a fragmentation of the self arises from the abandonment of traditional community in favor of the compartmentalization of modern social life into disparate social milieus. He argues that while individuals have come to have many different "social roles" that they live in various milieus, they have come to lack a sense of themselves as "individuals" per se, independent of their disparate social roles. In this, the self is not only fragmented in its own social roles, it is also divided from a broader sense of community and, he contends, from its own sense of its past and future.

For MacIntyre, this multiple fragmentation of modern selves, in turn, severely damages the potential modern selves have to engage in critical moral thought. MacIntyre notes, moral questions are often questions of "how to best find our way through conflict"—and thus moral thought on key questions is often "moral-cum-religious-cum-political-cum-economic."[8] As MacIntyre defines it, however, the capacity for moral thought arises only from our grappling with inner tension and conflict between different moral outlooks internalized within us. In his words, ". . . to be a moral agent is to have the potentiality for living and acting in a state of tension or, if need be, conflict between two moral points of view." MacIntyre argues that when there is conflict between these two moral worlds, that conflict forces the moral agents to "think their way through a series of more or less painful choices" or to find a way to circumvent those incompatibilities.[9] The result of this is the necessity for "practical thinking" in which the self questions assumptions, seeks novel approaches, and generally wrangles with the moral views available. Thus, tension between moral outlooks is productive as a necessary basis for critical moral thinking.

Yet for MacIntyre, the moral tension needed for critical thought is available only from the clash that involves "be[ing an] inhabitant of not just one, but of two moral systems."[10] In one system, I understand myself in terms of my multiple social roles, and in the other I understand myself as an individual per se, independent of those social roles. The second moral system is dominated by an internalized "common view" of what defines a good human being as one who has "an identity other than the roles that I occupy." To leave this is to "understand myself as someone who brings with her or himself to each role qualities of mind and character that belong to her or him *qua* individual and not *qua* role player."[11] On this view, it is the tension between *role-based* and *role-independent* moral outlooks that makes "the exercise of the powers of moral agency possible."[12]

For MacIntyre, these different moral systems must not be abstract and interior, but instead "socially embodied points of view," in which individuals are held accountable *by others* for their moral choices across different social milieu.[13] Yet, MacIntyre argues that modern social structures of compartmentalization do not produce for us cross-milieu communities. Thus our lives express a fragmented social order in which we have "become unable to recognize, let alone to transcend its limitations"—and so we "do not have the resources that would enable . . . [us] to move to an independent standpoint."[14] Thus, a socially grounded, internalized role-independent perspective is, according to MacIntyre, necessary for us to have the moral tension between role-based and role-independent moral worlds that critical moral thought requires.

For this reason, MacIntyre argues that the tension or moral conflict necessary to the exercise of moral agency is lacking in what he calls the "divided self"—a self made up of multiple and role-based identities associated with different social spheres of activity. MacIntyre argues that this "divided self" moves cleanly from one context to the next and answers the same moral question differently according to the moral codes of each different context without reference to the codes of other spheres, and without the scrutiny of reference to a global set of moral standards that exists outside of any of its identities or spheres.[15] In his words: "This divided self has to be characterized negatively, by what it lacks. It is not only without any standpoint from which it can pass critical judgment on the standards governing its various roles, but it must also lack those virtues of integrity and constancy that are prerequisites for exercising the powers of moral agency. . . . *there is nothing about the self thus divided that is liable to generate conflict* with what are taken to be the requirements of morality with the established social order."[16] To MacIntyre, a "divided self" with its various moral outlooks hopelessly segmented has no inner moral conflict, the necessary ingredient for moral agency—a problem that heightens the subject's propensity for moral lapse.

Finally, as a remedy to this complex problem, MacIntyre proposes that the degree to which individuals should shift among their multiple identities from one context to the next should be limited by two virtues that become prerequisites for all other virtues. These virtues are: *integrity* and *constancy*. *Integrity*, MacIntyre defines as the refusal of multiplicity through self-education such that "one is no longer able to be one kind of person in one social context, while quite another in other contexts." The person of integrity therefore sets "inflexible limits" on "one's adaptability" to the social roles that they may have occasion to assume.[17] *Constancy* also restricts the flexibility of the subject not only from one context to the next, but over time. The person who is constant pursues the same moral goods over time regardless of the social contexts in which they find themselves along the way.[18]

From the perspective of mestiza consciousness, and the framework of multiple identities developed so far in this book, there is much of value in MacIntyre's approach to the modern self and moral thought. Like MacIntyre, Anzaldúa also considers the compartmentalization of social spheres and social identities an entrenched habit of contemporary societies that should be critically reviewed and rejected in favor of more holistic approaches to self-understanding and self-presentation across social contexts.[19] MacIntyre and Anzaldúa commonly acknowledge that various social spheres construct subjectivities with a range of social roles that have a role to play in moral thought. Moreover, Anzaldúa, like MacIntyre in his early work, argues that individuals should have a sense of self that is rooted in the diverse communities in which they and their families have had a history.[20] Finally and most importantly, the approaches taken by Anzaldúa and MacIntyre to the self and critical thought coincide in locating the source of critical thinking in the tensions between internalized worldviews.

Despite considerable agreement in their approaches, there are three important ways in which Anzaldúa's account of mestiza consciousness departs from MacIntyre's approaches to the fragmented modern subject. First, in acknowledging community and socialization in different kinds of collective life to be important to identity formation, Anzaldúa sees commonality between social role-based identities and other kinds of social identities. For her, as in the framework of multiple identities developed in chapter two, social role-based identities such as the professional identities of professor or truck driver are associated with collective ways of life. Like other group identities, their lifeworlds include role-specific ways of being and outlooks that subjects internalize and identify with just as they do other community-based group identities. Consequently, social role-identities are in form—though not in content—the same as broad, community-based social identities such as ethnic, subcultural, religious, sexual or national identities.

Thus, mestiza consciousness considers social role identities to be functionally equivalent in form and potential significance to a subject's sense of self as other collective identities. Hence, one distinction between Anzaldúa and MacIntyre is that mestiza consciousness (and the framework I am building with it) regards a decentered subjectivity with multiple identities to include all kinds of identities as well as self-constructs that MacIntyre would regard as a role-identity or independent. For example, as I read Anzaldúa, her account of mestiza consciousness does not rule out the internalization of self constructs that do not originate from or specifically fall within a particular identity scheme. In her work, and in the framework I am building from it, an identity-independent isolated self-construct, such as "fair play" or "self-reliance," may be internalized and serve as a frame of reference alongside the content of identity related schemes. However, unlike MacIntyre, Anzaldúa does not hold that such identity-independent self-constructs a priori have a necessary or special role to play in critical thought above other intrapsychic elements.[21]

Second, Anzaldúa, like MacIntyre, contends that as a function of mestiza consciousness the subject should be aware of and able to consider its own acts of living different identities in varying contexts. She writes, "[W]hen you watch yourself and observe your mind at work you find that behind your acts and your temporary senses of self (identities) is a state of awareness that, if you allow it, keeps you from getting completely caught up in that particular identity or emotional state."[22] Yet, there is nothing in Anzaldúa's brief account of this state that indicates that it is itself an internalized standpoint or socialized frame of reference. MacIntyre's identity-independent standpoint is, however, by his account, not a cognitive abstraction or an internally selfcrafted viewpoint. Rather it is a socially derived and internalized way of thinking and being that is a collectively recognized, embodied, and sanctioned point of view that exists, for MacIntyre, independent of the subject's specific multiple identities.[23]

In contrast, Anzaldúa associates her distanced viewpoint with two concepts: the concept of *conocimiento* and the concept of *nepantla*.

Conocimiento is the Spanish word for knowledge or "ways of knowing." In Anzaldúa's account, we internalize knowledge of different lifeworlds through socialization in an array of different cultures as part of the ongoing processes of identity formation. As she stated in an interview, "You're not born a Chicana, you become a Chicana because of the culture that's caught in you."[24] As one "become[s] acquainted with all these [different social] worlds . . . you shift, cross the border from one to the other" based on your knowledge of the ways of being in different social spheres with which you identify yourself and are identified by others as a member.[25] In her words, "the work of conocimiento—consciousness work—connects the inner life of the mind and spirit to the outer worlds of action."[26] Thus, varied knowledge and memberships, identities, and daily identity enactments are bound up in the concept of conocimientos.

Diverse socialization often leads to identifications with various social worlds. Anzaldúa describes mapping the configuration of a particular person's multiple identities as circles on a page: "here is your race, your sexual orientation, here you're a Jew Chicana, here an academic, here an artist, there a blue-collar worker. Where these spaces overlap is nepantla, the Borderlands."[27] Nepantla is a word in Nahuatl meaning "the space in-between"[28]—it is the state of living in transition between worlds "as in transitions across borders of class, race, or sexual identity."[29] As I interpret Anzaldúa, being in a nepantilist state produces two different but related modes of thought: 1) learning and practicing "how to access different kinds of knowledges" including feelings, different moral outlooks, and images, and 2) the generative mode of "creating your own meaning or conocimientos,"[30] from the experience of accessing those different knowledges.

The difference between the positions of MacIntyre and Anzaldúa is subtle, but important to understanding whether the relationship among multiple identities can serve as a source for critical thought. By rooting her notion of a viewpoint for overlooking one's identity enactments in conocimientos, Anzaldúa locates a metaperspective on multiple identities not from outside of those multiple identities, but from within the knowledges that constitute those many identities. In this sense, for Anzaldúa, the critical thought arising from a distanced viewing of one's own identities does not depend—as it does for MacIntyre—on internalizing "an embodied standpoint" that is identity-independent. Instead, a distanced viewpoint is to be found in the diversity of multiple identities themselves and in the diverse knowledges of ways of being associated with each.

In developing her concepts of nepantla and conocimientos, however, Anzaldúa does not yet specify how the distanced viewpoints on identity they create are linked to the two modes of critical thought she names. She says only that for reconsiderations of existing viewpoints to come "there has to be some kind of opening, some kind of fissure, gate . . . a crack between worlds" that is at "the interface" of those worlds.[31] But how are we to understand the character and effects of such "cracks" at the interface of internalized knowledges? MacIntyre contends that a shifting between multiple identities—i.e. Anzaldúa's nepantilist state—provides no basis for critical thought because, from his perspective, shifting among compartmentalized identities produces no tension between the ways of being of those social identities. How, if at all, can living betwixt and between varying bodies of knowledge and ways of being associated with different social identities provide a meaningful basis for the practice of critical thought in the absence of identity-independent standpoints?

One possible answer, I would suggest, lies in the way that different lifeworlds and the identities within subjectivity are often not as relentlessly fragmented in the mind—or in the subject's lifeworlds—as MacIntyre asserts. Anzaldúa describes nepantla as living in-between worlds, in terms of the "overlap" of those worlds and identities.[32] This indicates that there are sometimes intersections in the knowledges— i.e. the meanings, values, and practices that make up particular communities and their lifeworlds—that will be internalized as common or related meanings by those who are members of both lifeworlds. In MacIntyre's emphasis on modern social fragmentation, he overlooks that there are frequently various intersections among the lifeworlds of distinct communities and thus potentially in the identities internalized in association with them. Yet not only social fragmentation, but also social sphere and identity intersections may be present in any of the three modes outlined in chapter two—i.e. additive and cross-cutting social influence, shared content, or intrapsychic or internal intersections in the mind. It is possible that such intersections may be the basis for inner tension and/or critical vantage points that are derived from—not independent of—multiple identities.

To investigate this possibility it is helpful to turn to examples. Once again, as in chapter two, Mary Waters' sociological study of West Indian immigrants to the U.S. offers important insight. In her study, Waters finds significant evidence of not only the multiple identities of immigrants, but also of the kinds of contextual identity shifts that result from grappling with how to live a life in-between different social worlds, as discussed by Anzaldúa. In an interview with a 15 year-old U.S.-born Trinidadian boy, for example, the boy describes his practice of varying his self-identifications with different social groups as part of negotiating his life between those groups. He states, "I think of myself as West Indian sometimes and American sometimes. . . . [Among my friends] some are West Indian and some are American . . . and they ask you what you are, you might say that you are American just to be with them. And then when you are with your West Indian friends, you might say you're West Indian to be with them."[33]

On its face, this quotation suggests the seamless kind of shifting among different social spheres without perspectives for judgments across those spheres that MacIntyre attributes to the "divided self." Yet, in this description, the young man describes his knowledge of the divergent expectations of different groups. Hence, contrary to the chronic lack of cross-milieu consideration described by MacIntyre, this young man's third person account suggests that he does not understand, much less apply, the standards or self-representations of one group without reference to the divergent standards of the other. Moreover, he is aware of his own shifts in self-presentation in different cases *and* why he makes them. This suggests two things. First, that Anzaldúa is correct to suggest that there are distanced vantage points from which those with multiple identities can interpret those identities and assess their identity enactments. Second, because the boy does not refer to his assessment as based on a third internalized standpoint, it suggests that his distanced point of view on his own multiple identity enactments is the product of the two identity schemes—American and West Indian—that he is discussing. While those two identity schemes are arguably fragmented—or at least originate in different social spheres—they have nonetheless become associated in his mind and his ways of thinking. In terms of Anzaldúa's concepts of conocimientos and napantla, here multiple knowledges (conocimientos) are analyzed vis-à-vis each other in the course of living back and forth and in between two social spheres (napantla). In that process, these identity schemes have come to intersect in his mind in intersecting self-constructs, such that they are at once bound together and yet distinct as ways of life as he understands them. Which is to say that even if their practices do not overlap within different social milieus—i.e. among his different groups of friends—his understanding of how each of his multiple identities and multiple lifeworlds are related internally and intersect within the self-concepts within his subjectivity. And this internal intersection gives this young Trinidadian American a distanced vantage point on both of his ethnic identities and thus a basis for critical analysis of them.

Based on this analysis, I contend that self-conscious awareness of the intersections among one's multiple identities can become the basis for a distanced view of one's own identity schemes and daily identity enactments based *only* on the subject's internalized knowledge of and engagement in different lifeworlds. Such a vantage point is what W. E. B. Du Bois is articulating, I believe, in his famous lines from *The Souls of Black Folk* quoted in this chapter's epigraph in which Du Bois refers to his account of double consciousness—a view of the multiple identities of Blacks not unlike Anzaldúa's account of mestiza consciousness. He writes, "It is a peculiar sensation, this double-consciousness, this sense of always looking at one's self through the eyes of others, of measuring one's soul by the tape of a world that looks on in amused contempt and pity."[34] Here, the color line defines white and Black identities as mutually exclusive. Yet subordinated American Blacks are socialized to learn and know not only the lifeworld of Blacks, but also the lifeworld of white society to the extent that they work in the white lifeworld, or otherwise have their life chances and daily interactions conditioned by the white lifeworld's norms and hierarchical values. Hence, double consciousness is a function of the way in which Black society and identity and white society and identity intersect in two ways, in Du Bois's knowledge (conocimientos) of the additive and/or crosscutting influence of the two worlds, and in the relationship in his mind of Black and white social spheres.

In practice, both influence-based and content-based intersectionality can, in turn, become the basis for seeing one's different identities as linked and intersecting in ones mind. Du Bois writes, "One ever feels his twoness,—an American, a Negro; two souls, two thoughts, two unreconciled strivings; two warring ideals in one dark body, whose dogged strength alone keeps it from being torn asunder."[35] Du Bois's anguished observation also indicates that identity scheme intersections can emerge from political and social conflict. Those intersections can, in turn, become common markers in the flow of resemblances within the stream of consciousness. That relay of resemblances in feeling is, as noted by William James in this chapter's opening epigraph, the one and only source of our sense of ourselves as individuals per se, in and over time. While MacIntyre seeks to locate this level of critical self-consciousness in a sense of self that we internalize from communities around us, reading James and Du Bois as the reference to intersectionality would suggest that this distanced sense of ourselves as individuals is always rooted in and derived from the ongoing functioning of consciousness (for further discussion, see chapter four).

Anzaldúa, like Du Bois, acknowledges that the process of "navigating the cracks"—especially between hierarchically ordered and mutually intolerant social worlds, such as divided ethnic groups—is "difficult and painful."[36] But in highlighting such border crossing, Anzaldúa points out that intersections of social worlds are becoming as common in late modernity as forms of social segmentation and compartmentalization. Shaped by globalization, mass migration, and hybridization in cultural borderlands, social groups and communities in modern complex societies increasingly overlap, sharing specific meanings, values, and practices, and often some group members as well. As Anzaldúa puts it "[l]iving in a multicultural society, we cross into each other's worlds all the time. We live in each other's pockets, occupy each other's territories, live in close proximity and intimacy with each other at home, in school, at work. We're mutually complicitous—us and them, white and colored, straight and queer, Christian and Jew, self and other, oppressor and oppressed."[37] Placed against this, MacIntyre's view that multiple identities and social milieu are generally fragmented is too one-sided a view of modern societies. If we look more closely, there are many intersections among various lifeworlds, and also many who live their lives crossing the social borders betwixt and between divided, and even conflicting, social groups and their spheres. These societal overlaps and intersections can construct overlaps and intersections among the multiple social identity schemes within subjectivity, thus mitigating identity fragmentation, and potentially providing a distanced vantage point on one's own identities that is rooted not ouside of, but within the materials of those identities.

The examples of intersectionality described above demonstrate the work that the overlapping or interrelation of ideas does within consciousness. The examples also demonstrate significant levels of contradiction in the content of the subject's multiple identities. In the case of the young Trinidadian man, his identities as American and West Indian are linked in his own subjectivity, but are rejected as incompatible by others. Du Bois feels an intense contradiction between his strivings as a Black man and as an American. These examples provide evidence that internalizing and living in between identities and lifeworlds with contradictory content can provide, not only distanced vantage points on one's own thoughts and actions, but also substantive contradictory material with which to critically consider the thoughts and actions of others.

Such was the case among West Indian immigrant youth in Mary Waters' study who identified with both American Blacks and West

Indians. One 17 year-old U.S.-born Bajan American man said, "Sometimes I get upset at my mother 'cause she use the term nigger, and I don't like that. . . . She has these feelings against black Americans because of how they treat her when she first came here. . . . But since I lived here, I know that it's not all of them that's that way. There's a few. But I know some Bajans, even my cousins, when I hang out with them, it's not so rosy, how my mother would say either. There's some Bajans that act as wild as black Americans."[38] Here the varied knowledge— the conocimientos—gained by living among both American Blacks and Bajans and the contradictions in meanings and practices across those social group boundaries give this Bajan American a material basis upon which to critically consider, reject, and act to resist the stereotypical and racist view of his own mother.

Clearly in this case, and in a number of other examples in Waters's study, the contradictory material within intersecting identity schemes and lifeworlds becomes the basis for critical thought and judgments that depart from powerful prevailing norms. In another example, a seventeen year-old Guyanese immigrant who emigrated at age six employed her multiple ethnic identities as Guyanese and American and their attendent contradictions to critically consider her parents' negative views of American Blacks, which she ultimately finds too one-sided to adopt herself. Asked if she accepted her parents' negative views of American Blacks she stated, "No, not really. They always look at the bad things. They never look at the good things, the positive things . . . the black kids that are in college, that are trying to finish high school. But they only look at the black kids that are in jail and that are dropping out. That's all they want to believe. They want to believe that Guyana is the best place to raise a child."[39] As these examples illustrate, having multiple identities and living in between the lifeworlds associated with them involves not simply identity fragmentation, but also intersections among distinct identities and social spheres that can provide those with multiple identities distanced vantage points for making a critical appraisal of their own identity-based thoughts and actions, as well as those of others. Moreover, the contradictory elements of those multiple identities and social spheres can provide substantive material from which to make critical judgments. In short, the contradiction of facts and interpretations can provide an important impetus and starting point for critical thought and judgments. As Anzaldúa stresses, living mutually exclusive or highly contradictory identities can thus hone, through practice, the subject's ability to grapple with and effectively manage specific contradictory elements of group identities and collective ways of life. The political significance of this ability to productively engage with identity contradiction will be addressed in chapters five and six.

Intersectionality and Identity Contradiction in Practice

If multiple identities within decentered subjectivity provide the moral tension necessary for critical moral thought, then they should also be able to support moral thought and action in the hard cases of moral lapse that MacIntyre discusses. For example, MacIntyre argues that in the divided self, role-based social identities are compartmentalized in their structure and by differences in moral norms across segmented social milieus. This compartmentalization prevents the tension necessary for moral reflection and establishes the conditions for stark moral lapse. As an example of this, MacIntyre describes the case of a scientist who in everyday life shifts among a number of different standards of truthfulness in different social contexts. At work in a corporate laboratory, the scientist quietly accepts the misrepresentation of his research findings by a profit-hungry CEO who promises to fire any scientist who objects to his lies. In the context of the scientific community, the same scientist adheres to a standard of total honesty in the representation of his data and holds all other scientists to a similar standard. Finally, the same scientist also leaves the laboratory at the end of the day for a cocktail party and enters effortlessly into a mode in which he exaggerates and fibs in a manner commonly acceptable to cocktail chatter.

That this scientist with a "divided self," can slide among these three different "ethics of deception," is proof enough, according to MacIntyre, that multiple role-identities are compartmentalized in ways that undermine moral capacity by giving the self the ability to "move from one context-based moral standpoint to another" and reach widely divergent moral judgments in each.[40] Yet MacIntyre simply states in this example that the scientist in question does not pause over—let alone offer a critical moral judgment on—the contradictory standards of honesty in which he is involved. However, to state that the scientist *could* behave in this way does not establish that such a person *must* act in this way, or that he would not have identity-based cognitive resources with which to do otherwise.

Consider again a scientist faced with collaborating in the lies of his CEO regarding research lest he be fired. MacIntyre states that this scientist and others with multiple roles have no "sphere" or "milieu available" from which to "scrutinize themselves and the structure of their society from some external point with any practical effect."[41] Yet a useful critical vantage point may be found not externally—but

rather internally, within the scientist's own set of multiple identifications. I would argue, through MacIntyre's own example, that intersectionality and multiple identities can make critical assessment
based on identity-based elements possible in at least four ways.[42]
Assume first, that the scientist does not experience his identities as
a scientist and a corporate employee (as opposed to a scientist in a
university or a government laboratory setting) as mutually exclusive.
Assume as well, that he identifies most highly as a scientist, and less
so as corporate employee. When faced with his CEO's request to collaborate in a deception, his identity scheme as a scientist would be
the most highly accessible to him as the frame of reference used to
consider right action.

However, as MacIntyre indicates, the man's identity scheme as a
scientist includes strict prohibitions against falsifying scientific findings. As his most accessible identity, it is to this cross-cutting set of
moral standards that the scientist is most likely to first turn. It is also
one that is in conflict with the demands of the CEO. The potential for
this moral inner tension is already implicit in MacIntyre's example in
the form of the CEO's threat to fire scientists who dissent. If all that
it takes to command deception in employees is to compartmentalize
the boardroom from the laboratory, then the CEO needn't threaten
his scientific staff. He need only gather them to the boardroom. The
threat is needless unless it is there to prevent the troublesome application of those opposing moral standards that the CEO feels his scientific staff is likely to hold dear and consider applicable to his request.

A second scenario for identity-based critique is also possible. For
this second case, assume instead that what leaps to mind first for the
scientist at the CEO's request is his identification with the corpora-
tion, despite the fact that he is highly identified as a scientist. This
makes his corrupt corporate identity active as his working-self. Yet,
once there, and as described in chapter two, the subject must still
make a judgment of fit—i.e. of relevance and appropriateness—of
that identity scheme that will be a function of not only contextual
norms, but also of the scientist's own identity-based goals, values,
principles, and endorsements.[43] Consequently, through his judgment of fit, the scientist also would have resources to judge his corporate identity and its value of deceit and he might then shift back to
his identity scheme as a scientist—the identity to which he is most
highly identified. This process of moving away from a recently primed
identity structure through critical reflection is a common finding in
identity salience studies in social psychology in which, given a few
moments, subjects will often shift from a recent experimentally cued

(or primed) cognitive and evaluative scheme to one that is more frequently salient—one with which they are often more highly identified.[44] In this way, the values of the identity schemes to which they are most highly identified can serve as a guiding force across a whole range of contexts.

My analysis of this example demonstrates that different identity schemes can provide divergent vantage points for critical moral reflection. However, it also suggests that the effectiveness of those available vantage points to the agent depends, in part, on *the content* and also on the agent's relative levels of identification with those available identity-based vantage points. For example, if the scientist were more heavily identified as a "corporate team player" and his identity scheme includes the view that profit should be made at all costs, then the relative accessibility of his corporate identity may be seen as a better "fit" for the circumstance. Through this assessment, he might—and he would have the internalized resources within him to do so—decide that the CEO's deception is morally acceptable and that lying is justified both in and outside of the lab.

In yet a third scenario, even strong identification with identity schemes that contained some morally lax dimensions would not necessarily lead to the application of poor moral principles. As mentioned in previous chapters in discussion of selective identities, social identities and their related lifeworlds are not generally constructed as internally consistent and uniform. The sets of meanings, values, and practices that comprise them may contain a variety of divergent and even contradictory elements.[45] In this case, the full range of cognitive, affective, and motivational constructs that might make up an identity as a "corporate team player" may include constructs of both honesty and dishonesty. Given this, any particular person who claims such an identity may do so in a given instance by honesty or dishonesty. MacIntyre indirectly acknowledges this himself when he refers to the former SEC commissioner who believed that honesty is ultimately profitable.[46]

The possibility of identifying selectively from a range of possible identity markers means that people can, when categorizing themselves as members of certain groups, disidentify with particular aspects of those role or group-based identities. They might do so especially when the common but optional defining characteristic of one identity threatens identification with another. Thus, if the scientist's identity as a scientist is very important to him, he could, from the vantage point of that desired categorization, recognize deception as a common component of corporate life, but also disidentify with such deception as something that threatens his claim to his social identity as a scientist.

In the fourth and final scenario, the distanced vantage point of the scientist's identities could emerge as a function of their constructions as mutually exclusive. The social identities of "research scientist" and "corporate employee" are, in some times and locations, constructed and experienced as mutually exclusive. Basic exploratory research only infrequently has the immediate commercial applications that corporations often value. Thus, the basic research that most scientists are initially trained to do in university settings and which they often favor is often at odds in its objective with the kinds of applied research that commercial enterprises privilege. This contradiction places the identification as a research scientist in frequent tension with the identity as a corporate employee as two intertwined but clashing ways of being, and this in turn binds them together in the mind of the scientist. Just as Du Bois ever feels his twoness as a Black American, the corporate scientist who is placed in the position of relying upon scientific principles that are simultaneously denied may feel her twoness as a corporate scientist.

For a scientist with mutually exclusive yet intersecting multiple identities, the request of the CEO to collaborate in the falsification of data could make simultaneously salient *both* her scientific identity scheme and her corporate identity schemes. Both frameworks then could be used as distanced vantage points for critique of the self's desires, the question at hand, and on the other as identity schemes. Elements of each framework could be borrowed across the boundaries of those identity frameworks and the possible transformation of each identity framework considered in light of the constructs of the other. A scientist in this scenario, or in any of the others, might not only resist participating in the CEO's deception, but also organize her colleagues to resist it as well as a means to rework the corporate culture of the company by infusing it with the values of honest scientific endeavor. In this, she could go beyond deciding on right action for herself alone, and go further still by defying the threat of her own termination from the company by organizing others to unmask and oust the deceptive CEO.[47]

This is not to say that during the processes of categorizing people never go along with others on elements that they might reject based on other identity vantage points. Yet, to follow along with others contrary to one's strongly held endorsements and in spite of the competing outlooks to which one has access is not a moral lapse rooted in *the lack of the possibility* of critical vantage points (as MacIntyre would have it). Structurally and (usually) in content, the diverse identity has vantage points present for critical moral reflection upon itself and social structures. Rather, this kind of moral lapse of following others to action one recognizes or could recognize as wrong is rooted instead in other failures such as wantonness and weakness of will.[48]

Given this point, the possibilities for critical thought produced by the diverse and flexible qualities of the multiple and decentered subject are not foolproof for producing critical thought in individuals. There are limitations to the ways in which multiple identities can foster critical thought. First, the possibility for critical reflection arising from identity-based vantage points cannot itself ensure right action will be taken, particularly when the *content* of those identities favor something normatively wrong. Nor can these structures ensure that people will even engage in moral reflection at all. Wantonness, as a lack of reflection upon our wants and desires, is always possible and the content or interconnections of multiple identities alone cannot ensure that a given person will make use of the critical capacities and resources within them. What the intersectionality and diverse content of lived multiple identities outlined here does ensure, however, is the *possibility* of having several distanced vantage points for critical reflection on difficult questions. This presents the *possibility* of critical reflection should a person choose to engage in it. In sum, contrary to what MacIntyre argues, the "divided self" with decentered and multiple identities has, by virtue of the (at least minimally) varying content of those identities and shifting among them in daily life, the resources and vantage points necessary to make critical moral reflection possible.

However, even if the intersectionality of diverse multiple identities can make critical reflection from a variety of identity standpoints possible, MacIntyre still argues that the moral lapses of those with multiple identities are rooted ultimately in the segmentation of lifeworlds that inevitably shape the self and constrain its possibilities for agency. MacIntyre's view that segmentation and insularity are widespread and promote general disregard and resistance to the cross-fertilization of moral standards across different social contexts is valuable and persuasive. The extent of such insularity, however, is an empirical question, and it may not prevail in every given place and time. Moreover, I would grant to MacIntyre that social constructions that successfully subvert human interest in and commitment to critical moral thought and right action are likely to produce moral failure regardless of the basic attributes of multiple identities.

While MacIntyre's concern with fragmentation and insularity

is valid, at the same time, one of the virtues of Anzaldúa's account of mestiza consciousness is that it points out how the diversity of moral frameworks available to us in modern cultural borderlands means that no single moral framework—good or bad—need ever be ultimately total in its reach and influence on us. In an increasingly globalized world that is marked by overlapping cultural borderlands and frequent cultural displacement, there are few social contexts that are so isolated that aspects of other social worlds do not often touch them. Thus, while the social segmentation that MacIntyre bemoans does exist, it is also countered in various ways by equally unrelenting dynamics of social amalgamation and even homogenization. These dynamics combine to produce a cross-cutting character to social life that is present even in MacIntyre's own example, in which the use of scientific data is not simply a scientific matter. It is also an economic issue, a matter of personal integrity, and a matter of politics involving economic exploitation. As such, identity frames of reference from all of these social domains are justifiably relevant to the moral deliberations involved in scientific disclosure.

Nonetheless, MacIntyre also argues further that the morally damaging insularity of social segmentation cannot be overcome by moral accountability to others regarding actions that take place in different social realms. Yet, it is not hard to think of examples of people who publicly criticize and challenge the actions of those who act in one context in a manner that is morally at odds with their actions in another.[49] An entire transnational social movement, for example, was built around critically challenging Phil Knight, the CEO of Nike, for selling shoes in the United States using slogans promoting "women's empowerment" while fabricating those shoes in Southeast Asia using the labor of women working in sweatshops. In sweatshops producing for Nike, women endured far-below-subsistence wages in conditions where physical beatings, sexual harassment, and coerced overtime were commonplace.[50]

Moreover, while insularity and segmentation among social realms in contemporary social life can undermine cross-context accountability, those social realms also frequently intersect in shared domains of action, overlapping relations of cause and effect, and common personnel who may *with effort* extend moral and/or political accountability across different social domains. For example, historically, some scientists have insisted on cross-context accountability for the use of their work regardless of the personal consequences. Even if cross-context insularity is as common as MacIntyre contends, this does not eliminate *the possibility* that those with diverse or multiple identities can, by virtue of their different identity-based vantage points, bring various moral standards to bear on social contexts where they are not commonly applied and to do so in spite of prevailing norms of social compartmentalization.

The Case of J: Identity Diversity, Salience, and the Moral Atrocity

If having a range of multiple identities—especially identities with contradictory elements—can provide the tension needed as a basis for critical moral thought, then how effective is that tension as a basis for moral decision-making when moral choices have political consequences, including moral atrocity? MacIntyre argues that the quality of moral thought and judgment arising from multiple identities—especially multiple role-based identities—would be fairly low. He illustrates this argument with the case of "J," a Nazi collaborator. MacIntyre describes J as a man who "like everyone else, occupied a number of roles."[51] These social roles included treasurer of a sports club, a non-commissioned military officer in wartime, and a railway engineer. In the latter role, J was carefully instructed by his superiors never to inquire into the content of the freight his trains carried. Following these commands, J later failed to question the circumstance when his trains carried Jewish prisoners to extermination camps. When questioned about this after the Holocaust, J sincerely replied, "I did not know. It was not for someone in my position to know. I did my duty. I did not fail in my responsibilities. You cannot charge me with moral failure."[52] MacIntyre asks whether J's defense is an adequate moral defense. He seeks the answer in the social structures that inform and animate J's several role-based social identities.

As MacIntyre extends his analysis of the case of J, however, he understandably does not wish to conclude that J is not morally responsible for what he has done. Thus to make J morally accountable, MacIntyre argues that while the divided self may *seem* compartmentalized "it can never be dissolved nor dissolve itself *entirely* into the distinctive roles that it plays in each compartmentalized sphere of activity."[53] In making this argument, MacIntyre acknowledges himself to be shifting to the view that there *is* interconnection among multiple role-identities that make it possible for the subject to engage in two further tasks. The first task is one of "managing its transitions from one role to another" and the second is to manage the exact way in which one will enact each role-identity.[54] For MacIntyre, the need to manage one's multiple identifications introduces "a virtue that is a newcomer to the catalogue of the virtues: adaptability [or] flexibility, [that involves] knowing, chameleon-like, how to take on the color of this or that social background."[55]

This shift in MacIntyre's characterization of the "divided self" brings his account quite close to Anzaldúa's account of mestiza consciousness as he newly emphasizes the subject's conscious ability to shift among different identities in different contexts. Although neither Anzaldúa nor MacIntyre specify exactly how this "management" of multiple identities takes place (I discuss this process in chapters two and four), MacIntyre argues that because the self must manage *all* of its identities, a person who attends to the precepts of only *one* of his or her identities in a given context is exercising a kind of rigid discipline. This rigidity requires a "habit of mind" that actively engages in the compartmentalization of the self into its various identities.[56] This habit of mind produces "active refusals and denials" that implicate the person in the moral trespasses those compartmentalizations and active refusals create.[57]

In MacIntyre's analysis of J, it was his active refusal to examine and to question his role as an engineer that implicates him in the moral crimes of the Holocaust. In other words, J's lack of knowledge was *active* and, therefore, it was a part of his own moral choices for which he may be held accountable. MacIntyre thus contends that J actively engaged in a set of identity-based refusals and denials that implicate him and render him responsible for the moral atrocities in which he has collaborated. Not incidentally, Anzaldúa also considers such rigidity a source of risk and potential political disaster. In poetic style she described the virtue of flexibility associated with mestiza consciousness as an antidote for habitual rigidity of thought. She writes, "[o]nly by remaining flexible is she [la mestiza] able to stretch the psyche horizontally and vertically," thus disrupting rigid mindsets that "are supposed to keep the undesirable ideas out." Such rigid mindsets are "entrenched habits and patterns; [and] these habits and patterns are the enemy within. Rigidity means death."[58] So it apparently was in the case of J.

MacIntyre's conclusion that J had a degree of control over which of his multiple identity schemes in which to think and act in the world at different moments is persuasive, and similar to what I have argued above. Less plausible, however, is MacIntyre's claim that J is implicated because he cordoned off the multiple and conflicting moral frameworks within his subjectivity that would have aided him in making superior moral judgments. This is because among J's multiple identities, it is difficult to see what his conflicting frame of reference would have been. Instead, it seems more likely that, as MacIntyre has presented the case, J's multiplicity was not *willfully too compartmentalized,* but rather that his multiple identities were *too insufficiently diverse* in their range and *too insufficiently conflicted or contradictory* in their moral content to support anything but a simplistic and wholly inadequate level of moral reasoning. These insufficiencies of *content* helped strip away the element of moral tension necessary for moral agency and autonomy despite the structural basis of multiple identities and their potential vantage points.

Let us look again at the supposedly "different" identities that J is said to have had. J was a soldier and officer, a father, a sports fan, a sports club officer, and a railway engineer. Moreover, in MacIntyre's words, "[E]ducation had inculcated into J" the "fundamental moral beliefs"[59] of *duty* and *responsibility* in which we are held morally accountable to others as "each of us owes it to others to perform her or his assigned duties and to discharge her or his assigned responsibilities."[60] On its surface then, J seems to have the type of moral make up that MacIntyre first applauds. Such a make up *should* have generated a moral tension within J—i.e. a tension between the contours of his social role and identities and his identity-independent moral code. Hence MacIntyre concludes that it had to be J's rigid "habits of mind" that prevented inner moral tension from engendering moral agency and good moral judgment.

What moral tension or contradiction, however, could have arisen among J's social identities and his categorical moral convictions? Yes, J was a father. But what kind of father was he? The traditional model of the father is a patriarchal one where the authority of the father is supreme and must always remain unquestioned. Duty and responsibility on this model require sons, daughters, and wives to follow the law of the father without question. Yes, J was also a soldier. Yet, here too is a patriarchal regime that replicates the law of the father in the unquestioned authority of those who rank highest in the chain of command. Good soldiers and military officers do not question the orders of their superiors. Their role and responsibility is to follow orders. It is their duty to assume that those who have issued their orders have done so in the name of vanquishing a common foe. This aim of vanquishing a common foe (at least metaphorically) is also presumably the primary concern of J's sports club. We know nothing about this club from MacIntyre's account other than that J has a place of responsibility in it. Yet, if it is like some others of its kind, conceivably this club is devoted to sports in which vanquishing a foe is valued above all else, often to the exclusion of moral concerns regarding inflicting physical pain or respecting human dignity and equality.[61]

Lastly, J was also a train engineer. In this capacity, J was instructed to follow orders without question as his duty and responsibility. Yet, compared with his other social roles and identities as father, soldier, and sportsman, the dictates of J's identity as engineer to follow orders uncritically and without question are not fundamentally different from his other identity schemes. Although the contexts of each of his social roles vary—home, battlefield, sports field, train yard—all are built upon similar meanings, values, and practices. They are all built around the ultimate values of basic reverence and deference for hierarchical authority and most importantly for the "rule of the father" that brooks no disobedience.

In terms of J's critical capacity, therefore, each of J's social roles and identities share a common moral outlook to an extensive degree. This high degree of commonality among J's social identities and his non-role-based moral convictions undermine the degree to which any significant moral tension can arise among his multiple social identities or among those identities and his internalized identity-independent moral convictions. Without significant differences and meaningful contradictions among his various identities, J had no competing or conflicting moral frameworks from which to critically reflect upon his different internalized ways of thinking or the actions rooted in them. Lacking all but the most superficial diversity among his frames of reference, J, though able to take different identity-based vantage points to evaluate his actions and consider his circumstances, possesses only vantage points that contain basically the same moral constructs and similar cognitive, affective, and motivational components related to a common ultimate value of adherence to patriarchal authority. Yet, as MacIntyre himself argues, moral agency depends on there being moral tension and conflict within the self. Thus without significant variation in his multiple identities J is left without the basic ingredient for agency and with few, if any, resources for the critical reflection at the heart of critical thought on political and moral questions.[62] In short, J's multiple identities are all basically moral equivalents, all variations on the same moral theme. Thus, they do not furnish enough moral tension for J to employ his basic capacity for critical thought, and by it choose to deviate from the norm of obeying orders that was fundamental to all of his various identities. As J's moral luck would have it, his untroubled identification with patriarchal authority made him the perfect Nazi stooge.

If my analysis—which accepts MacIntyre's emphasis on the need for inner contradiction—is plausible, then it raises another question regarding multiple identity formation and its relationship to political life. How, in the social diversity of late nineteenth and early twentieth century Germany, at a time when J would potentially have been exposed to many different ways of being and thinking, did J nonetheless end up with a collection of more or less homogeneous identities? How is it that while the Nazi rise to power did not go uncontested in pre-war Germany, J seems to have turned a deaf ear to criticism leveled at the Nazi regime and its genocidal anti-Semitism? Potential clues to answering this question may be found in social psychology. Some social psychologists have suggested that when all, or nearly all, of a person's array of self-constructs reinforce a particular pattern of thought or set of attitudes—e.g. a patriarchal mindset or egalitarian outlook—those self-constructs became a mutually reinforcing set of compound frames of reference via which everyday interpretative and cognitive processes take place. In and through that compound set of mutually reinforcing identity schemes, the subject is more likely to accept messages and information that are compatible with their existing perspectives and to screen out and/or reject messages and information that are not.[63]

Moreover, when a strong majority of identity schemes are more or less similar, the same perspectives and values are accessible and salient for use throughout the day. Extensive research indicates that when particular information or self-constructs are *chronically accessible* to us, information that is relevant to those chronic constructs draws our attention in automatic, or unconscious, attention responses. As one researcher put it, "it appears that for aspects of one's life one *frequently thinks about*—values, important dimensions of one's self-concept and the behavior of others, and attitudes—the presence of information related to those aspects automatically attracts our attention. These forms, then, are more likely than others to be noticed, thought about, and remembered . . . "[64] In the case of J, because all of his identity schemes had a basis in patriarchal rule, that patriarchal perspective would be chronically accessible, making like information such as Nazi rhetoric and action more likely to draw his attention over competing and contradictory information.[65]

As a corollary, when faced later with divergent information and alternative viewpoints regarding the Nazi regime, it would have been easiest for J to choose to interpret that contrary information in terms of his patriarchal worldview. In so doing, he may have screened out or misinterpreted important discrepant information on the job, and failed to listen to or seriously consider non-patriarchal, anti-fascist interpretations and critiques of Nazi policies. If so, then, while J may have heard alternative anti-Nazi viewpoints, given his existing configuration of multiple identities he would have been unlikely to have *listened* to them, much less been willing to internalize or identify himself with those alternative viewpoints, as did those Germans who actively resisted the genocide.

On this reading of J's conduct, Hitler might be seen as having mobilized people by activating identifications with anti-Semitism that already existed—perhaps more or less latently—in social groups and among many Germans.[66] Regarding the Germans who resisted the Nazi regime at the risk of their own lives, the question then becomes: What aspects of their subjectivities were made salient by Nazi efforts to activate anti-Semitism as a politically mobilizing factor? Did a deep or casual identification with Jewish or other persecuted groups become salient? If so, did this identification arise from intermarriage, friendship, or other social connections? Or perhaps were isolated self-concepts of equality or nonviolence that intersected with German cultural or national identities made salient by Hitler's rise to power? In any case, considered in this way, a framework of multiple identities may add to the tools we currently have for understanding turns in fascist politics.[67]

In sum, it may be that past a certain threshold of multiple identity homogeneity, it becomes more difficult to unsettle the sustained salience of homogeneous identity schemes already in the subject, or to add to the subject's diversity of identities through successive socialization. Excessive and stable homogeneity prevents, or at least makes less likely, the internalization and development of divergent identifications because divergent ideas, critical viewpoints, and other information inconsistent with previously internalized outlooks are more likely to be screened out or not draw attention.[68] This, in turn, eliminates or minimizes the inner conflict of perspectives, and makes the distanced vantage points necessary for *critical* thought more difficult, if not impossible, to achieve. In addition, past a certain threshold the mutual reinforcement of similar self-constructs could muffle the unsettling effects of intra-group variations and intra-identity scheme variations such as those discussed in scenario three above. In the case of J, although different and competing non-patriarchal ways of thinking and being were present in his society, it would have been easiest for him to favor those identities he already had, and to disregard—or brace himself against—the insights of other lifeworlds that contained alternatives.

Within this approach to multiple identities and critical thinking, however, much of the political impact of homogeneous multiple identities depends on what specific meanings, values, and practices a person's fairly homogenous self-constructs contain. If the content of all of a given subject's self-constructs valorize diversity and respect for human rights and dignity, for example, then the fact that they have homogenous multiple identities may only mean that those subjects tend to screen out messages and values of intolerance.[69] Politically that may have only positive implications. I do not claim to know where the minimum threshold for identity diversity might lie. It may be that the minimum level varies for each of us and even small aspects of subjectivity may make a difference in our judgments and unconscious reactions in extreme circumstances. In any one person's case, the history of their identity formations may be so influenced by unique personal identities, chance events and encounters, aesthetic and other affective judgments, and vague idiosyncratic influences, that individual cases do not bear generalization.

In the end, my alternative analysis of J's moral failure leads to some of the same conclusions reached by MacIntyre. I agree that J probably did not know what he had done. Moreover, I agree with MacIntyre that J did not, and apparently could not, have exercised critical moral thought and agency.[70] Unlike MacIntyre, however, I do not attribute J's lack of critical moral thought to his multiple identities or to his willful and excessive separation of his own social roles and identities—although I agree with both MacIntyre and Anzaldúa, that such willful rigidity may undermine critical thought in a destructive manner. Rather, I attribute J's failure to the homogeneity of his subjectivity and his lack of *meaningfully* diverse and even contradictory multiple identities. This lack is something for which not only J, but also the society at large, are responsible.[71] The catastrophic nature of the moral failure in the case of J further suggests that there can be great deal at stake in ensuring that citizens of a democratic regime have meaningfully diverse sets of identifications. For it is upon that diversity—whatever configuration it may have—that I would argue the capacity for critical thought depends. Moreover, my analysis suggests that politically there is a great deal at stake in attending carefully to the ways in which some prevalent identity schemes or other self-constructs are made salient in the course of public life. I return to the political implication of multiple identities in the concluding chapter. In the next chapter, I take up again the idea of identity contradiction and investigate how, if at all, a decentered and multiple subjectivity can be at once diverse and contradictory, as well as a cohesive whole.

CHAPTER FOUR

The Two-Tiered Cohesion of Decentered Subjectivity
A Herdsman's Maps and the Politics of Disordered Contradiction

[T]hey say, the Self is nothing but Unity, unity abstract and absolute, so Hume says it is nothing but Diversity, diversity abstract and absolute; whereas in truth it is that mixture of unity and diversity which we ourselves have already found so easy to pick apart.
WILLIAM JAMES, *Principles of Psychology*

Our choice is not limited to either a "masculine," overly differentiated, and unitary self or no self at all. We should be suspicious of those who would revise history (and hence our collective memory) to construct such flawed alternatives.
JANE FLAX, *Thinking Fragments*

It is only when an agent takes the unification of his traits, his thoughts and his actions, as a central project that he is capable of self-deception and *akrasia*. A person who just is a loose confederation of habits is an agent only in the loosest sense. For someone to be capable of *agency in the strong sense,* to hold himself responsible for avoiding self-deception and *akrasia, requires that he*—or at any rate some relatively central set of his habits—*reflexively underwrite his integrative processes.* He must declare his various friendly neighborhood habits to be one city, the *I.*
AMÉLIE OKSENBERG RORTY, "Self-Deception, *Akrasia,* and Irrationality"

In the previous chapter, I set out reasons for regarding identity contradiction as a necessary and valuable resource for critical and creative thought. Yet, as Gloria Anzaldúa has stressed, the value of identity contradiction is also contradictory. For while identity contradictions are necessary, and at times fruitful for critical thought in socially constructed subjects, they nonetheless also represent divides and fragmentations within the psyche that can be an unwelcome source of pain and confusion. Perhaps even more importantly—and as I shall contend throughout the remainder of this book—the primary political implications of multiple identities result largely from how individuals choose to cope with their identity contradictions, especially those contradictions that have been internalized within ongoing political conflicts.

Given the political significance of identity contradictions, it is important to situate identity contradiction within a broader understanding of the overall cohesion of a decentered and multiple subject. If identity contradictions are intellectually valuable *but also* fragmentary, can identity contradictions be compatible with the wholeness of a decentered subject? Can multiple identities that contradict each other hang together as a whole despite the contradictions among them? This chapter is dedicated to proposing an answer to these questions. In it, I offer a theoretical framework for the cohesion of a decentered and multiple subject that incorporates identity contradiction and illuminates the character of personal identity.

Overall, I will suggest that a multiple and decentered subjectivity that includes identity contradictions can and does cohere as a whole on the basis of two general characteristics. Each of these characteristics offers a different mechanism and tier of cohesion for the subject. The *first* of these tiers involves how subjectivity hangs together minimally, but inevitably, as a complex self-system. I contend that the activity of this self-system is the basis for one's sense of self-continuity in and over time, and thus for one's unique relationship to oneself that we refer to generally as "personal identity." Because the cohesion of a self-system is inevitable and continues independent of the second tier, I argue that system integration is alone sufficient to make the decentered subject cohesive as a diverse and decentered whole.

In contrast, the *second* characteristic that produces cohesion in the decentered subject is much more variable. This mechanism lies in the different degree of positive intersection and integration among all of the multiple identities and various other self-constructs within subjectivity. These intersections can be internalized *passively* as a function of social construction (i.e. societal integration or fragmentation of the self) or can be generated *actively* by subjects as acts of self-fragmentation or self-integration. It is in this second tier of passive and active intersection and contingent and changeable fragmentation that the political relevance of identity contradictions—and of how people handle those contradictions—becomes evident.

With the aim of describing the place of identity contradictions within the overall character of the cohesion of subjectivity, this chapter is divided into three parts. In part one, I develop an account of the first tier of self-cohesion by relating the five-part self-system introduced in chapter two with a formal theoretical account of "personal identity." To do so, I turn to classic work in psychology by William James, his metaphor of the herdsman, a metaphor that I adopt and utilize throughout the remainder of the book. James's herdsman metaphor is useful for understanding the first tier of self-cohesion, but it is not effective for fully understanding the second tier, which requires closer attention to identity contradiction as part of specific kinds of embodied thought, feeling, action, and habits.

To explore this second tier of self-cohesion, I turn in part two to Amélie Oksenberg Rorty's work on inner contradiction, *akrasia*, and self-deception. Rorty offers a different metaphor of inner diversity involving two city maps—one reflecting a centrally planned city, the other an unplanned medieval city. Based on an analysis of Rorty's metaphor, I sketch a framework of this second tier of self-cohesion.

Finally, in part three, and based on the frameworks of self-cohesion developed in parts one and two, as well as writings by Rorty and Jane Flax, I investigate the possibility that the ways in which individuals manage their identity contradictions can have important political consequences in the form of conflict-related acts of self-deception and akrasia. Analyzing Gloria Anzaldúa's writings and other examples, I also describe how politically significant identity contradictions may be present in subjects in relatively homogeneous contexts. I then offer a five-part typology of identity contradiction, through which I further illustrate the connection between political life and the identity contradictions potentially within decentered subjectivities. I close the chapter by considering how identity contradictions can shape patterns of political interpretation that may, in turn, obscure politically relevant interconnections among social groups that are supposed to be deeply divided.

Multiple Identities, Personal Identity, and a First Tier of Self-Cohesion

The question of how identity contradictions relate to the integration of the self has long been a matter of philosophical debate. In chapters five and six, I will consider at length how some of the most influential philosophical approaches to self-integration compare to the framework of integration that I am offering in this and the next two chapters. For the moment, however, I will simply begin by contending that there are two characteristics of multiple identities that are responsible for how a decentered subjectivity with multiple identities can be considered a whole despite whatever inner diversity and contradictions it may have.

The first of these characteristics, introduced in chapter two, is that multiple and decentered subjectivity functions as a complex five-part system in which the multiplicity of internalized self-constructs can become salient alternately and contextually in a way that binds the multiplicity of dimensions within subjectivity together. The co-hesion provided by the workings of this five-part self-system is alone sufficient to give decentered, multiple and contradictory subjectivity a degree of wholeness and self-perceived continuity that encompasses the full spectrum of its diverse quality. To lay out the character of this cohesive characteristic, it is helpful to relate this explanation to the familiar concept of personal identity.

If personal identities are the unique identities that we have with specific individuals (e.g. father, friend), then *personal identity* is the unique relationship that a person has to himself or herself. In that unique relationship with oneself, individuals commonly feel a sense of self-continuity—as sense of being the same person over time—even when they have changed quite dramatically. Western philoso-phy has long struggled to account for the sense of self-continuity that accompanies the obvious changeability and diversity of the self. Yet to regard the self as including a *multiplicity* of identities, as I do in this work, further complicates the longstanding question of the grounds of personal identity, in that a theory of multiple identities must account not only for multiplicity of the self *over* time, but the multiplicity of the self in time as well.[1] My aim here is not to solve this longstanding philosophical problem, but rather to offer one possible approach to understanding personal identity with reference to the cohesion of multiple identities, by building on existing accounts of personal identity.

To consider the character of personal identity with regard to mul-tiple identities, it is useful to turn to the work of William James. As stated in this book's introductory chapter, William James famously argued that an individual "has as many social selves as there are dis-tinct *groups* of persons about whose opinion he cares." James stated that different selves become relevant in different contexts such that a person "generally shows a different side of himself to each of these dif-ferent groups."[2] Moreover, as the first epigraph of this chapter shows, James also considered subjectivity to be a mixture of elements that at once unite and divide the self even as the self remains a whole. In adopting this position, James was responding to David Hume and to Hume's bundle theory of the self. Hume regarded subjects as "noth-ing but a bundle or collection of different perceptions" that pass very rapidly in "perpetual flux and movement."[3] Hume argued that when individuals imagine the bundle of passing perceptions as resembling one another, then this imagined resemblance becomes the basis upon which an individual perceives himself or herself to be a whole self with continuity over time. For Hume therefore, it is imagining ourselves to be a whole over time that is the basis for our personal identity.

William James argued however, that while Hume rightly empha-sized the diversity of the subject, Hume took a position that was too extreme when he argued that nothing but fanciful imaginings unite a person's disparate social selves into a whole.[4] Thus, while James agreed with Hume that personal identity is *in part* a function of re-semblances among different aspects of the self, he argued that this sense of resemblance is not solely a figment of imagination. Rather, the sense of resemblance among one's many perceptions is based in the activity of what might be called thought-in-the-moment. James designates this thought-in-the-moment—the present mental state—with a capital letter as "judging-Thought." For James, the *activity* of judging-Thought is a cognitive motion that "binds the individual past facts with each other and with itself," and this binding of di-verse elements by judging-Thought unites the self as a whole unit.[5] That binding encompasses *both* connection and separation, what I have been referring to here as the integration and fragmentation of subjectivity.

James describes the subject's combination of unity and diversity through a debate between his psychologist's formal reasoning, and the reasoning of "common-sense." As if to demonstrate his over-all point, James genders common sense female, and in the ensuing debate, his masculine thinking is held to account by the feminine mind more gifted in the insights of common sense.[6] In the exchange between the two modes of gendered reasoning, James grapples with the problem of the unity of consciousness through the metaphor of "the herdsman." In James's metaphor, the herdsman is the owner of a herd of cattle that carry his herd brand. Each head of cattle represents the various selves—i.e. what I have been calling identity schemes and self-constructs—within subjectivity. The mark of the herd brand is judged and given by Thought, based on a sense of warm affective re-sponse felt toward each creature that belongs to him. The brand is at once the sign and the cause of our knowing that these cattle be-long together and belong to the herdsman.[7] As part of the herd, cattle themselves scatter and meander. Although they are branded, they do not stick together as "[e]ach wanders with whatever accidental mates it finds. The herd's unity is [thus] only potential, its center ideal, like the 'center of gravity' in physics, until the herdsman or owner comes."[8] In the ensuing dialogue, however, common sense insists that while the owner/herdsman is *not* a substantial or transcendental owner, he must nonetheless be more than simply an auto-coalescing part of a stream of thoughts and feelings. In other words, common sense holds that the herdsman must be more than part of a flow of thought that has no *medium* of cohesion.

James grants the feminine mind her point and suggests that judging-Thought be considered that medium of cohesion, and that judging-Thought is conceived of as a relay of successive owners of the cattle. In that relay, each owner as judging-Thought-in-the-moment is *not* transcendental or identical with the previous owner in-its-moment. Rather the new owner has "merely inherited his 'title.'"[9] The birth of each judging-Thought from moment to moment coincides exactly with the death of the judging-Thought of the previous moment. Each moment of judging-Thought, thus *"find[s]* the past self already its own as soon as it found it at all, and the past self would thus never be wild, but always owned, by a title that never lapsed."[10] As James puts it, "[w]e can imagine a long succession of herdsmen coming rapidly into possession of the same cattle by transmission of an original title by bequest."[11] In the process recounted in the herdsman metaphor, the perception of "sameness running through the ingredients of the self" and the "thread of resemblance" that together seem to unite the multiplicity of subjectivity into a whole, though disparate herd, is *not merely imaginary.* Instead it is based on a sense of self-continuity that springs from the phenomenological activity of judging-Thought. The unique relationship that we have to ourselves— i.e. "personal identity" per se—is therefore grounded in the activity of thought-in-the-moment as it links and binds all that is within its purview (i.e. within subjectivity) to each other and also to itself.[12]

James's herdsman metaphor for personal identity is a good basis for illustrating how multiple identities and the contradictions among them can co-exist without eliminating our sense of being a whole self in and over time. It is possible to build on James's argument by relating it to the concept of salience from Social Identity Theory, and the idea that identity schemes are socially constructed—theoretical outlooks not yet available in James's time. In combining these theoretical elements, I maintain with James that the activity of thought-in-the-moment, or judging-Thought, is the phenomenological basis of personal identity. But using the concepts of accessibility and salience from Social Identity Theory, I would further specify that thought-in-the-moment is this basis because its activity stands in a relationship of access to all of the multiple identity schemes and self-constructs within subjectivity. This access, I would argue, has a binding quality that springs from the phenomenological activity of judging-Thought as judging-Thought maintains *a thread of varied salience*. Each turning of salience from one moment or context to the next channels a framework of thought that belongs to the self—i.e that has a herd brand. But judging-Thought always only channels those frameworks, because as a raw capacity for cognition it *can* only channel—and put into play as the working-self—elements from the diverse reservoir of self-constructs that comprise a multiple and decentered subjectivity. Consequently, a scheme of thought, feeling, and action that is *known to oneself as oneself* is always salient and recognizable as oneself through the activity of judging-Thought. Therefore, even if from moment to moment, and/or over time, the dimension of self that is salient in a given moment is quite different or even contradictory to others that are or have been salient, there is always *a continual basis for self-recognition in each moment*.

On my account then, the sensation of self-continuity—the feeling of personal identity—arises not so much from an imagined or recognized thread of resemblance as Hume and James argued, but rather from the thread of continual self-recognition of diverse elements of subjectivity as they are channeled by judging-Thought—as raw capacity for introducing varied patterns of cognitive, affective, and motivated thought. This continual thread of recognition has a binding quality that encompasses identities and self-constructs that may range from highly integrated to deeply fragmented. Because judging-Thought links these in a connection of access to the totality of self-constructs and identities within the subject, it is this relationship of access that links diverse identity schemes to thought-in-the moment and to each other, even when various elements are *not* salient in a given moment.[13] The binding access of judging-Thought thus creates a connection among all the multiple self-constructs and identities within subjectivity that does not depend on any other intersections among the multiple identities within subjectivity that might also exist. For at a minimum, even highly fragmented identity schemes and self-constructs are bound to each other via their common connection of accessibility to thought-in-the-moment. The result is a self-perception of wholeness and self-continuity that encompasses all the multiple elements within subjectivity as "me" even if those identities are quite distinct and little interrelated.

It is possible to further refine James's account of personal identity as a divergent whole by considering three key terms from James's metaphor—title, bequest, and brand—in terms of multiple identity schemes. As James argued, at any point in time the subject can be said to have a "title" to the multiple identities and self-constructs within

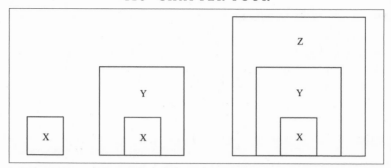

4.1. Successive moments of consciousness: each experience leaving its mark.
Figure derived from one by William James (*Principles of Psychology*, 321).

himself. This means that the subject is formally the owner of the diverse elements of himself, i.e. they *belong* to him by virtue of being internalized within subjectivity. In addition, the notion of bequest describes *how* those multiple elements have come to belong to the subject: they came to him not through special effort of his own but as an inheritance in which he merely comes into possession of elements of self that had been previously possessed by earlier moments of judging-Thought. That is to say, a "bequest" is not necessarily a conscious act, but rather is the remaining impression in subjectivity of a socially constructed and internalized element. For example, three successive moments of judging-Thought might bequest their objects of thought as shown in fig. 4.1.

In this figure X, Y, and Z represent successive thoughts with a lettered object of judging-Thought within it. Each object of thought creates an impression in subjectivity that is internalized as a self-construct. In James's words, X, Y, and Z would each "stand for three pulses in a consciousness of personal identity," but yet they are "all something different from the others."[14] Nonetheless, even as each pulse of consciousness varies from the others, Y would know and contain X. Likewise Z would know and contain Y and X. Thus, as James puts it with reference to Kant, "[e]ach Thought is thus born an owner, and dies owned, transmitting whatever it realized as its Self to its own later proprietor."[15] In this way, "[t]hree successive states of the same brain, on which each experience in passing leaves its mark, might . . . well engender thoughts differing from each other . . ." and at the same time know and contain a wide diversity elements that may or may not be related to each other beyond their relationship of access to judging-Thought.[16]

While the relationship between *title* and *bequest* may account significantly for the combination of diversity *and* wholeness in the self, I contend—as James does not address either of these issues—that the political implications of multiple identities lie more in the relationship between the terms of *title* and *brand*. Recall that in James's account, the notion of brand symbolizes an affective connection—present or past—with elements of the self that belong as part of subjectivity. All of the multiple elements within subjectivity thus have a herd brand. That brand symbolizes that those elements belong together and belong to the self, who is the metaphorical owner. However, if this relationship is parsed still further, it is possible to recognize that while a herd brand may symbolize the fact of belonging within subjectivity—i.e. the rightful purview of the herdsman—a bequeathed title may exist even when *claims* to ownership are absent. Suppose, for example, a wealthy woman dies owning a piece of property that is not recognized and claimed by her estate. If the title to the property eventually emerges in her name, her ownership—that is her title—is complete without her having made a claim to ownership. Thus, in a legal sense, a title symbolizing formal ownership of an object may exist and establish *effective and durable* ownership that is nonetheless independent of a title holder's claims to ownership, claims that an owner may fail to make or make belatedly.

As we shall see in part two of this chapter, the possibility of possessing multiple identity schemes that one has inherited by bequest, without claiming or recognizing that ownership, is a politically significant characteristic of multiple identities. Before explaining how this is so, however, it is first important to look at three other characteristics of multiple identities that James's account of personal identity suggests. First, the basis for the cohesion of a decentered subjectivity is not an Arch-Ego or other core self. While James does entertain the possibility that such an Arch-Ego exists, his metaphor of the herdsman as an activity generating cohesion does not require it.[17] Rather, James is explicit that the "'owner' symbolizes here that 'section' of consciousness, or pulse of thought, which we have all along represented as the *vehicle* of the judgment of identity."[18] Thus, judging-Thought is the locus of cognitive, affective, and motivational function that is simply, but importantly, *only* the realized raw *capacity* for thought-in-the-moment. As such, judging-Thought *has no necessary or specific content or shape*. Its *only* content is the content that is given to it moment-to-moment by the identity schemes and other self-constructs that become momentarily salient as frameworks for thought and action.[19]

Second, James's argument regarding judging-Thought as a bare capacity for cognition dovetails well with the five-part sub-system definition of subjectivity offered in chapter two. In that chapter, I defined subjectivity conventionally as a system comprised of five subsystems of embodied capacity for thought and feeling. These five interconnected subsystems are: 1) *the cognitive system,* involving thought and pattern recognition, 2) *the affective system,* involving feeling, judgment, and emotion, 3) *the motivational system,* roughly involving the capacity for goal-oriented thought and action, 4) *the motoric system,* involving habits as over-learned routines of thought or action, and 5) *the psychophysiological system,* involving the interconnection of bodily functions such as breath and heart rate to the other four systems.[20] I suggest that this five-part system of subjectivity can be usefully combined with the notion of "salience" and James's conception of "judging-Thought" to generate an expanded account of the activity of judging-Thought in which judging-Thought is considered to be a locus of cognitive, affective, and motivational capacity that is mediated by bodily reaction and habituated thoughts, feelings, and actions.

Third, if plausible, such an expanded notion of judging-Thought would shed different light on the character and source of human agency, than a unitary or centered account of the subject. If the basis of personal identity is rooted in the activity of judging-Thought and the binding access of that activity, then more broadly personal identity is rooted in the capacity for thought-in-the-moment. That capacity for thought encompasses embodied, and potentially habituated, processes of cognitive, affective, and motivationally based thought. Further still, that capacity for cognition, affect, and motivation based thought could encompass thoughts that involve making selections from a range of possibilities—or what we conventionally call "choice." It follows from this, that because human *agency* is commonly defined as the capacity to choose, and because that capacity to choose is rooted in the activity of judging-Thought as a raw, inborn, capacity for thought-in-the-moment, my account of decentered and multiple subjectivity *presupposes human beings to have agency* by virtue of that raw capacity. I make this presumption, moreover, in a manner consistent with the background assumptions—overt or not—of other poststructuralist accounts of the self, most notably that of Michel Foucault's later works.[21] I further discuss and defend this assumption in chapter six. As a caveat, however, the presumption of agency in decentered subjects makes no claim as to the use of that capacity.

If decentered subjectivities have an inborn capacity for thought and agency, how, *if at all,* an agent will employ that raw capacity cannot be fully anticipated philosophically. People may have raw capacities that they do not use, or use well. I am only arguing therefore, that the first basic tier of the cohesion of decentered and multiple subjectivity lies in the five-part self-system common to every person. That self-system is the locus of the bare capacity for thought and choice, and following William James, I have labeled that capacity judging-Thought.

Identity Contradiction, Intersectionality, and a Second Tier of Self-Cohesion

Part one of this chapter discussed the first tier of self-cohesion—a self-system that gathers a decentered and multiple subjectivity into a self-recognizable whole. This second part of the chapter describes a second level and source of self-cohesion. Unlike the cohesion of a self-system—which is inevitable and the same for all subjects—this second level varies in degree and specificity from one individual to the next, as well as potentially varying for specific individuals over time. Moreover, unlike the cohesion of the self-system in which the basis of cohesion is the binding access of potential salience that lies in part beyond the subject's conscious control, the second tier of cohesion is based in the constructed intersections among identity schemes and other self-constructs. On this second level, identity contradictions and intersections and how individuals respond to them play important roles both in the degree of self-cohesion and in the political significance of that degree of integration.

Unfortunately, the metaphor of the herdsman that was so useful in part one of the chapter is of limited value in what it can reveal about this second tier. James was interested in discovering how inner diversity could be reconciled with overall unity in any subject. For this purpose his metaphor of the herdsman need not make reference to the particular character of the different "social selves" within the subject, or how those "social selves" are interrelated. Both of these, however, are central to the second level of self-cohesion. Nonetheless James's herdsman metaphor is rich enough to generate some useful clues about specific multiple identities if it is read more generally than I have done so far. On the whole, after all, James equates multiple identities within the self with branded cattle that are overseen—or more precisely, on my analysis, administered—by a herdsman. By nature herd cattle are generally wayward, yet also liable to form themselves into accidental and randomly wandering groups. A particular herd may be made up of bulls, cows, and calves of different dispositions, and individual cattle often have their own inborn characteristics, in which some may be prone to violent charges, while others are calm and docile. Collectively, herd cattle can be startled into stampedes deadly to themselves and others. Unlike working dogs, they are not always reliably loyal to a herdsman, but unlike cats, cattle can be herded and moved in one direction *if and only if* the task is attended to continually.

In terms of the second tier of identity cohesion, this metaphor is somewhat apt. If multiple identities are like cattle, then if they are poorly overseen, they too may be prone to independent activity scattered across a broad range, and subject to random and aimless combinations that may escape the control of a herdsman. Moreover, multiple identities may be diverse, of different disposition, and mutually influencing in potentially unexplained and dangerous ways. For within virtually all decentered and multiple subjectivities there are multiple identity schemes, identity fragments, semi-independent beliefs, desires, fears, motivational schemes, various habits, and patterns of perception and interpretation that are socially constructed and internalized in memory as each individual's full herd of self-constructs. As it happens, this unruly mass of self-constructs also has a wayward potential. Moreover, that wayward potential has direct political implications for how people act and interact interpersonally and politically. As I shall argue below and in later chapters, it also has implications for the propensity of individuals and groups to consistently act upon deeply held social and political principles, such as those of social justice and equality.

Beyond these generalities, however, James's herdsman metaphor tells us little about the specific content of wayward identity schemes or their potential relationship to one another. It lacks the imagery of differentiation among identity schemes within the herd that would illuminate identity contradictions or linkages among specific cattle in the herd. Yet, specific contradictions and the types and degrees of intersectionality among particular identity schemes and self-constructs form the variable and contingent basis of self-cohesion in the second tier. To gain insight into these aspects of the second tier self-cohesion, therefore, it is useful to turn to the writings of philosopher Amélie Oksenberg Rorty, who extensively addresses inner diversity and the consequences of internal contradiction.

Amélie Oksenberg Rorty, like William James, explains the inner diversity of the self and its functioning with a metaphor. Her metaphor is one of two city maps that present different parts of the same metropolis—a metropolis that also represents an internally diverse subjectivity. One of the two maps is of a planned city. The other is of a disorderly medieval city, and the map of the planned city is superimposed upon the thriving medieval one. As the privileged representation of the self, the planned or "radiant city" is pristine, centralized, and orderly. At its center is the seat of government from which long boulevards spread out like spokes from city center to suburb. Its governmental branches are "presumed to act from a single set of rules, with clearly defined priorities fixed by a classical conception of rationality."[22] Likewise, its grand boulevards presumably deliver to each distant area of activity "regulations by the same systematic rational plan" for its activities.[23]

Beneath this respectable and ordered urbanity of the self, however, is a bustling medieval area very different in character. This medieval city-self has no orderly boulevards linking its various regions, which may be fragmented from each other and unfamiliar across various divides. This part of the city-self is a mass of "relatively autonomous neighborhoods, linked by small lanes that change their names half way across their paths," it is a "loose confederation of quite different neighborhoods, each with its [own] distinctive internal organization . . . [and] different conditions for entry," in a lively, diverse area.[24]

The items on *both* maps together represent the totality of different self-constructs within a single multiple and decentered subjectivity. The contents of both maps can obstruct or advance the operations of those on the other. While Rorty focuses in particular on habits—especially behavioral, interpretive, and evaluative habits—the self-constructs on these maps could logically include identity schemes, as well as all of the other kinds of self-constructs commonly found within subjectivities. In everyday life, the habits and other self-constructs on either map may become salient as the framework for thought and action. Despite the privileging of the planned city map, both maps thus contain effective parts of the self.

While these two maps and their contents are common to virtually everyone, Rorty points out that they are not equally well recognized. For the most part, philosophers, like the rest of us, tend to privilege the material on our planned city maps. As discussed in chapter three, for example, communitarian Alasdair MacIntyre regards the neat and coherent narratives of our lives as not only the best way to weave our inner diversity together, but also the best way to bring to center stage in our lives the values that we *intend* to follow. Privileging the elements of the planned city map highlights for ourselves the parts of the self that we readily acknowledge and seek to live by. But Rorty suggests that emphasizing these readily avowed parts of the self has the effect—intended or unintended—of leaving

a great many other *actual and effective* parts of one's subjectivity unrecognized and unattended.

A self-understanding that attends only to the planned city-self
will tend to ignore the influential presence of rough neighborhoods,
intolerant guilds, slovenly gangs, lonely alleyways, corrupt precincts,
red-light districts, and circles of battered women and misfit men that
are also potentially part of one's medieval city-self.[25] Like wayward
cattle that wander unattended, these overlooked aspects of the self
can become salient and serve from time to time as frameworks for
thought and action whether they are avowed as part of our self-maps
or not. Moreover, if and when there is a disjuncture between what
prevails on our planned city maps and what takes precedence on
one's medieval map, that disjunction can often represent an internal
identity contradiction—i.e. a conflict between two or more identity
schemes or self-constructs. Thus, when self-constructs on the medieval map go unacknowledged, specific identity contradictions may
also go unacknowledged, increasing the likelihood that those contradictions will be poorly handled, or not addressed at all.

Rorty discusses two important consequences of mishandling
identity contradiction: akrasia and self-deception. *Akrasia* refers to
acting intentionally and voluntarily in ways that depart from what
a person regards as their preferred course of action in that kind of
situation. Akrasia may involve either practical action or psychological action such as interpreting or choosing. *Self-deception* "involves
deception of the self, by the self, for or about the self" such as at once
believing X *and* believing not-X (or denying belief in X).[26] While
recognizing the conflict between X and not-X at some level, the
agent denies the conflict's existence in the interest of preserving a
cherished notion (good or bad) of how they understand themselves.
Self-deception and akrasia both result in recognized or unrecognized
discrepancies between beliefs and actions, between words and deeds.
Unlike akrasia, however, self-deception will often be vigorously denied and possessively guarded as part of one's cherished self-image.

In her analysis of both phenomena, Rorty emphasizes that akrasia and self-deception are almost entirely the consequence of coping
with conflict or inner contradiction. When grappling with contradiction or conflict, akratic options may be chosen—voluntarily and
actively—on a variety of grounds, including habit, or embodiment-
inflected motivations such as a fatigue-driven desire to respond
quickly to a conflict. As Rorty argues, however, when faced with contradictions, akratic thoughts and behaviors are often *not those that
are strongly preferred*. Rather, the primary attraction of akratic action

is of its being "a strongly entrenched habit," or the least difficult resolution to a contradiction. In either case, "the akratic course is thus *the easy course.*"[27] On the whole then, acting akratically against one's preferred principles, according to Rorty, is often a function of one's failure to grapple well with inner contradictions. As Rorty emphasizes "[w]hen an agent is conflicted *without a taste for conflicts* and *without approved strategies* for resolving them, then akrasia sometimes provides a way out."[28]

As with akrasia, the failure to grapple effectively with internal contradiction is also at the heart of self-deception. Self-deception happens in two ways: self-care under conditions of uncertainty, and rigid adherence to motives or beliefs that one is actually finding suspect. First, under circumstances of uncertainty—such as political conflicts, changing social conditions, challenging marriages or work life—it may at times become useful to us to manipulate ourselves by way of a self-deception. In that self-manipulation, we tell ourselves that the outcome of the uncertain circumstance is—or will be—what we wish. We tell ourselves that "everything will be okay" even and especially when there is reason for doubt. This kind of self-deception is heartening and potentially benign in that it can help us to maintain loyal and enthusiastic effort beyond what would otherwise be our emotional limit. If at some level individuals see that they have deceived themselves, they may nonetheless persist in the projection for the sake of their comfort, "being careful to hide the traces of the enlarged slightly misleading description, the carefully preserved myopia, the averted gaze."[29]

The second kind of self-deception typically involves rigid clinging to motives or beliefs that have to some degree already become suspicious or otherwise seem untenable to us. In some cases, resisting modification of beliefs and actions in the face of radical doubt is adaptive. Conservatism can make sense when it is important to keep options open in light of risk or uncertainty. But this can easily veer into self-deception in which contradictory facts are recognized, but compartmentalized (i.e. ignored) with active resistance on the part of the subject to attend to those facts as a basis for self-correction. That rigidity may remain unrecognized on an indefinite basis. Or it may be recognized but then "judged to be worth the cost."[30] In some cases, self-deception of this kind (like akrasia) when self-obscured may be the best choice among a range of bad options for a person suffering in miserable conditions. In other cases, self-deception is instead the product of unwillingness on the part of the self-deceiver to address contradictions, or uncertainty on their part regarding how to address those contradictions. In both cases, self-deception can result in the sustained betrayal of deeply held beliefs. That betrayal, whether or not it springs from inner contradiction, will *create* contradiction in the self by fragmenting one's beliefs from one's actions.

Rorty's analysis suggests that contradictions are challenges very commonly faced by individuals. The question then becomes, what kinds of identity-related contradictions are there? While Rorty does not supply a framework, I would argue that there are at least five types of identity contradictions. The first of these types of identity contradiction are *perspective dependent contradictions.* These contradictions appear to us depending on the perspective that one takes to consider a circumstance (for example, a vegetarian who hunts).

Second are the *normatively accepted contradictions,* contradictions that are generally accepted as part of everyday life, such as the contradiction of the Christian soldier who is bound by faith not to kill, but committed in his profession to kill if necessary.

Third are *competing demand contradictions* that involve conflicts and contradictions arising from balancing the competing demands and commitments of one or more social identities or groups.

Fourth are *contested terrain contradictions,* contradictions that arise when the values and practices of two or more social groups and identities are in the process of social transformation. In such cases, people who have changing identities are caught in the contradictions that emerge between the old and new demands and the emerging practices of those identities. For example, many working women in the U.S. today feel strong contradictions between their identities as mothers (who have traditionally stayed at home), and their identities as working women who spend long hours away from home. When social change is uneven, workplace accommodations and social and institutional supports may remain inadequate even as family practices change. As long as working parents live in a world that is organized as if they do not *both* work and parent, they will struggle with the contradictions and contested practices of identifying themselves as working people who are also strongly identified with their children as responsible parents.

Fifth, *mutually exclusive contradictions* are contradictions in which pairs or clusters of identities are socially constructed and therefore widely regarded as mutually exclusive. Having one of those identities is supposed to rule out having the other(s). In the United States, for example, the color line defines Black racial identity as mutually exclusive with white racial identity, as typified by the one-drop rule.[31] Mutually exclusive identity contradictions are not limited to racial or ethnic identities, however, and may also include religious, class, national, subcultural, and any other identifications that are together regarded as zero-sum.

Second Tier Cohesion of the Self

With Rorty's city map metaphor, a typology of identity contradictions, and a sense of the consequences of mishandled identity contradictions in mind, it is possible now to situate identity contradiction within a broader account of the second tier of self-cohesion. This second tier, I would argue, is a variable form of self-cohesion, for, as stated earlier in this chapter, this second tier of self-cohesion is not based on the binding access of potential salience common to all self-constructs. Rather it is based on variable and contingent forms of intersection—i.e. interconnections of different kinds—that exist in and among different identity schemes and other self-constructs within subjectivity. To explain this variability, it is necessary to say more about the character and sources of intersections among multiple identities and other parts of the self.

Recall that in chapter two, I refined present accounts of intersectionality by breaking it down into three forms of intersectionality. First are influence-based intersections, in which social groups have converging influence on selves and social life. These include additive or reinforcing intersections and also cross-cutting influence or negative association, the latter of which produce intersections that are based on fragmentation. Second are content-based, consisting of shared content of some kind—e.g. ideals or practices—among social groups or internalized constructs. The third are internal or intrapsychic intersections, which are the connections and associations among different identity schemes and other self-constructs in our own minds and self-understandings. These intersections may or may not correspond to those that prevail conventionally in social life. Thus, intersections of different kinds exist within and among groups and entities in social life and within and among different self-constructs within our subjectivities.

If intersections among self-constructs are the basis for the second tier of cohesion, then what are the sources of those intersections? From a constructivist perspective, including the assumption of agency I made in part one of this chapter, I would argue that internal intersections become part of subjectivity in two ways. First, they can be internalized by subjects in and through social construction of subjectivity via language-mediated processes in everyday social life. I will label these inner intersections *societal or passive intersections,* in that they have been internalized from social life more or less passively and left unrevised by individuals themselves. Second, intersections can also be generated *actively* through the conscious activity and agency of the subject. Chapters five and six will focus in detail on this active form of self-integration, which I call integrative selfcraft. In my account, different types of intersections can either disconnect and fragment or link and integrate different elements within the self.

Thus, there are four potential kinds of intersections within subjectivity: active self-integration, active self-fragmentation, societal self-integration, and societal self-fragmentation. Based on this typology of fragmentation and integration of the self, the second tier of self-cohesion may be rendered in Fig. 4.2 as follows.

In Fig.4.2, the line down the middle of the sphere represents the separation between the *fragmentation* of inner elements on the left, and the *integration* of inner elements on the right. The upper left portion of the sphere represents societal or passive fragmentation of elements in subjectivity. The lower right portion of the sphere represents societal or passive integration of subjectivity. The lower left portion represents active self-fragmentation including the forms of akrasia and self-deception discussed by Amélie Oksenberg Rorty. The upper right portion of the sphere represents active self-integration produced through integrative selfcraft. Finally the sliver at the bottom of the

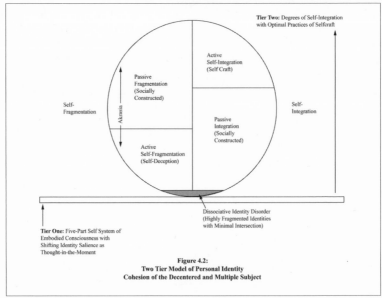

Figure 4.2:
Two Tier Model of Personal Identity
Cohesion of the Decentered and Multiple Subject

4.2. Two-tier model of personal Identity: cohesion of the decentered and multiple subject sphere represents highly self-fragmented subjectivities such as those found in dissociative identity disorders. The first tier of self-cohesion is represented as the baseline at the bottom of the figure. The orientation of the sphere above the plane of self-system integration represents how the second tier of self-cohesion is a supplementary form of cohesion that has varying degrees because subjects may have different configurations of intersections that either integrate or fragment their different identities.

These intersections vary on the basis of the configurations of multiple identities that a person has, and on the character of the linkages between those identities as they are constructed in a given place and time. In chapter two, for example, I discussed the experience of the second-generation Haitian America woman, Claudia. While Claudia identifies as both Black and ethnically Haitian, her racial and ethnic identities intersect negatively and are socially constructed in her school environment as mutually exclusive. That construction of mutual exclusivity at once divides these racial and ethnic group categories, but also associates those categories through a negative interrelationship, in which to be Haitian is not to be identified as Black and vice versa. Likewise Black identity for Claudia intersects with working class identity while ethnic Haitian identity intersects with upward mobility and rising class status. For the most part Claudia, who is 17 years old, has merely internalized these intersections from social life with her school friends. At the same time, despite the social embargo on identifying as both Black and Haitian she nonetheless chooses to do so by switching back and forth among her multiple ethnic and racial identities depending on her context. In doing so, Claudia is actively choosing to integrate her Haitian ethnic and Black racial identities despite the fact that those identities are constructed as fragmented in the broader society. While she may be seen as engaging in an act of self-integration, she is also uncertain of the value or legitimacy of her doing so. When she describes her linguistic code-switching between groups she begins by saying, "I'm ashamed to say this, but my accent changes."[32] As an example of self-integration, Claudia seems to actively integrate her Black and Haitian identities but also appears to do so in a way that nonetheless— and contradictorily—retains as part of that positive intersection of identities the idea that she should not claim both Black and Haitian identity schemes—hence her feeling of shame.

In this second-tier framework, akrasia and self-deception are forms of *self*-fragmentation. They are fragmentations of ourselves in which we ignore, separate, disconnect, or disavow identity schemes or other self-constructs within us as a method for grappling with painful contradictions and/or conflicts that come to the self through everyday social life. Self-fragmentation disrupts or prevents the formation of whatever intersections there might otherwise exist among specific self-constructs in the passive (or societal) integration of the self. Amélie Oksenberg Rorty argues that self-deception and akrasia are quite common as a means of coping with contradiction, and are potentially more widespread than we realize or would like to admit. Yet, at least among philosophers, akrasia and self-deception are often ignored or dismissed as "irrational" and therefore not something to which everyone is ultimately susceptible. My account of multiple identities would suggest that given the multiplicity of the subject and the socially constructed quality of identity contradictions, everyone is subject to akrasia and self-deception depending on how they respond to the identity contradictions that they may have.

Yet this susceptibility to akrasia and self-deception does not arise from having multiple identities per se, but rather from contradictions among identities. Those contradictions may exist between the identities on a subject's planned and medieval maps, especially if subjects tend to ignore identity schemes or mismanage their identity contradictions in self-fragmenting ways. Such agents do not seek to actively integrate all self-constructs within their subjectivity—that is, to put all of their constructs on a single map of interconnected elements. As Rorty notes in the epigraph to this chapter, not everyone will engage in such self-integration—a practice which is ultimately optional. For the purposes of self-cohesion a person can be simply integrated on a system basis only. But one who thinks and functions in daily life as a "confederation of habits is an agent only in the loosest sense."[33] She argues that to be an agent in a stronger sense requires that a person "underwrite his integrative processes," a process that I will explore in the next two chapters as the process of integrative selfcraft.

This argument that susceptibility to akratic and self-deceptive action involves multiple identities should not lead to the conclusion, however, that self-fragmentation is only the product of individual irrationality or mental illness. Rather, as Rorty demonstrates persuasively, both self-deception and akrasia take place via *normal* psychological processes, processes in which all of us necessarily engage in and which in many instances are vital components of a well-adapted life. As she points out, the problems of self-deception and akrasia do not arise from abnormal psychology or irrationality, but rather from how subjects succeed or fail to either actively acknowledge their own inner diversity, and/or successfully cope with the contradictions that may exist among the self-constructs within themselves. When applied to an extreme degree, this kind of coping mechanism can become the source of severe social maladaptation. Very rarely self-fragmentation results in dissociative disorders. However, dissociative disorders are distinct and should be distinguished from multiple identities as multiple identities are manifest in the vast majority of instances.[34]

Within psychology broadly, *dissociation* is defined as "the separation of an idea or thought from the main stream of consciousness."[35] Psychic elements that are "associated" have some interconnection between them. Those psychic elements that are "dissociated" are relatively separated and isolated from each other. Under normal circumstances, dissociation is a common feature of daily life for everyone. The performance of mundane chores while daydreaming is an everyday example of the human capacity to cordon off some aspects of experience, knowledge, or thought to a domain outside of primary consciousness. The capacity for dissociation is thus an important coping mechanism. In the context of an accident, for example, a person who is hurt may still rush to help others—and having dissociated their pain—will become aware of their own injuries only after the danger has passed. While the capacity for dissociation is not fully understood, it is thought that dissociation may be produced via a mild, self-induced trance.[36]

While dissociation is a common and normal psychological coping mechanism, dissociation can, like other self-regulatory functions, develop a pathological and habituated form. The list of dissociative dysfunctions is long. Dissociation is considered a symptom of a wide range of diagnosed psychopathologies, including eating disorders. Moreover, clinical psychology recognizes a collection of what are called "dissociative disorders." These disorders are defined by "a disturbance or alteration in the normally integrative function of identity, memory, or consciousness. The disturbance or alteration may be sudden or gradual and transient or chronic."[37] Among this list of disorders, Dissociative Identity Disorder (DID) has been repeatedly invoked in the debate over multiple identities. While the clinical debate concerning the character and even existence of DID continues, it is worthwhile in the philosophical debate over multiple identities to situate DID as a phenomenon related to, but quite distinct from, everyday manifestations of multiple identities, including identity configurations that contain significant identity contradictions.[38]

To Illustrate this distinction, Dissociative Identity Disorder is defined as a post-traumatic stress disorder. Cases are considered extremely rare, and of the known clinical cases approximately

90 percent of the afflicted are women. Of those women, an estimated 97 percent have been the victims of prolonged sexual abuse as children.[39] In these cases, the trauma of abuse is thought to produce a need to psychologically "escape" the unavoidable experience of rape or torture. The common capacity for dissociation provides the abused child with a way to cordon off bodily experiences from the center of consciousness, and thus to survive painful abuse *without* lapsing into psychosis. As a result of self-induced dissociative states, traumatic events may be endured in trance and not consciously remembered once the event has passed. In this way, dissociation is used as a coping mechanism for survival of repeated trauma and abuse.

In the case of DID, this use of dissociation to cope with severe abuse trauma becomes habitual. In such cases, a set of different identity schemes are formed and dissociated from each other. Like non-dissociated identity schemes, each of these dissociated identities or "alters" is typically associated with different contexts, social roles, or various life functions. For example, a particular "alter" may be the primary identity scheme that experiences and is the repository for all memories of inflicted pain. Another may be an identity scheme that deals with a particular parent or sibling. Other identity fragments may form so as to be responsible for homework or religious practices. The practical manifestation of this radical form of self-fragmentation in social life can be extreme social maladaptation.[40]

However seemingly bizarre, sensationalized, and even still denied DID may be, it is understandable as a mode of coping with intense contradiction *without* veering into psychosis. Just as for the miserable person for whom akrasia and self-deception are the best of bad options under hopeless conditions, the development of DID from the chronic trauma of child sexual abuse makes sense from the perspective of pre-mature rationality. At an early age, children do not have a mature "taste for conflict" that Rorty refers to as necessary for grappling well with contradiction and conflict. Yet, conflict reaches the child in the form of repeated violent assault. Morally immature, children also lack their own "approved strategies for resolving [conflict]" such as the contradiction between physical safety in some relationships and the violations experienced in others.[41] Dissociative response represents a way to relieve the anxiety of that contradiction by cordoning off a pain-bearing identity fragment from other conscious aspects of the self. When that fragment is made salient by abuse that "receptacle" for trauma is a strategy to *avoid* falling into psychosis. Thus, the difference between the normal psychology of those with multiple identities and the normal—though severely maladaptive—

psychology of those with Dissociative Identity Disorders is the latter's rare and extensive *degree of self-fragmentation.*[42] For those with DID, the degree of self-fragmentation has reduced intersectionality to a desperate minimum.

Politics and a Life of Disordered Contradiction

So far in this chapter, I have argued that decentered subjectivity coheres at two levels. The first level is one of self-system cohesion, in which the identities and other constructs within the self are bound together by their common potential to become salient as the framework for thought and action in a given moment. This is a certain and necessary level of self-cohesion and is present even in subjects with highly dissociated identities. The second level of cohesion involves the varying intersections—i.e. specific associations and interconnections—among the multiple identities and other self-constructs within subjectivity. As sketched in Fig. 4.2 above, these intersections may be either internalized from social life or the products of self-fragmentation or self-integration.

With this dual framework in mind, it is possible to explore some of the connections between political life and multiple identities as they relate to identity contradictions. Much of the source of these connections can be found in the close interrelationship between social and political conflicts and the identity contradictions that they can produce in individual subjectivities. The origin of Dissociated Identity Disorder in child sexual abuse, for instance, is an extreme example of how the fragmentation of subjectivity is partly a consequence of societal fragmentation—specifically in this case, the violence of patriarchy visited upon female children. To consider the political and personal consequences of how forms of social fragmentation shape the multiple identities and identity contradiction of subjects, it is helpful to turn to the work of Jane Flax. As a practicing psychotherapist, philosopher, feminist, and political theorist, Flax "juggles at least four identities and practices" each with their own distinct, divergent, yet also interrelated perspectives.[43] Thus, I regard Flax, like Gloria Anzaldúa, to be a borderlands thinker in that she brings a rare combination of identity schemes, professional perspectives, and academic expertise to her scholarship.

In her book, *Thinking Fragments,* Flax underscores the special quality of our current moment in human history as one in which we are rethinking our traditional understandings of the self, gender, knowledge, and power in light of the inadequacies of those traditions and their past destructive consequences. In this disorienting transition Flax argues, feminist theory, psychoanalytic theory, and postmodernist philosophy each provide three important lenses for analyzing the current state of this transition, our place in it, and our potential responses to it. Yet, Flax argues that none of those lenses are alone adequate to the task at hand. Moreover, each lens is itself in need of critique from the perspectives of the other two. Thus, in *Thinking Fragments,* Flax juxtaposes and analyzes all three perspectives— feminist theory, psychoanalytic theory, and poststructuralism—to locate the critiques and supplements that each offers the others. The result is an extensive, detailed, and nuanced work that rewards careful reading, and offers many more important insights than I have the opportunity to engage here.

For my purpose of exploring the political and personal significance of social fragmentation and its production of identity contradiction, three of Flax's points are of greatest relevance. First, Flax unites and applies to politics a point that both Gloria Anzaldúa and Amélie Oksenberg Rorty make separately, namely that the fragmentation of the self is not only a function of self-fragmentation, but also arises from the fragmentation of society in which we are socialized. Modern societies, Flax emphasizes, are *both* pervasively ordered *and* socially fragmented. Societal fragments, *especially* along the lines of social conflicts and group hierarchies of all kinds, become constructed into subjectivities *creating connections and disconnections of many kinds within us.* As discussed in chapter two for example, the pervasive ordering of race with class can conflate group categories until some associations—such as the association of Black identity with poverty—become part of our subjectivities. When social fragmentations arise from politicized group conflicts or hierarchies of race, sexuality, or gender, those political conflicts can forge identity contradictions within ourselves.

From this point a second one follows. When social fragmentation generates identity contradictions, as Flax indicates, self-fragmentation and societal fragmentation can become mutually reinforcing—each sustains the other. In this mutually constructive relationship some social conflicts produce identity contradictions in subjectivity. In turn, because subjectivity is construct*ing,* as well as constructed, subjects may contribute to specific social conflicts on the basis of the identity conflicts within themselves. For example, Flax notes that psychically and socially "[h]omophobia is used to enforce repression of aspects of desire, sexuality, and relations with others."[44] In other words, as homophobia and the subordination of lesbian, gay, bisexual, transgender, queer, and intersex people fragment social life in the U.S. those who may have same-sex desire may not recognize or explore those desires or may express them in violence or hate because of their internalized notions of fear, anxiety, or hatred of homosexuals. Here, the fault lines that divide society divide the psyche as well, and may produce thought and action that reinforce social and political conflict and sustain heterosexist social fragmentation and group political conflict.

Evidence for the relationship between identity contradiction and politically relevant attitudes can be found in a controlled research study of men who identified themselves as homophobic. Researchers measured penile circumference of male research subjects during exposure to a variety of sexually explicit videotapes. The homophobic men exhibited strong arousal to male homoerotic imagery, while a control group of non-homophobic men exhibited no arousal to the same male homoerotic imagery. Despite the obtrusive presence of the research apparatus on their phallus, the homophobic men categorically denied experiencing any arousal from the homosexual imagery, suggesting not only a contradiction between their stated desires and their actual desires, but also either poor self-awareness or the employment of self-deception as a means to respond to that inner contradiction.[45] In either case, it would seem that for these men, as Flax put it: "[r]elations of domination are transformed into prohibitions upon thought."[46] In turn, those inner prohibitions may be channeled back into society in fragmenting attitudes and actions.

In a third and related point, Flax argues that the failure to recognize how internalized social and political conflicts can operate within us as identity contradictions is likely to cause various myopias. Flax illustrates this point by considering the peculiar blind spots in each of the three intellectual lenses that she considers. Such myopic blind spots were particularly present in each case with regard to gender. Flax persuasively demonstrates that both psychoanalysis and postmodernist thought are marred in that both—or rather the male thinkers that have dominated both—have failed to grapple effectively with gendered, and especially female, experience. In this failure, while thinkers in each arena purport to analyze the self and social construction, those thinkers overlook how internalized constructions of patriarchy have shaped their own systematizing thought, thereby producing peculiar omissions and gaps in their writing.[47] Michel Foucault, for example (whose work significantly informs both Flax's scholarship and this book) presents *The History of Sexuality,* Vol I. with virtually no focused discussion of women. Even from a homosexual perspective, that is a fairly striking omission given the topic of his book.

Yet, feminist theory is not exempt from the myopias introduced by patriarchal gender socialization. While feminists often strongly identify with anti-patriarchal meanings, values, and practices, patriarchy still exists as a constructing social force. Thus as Flax stresses, "[i]nasmuch as women *have been* part of all societies, our thinking [as feminists] cannot be free from the modes of self-understanding of the cultures in which we live. *We as well as men* internalize the dominant gender's conceptions of masculinity and femininity."[48] Hence, the internalization of both patriarchal and anti-patriarchal conceptions of femininity as well as other tensions of gendered life produced in feminists "contradictory feelings about sexuality, motherhood, and autonomy that enter into the structure of feminist discourse."[49] Feminist theory, like psychoanalysis and poststructuralism, is also a scholarly domain that is "marked by ambivalence, omissions, and gaps" and outright contradictions in feminist treatments of female and male embodiment, gendered divisions of labor, kinship ties, masculinity and male parenting, female sexual desire, and the public/private divide, to name only a few.[50]

In general, however, feminists have not often been eager to engage with such criticisms, often persisting in instead the two intellectual moves that Flax contends produce erratic argumentation within feminist scholarship. These two moves are: 1) positing the idea that there is "only one perspective [that] can be 'correct' or 'properly feminist'" and, 2) the failure to consistently see gender as a *relational* identity category. The first of these involves the impulse to prematurely resolve contradiction by closing off ambivalence, multiplicity, and potential contradiction in feminist analysis. Unfortunately, feminist responses to Flax have, at times, ignored or reenacted this key critique of feminist analysis rather than grapple effectively with her arguments. In her influential response to Flax, for example, Seyla Benhabib does not address Flax's gender-based critique of poststructuralist and psychoanalytic perspectives. Rather, she reads Flax as having offered a celebration of postmodernism that is hazardous to feminism, ironically on the grounds that it "can be interpreted to permit *if not contradictory then at least radically divergent strategies*" which might "eliminate not only the specificity of feminist theory but place in question the very emancipatory ideals of the women's movement altogether."[51] This response (and I chose it because Benhabib's work has taken a more contradiction-accepting and constructivist turn in recent years) exemplifies the feminist discomfort with contradiction that Flax had pointed out. As Flax persuasively argues, such premature attempts to close off contradiction often do not resolve contradiction or ambivalence as much as they tend to simply displace those contradictions to the under-theorized margins of feminist discourse.[52] To express this using Rorty's map metaphor of subjectivity, gender contradictions that are simply pushed off the centralized map by premature closure are likely to reappear on the medieval map, potentially resulting in contradiction between those elements and the sometimes salience of "medieval" self-constructs that the subject does not recognize or avow.

Flax's analysis is useful for analyzing how different responses to identity contradictions can have implications for everyday social and political life. To illustrate this practical dimension, let me turn to the second problematic feminist practice of failing to regard gender identity as relational. If gender is considered to represent "a set of opposite and inherently different beings" rather than "a social relation," it can be difficult, as Flax puts it, "to identify women's or men's full part in and how we are affected by particular societies" or, I would add, to recognize both men's and women's contributions to the full range of current patriarchal or feminist practices.[53] Since the beginning of the feminist movement in the United States, American men, women, and children of all backgrounds are highly likely to have internalized *both* patriarchal and anti-patriarchal meanings, values, and practices as part of their principle gender identities and other gendered self-constructs. Thus, both men and women are likely to have both patriarchal and anti-patriarchal self-constructs within their subjectivities.

However, if men and women do not consider their own gendered attitudes and behaviors *relationally,* and on a continuum of constructed gendered meanings scaled from feminine to masculine— but instead on a gender binary male/female—it can become difficult to see how both patriarchal and anti-patriarchal norms and current gender conflicts shape all of us in varied ways. Failing to see gender relationally tends to lead to the construction of all men as patriarchs and all women as either anti-patriarchal feminists or the victims of patriarchy. Yet, if *both* men and women have contradictory gendered self-constructs—including feminine, masculine, patriarchal and anti-patriarchal elements—within their multiple identities, it is not only possible *but probable* that at least some men at times express their gender identity or identities through feminine and/or anti-patriarchal norms, and that at least some women express their gender identities through traditional masculine and/or patriarchal practices.

Furthermore, as noted in chapter one, and as confirmed even by Samuel Huntington in his approach to multiple identities, all social identities are relational. This means that, in practice, gender identities, like other social identities, can only be successfully claimed if gender identity claims are recognized and accepted by others both inside and outside the social group in question. Thus, for a professional woman who seeks to claim a female gender identity in the workplace, doing so requires recognition of her female gender identity by *both* women and men at various times and in various interactions. How that gender recognition is to be achieved, and on what basis, varies. In patriarchal orders, women often gain needed recognition from men and boys through at least three traditional means: heterosexual desire, recognition of female beauty, and/or maternalistic influence and care. All three of these forms of relational, gendered interaction involve female attentions to men that may in many circumstances—such as a workplace—sustain male privilege. Non-patriarchal forms of gender recognition might take alternative forms.

What can these observations on the relational quality of gender identity contribute to our understanding of the political implications of multiple identities and identity contradiction? I would argue that these observations, combined with discussions earlier in the chapter, contribute four major points. First, deep and ongoing group political conflicts within a political regime are likely to construct into the subjectivities in the regime fragmentations, multiplicities, and/or contradictions that reflect those conflicts. Once subjects have been socialized to group conflicts and divisions, it is not possible to eliminate from the mind the impressions internalized through socialization. Those encodings remain, although their degree of accessibility and their intersections may change.

Second, the manifestation of group conflicts within the psyches of members of a regime often leaves those individuals with contradictions among their multiple identities and various self-constructs with which they must grapple. As stressed in chapter three, however, these identity contradictions should not be seen as solely negative, but also as potentially positive, as needed resources for critical and creative thought.

Third, as discussed above with reference to homophobia, how people within a regime handle the conflict-derived contradictions among their multiple identities and self-constructs will shape how they think, act, and interact with others. The practical consequences of how they grapple with their identity contradiction, in turn, shapes what contributions they will make to the ongoing social and political conflicts from which their contradictions emerged. Keeping Amélie Oksenberg Rorty's work on akrasia and self-deception in mind,

I would argue that there are four general ways that individuals can cope with their identity contradictions, each of which have different consequences for how people contribute to the ground level terrain of political and social conflict.

These four different ways of dealing with identity contradiction are: 1) to remain consciously unaware of the contradiction, 2) to cope with the contradiction akratically, 3) to cope with the contradiction self-deceptively, and 4) to grapple with the contradiction in a self-integrative manner, either resolving the contradiction or finding strategies for managing it through ambivalence, flexibility, or forms of selfcraft. The first of these—remaining unconscious of the contradiction—involves maintaining a passive and non-self-reflective approach to the contradictions that have come to exist within one's self through social construction. This may take place when individuals have no established value priorities—i.e. they are what philosophers refer to as wantons—or have established priority systems but are—as Social Identity Theory theorizes—not aware of their contradictory identities schemes because those schemes are *not ever* simultaneously salient.

For example, if a man has internalized both patriarchal and non-patriarchal gender schemes in his exposure to gender conflict, his gendered interactions may take patriarchal forms in some moments and non-patriarchal forms at others. Whatever gendered frame of reference becomes salient for him from moment to moment will guide his responses. That salience will be a function of his response to social cues and other variable factors, as discussed in chapter two. The practical result will be a kind of gendered moodiness in which gender expression and interactions will be "all over the map," depending on what frames of reference happen to become salient at a given moment, ranging potentially from frankly feminist to rankly patriarchal.

The second and third ways of addressing identity contradiction involve akrasia and self-deception. Both akratic and self-deceptive responses to identity contradiction involve engaging in active forms of self-fragmentation beyond whatever inner fragmentation or integrations they may have gained passively from social life. To illustrate this we can turn again to the example of gender contradictions in feminist and patriarchal gender identity schemes. Because feminist identity is generally constructed around the disavowal of patriarchal modes of conduct, the virtually inevitable presence of internalized patriarchal identity schemes within the subjectivities of a highly-identified feminist can create an intensified internal contradiction that is painful as well as difficult to manage. As Rorty suggests, in general, when individuals face personally challenging conflicts and contradictions "without a taste for conflicts and without approved strategies for resolving them" then akrasia may be an understandable, if problematic, way in which to cope with those contradictions.[54] A feminist scholar, for example, who consciously lets a handsome, but domineering male student dominate her seminar, is acting akratically with regard to her feminist identity and commitments. Yet, she may do so routinely because it is easier to let patriarchal patterns persist in the classroom than to painfully establish non-confrontational but effective ways to quiet male speakers and draw out intimidated female students.

However, if the gender akratic feminist engages in favoritism toward young men, doing so *consciously* would strongly contradict feminist identity in ways that some feminists might find particularly painful. When this is the case, self-deception can provide a way out of this painful identity contradiction, in that a feminist may self-deceptively refuse to see the pattern of male privilege in her own (potentially habitual) behavior. Her gendered self-deception could cordon off her awareness of her internalized patriarchal female mode. Yet, that frame of reference may nonetheless become salient from time to time. It may be cued perhaps by a male student's looks or manner that makes salient for the feminist a gendered wish to obtain his male-gendered recognition of her *as a woman*—and thus the use of traditional patriarchal forms of female attentions to men. Because, as Rorty notes, self-deceptions are often viciously guarded as a constitutive part of one's treasured sense of self, a highly-identified feminist who is self-deceived about her patriarchal practices is likely to respond with hostility to any friendly efforts by others to point out and help her to correct her gendered (mis)conduct.[55]

Fourth, people may also choose to engage in self-integration through the practices of integrative selfcraft as discussed in chapter six. In such selfcraft, identity contradictions are grappled with directly and either resolved after significant engagement or they come to be managed through various strategies as discussed in chapter five.

Passive and self-fragmentary approaches to conflict-produced identity contradictions can result in conduct that may be, metaphorically speaking, "all over the map." I will discuss a set of specific political consequences of this, and of active integrative selfcraft, in the concluding chapter of this book. In the meantime however, it is relatively easy to see how passive and self-fragmentary responses to identity contradictions can result in political decision-making that is at best moody, and at worst involves akratic and/or self-deceived betrayals of the political principles that members of a society believe they hold dear. How individual feminists grapple with the almost inevitable contradictions between patriarchal and non-patriarchal constructs within their subjectivities will play out in their conduct as individuals and at the collective level within the community of feminists as a whole. Gendered moodiness, gender akrasia, and gendered self-deceptions can result in practices that reassert patriarchal practices one day while opposing them the next.

My argument here differs from Alasdair MacIntyre's argument regarding societal fragmentation and impaired political decision making discussed in chapter three. While I agree with MacIntyre that people in modern fragmented societies can be inconsistent in their actions on points of moral and political significance, I disagree with him that the source of this problem is multiplicity of identities or diversity of societies, per se. Rather, the cause of problematic inconsistencies is rooted in how individuals grapple with the diversity and contradictions within themselves and how, on that basis, they contribute either to social or political fragmentation or to integration and social justice objectives. It is in the interest of emancipatory, social justice goals, that Flax—like Gloria Anzaldúa—urges feminists to learn "to tolerate, invite, and interpret ambivalence, ambiguity, and multiplicity, as well as to expose the roots of our needs for imposing order and structure no matter how arbitrary and oppressive these [imposed orders] may be."[56] In the next two chapters, I will explore the alternative to passive and self-fragmentary approaches to multiple identity contradictions presented by integrative selfcraft. As I shall argue, self-integration offers the possibility for subjects to directly address how political conflicts shape their multiple identities, and also provides them with the means by which to shape which of their multiple identity schemes most influences their daily thoughts and action.

CHAPTER FIVE

Ambivalence and Life Projects
Love, Politics, and Self-Integration in *Casablanca*

... politics and ethics require neither homogeneous subjects nor
uniform collective standpoints. They do entail attention to ... multiplicity, taking into account each subject's multiple, interwoven locations as authority, resistor, and determined subject who articulates
and is spoken by specific social vocabularies.
JANE FLAX, "On Encountering Incommensurability"

Lacking the assurance of righteousness and transparency to ourselves and others, we must act anyway. This fosters both the freedom
and tragedy of action in political and social contexts.
JANE FLAX "Ethics of Multiplicity"

... the liquidation of the self into a set of demarcated areas of
role-playing allows no scope for the exercise of ... virtues in any
sense.... And the unity of a virtue in someone's life is intelligible
only as a characteristic of a unitary life, a life that can be conceived and
evaluated as a whole [as a].... self whose *unity resides in the unity of
a narrative which links birth to life to death* as a narrative beginning to
middle to end.
ALASDAIR MACINTYRE, "Unity of Human Life"

In this chapter, I examine two competing approaches to self-
integration reflected in the epigraphs above by Jane Flax and Alasdair
MacIntyre. My aim is to investigate the overall character of the self-
integration of multiple identities. Are subjects best self-integrated by
building a tightly unified, conflict-free subjectivity centered by a life
narrative or other element as MacIntyre and other philosophers have
argued? Or is there a free-form mode of self-integration that can accommodate contradictory and divergent aspects of the self and allow individuals to draw moral and political direction creatively from
their contradictions? Is there one mode of integrating the self that is
suitable for everyone, or are there different modes that may suit different people?

The Western philosophical tradition has favored the first
approach—one that resolves identity contradictions and/or centers
the self through self-narratives. Harry Frankfurt, Alasdair MacIntyre,
and Charles Taylor, for example, have contended that some form of
self-imposed order must be brought to the self or it may collapse from
the strain of its own internal contradictions. These philosophers view
the personal risks of fragmentation to be extreme, and in different

ways each has argued that the self must be integrated in ways that make it largely conflict free. In his work on autonomy, for example, Harry Frankfurt recommends the resolution of all inner contradiction through the formation of a rank-ordered set of self-guiding endorsements. Alasdair MacIntyre argues that integration should invoke consistency through an all-encompassing life narrative that brings complete intelligibility to the subject. Charles Taylor has argued that subjectivity must be integrated through overarching moral choices that reflect authentic aspects of the self and provide self-fulfillment.[1]

In contrast, and as discussed in chapter four, Amélie Oksenberg Rorty has argued persuasively that subjects can in fact muddle though more or less adequately without taking up the project of attempting to integrate the various aspects of their subjectivities or with only quite poor self-integration. When such subjects face internal contradictions, their lack of self-integration can lead them to engage in akrasia and self-deception (benign or harmful) as a result of their passivity toward, or mishandling of those contradictions. In addition, Jane Flax and Gloria Anzaldúa have argued against the view that effectively handling contradiction always requires unambiguous resolutions of identity contradiction. Rather, they suggest that within broad limits *ambivalence* and the acceptance of the ambiguity and inconsistency often associated with ambivalence can be productive as ways to effectively manage trenchant, identity-related contradictions. Moreover, they argue that ambivalence toward lasting identity contradictions can preserve the productive tensions and resources for creativity that unresolved contradictions can furnish (for a discussion of identity contradiction as a resource for critical and creative thought, see chapter three).[2]

In the pages that follow, I draw elements from both of these two contradictory approaches to self-integration, and introduce a notion of self-integrative *life projects* in which self-chosen endorsements are loosely interwoven into broad self-guiding projects that serve as a basis for integrating the self. I argue that while self-chosen rank-ordered endorsements, narrative unity, and self-fulfilling authenticity may have roles to play for some individuals in their particular processes of self-integration, these three elements alone are inadequate to contain the complexity of self-integration of multiple identities. This inadequacy is especially acute under those circumstances of conflict or contradiction in which a person's multiple identities are socially constructed as mutually exclusive, or when their life projects have become contradictory due to social, political, or interpersonal conflicts beyond their control. Under these circumstances, enduring contradiction, ambivalence, and ambiguity can play important roles in the self-integration of multiple identities. In short, contrary to the prevailing philosophical view, at times lasting internal contradictions and inconsistencies can be markers of *effective* efforts to self-integrate multiple identities in contexts of conflict and contradiction.

This chapter is divided into two parts. In the first part, I investigate the role of ambivalence in self-integration. I apply the views of Jane Flax and Gloria Anzaldúa on the usefulness of ambivalence to the alternative viewpoint in favor of the wholehearted observance of rank-ordered endorsements as necessary to self-integration offered by Harry Frankfurt. Frankfurt's model of ranked endorsements rules out both ambivalence and inconsistency toward one's endorsements for a well integrated self. In my analysis of the role of ambivalence in self-integration, I consider the experiences of two individuals— Christian Park and María Lugones—both of whom appear to have integrated multiple identities that are considered to be mutually exclusive. Based on their experiences, I offer three specific ways in which the ambivalence and inconsistency ruled out by Frankfurt can play a significant self-integrative role, *especially* when individuals seek to integrate identities that are constructed as mutually exclusive within ongoing social or political conflicts. At the close of part one, I sketch a framework of *self-integrative life projects* as an alternative to rank-ordered endorsements as a means of self-integration.

In part two of the chapter, I explore how a life-projects approach to self-integration relates to frameworks that employ *self-narrative* and *authentic self-fulfillment* as self-integrative frameworks—such as those frameworks advanced by Alasdair MacIntyre and Charles Taylor respectively. Through a reading of the film *Casablanca,* I illustrate how the process of self-integration of multiple identities is always in motion and subject to disruption and disintegrative setbacks induced by contradictions arising from conflict or trauma. Recovering lost self-integration—like the pursuit of self-integrative projects that build new levels of integration—may require ambivalence, inconsistency, and enduring contradictions that allow subjects to reestablish and reintegrate themselves through life projects that contain and sustain integrative contradictions. For example, integrative life projects may make use of aspects of ourselves that we neither endorse nor with which we are highly identified. As such, self-integrative projects as I define them are held together in part through ambivalence and inconsistency that may contain, but also complicate and even subvert the forms of unifying self-narrative and self-fulfilling authenticity that are advocated by MacIntyre and Taylor.

Conflict, Integrative Ambivalence, and
the Limits of Wholeheartedness

Self-integration is largely about making choices between competing desires. In common with other philosophers, including constructivists, Harry Frankfurt has argued that conflicting desires may come to exist within us from outside of ourselves like an "involuntary spasm" that erupts in our bodies through no effort of our own.[3] Frankfurt further argues, however, that when a conflict exists among a person's desires "unless this conflict is resolved, [. . . the person] has no preference concerning which of his [everyday] first-order desires is to be his will. This condition, *if it is so severe that it prevents him from identifying himself in a sufficiently decisive way* with *any* of his conflicting first-order desires, *destroys him as a person.*"[4] In Frankfurt's view, inner contradiction thus "tends to paralyze [. . . a person's] will and to keep him from acting at all, or it tends to remove him from his will so that his will operates without his participation. In both cases *he becomes . . . a helpless bystander to the forces that move him.*"[5]

For Frankfurt, the remedy for the potential paralysis of inner conflicts and contradiction is to resolve all inner contradictions and conflicts through a process of endorsing and identifying oneself with a set of desires and principles. One's chosen desires and principles are then hierarchically ordered so as to become one's "higher order" or self-governing desires which would, by definition, include any desires that are related to specific identity schemes. In Frankfurt's words, when the self "identifies with a desire, [he thereby] *constitutes himself*" and willfully integrates himself into a whole from the materials that "happen to occur in the history of his body."[6] For Frankfurt this process of self-constitution through self-identification with chosen desires and principles *is* the process of self-integration. However, for the process of self-integration to be complete, Frankfurt sets forth two additional requirements. First, self-integration requires resolving the conflicts among one's higher desires (those we think of as guiding our everyday choices) by placing them in a *"single ordering."*[7] This conflict-free ordering assigns a *specific rank-order* and consistent hierarchical priority to one's set of endorsements.

Second, Frankfurt argues that a person's rank-ordered endorsements are only self-integrating if a person is *wholehearted* about observing those endorsements. Therefore, two additional components are also needed as a part of wholeheartedness: 1) *consistency,* or the act of establishing and following a consistent set of guiding principles, and 2) the *elimination of ambivalence,* especially in the assignment of "outlaw" status to any and all desires that the subject does not identify with and does not endorse.[8] For Frankfurt it is "these [two] acts of ordering and of rejection—integration and separation"—that " . . . create a self out of the raw materials of inner life."[9] Thus, in Frankfurt's model of the well-integrated subject, inconsistency is the failure to firmly rank order one's higher order preferences. Ambivalence is the failure to *completely disavow* what we do not endorse. Both of these failures undermine the wholeheartedness that Frankfurt regards as necessary for successful self-integration.

Yet, as I argued in chapters two and three, the ambivalence and inconsistency that Frankfurt rules out as detrimental to self-integration are often characteristic of how multiple identities are lived in everyday life. Gloria Anzaldúa identifies ambivalence as a key characteristic of mestiza consciousness, an asset in our capacity to shift among multiple social spheres, and for gaining critical and creative insights from identity contradictions. Anzaldúa's emphasis on ambivalence and "tolerance for ambiguity" suggests that the ambivalence and inconsistency ruled out by Frankfurt can, at times, be important tools for those who seek to integrate endorsements that are drawn from disparate identity schemes.[10]

Consider for example, the experience of a young Korean American man named Christian Park. Park describes living his Korean and American ethnic identities as a process of continual movement and variation in which he prioritizes different cultural worlds at different times, shifting among multiple spheres, in which his various endorsements have different priorities or valences. Interviewed for the documentary *Between Two Worlds,* Park stated:

> Being between two worlds . . . some people say, might give you power. But on the other side, you have no firm ground, a so-called homeland or any places that they will accept you as who you are, . . . [a place where] they don't question you—you are Korean, you are American. Well, we don't have that place. We are always drifting here—if it's comfortable here, I'll stay, but not permanently. So I move to the other side. So you wonder about your identity and you have to ask constantly . . ."who am I?" And the problem is . . . I don't think I'll find an answer.[11]

At first glance, Park's statement seems to indicate that a lasting contradiction between his multiple ethnic identities has made Park into the kind of "helpless bystander to the forces that move him" that rightly concerns Harry Frankfurt. Park seems to simply drift from place to place doing what is comfortable without reference to established endorsements or self-grounding principles. Yet, such a conclusion becomes implausible in light of Park's nuanced references to the actual *sources* of his ambivalence toward his ethnic identities and the reasons why he engages in restless inconsistency in living his multiple identities. Park's restlessness does not arise from his inconsistency toward what *he* values. Rather, from his words we can gather that Park has formulated a set of established endorsements that prioritize two of the self-identifications given to him socially: he is Korean—he is American.

Yet while Park may firmly endorse these identifications as ways of being for himself, he indicates that there is virtually no social context in which he can depend on others to accept and not "question" his particular combination of endorsements. As Park states, he finds no places in which the people he meets and knows "will accept you as you are." Instead, he routinely encounters skepticism and challenges from others who demand an account of why Park believes he can unite two ethnic identities that are regarded *by them*—though not by him—as incompatible. Therefore, the source of Park's inconsistency and ambivalence regarding his identity claims and expressions does not arise from his hesitation toward his endorsements. Rather, his inconsistency and ambivalence are brought about by the daily tensions of ethnic conflict. Like other group conflicts, that conflict is carried out, in part, through social constructions that define his two ethnic identities as mutually exclusive and contradictory. In turn, those widely accepted constructions lead *others* to challenge Park's identity-based choices. In other words, as with other border-crossers discussed in chapter two, the challenges to his endorsements that Park experiences are based on the politicized views of others, in which the norms and practices of Korean and American social identities cannot be harmoniously united.

In response to Harry Frankfurt's approach to self-integration then, Park may in fact—as Frankfurt contends is necessary—wholeheartedly endorse the meanings, values, and practices of his ethnic identities as guiding for himself, and yet *still* feel a sense of inner conflict based on the identity challenges he receives from others. His strong self-endorsements alone cannot change the broader social context of ethnic hierarchy and conflicts that are the basis upon which the contradictions he describes emerge. Thus, however wholehearted in his endorsements he may be, as Park notes, he must grapple on a daily basis with the conflict-induced contradictions among his identity-related endorsements. In comparison, others whose multiple identities are socially constructed as compatible or nested seldom feel that "who they are" is going to be challenged by others in the manner that Park routinely endures.[12]

On the whole, group social and political conflicts often generate conditions that force border-crossers, such as Park, who identify across conflicted social group boundaries, to struggle against the challenges of others as they try to self-integrate their conflict-related multiple identities. Scholarly research in various fields indicates that politicized group conflicts such as nationalist movements or ethnic group conflicts often involve redefining and socially (re)constructing specific groups or cultures as opposed and incompatible *in spite of commonalities* that may also exist between them.[13] Over time, conflict-induced constructions of group or "cultural incompatibility" become normative as the "common sense" causing commonalties among divided groups to become increasingly obscured. At such a stage, it may be that only those who identify robustly with both cultures—e.g. border-crossers such as Christian Park—are likely to be continually aware of those group commonalities.

For example, British colonial rule in India constructed British cultural identity and Indian cultural identity as mutually exclusive and hierarchically ordered as a means to establish and maintain sovereign power. In his efforts to end the Raj, however, Gandhi—who was born and raised in India and also educated in England—highlighted these politicized and binary cultural constructions. Gandhi argued that Indian civilization, although widely different from British culture in many respects, in fact shared with British culture a significant number of key values derived from common pre-modern traditions. Moreover, Gandhi persuasively argued that in some ways, Indians were more consistently and strongly observant of those common values than many Britons. Indians simply exercised those values in ways that are inflected by Indian cultural and subcultural norms.[14] Politicized and conflict-derived constructions of mutually exclusive social identities such as those in British colonial discourse are not uncommon. In chapter one, for example, I discussed that while Latina/o ethnic cultural identity is often constructed as mutually exclusive with "American" identity, Latino and Euroamerican ethnic groups in the United States nonetheless seem to share a range of priorities with regard to family life, personal responsibility, religiosity, patriotism, and other factors. Many of the differences that do exist seem to be differences of degree and priority, rather than of irreconcilable perspectives.[15]

What do these patterns of conflict and resistance mean for processes of self-integration? For the purposes of self-integrating multiple identity schemes including those defined as mutually exclusive, I would suggest that in any instance in which it is possible to locate overlapping, or divergent but reconcilable values and practices among two or more divergent identity schemes it is possible for individuals to devise a set of self-guiding endorsements from among the various contents of their mutually exclusive identities. Let us say, for example, that for Christian Park both of his ethnic identifications include, to varying degrees, meanings, values, and practices that favor the pursuit of higher education. If Park chooses a desire for higher education as a self-guiding endorsement, that endorsement, in turn, creates an intersection among those two ethnic identity schemes. His identities are now associated by the endorsement, which in its conscious acknowledgment and exercise constitutes a positive or reinforcing intersection between the two.[16] In this way, Park can self-integrate two supposedly mutually exclusive identity schemes. Moreover, through his choices of endorsements, he may construct his subjectivity—at least in part—at the intersections between American and Korean cultures as a cultural hybrid that both retains its antecedent identities but *also* sustains a hybridized one that is not simply a sum of its parts but a syncretic fusion of distinct cultural schemes.[17]

In this approach, each endorsement that is drawn from multiple identities can create intersections among those multiple identities. In addition, other integrating intersections can be created when endorsements are made relevant to other identity schemes. For example, for Christian Park, his educational endorsement forms an intersection between his ethnic Korean and ethnic American identities. If he applies that ethnically-derived endorsement to his work life by choosing part-time work over other preferred employment to attend school, then his educational endorsement can also create an intersection between his two ethnic identities and his professional identity. As discussed in chapter two, I have argued (contrary to Social Identity Theory) that when intersections create associations among specific identities within subjectivity, those intersecting identity-schemes have the potential to become co-salient as the frame of reference at a given time *even if they contain contradictory elements.* This potential for co-salience is an important manifestation of self-integration, because it represents the potential for revised intersectionality to reverse oppression-derived or other problematic fragmentations within the self. This means self integration makes use of common content among diverse identity schemes. In some cases, however, such linkable dimensions may not exist.

While it is often possible to self-integrate mutually exclusive identities based on group commonalities, at times profound and irreconcilable differences do exist among the collective identity schemes that individuals wish to integrate. In some cases, diametrically opposed values among social groups are used to define the social boundaries between those groups, thus making acceptance or rejection of those boundary-setting precepts indicative of who may claim group membership. An example of this can be seen in an essay by philosopher María Lugones entitled "Hispaneando y Lesbiando" in which she responds to a white philosopher's call for lesbian separatism. Lugones identifies as both a lesbian and a Latina—and more specifically as a Latina immigrant grounded in the U.S. and its racial (and once colonial) social structures as they exist "in rural *Nuevomejicana* villages."[18] In the essay, Lugones describes how, in her experience, her social identities of Latina and lesbian have often been constructed as mutually exclusive. In that construction, homosexuality has been seen as largely anathema within Latina/o cultures, such that claiming lesbian, gay, or queer identities throws into question one's claims to ethnic group membership on the basis of homophobic and heterosexist norms. Likewise, Lugones's essay argues—politely but clearly—that lesbian separatism suffers from a not uncommon problem in Euroamerican-dominated lesbian communities, that the cultural concerns and values of Latinas are often marginal, ignored, or implicitly or explicitly denigrated as unimportant or dispensable.

Lugones argues that given her strong commitments to her identities and life as *both* a lesbian and a Latina, she must find approaches to these two cross-cutting forms of marginalization—one homophobic, the other ethnocentric and potentially racist given its colonial history. On one hand is the challenge that within rural *Nuevomejicana* contexts, she and other lesbians "will not be heard as real participants" in the Hispana community's struggle against ethnic subordination "if openly lesbian" in their self-presentation.[19] In other words, to emphasize her lesbian identity in rural *Nuevomejicana* communities is to potentially lose her membership as a group insider in the struggle against racism and ethnic subordination in those contexts. On the other hand, to participate solely in lesbian communities dominated by non-Latinas is also to suffer the inattention within lesbian communities to her ethnic concerns with sustaining Latina/o cultures.[20]

For María Lugones then, living her Latina and lesbian identities requires finding ways to embrace and live her life as a lesbian and a Latina without accepting the mutually denying homophobic and ethnocentric precepts that often prevail in both *Nuevomejicana* and lesbian social spheres. Lugones states that she is not sure if retaining both her lesbian and Latina identities amounts to *integration* of herself. But of the possibility of living both identities she states, " [b]ut it seems clear to me that each possibility need not exclude the other *so long as* I am not a unitary but a multiplicitous being."[21] As I have been arguing, however, the project of linking together identities that have been socially constructed as mutually exclusive is very much a part of the project of self-integration of multiple identities. In that project, the goal is not to create a unitary self that is without contradiction, but rather to create an integrated but diverse and multiplicitous subjectivity that can draw creatively from whatever contradictions it retains.

Fortunately, when Lugones and other would-be self-integrators face the prospect of marginalization as an obstacle to self-integration, the complexity of self-identification processes can be an asset in overcoming those obstacles. Specifically, and as described in chapters one and two above, self-identification can involve forms of *selective identification* that do not require a wholesale acceptance of all possible aspects of a particular social identity as those aspects exist in a given time and place. Recall from chapter one that in Fredrik Barth's classic account of ethnic group identity, identifying with a social group means, 1) practicing in one form or another at least a subset of the diacritical expressions of the identity, and 2) making a claim of willingness (explicitly, or more often implicitly) "to be judged, and to judge oneself, by those standards that are relevant to that identity."[22]

The significance of selective identification for practices of self-integration is that it is not necessary for Lugones or anyone else to use *all* of the diacritical markers associated with a group identity. In every moment in which an identity claim is made and is open to recognition or rejection by others, presenting a subset of group markers is sufficient for a claim to group membership to be accepted and/or for a social group boundary to be invoked.[23] Moreover, it is possible for Lugones or any one else to use *different identity markers at different times* to invoke a recognizable claim to a group identity. For example, Lugones might project self-identification with the ethnic group boundary variously in different contexts, using language in one instance, dress in another, surname and residence in yet another. As discussed with reference to ethnic code switching in chapter two, this practice of differential self-presentation is not uncommon. In her study of phenotypically Black second-generation West Indian immigrants, for example, Mary Waters found that those immigrants who were highly ethnically identified and who objected to being seen only as American Blacks often found ways, through dress and vocabulary, to overtly signify their ethnic identity in some daily contexts but to downplay their ethnicity in others. Immigrants report using such variation in part to avoid suffering the racial subordination experienced by non-immigrant American Blacks.[24]

In addition, while social group members may share knowledge of common group symbols and rituals, they need not necessarily give the exact same meanings or expression to those group symbols at all times. Rather, specific individuals or families within a social group may bring their own meanings to ostensibly shared concepts. A cultural holiday, for example, may be held in common, but practiced in ways that are inflected by various specificities. From house to house, all families may be serving enchiladas, but next door the grandmother from Veracruz has filled them with seafood and the family from Santa Fe across the street has made them flat.[25] As anthropologist Anthony Cohen argued in his classic work on the social construction of communities, the processes of group formation and identification through boundary maintenance always commit a generalization—i.e. present an *approximation myth*—that maintains the boundaries of the social group through incorporations and exclusions that are rendered symbolically, but which still leave considerable room for various interpretations of "common" and identifying group symbols and beliefs. These mythic group symbols and beliefs are also, at various times and in various ways, invoked to represent the cohesion of the social group. The upshot is that while approximated group boundaries may contain significant uniformity, they also contain significant diversity, complexity, and differentiation, and can show significant change over time without risking discontinuation of the group. For whatever their variations, groups persist over time as long as there is someone who claims the boundary of the group, whatever its current content or membership.

The importance of these two levels of selective identification—the individual and the collective levels—for self-integrating truly contradictory multiple identity schemes is that individual claims to given group identifications can, in principle, tolerate wide variation without eroding group cohesion or existence.[26] Therefore, Lugones may select, modify, and differentially interpret Latina group norms and markers and still successfully claim group identity in given contexts. By exercising selective identification, Lugones may *personally* reject the homophobic, heterosexist, and ethnocentric group norms of her *Nuevohispana* and lesbian communities—acceptance of which would fragment her sexual from her ethnic identities. She does so by conceiving—against social norms—a personal or inner intersection in which *she can understand herself* as both and at once a Latina and lesbian. In her essay, Lugones states repeatedly that this intersection is manifest in her daily choice not to abandon either identity, but to practice both in different spheres regardless of group prohibitions on doing so. And yet those prohibitions remain, and she must continue to cope with them.

How does Lugones cope with those prohibitions on the self-integrative choices she has made? Although she does not specify her exact methods, Lugones is clear that she will not be heard as an insider in *Nuevohispana* contexts as an "out" lesbian. Yet, because she does not advocate the secrecy of closeted sexuality, the suggestion seems to be that she does not emphasize her sexual identity in *Hispana* contexts, leaving her sexuality ambiguous because unspecified. There is textual evidence for this in her comment that while she has kin she is also without kin. She writes:

> When lesbians of different cultures get together. . . . I have the clear sense of our being without kin as we are lesbian. That we have left our kin and, in a significant sense, our people in communities that will not recognize us as fully their own as lesbians [*sic*]. I do not know if anglo lesbians have this sense, but they do not *express* it frequently. Hispana lesbians express constantly an ambivalent attachment to *lo nuestro* [our own].[27]

The reference to constant expressions of ambivalence and "ambivalent attachment" in this quotation suggests that Lugones is also allowing ambivalence to serve as another strategy, in addition to selective identification, to hold her multiple identities together. For Lugones, the identities that she has integrated via selective identification and hybrid endorsements nonetheless come under renewed pressure of fragmentation in broader social contexts, and as she states, she routinely encounters and responds to this pressure with ambivalence. As such, when her interconnection of lesbian and Latina identity is constantly denied by family members who are close to Lugones, ambivalence allows her to implicitly continue to acknowledge and accommodate that denial, but also not accept its message as one with which she will identify herself. To fail to accommodate familial denial would be to let go of family connections that are important to her, hence ambivalence plays an integrating role in helping her to maintain identifications and commitments that are in tension.[28]

If ambivalence, selective identification, and ambiguity in self-presentation are three mechanisms for integrating mutually exclusive identities, the question still remains how specific intersections can be produced among those identities, when there are no affirmative inter-sections inherited from social life. In other words, upon what basis *in the mind* can positive identity intersections be established among mu-tually denying identities? One clue may be found in Lugones's essay in which she advocates the rejection of lesbian separatism with an ap-peal to the overall aim of resisting racism and ethnic subordination of Latinas on one hand, and the establishment of robust lesbian plural-ism and the affirmation of lesbian life and identity on the other. Both of these programs—namely her anti-racism/anti-ethnocentrism and her anti-heterosexism—I would suggest constitute a "life project" to which Lugones is deeply committed and it is upon the basis of that life project that she is able to craft positive intersections between her mutually denying identities.

A *life project* may be thought of as a life goal or commitment—a passion or broad overarching desire—that animates our life choices consciously (and also potentially unconsciously, as I shall argue later in this chapter and in chapter six). More specifically, the passion of a life project is an intermediate kind of desire and endorsement that falls below the level of answers to broad existential questions—i.e. "what is humanity's purpose on earth?"—and above more narrowly defined sets of guiding endorsements or everyday desires and impulses such as "I'm working for a promotion at work." In this middle ground, a life project could be defined as a person's one-line obituary. It is the sentence that describes the passion, concern, or project that drives a person in life. For example, William Butler Yeats spent his adult life cultivating a mastery of poetic form. Judging from his spiritual pursuits, including his interest in the occult, it is clear that Yeats did not consider poetry itself to represent the meaning of life at an exis-tential level, or to reveal life's mysteries as Yeats perceived them. Nor was poetry merely a narrow concern for Yeats, in which he toiled as a means to other interests. Rather poetry was an overarching pursuit that linked many of Yeats's narrower—and often passing—interests. Over time, poetry also led him to explore different areas of history, literature, aesthetic theory, and to thematize different political and gendered perspectives. Poetry was likewise a principle basis of con-nection between himself and his circle of literary friends, including Ezra Pound, Arthur Symons, his benefactress Lady Augusta Gregory, and his celebrated attachment to Maud Gonne.[29] Given the signifi-cance and intensity of Yeats's pursuit of romantic love in his lifetime, the search for romantic love arguably may be considered a second life project for Yeats. If so, this suggests that a person may have more than one life project, though given the practical constraints of even a very full life, perhaps not more than two or three at most.

Returning to the case of María Lugones, I would suggest that while not everyone may develop a life project of the kind that Yeats's poetic lifework represents, Lugones too has a life project that animates her life choices. As a feminist philosopher and a politically engaged scholar and activist, Lugones describes herself in many works as committed to resisting all forms of social subordination including, but not limited to, the subordination of Latinos and gay, lesbian, transgender, bisexual, and queer peoples.[30] Her emphasis on resisting *all* forms of group subordination is potentially borrowed from and contributes to Chicana and U.S. Third World feminisms in which the project of addressing systematic forms of subordination by opposing *all* forms of social subordination has become a central tenet.[31] Whatever its origin, however, Lugones's life project of resisting all modes of subordination seems to play an important self-integrative role as she lives her self-integrated identities in contexts of conflict.

If it is plausible to see Lugones's self-identified commitment to resisting all kinds of group subordination as a life project, it follows that Lugones forms intersections between her various endorsements and identity schemes by considering there to be an important and necessary intersection between struggles against racism and struggles against homophobia and heterosexism. *Her life project of anti-subordination* thus becomes the self-generated basis for an intrapsychic intersection within Lugones's subjectivity between her "mutually exclusive" Latina and lesbian identities. That link is self-integrating in that it is through her commitment to the intersection of her anti-racist/anti-ethnocentric *and* anti-homophobic endorsements that Lugones seems able to remain highly identified with both identities despite constant challenges to and denial of her combination of identities.[32] Further, despite the challenges, the intersections associated with her self-guiding endorsements and identities may be reinforced for Lugones whenever she *acts upon* her anti-racist/anti-ethnocentric *and* anti-homophobic endorsements in the social spheres most resistant and in need of them. Moreover, in terms of political change, by engaging in her own self-integrative life project to integrate her own identities, Lugones's everyday thoughts and actions openly reject and disavow the mutual group hatreds between Latinos and lesbians, even as she acknowledges and works around those mutual forms of intolerance in her continual efforts at resisting group subordination meted out by these and other groups.

The integrative possibilities introduced by selective identification and integrative life projects return us to the question of whether or not self-integration can be achieved without the kind of integrative whole-heartedness that Harry Frankfurt values. Is it possible that under some conditions, inconsistency, flexibility, and ambivalence have greater integrative value than wholeheartedness, which rules out inconsistency and ambivalence? Could ambivalence and inconsistency have integrative value when individuals seek to self-integrate multiple identities containing contradictions under conditions of group conflict?

As Lugones notes she—and potentially many others—has *established or committed herself* to her self-chosen, self-integrating endorsements but does so with ambivalence toward her group belongings and/or inconsistency in her self-presentation from one group setting to another. On one hand, Lugones is highly identified with her life project and the identities and ways of life it links. In that sense she could be seen—even by Frankfurt's criteria—as wholehearted in her commitment to exercise her anti-racist, anti-homophobic endorsements in her everyday intellectual, political, and personal life. On the other hand, because Lugones is engaging in the self-integration of identities of groups in conflict, her self-integrative choices are often contested in everyday contexts. That contestation places Lugones as self-integrator into the position of having to either reverse her choices, or repeatedly *act strategically to defend and/or otherwise protect the daily practice* of those endorsements in everyday interactions among those divided groups.

Based on this analysis, I contend that it is in the practical strategic defense of her self-integrative choices that ambiguity in self-presentation of her sexual identity and ambivalence toward her ethnic group membership become instrumental in helping Lugones cope with the challenges presented by *practicing* the endorsements and identities of the life project that integrates her multiple identities. In other words, in contexts of politicized group conflict, ambivalence and inconsistency can and often do play a significant role in the self-integration of multiple identities when individuals draw endorsements from and attempt to self-integrate diverse social identity schemes.

This conclusion regarding the usefulness of ambivalence is relevant to *any* circumstance in which individuals attempt to integrate multiple identities that are constructed as mutually exclusive in politicized conflicts, even those in which identity schemes do have commonalities. For example, Christian Park—as a person who identifies himself with two ethnic groups and divided communities—describes

himself as being continually at risk of scorn, conflict, and contradictions induced by those he encounters—ranging from family members
to strangers. The conflicts and contradictions induced by those he encounters affect Park; he describes himself as bracing for routine conflict and learning to cope with its contradictions effectively through
flexibility in his self-identifications and ambivalence about his group
belongings.[33] Here again, it is in the self-defensive coping with attacks and contradictions incited by others that the ambivalence and
inconsistency toward endorsements ruled out by Frankfurt can become useful as integrative tools not only for deriving and weaving
together integrating endorsements, but also for support in observing
those endorsements consistently in cases of conflict.[34]

Consistent with this point, Gloria Anzaldúa previously un-
derscored the vital role that ambivalence, flexibility, and tolerance
for ambiguity play in how individuals with mestiza consciousness
grapple with the daily contradictions that they face. Similarly, Jane
Flax has drawn upon her background in psychoanalytic theory to
make the argument that "ambivalence is an appropriate response
to an inherently conflictual situation."[35] Flax further contends that
philosophical inquiries into widespread maladaptation to contradictory or conflictual contexts should therefore look carefully at *the
sources of ambivalence,* for within broad limits "[t]he problem lies not
in the ambivalence [itself], but in premature attempts to resolve or
deny conflicts."[36] Based on the importance of ambivalence stressed
by Anzaldúa and Flax, I would further specify that ambivalence and
inconsistency can play three specific self-integrative roles that help
individuals grapple effectively with identity contradictions.

First, for those who identify with two or more conflicting or hierarchically ordered social groups, ambivalence toward one's membership in social groups with which one is strongly self-identified can help
subjects sustain the inevitable pain of identity challenges. This can aid
self-integration of multiple identities when social hierarchies, political conflicts, or social changes produce tensions in group life causing
some to challenge the identity claims of others. In such cases, a specific
identity contradiction emerges in which one's sense of "Being"—i.e.
whom one understands oneself to be as a self-integrated person—and
one's claims to belonging and membership in specific social groups
are contested by others on the basis of politicized group conflicts.

When faced with identity contradictions of being and belonging in everyday life, ambivalence can allow individuals to feel both
attachment *and* detachment to their group and interpersonal commitments. Such ambivalent attachment allows subjects to respond to

that contradiction, not through premature resolution, but through various flexible responses tailored to different occasions. Armed with simultaneous attachment *and* detachment to group membership, embattled self-integrators may shift from relinquishing their claims to an identity in favor of group belonging in one instance, to sacrificing group belonging in favor of how they wish to be in another. In this way, it is self-integrative for Hispana lesbians to, as Lugones puts it, "express constantly an ambivalent attachment" toward their families and ethnic groups. Moreover, by facilitating ambivalent group attachments in this way, the virtue of a high tolerance for ambivalence and ambiguity discussed by Anzaldúa also makes way for the use of flexibility in self-integration (this is discussed further below).

However, ambivalence toward one's own group memberships and strongly held identities accomplishes more toward self-integration than helping self-integrators cope with contradictions of being and belonging. In Lugones's case, there is also an identity contradiction in identifying herself with self-denying groups. Although she is a lesbian, Lugones strongly identifies herself as a Latina and thus with a culture that has largely refused to recognize lesbians. By choosing to associate herself with a homophobic and heterosexist culture as part of her life project, Lugones places herself in the contradictory position of seeming to welcome and be "willing to be judged" by others according to a value system that she also vocally criticizes and rejects in her scholarly work and activism as "outlaw" to her endorsements.

Lugones knows and acknowledges that in *Nuevohispana* spheres, others that she encounters will assume that she accepts homophobic outlooks. In Frankfurt's model Lugones's approach could be seen as a disintegrative failure of wholeheartedness, in that Lugones has not ruled out for herself participation in spheres that endorse what she rejects. Yet, while Lugones does wholeheartedly refuse to accept homophobic values as part of her endorsements, it is by maintaining ambivalence toward her membership in homophobic communities that she may retain active allegiance to Latina/o communities as part of her life project of anti-subordination, in spite of the contradictions of association doing so presents. Paradoxically, in contexts of conflict, it is through ambivalence that Lugones may not only self-organize her multiplicity in a meaningful way, but also place herself in a position to work for change in both lesbian and Latina spheres and to link those spheres in her own life despite ongoing conflicts.

The second integrative role for ambivalence in sustaining those with multiple identities is *self-protective or conflict preempting inconsistencies in self-presentation* across varying contexts. Such inconsistencies may also aid those who face challenges to their being or belonging as a function of group conflicts to maintain their self-integration. Flexibility and inconsistencies allow those who are integrating mutually exclusive identities to claim those identities to different degrees depending on the conflicts they are facing at a given moment. Park refers to this type of inconsistency when he describes shifting back and forth between social worlds to manage identity challenges when levels of rejection become too great for him to handle. While he seeks temporary relief and comfort by claiming his identities differently at different times, this flexibility is also aided by ambivalence because Park does not fully expect to find lasting peace, acceptance, or rest for his sense of being, although he seeks such peace though flexibility.

In addition, in political terms inconsistency can allow for "border-crossers" who are trying to integrate mutually exclusive multiple identities in contexts of conflict to choose *not* to present or to not *fully* present their self-identifications in exactly the same way in every context *as a means to circumvent subordination or make less-than-overt interventions in that conflict.* This kind of self-integrative inconsistency in self-presentation could be called preemptive inconsistency. For example, an out Latina lesbian with the same anti-subordination life project as Lugones might attend Thanksgiving dinner at her grandmother's home and introduce her lover as her "amiga/friend" rather than as her "novia/girlfriend." In so doing she *consciously* allows conservative, and potentially homophobic family members to ascribe varying interpretations to her sexual relationship. Her strategy is that if her family welcomes her lover as a friend at a family gathering as significant as Thanksgiving, she is potentially in a much better position to recruit their acceptance of her lover as her life partner at a later stage. On Frankfurt's model of rank-ordered endorsements, however, inconsistency is a disintegrative failing because it represents a failure to live by top-rank-endorsements of anti-subordination. Her lesbian identity and pride have been sacrificed and subordinated to keep family peace and placate homophobic individuals.

However, her inconsistency can be seen as self-integrating if her inconsistency in self-presentation is understood as an intentional self-presentation rooted in both her anti-homophobic lesbian identity and her life project of anti-subordination. On these grounds, her inconsistency represents a conscious and self-reflective strategy in which she has considered her possible actions carefully in light of the multiplicity of social hierarchies and narratives of group conflict within which she, her lover, and her family stand at a specific moment in socio-political time.

As a conscious, self-reflective inconsistency, mild (mis)represen-
tion of her sexual identity is a way to "negotiate" several conflict-
induced obstacles to her goals. On one hand is the risk of ostracism
among lesbians who might be critical of her choice to cloak her relationship and sexual identity. On the other is the risk of familial tension and homophobic rejection. Yet from a life project perspective,
if she is committed to anti-subordination, it *is* self-consistent for her
to attempt to lay the groundwork for potential full acceptance of her
lesbian life and identity among her family members later on.

This example illustrates how the concept of self-integrative
life projects can be useful for illuminating how it is possible to
self-integrate highly divergent multiple identities. Life projects—
intrapsychically comprised of sets of variously interconnected endorsements oriented toward an overarching goal or passion—depart
from Frankfurt's model of rank-ordered and wholeheartedly observed individual endorsements. In that model, when integration is
established through rank-ordered endorsements, one either observes
or betrays those ranked endorsements. Betraying one's endorsements
*dis*integrates subjectivity. In contrast, the life projects approach I
am offering here accepts that individuals may occasionally forward
their life projects through their less-than-laudable—and therefore
unendorsed—capabilities, such as the capacity for deception. Moreover, a life project approach accepts that not every action one may
take in a given day will contribute directly, positively, or in immediate
ways to one's life project(s). As a practical matter, building projects of
all kinds often involve elements of destruction. Sites must be cleared;
errors are made, and later corrected. A casually observant passerby
may see only contradiction in iterations of building and removal,
whereas the thoughtful, confident builder may see non-linear progress toward her broader vision. Life projects as integrative tools make
room for actions that are marked by ambivalence and inconsistency
and which may *appear* to betray one's endorsements, but which in
fact may express attempts to effectively integrate multiple identities
and commitments in deeply contradictory and conflictual contexts.

Finally, there is also a third integrative role for ambivalence and
inconsistency. If ambivalence and inconsistency in self-identification
and presentation can play a vital role in managing conflict and contradiction, then *flexibility in the priority of endorsements*—rather
than the strict rank-order advocated by Frankfurt—may help those
with mutually exclusive identities to produce consistently sound
judgments and actions that are in keeping with their endorsements
and life projects in conflictual contexts. María Lugones, for example,

is highly identified with politicized struggles against all forms of social subordination. But pursuing that life project consistently and effectively may require her to act *with different priorities across different contexts.*[37] The wholehearted exercise of her anti-racist endorsements often involve activities that are localized in lesbian social settings, while her anti-heterosexist activities are often localized in Latina/o social settings. Pursuing her endorsements and life project thus may require that she actually counter-identify as a lesbian in some Latina contexts and counter-identify as a Latina in some lesbian contexts, braving marginalization in both realms to make anti-racism salient in some unreceptive spaces and anti-heterosexism salient in others.[38] While Lugones may be flexible in how she prioritizes her endorsements, she would not deny the importance of *both* endorsements and their significance in her life projects in any context. Given this, Lugones has a strong reason *not* to establish a strict or rigid rank-order priority among her higher order desires as Frankfurt suggests.

Contradiction and Self-Integration in Casablanca

On the account of the self-integration of multiple identities that I am offering, individuals establish endorsements that are loosely self-organized and linked into broad, self-guiding, life projects. In the process of self-integration, individuals reshape the existing intersections among their multiple identities as needed and pursue their self-integrative projects on an ongoing basis. They observe as much as possible their endorsements while remaining vigilant and self-reflective about the influence on their daily thoughts and actions of those aspects of their subjectivities that they do not underwrite. Yet, they also retain a willingness to utilize the qualities of themselves that they do not generally endorse should their life projects demand it. In terms of the metaphors used in chapter four, this practice of self-integration is analogous to the herdsman culling from his herd those animals for show that he judges to be best, while he continues to attend to the activities and needs of the remainder of the herd. Alternatively, it is like the city planner who lays out and walks her high streets, but is also knowledgeable and engaged with the impoverished neighborhoods, obscure, damaged alleyways, and busy cross streets of the rest of her personal metropolis.

This approach to understanding self-integration of a multiple and decentered subject both differs from and has commonalities with accounts of self-integration advanced by Alasdair MacIntyre and Charles Taylor that center the self on "self-narratives" or conceptions of self-fulfilling authenticity respectively.[39] In his concept of "narrative selfhood," Alasdair MacIntyre advocates a concept of the "narrative self" in which the intelligibility of our selves (and others) is necessarily derived from an inclusive self-narrative that "runs from one's birth to one's death."[40] For MacIntyre, narrative selfhood involves accountability. We must be "open to being asked to give a certain kind of account of what one did or what happened to one" and also of being always able to "ask others for an account" of themselves.[41] Inclusive and overarching self-narratives render the self an integrated and coherent self, to the extent that one's self-narrative is integrated and logically coherent.

Although MacIntyre acknowledges the potential multiplicity of nested self-narratives, he considers the consistency-generative role of self-narrative to rule out the possibility that inconsistent or contradictory narratives can accurately reflect the self. Moreover, his definition of narrative selfhood excludes the possibility that refusals of self-narrative can be expressive of the self. It also rejects the idea that the intentional rejection of narrative accountability can *sometimes* set fruitful conditions for the growth of key elements of subjectivity, especially under conditions of conflict or contradiction. All three of these possibilities overlooked by MacIntyre are discussed at the end of this chapter as ways that affirm the value of self-narrative in self-integration, but also sketch its limitations for integrating multiple identities under conditions of conflict.

In another framework of self-integration Charles Taylor argues that selves should be organized through endorsements or "strong evaluations" of broad overarching principles, which he calls "hypergoods."[42] For Taylor, "strongly valued preferences" define identity.[43] In addition, those strong preferences are not simply a matter of choice, but are also potentially inherent or "authentic" to the self. However, knowledge of the authentic elements of ourselves and our identities is not generally found by us "in isolation;" rather we "negotiate it [i.e. knowledge of our authentic elements] through dialogue, partly overt, partly internalized, with others."[44] If and when we discover our authentic elements, however, and make them our guiding preferences, living our authenticity is not only integrating, but also self-fulfilling in that it is an expression of what is "true" of ourselves.

Yet, Taylor's account of identity and authenticity—like MacIntyre's narrative selfhood—is focused on making identity "coherent" in such a way that it leaves no room for contradictory identities or hypergoods. Just as MacIntyre acknowledges the multiplicity of nested self-narratives, Taylor too recognizes the multiplicity of the self, but at the same time asserts that multiplicity will be typically nested and compatible. He writes, "Thus it may be essential to the self-definition of A that he is a Catholic and a Quebecois; of B that he is Armenian and an anarchist." And "I spoke of identifying oneself as a Catholic or an anarchist, or as an Armenian or a Quebecois. *Normally, however, one dimension would not be exclusive of the other.*"[45] But as I have stressed throughout this work, the various elements within subjectivities often involve contradictions.

The commonplace quality of identity contradiction, as I shall argue in detail at the end of this chapter, creates limitations on the degree to which authentic self-fulfillment realized through endorsements can serve as a basis for self-integration of decentered subjectivity. Consequently, from the outset of this discussion, I grant that the coherent and encompassing self-narratives and authentic self-fulfillment described by MacIntyre and Taylor may *sometimes* play important roles in self-integration for some individuals at certain times. Yet, I will argue also that both coherent self-narratives and authentic self-fulfillment may be compromised when the intersections among multiple identity schemes—or our attempts to shape or reshape those intersections—are conditioned by circumstances of social conflict or contradiction. In addition, both may be compromised when an individual's multiple identities are compatible and nested, but political conflicts place a person's life projects in direct contradiction.

Consider, for example, the widely beloved film *Casablanca*. Umberto Eco has interpreted the force and enduring fascination of the film as arising from its truly haphazard combination of divergent narrative elements—all of which are drawn from the literary panoply of "tried and true" elements.[46] Multiple archetypes, multiple storylines, multiple clichés, many symbols, struggles, and passions are all crowded together in the film such that impulse and instinct have apparently overtaken pre-meditated filmcraft. In the process, *Casablanca,* as Eco points out, is a film that "made itself" "beyond the control" of its actors and authors. And from this uncontrolled amalgamation there has emerged a raw convolution of human narrative that "has spoken in the place of the director."[47] It is that untamed narrative, Eco argues, that succeeds in touching and captivating audiences. *Casablanca* succeeds *despite its failings* as a consistent logical narrative, the kind of consistent narrative praised in film and aesthetic theory as well as by philosophers of the narrative self.

For Eco, the peculiar magic of *Casablanca*'s raw, choppy narrative is that it makes audiences willing to "accept it when characters change mood, morality, and psychology from one moment to the next."[48] In terms of aesthetic and narrative theory, such rapid shifts in mood, morality, and psychology of characters are flaws that mar filmmaking and which films more aesthetically accomplished than *Casablanca* avoid—films that nonetheless do not have *Casablanca*'s iconic and monumental appeal.[49] While Eco sees the portrayal of inexplicably shifting psychology as damaging to *Casablanca*'s aesthetic, my argument throughout this book has been that such continually shifting mood, morality, and psychology is the quintessential daily manifestation of an individual's multiple identities. Whether in the course of a single conversation or across multiple social contexts, multiple identity schemes—as our multiple internalized psychologies—continually shift in response to often subtle, salience-shifting factors.

Casablanca thus reflects the kinds of shifts in identity salience that we frequently experience, but much less frequently notice or acknowledge. Consequently, I would suggest that it is not in spite of portraying these psychological inconsistencies in a convoluted nonlinear narrative that *Casablanca* succeeds: it is *because* the film portrays those inconsistencies of self in a realistically non-linear manner that it succeeds. Likewise, the film unconsciously addresses the question of self-integration that is consciously addressed in this chapter. *Casablanca*'s principal characters—Rick, Ilsa, Laszlo, and Renault—like the rest of us, all face the need to grapple with identity contradictions, and encounter the question of how (and even whether or not) to integrate their own multiplicity through various life projects. As if referring to a *dis*integrated subject, Sydney Greenstreet's Señor Ferrari declares *Casablanca*'s anti-hero Rick, played by Humphrey Bogart, to be "a difficult customer"—so much so that "no one ever knows what he'll do or why."[50] By reputation at least, Rick's conduct seems to be all over the map.

Still, though jaded and cynical, Bogart's Rick consistently describes himself as apolitical—loudly avowing hermit-like political neutrality. The political problems of the world are not in his department, even as he lives in the midst of World War II. However, from its beginning the film's narrative is riddled with Rick's performative contradictions. His supposed indifference to the political conflicts around him is repeatedly belied by his microresistance to the Nazi regime from inside his saloonkeeper's realm. In the film's early scenes, Rick casually refuses café credit to German soldiers, and confrontationally bans an affluent German banker from his gambling room. While Rick declares himself *selfishly* apolitical to Victor Laszlo, moments later it is Rick's leadership from the shadows of the café—vis-à-vis his orchestra, whose members display overt loyalty to Rick, *not* to Laszlo—that makes possible Laszlo's display of symbolic political resistance in the singing of "La Marseillaise." Furthermore, with the closure of the café, it is Rick who bears the immediate cost of Laszlo's strategically questionable bravado, a cost that Rick *unselfishly* refuses to redistribute to his staff.

Such examples of the contradictions between Rick's political words and deeds are numerous, and several portray seemingly intentional ambivalence in his self-identifications. For example, Rick reasserts his political neutrality to the Nazi henchman Major Strasser. Yet in the scene's interaction, Rick uses overt ambivalence with regard to the identities and political endorsements he professes—claiming to be a drunkard without political sympathies. This professed ambivalence has an empowering role in Rick's response to Strasser. For through his sardonic and evasive replies to Strasser's interrogation, Rick inserts a level of ambiguity in his position and thus stakes out for himself a level of unpredictable independence in his relationship to the political authority of both Vichy France and Nazi Germany.[51]

That ambiguous position serves Rick well in the narrative's climax. Not only does Rick display self-contradictory conduct with regard to *anti-fascist political convictions,* he also performs contradictorily regarding other political principles. Rick is willing to run a lucrative illegal gambling hall that happens (through its rigged roulette wheel) to help keep him in favor with his friend, Captain Renault, the corrupt prefect of police. At the same time, Rick refuses to engage in black market activities that exploit the refugee traffic of wartime Casablanca. When Ferrari proposes such black marketeering and asks Rick to sell him the services of his Black friend Sam—Rick replies "I don't buy or sell human beings" and pointedly lets Sam make his own choices regarding Ferrari's lucrative offer of employment, even as he simultaneously shelters Sam from Ferrari's imposing manner by moderating the exchange.[52] This and other scenes between Rick and Sam suggest that they have a complex interracial friendship characterized by mutual relations of care and responsibility that are nonetheless also complicated, and sometimes cross-cut, by hierarchical relationships of paid labor and exchange.

In terms of *gender justice,* Rick's statements and actions likewise appear contradictory. Rick is fully aware of Louis Renault's sexual exploitation of female refugees and he does nothing to intervene. Yet his jaded neutrality recedes when he is touched by the agony of the young Bulgarian bride faced with a choice between succumbing to Renault's advances and allowing her and her husband's hopes of escaping the war to die. In the course of their conversation, Rick is visibly moved in mood and psychology from a morose flippancy at the beginning of her inquiries regarding Renault, to an open emotional distress when she describes her proposed loving sacrifice. The proposed sacrifice resonates painfully with—and presumably makes salient—Rick's own lovesick state. Falsely believing that no one ever loved *him* enough to make a similar sacrifice, Rick's ultimate response to the bride's dilemma is an out-of-character (but only apparently out-of-character) "gesture to love" in which he engages in public dishonesty to aid the young couple. The contradictions of this honorable act are manifold: Rick must openly compromise the honest image of his rigged roulette wheel to keep the conflicted young bride an honest woman.[53] The contradictions only increase as Rick endures the opposing interpretations of his action in the social borderlands of the café. His action earns him the jubilant praise and deepened affection of Carl and Sasha, and a sharp rebuke from his friend Renault.[54]

In all these areas of self-contradiction, ambivalence, ambiguity, and flexibility play a prominent role in how Rick interacts with others throughout most of the film. His words and actions exhibit all three of the means outlined above in which ambivalence and flexibility help in the management of identity contradiction. First, Rick is clearly ambivalent and evasive about his claims to important group memberships. While he has named his place of business the Café Américain, when asked about his nationality by Major Strasser, he declines to claim American national identity and instead refers to himself "as a drunkard." Second, he engages in self-protective or preemptive inconsistencies. For example, when Renault asks him why he came to coastal, but dry Casablanca he answers the question with an implausible evasion, pensively stating that he "came for the waters." And third, Rick's endorsement priorities undergo both minor flexibilities and major shifts in the course of the film.

If Bogart's Rick is a walking contradiction, the question remains whether the disparities in his conduct are as inscrutable as Ferrari claims or whether they can be attributed to some form of self-fragmentation. Is Rick wantonly without conviction like Renault, who declares himself to blow with the wind? Is he akratically weak-willed toward his politically neutral convictions, or self-deceived about where his priorities really lie? A poll of Rick's fellow characters in *Casablanca* would certainly favor self-deception. Renault, Ilsa, and Laszlo all remind Rick at various times, of his record of political resistance to fascism in Spain, Ethiopia, and against the Nazis who placed a bounty on him in Paris. Rick's life history suggests that he had adopted resistance to fascism as a life project before arriving in

Casablanca. But in Casablanca, he continually denies that project in his self-narration even as he cannot seem to fully resist the impulse to anti-fascist political intervention in his life as a saloon keeper. In their argument over the letters of transit, Ilsa pointedly reminds Rick of his past political convictions. He states, "Do I have to hear again what a great man your husband is, what an important cause he's fighting for?" Ilsa answers emphatically, "But it was your cause, too. In your own way you were fighting for the same thing."[55] Laszlo goes still further, charging Rick with self-deception directly when Rick questions the worth of political resistance and suggests that if the world were to die it would be out of its misery. To this last piece of cynicism Laszlo replies, "Do you know how you sound Monsieur Blaine? Like a man who is trying to convince himself of something he doesn't believe in his heart. . . . I wonder if you know that you're trying to escape from yourself—and that you'll never succeed."[56]

In addition to the opinions of other characters and the numerous disjunctions between Rick's political word and deeds, there are also other clues in *Casablanca* that suggest Rick is potentially engaged in active self-deception regarding his political convictions. Various pieces of dialogue convey that since arriving in Casablanca, Rick has deliberately obscured or belittled his political history, which itself contradicts his stated disinterest in the problems of the world. For example, Rick's unprovoked belligerence toward Ugarte, played by Peter Lorre, in the opening café scene immediately portrays Rick as highly protective of some kind of self-reinvention. Their conversation immediately follows from Rick's confrontation with the German banker at the gambling room door. Ugarte begins:

"You know Rick, watching you just now with the Deutche Bank one would think you've been doing this all your life."
(Rick, harshly) "What makes you think I haven't?"
(Ugarte, uncomfortably) "Oh, nothing. But when you first came to Casablanca, I thought . . ."
(Rick, intimidatingly) "You thought what?"
(Ugarte, cringing in retreat) "What right do I have to think, huh?"[57]

In this odd and seemingly random exchange, Rick tensely privileges his saloonkeeper's role through the combative denial of any other possible past. Yet the scene's refusal bears a layered—and apparently unintentionally—contradictory meaning, because the confrontation that elicited the dialogue is at once contrarian as an act of professional saloon keeping, and quite intelligible as an act of politicized microresistance. This gives ambiguity to the meaning of the "this" that refers to whatever it is Rick may have actually been doing his whole life: is it barkeeping or confronting fascists? The sharp and defensive quality of Rick's reply to Ugarte's mild and merely conversational probing bring back to mind Amélie Oksenberg Rorty's argument (discussed in chapter four) that when cherished self-deceptions are in some way questioned, highly motivated self-deceivers may often act aggressively to "hide the traces" of those self-deceptions.[58]

If Rick is lying to himself about the value he places on anti-fascist political struggle as a life project, his motivation for that self-deception seems to be connected to how he perceives the relationship between that political project and his other apparent project of committed love—a project focused entirely on his romantic attachment to Ilsa. It is not until Rick's conversation with Ilsa in the bazaar that it becomes possible to identify the potential source of Rick's pseudo-abandonment of politics, which would suggest lies in his misperception of why Ilsa abandoned him in Paris. In his first private and *sober* words to her he asks, "Did you run out on me because you couldn't take it, because you knew what it would be like hiding from the police, running away all the time? . . . Well I'm not running away any more. I'm settled now. Above a saloon it's true. But, walk up a flight."[59] These words suggest that in Rick's mind, Ilsa's abandonment and what he (falsely) believes to be her loss of love for him, has come as the cost of his political commitments. If so, then this misperception and the trauma of this loss could have established in Rick's mind a powerful conflict between love and politics—the two life projects that had previously been self-integrative for him.

As the narrative unfolds in its non-linear fashion, it becomes clear that all three members of the film's love-triangle have faced—and still face—this same central conflict between love and politics. For Ilsa, Rick, and Laszlo, the second World War has set their life projects of *committed love* at loggerheads with their life projects of *political resistance* to fascism. Yet all three have evidently grappled with that conflict differently. Both men have chosen to engage (in Jane Flax's words) in "premature attempts to *resolve* or *deny* [their] conflicts."[60] Only Ilsa seems to grapple with the contradiction directly and effectively.

Victor Laszlo, for example, seems to deny that there is any possible conflict between his political project and his project of marital love. Throughout the film he appears oblivious to the fact that the demands in time and attention of his politics may reasonably be expected to take a toll on the emotional foundations of his marriage and Ilsa's romantic attachment to him.[61] Setting Laszlo's year of resistance in a German concentration camp aside as both involuntary, and unassailable, the limited time he spends with Ilsa on-screen is, with very few exceptions, marked by a kind of formality that suggests emotional distance. His expressions of care seem sincere, but also perfunctory and tepid (the only kiss he gives her while they are alone is a kiss on the forehead as he departs for an underground meeting—not quite an expression of passionate love and desire for a beautiful woman). Laszlo is unperturbed when Renault flirts openly with his wife before him, and for a skilled resistance fighter he is strangely unassertive in attempting to discover the nature of Ilsa's obvious attachment to Rick. Even if Laszlo does not wish to assign blame to anyone, strong curiosity about Ilsa's feelings and needs would nonetheless be appropriate. Together, these elements suggest a high level of inattentiveness on Laszlo's part toward his wife and a favoring of his political life that sits uncomfortably with his continued declaration of love, and retention of her hand.

In contrast, Rick—who *is* the rank sentimentalist Renault suspects him of being—does not deny the conflict between his projects of love and politics, but rather prematurely resolves that conflict in favor of love. Consequently, he fails to engage realistically with the political facts that endanger him and Ilsa in Paris. The warfront has moved, and Rick must move with it in order to survive. Yet, when in Paris Sam reminds Rick that the arriving Germans will soon be looking for him due to the bounty on his head, Rick irreverently replies, "I left a note in my apartment. They'll know where to find me."[62] As he joyfully turns away from Sam back to Ilsa, he turns his back on how his political project has heightened for him the present dangers of the war. In response to Ilsa's agonized concern for his safety and pleas that he flee Paris, Rick pours more champagne, proposes marriage, and showers her with adoring attention. Faced with a conflict between his project of love and the nature of his politics, Rick refuses to compromise the constant attentiveness he regards as indispensable to lasting romantic attachment.

Rick's privileging of his project of committed love for Ilsa continues long after she has left him, and its failure distorts his social functioning. Whatever charismatic efficacy Rick manages to achieve in Casablanca, he remains a lovesick, socially erratic wreck until Ilsa's love and sacrifice for him are finally revealed. In his post-Paris mode Rick not only denies his politics and has no interest in other women, he also becomes interpersonally isolationist—a fact observed by both Renault and Ferrari. His compulsive isolationism takes two forms:

his refusal to participate appropriately in conventional rituals of social interaction, and his consistent refusal to impart any personal information to others, including trusted friends. His refusal to drink
socially with others, for example, is extreme enough to give offense.
Moreover, in various scenes he appears publicly in a pensive, disengaged reverie that render him anti-social, despite the fact that he is
both socially skilled and in the business of facilitating social life for
others.[63] While Renault is arguably Rick's closest friend, Rick is evasive with him about his past, including his famous declaration that he
came to Casablanca for the waters.

Although the source of Rick's isolationism is difficult to discern
at first, when Ilsa suddenly returns, Rick's attentiveness to her *and*
his willingness to engage gracefully in social rituals likewise suddenly return.[64] The first thirty-one words that Rick speaks to Ilsa in
the café—which include the description of her apparel at *La Belle
Aurore*—are more charged with passion, love, and desire than all of
the words spoken to her by Laszlo combined. However, these restora-
tions in social ability do not at first lead to greater efficacy in Rick, but
instead to increasingly erratic and self-destructive behavior. Although
Ilsa is subtly, but unmistakably, receptive to Rick's attentions even in
front of Laszlo, Rick is inexplicably blind to her marital risk-taking
on his behalf. Pained by what he takes to be Ilsa's passionate love for
Laszlo, he salves that pain with dramatically increased drinking on
the night of her return and thereafter. In the social borderlands of the
café, Rick's changing drinking habits are seen as negative by his loyal
staff, but are applauded by Renault as a sign of Rick's improved sociability. While the dispute goes unresolved, the shift also negatively
affects his interactions. It is while drunk and feeling angry self-pity
that Rick cruelly refuses Ilsa's first overture of explanation with the
brutal insinuation that she is a whore.[65]

Of the three lovers only Ilsa finds a way to balance the contradictory demands of passionate love, marital responsibility, and political
resistance that have been placed on cross-currents by the war. Her
decision to deceive and abandon Rick saves her beloved Rick's life,
secures to Laszlo what she is committed by marriage to provide, and
contributes to the war effort by ensuring that both political actors
and herself survive for later struggle. The productivity of her creative
solution under constrained circumstances is a product of the contradictions and tension among her motivations which clearly inform her
actions in different ways. Yet, Ilsa's creative solution comes at enormous emotional and personal cost. With it she must then maintain
and cope with the inner contradiction of romantically loving a man

she has abandoned, and living with a husband she respects and admires but does not romantically love.

Yet, in his interpretation of *Casablanca,* Umberto Eco denigrates Ilsa as a mere intermediary such that "[s]he herself is not a bearer of positive values; only the men are."[66] Conversely, reading the film in light of multiple identities and the challenge of interweaving contradictory identity schemes and life projects under conditions of conflict, it is actually Ilsa who is the moral center of the film. Only Ilsa exhibits the personal strength and creative engagement necessary to initially meet the *full range* of her self-chosen political and ethical commitments. Moreover, contrary to Eco's view, it is by providing a positive example of the value of life commitments to love *and* anti-fascist politics that Ilsa favorably influences other characters—especially Rick, and through Rick also Renault. It is in her intimate revelation to Rick of her sacrifice and enduring love for him, that Ilsa illustrates for Rick the possibility of reconciling his projects of romantic love and political resistance. Rick subsequently proceeds to amass—quite creatively—the ingredients necessary to emulate *her* original, politicized loving sacrifice. In so doing, he once again recognizes and *re*integrates his self-fragmented projects of love and politics by reworking in his mind the perceived intersection between those projects. In that revised intersection, politics is no longer seen as a poison to romantic love, but at times also the express manifestation of that love.

With this revised intersection as a footing, Rick improves his self-integration by ceasing to deny his political convictions. In this, he also seems to regain consistent efficacy, as his conduct shifts from the erratic, mojo-less, semi-function of intrapsychic disarray, to the effective motivation and concerted action of a confidently self-directed, yet also comfortably interdependent person. To the extent that Rick has recrafted and laid claim to the intersection between his love and his politics, his doing so has reinvigorated his politics, his romantic love, and his respect for Ilsa. The tragic part of this triumph is that Rick cannot acknowledge his debt to Ilsa explicitly—either because he does not yet see it, or because he feels he cannot reveal it strategically if he is to succeed in sending her away. Instead, he disavows the significance of their love vis-à-vis the problems of the world and condescends to the very woman who has saved him (by formerly jilting him) so that he may bring about her escape (by now pseudo-jilting her). Renault relieves this convoluted tragedy by assuring Rick, and the audience, that Ilsa recognized Rick's "fairy tale" of non-nobility to be an expedient lie.[67]

Self-Integration in Relation to Ranked Endorsements, Narrative, and Authentic Self-Fulfillment

Renault hails the moment of Rick's successful self-integration of his love and politics by remarking: "Well Rick, you're not only a sentimentalist. But you've become a patriot." To which Rick blithely replies, "Well, it seemed like a good time to start."[68] Indeed. Perhaps it is always a good time to start self-integrating whatever counterproductive intrapsychic fragmentation we might have inherited socially, or generated for ourselves. Based on my preceding analysis, I would agree with Frankfurt, MacIntyre, and Taylor that in the process of self-integration rank-ordered desires, self-narrative, and/or authentic self-fulfillment may play integrative roles at different times for different people. However, all three of these means also can be counterproductive to self-integration, especially when the consistency imposed by these methods requires "resolving" contradiction prematurely.

With regard to rank ordered desires, for example, Rick's self-deception in Casablanca arises from the imbalance of his projects of politics and love for Ilsa. Rick's failure to balance these, however, is a consequence of his hierarchical rank-ordering of his romantic and political endorsements in which Rick privileges romance over wartime concerns. His rigidity in observing this rank order denies to Ilsa the possibility of confiding in Rick as she wishes to, and forces her to act unilaterally in a manner protective of Rick but nearly fatal to his projects of romantic love and politics. Rick responds to the heartbreak induced by his own rigidity by deliberately fragmenting his love and politics, aggressively disavowing politics after Paris as he post-traumatically reinvents himself from loving "Richard" to cynical "Rick."

Yet, Rick's against-the-grain self-disintegration can only be sustained through noisy self-deception regarding the political concerns he still ultimately feels and acts upon, and his still secretly privileged romanticism. If Amélie Oksenberg Rorty is right to regard self-deception and akrasia as symptoms of conflict—Rick's self-deception and self-fragmentation in relation to his political predilections are rooted in his failure to grapple effectively with the contradiction between his love for Ilsa and the demands of the war. Firmly rank-ordering his desires contributed to this debacle. While Rick's failure is partly due to poor judgment—it is also a failure that reflects the hazards and limitations of relying on rank-ordered desires for self-integration, especially under conditions of conflict.

In contrast, Ilsa's efficacy in Paris demonstrates the value of responding to contradiction with the aid of ambivalence and flexibility. While it is impossible to determine clearly from the film, it is reasonable to infer that Ilsa grappled extensively with the contradictions of her situation in order to respond effectively to those contradictions. Our only clue is her own cry to Rick, "The day you left Paris . . . If you knew what I went through. If you knew how much I loved you, how much I still love you."[69] Moreover, Ilsa's strength in sustaining the challenges of her contradictory commitments over time—despite their personal costs—seems to be aided by her use of ambiguity. For instance, when asked by Laszlo to describe Rick after their first romantically charged encounter in the café, Ilsa is at once self-contradictorily evasive and unnecessarily forthcoming when she states, "Oh, I really can't say. Though, I saw him quite often in Paris."[70] This kind of strategically motivated ambivalence and ambiguity is what Anzaldúa meant, I believe, when she emphasized the importance of cultivating a "tolerance of ambiguity" in order to live multiple identities effectively. It is arguably also what Jane Flax is emphasizing when she cautions against the impulse to resolve contradictions prematurely.

The life project intersectionality-assisted account of self-integration outlined here takes a different approach to contradiction than rank-ordered endorsements. In practice, the model offered here often would not—and need not—put an end to contradiction or to the fluid inconsistencies of a life project oriented subject. It would instead hope to increase the likelihood that the contradictions and inconsistencies of the subject would be more consciously felt and understood by him or her, and more productive to the subject's lifelong projects. Honorably sending Ilsa to safety with her hero-husband required skillful lies and deceit from Rick. Rick is an honorable man, who fortunately for all, had some handy skills associated generally with *dishonor*. Rick lies, steals, cheats, and ultimately kills (but only in self-defense) to forward his good causes of love and political resistance. He ultimately does sell human beings—Carl, Sam, Sasha, and Emile, and particularly Sam—to protect them all from bearing the costs of his choices. To eschew these contradictions or condemn Rick for them would be to ignore how consistent these actions are with his life projects, and the multiple identifications those projects involve.

Consequently, any mode of self-integration that cannot accommodate inconsistency and lasting contradiction will be inadequate when project or identity-related contradictions are unavoidable, such as in contexts of social or political conflict. With regard to integrative self narrative advocated by MacIntyre, for example, Ilsa and Rick's mutual embrace of love-by-rejection is a useful illustration of why MacIntyre's account of narrative consistency is inadequate as a means to explain, much less integrate, the self. A notion of love-by-rejection is incoherent, and narrating it requires inconsistency. Yet in *Casablanca*'s scheme of unavoidable contradiction, love-by-rejection is how the protagonists hold their complex projects and multiple identifications together. Moreover, as discussed above in my reading of the film, Rick can be seen as employing ambiguity and flexibility to cohesive effect even while his life projects are significantly fragmented following his loss of Ilsa in Paris. As discussed above, during that time Rick employs all three modes of integrative ambivalence and flexibility. Moreover, all three dimensions of ambivalence and flexibility aid Rick in various ways in pursuing his life projects of resistance to fascism and search for committed love or coping with the pain of the contradictions that he faces.

The important place of contradiction, inconsistency, and ambivalence in self-integration through life projects throws into doubt the degree to which coherent or comprehensive narrativity—that is, narrative identity—can be seen as the sole means to integrate the self. Most of the film's most meaningful exchanges are so contradictory that many cannot be contained and related in any logical or consistent narrative or set of nested or compatible narratives. From the anti-social pleasure peddler who refuses the business of bankers, to episodes of public cheating that champion fidelity, to the constant lies of honorable men and women, the identity expressions vital to *Casablanca* do not—as Eco also notes—fit into a concisely consistent or logical narrative.

Instead, the effective narrative options are reduced to multiple and contradictory storylines or undulating, mutually dependent tales that make little sense placed side-by-side or superimposed on one another. Nonsensical utterances expose the untamable quality of the character's valid self-expressions. Carl rejoices by the roulette table watching Rick help the Bulgarian couple. A worried gambler disrupts his joy by asking, "[a]re you sure this place is honest?" With consternation and apt incomprehensibility Carl replies, "[h]onest? As honest as the day is long," as he turns away busily with an anxious expression.[71] However, just because the expression of multiple identity schemes may exceed the limits of logical and consistent narrative organization, it does *not* follow that the self-reflexivity needed to produce self-integration cannot cope with deep contradiction. On the contrary, this reading of *Casablanca*—especially regarding Rick's successful reintegration—suggests that the better we become at integrating our multiple identities through life projects in contexts of conflict the more likely it may be that the daily manifestations of that integration will involve contradictions that will exceed consistent logical narrativity.[72]

Like rank-ordered endorsements and coherent self-narrativities, authenticity and self-fulfillment also have their limits and drawbacks for self-integration. Charles Taylor's account of authenticity, and the self-fulfillment arising from it, is helpful when people's identities and overarching principles are nested and compatible. My reading of *Casablanca* suggests that there may well be aspects of each self that are "authentic" to them in that—however those elements arrived in the subject—are not significantly malleable. Rick's impulses of love for Ilsa and anti-fascist politics come back to him however much he denies them. But self-integration on the basis of such authenticity may be anything but self-fulfilling if it must incorporate conflict-induced contradiction.[73] It simply does not follow that the expression of authentic qualities of self through the self-reflexive pursuit of life projects or overarching "hypergoods" will result in the self-fulfillment that Taylor associates with expressions of authentic self.

In the case of Rick, Ilsa, and Laszlo in *Casablanca*, expressions of their authentic political selves come at tremendous cost to their self-fulfillment as a consequence of the conflict of the war. Beneath the rhetoric and self-authentic action of the closing scene, for example, none of the three are self-fulfilled. And while Eco ridicules the inconsistency and implausibility of rapidly changing mood and moral/psychological expression in the film, the faces of the members of the film's love-triangle beautifully capture the actions—at once authentic and committed—of each, and the profoundly unfulfilling quality of those actions. Rick's love for Ilsa is the most authentic and immutable thing about him. And while that love is certainly expressed in some way by ensuring her safety, the grimace of pain that flitters across his face as he urges her and Laszlo to the plane speaks volumes about the loss of self-fulfillment his authentic self-integration has cost him.

Laszlo too has perhaps discovered that his political activity has likely cost him the *heart* of his wife though not her honorable hand. His blank-faced observance of Ilsa's tearful and obvious distress at the prospect of leaving with Laszlo for America instantly morphs into a smug condescending speech to Rick about their joint political struggle. Nonetheless, only a Herculean effort at self-deception could convince Laszlo now that Ilsa is as in love with him as she is with Rick.

And finally, as she turns away from Rick to Laszlo, Ilsa's face displays a mild, sweet smile, perhaps one of comfort for her husband. Her expression momentarily warms in its intensity as she turns away from Laszlo and looks forward, reflecting perhaps on the act of loving sacrifice that is making their escape possible. But as she strides to the plane, an errant tear catches the light and Ilsa's face falls. She assumes a look of pensive disengagement not unlike that worn by Rick on the platform in Paris when he too had been abandoned against his will as an expression of the love of a beloved.

Through the experiences of Christian Park and María Lugones, and through a reading of *Casablanca,* I have investigated in this chapter various modes of identity integration and formulated a life project model of self-integration in which self-produced intersectionality plays a significant role. What cannot be investigated though the sources examined here, however, is the actual embodied and intrapsychic process of self-integration as it takes place in everyday cases. *Casablanca,* for example, does not portray Rick's experience in the twelve hours or so between Laszlo's arrest and Rick's conversation with Renault in which he begins to orchestrate Ilsa and Laszlo's escape. Rick is asked by Ilsa to think for all of them, but what then? What were the cognitive-affective-embodied processes involved in Rick's active *re*integration of his life projects and his identities as a lover to Ilsa and an anti-fascist? If we had seen it, would Rick's process of letting go of his self-deceptions have been painful and traumatic, or cathartic, peaceful, and joyful? Was the process of self-integration quick or extended? What were the stages of self-transformation, if any? What elements helped or hindered the process? Was engagement with others essential? If so, what kind of engagement? Answering these questions definitively is far beyond the scope of this project. However, in the next chapter, I offer a preliminary assessment of these questions in which the process of self-integrating of multiple identities is examined in relation to the personal process of self-transformation, and the political processes of social and political change.

CHAPTER SIX

Selfcraft

Love and Politics in the Self-Integration of Multiple Identities

Soy un amasamiento, I am an act of kneading, of uniting and joining that has not only produced both a creature of darkness and a creature of light, but also a creature that questions the definitions of light and dark and gives them new meanings.
GLORIA ANZALDÚA, *Borderlands*

In the previous chapter, I argued that self-integration of multiple identities is fostered by ambivalence and flexibility, and that integrative life projects offer a means by which to integrate contradictory elements of the self which rank-ordered endorsements and coherent life narratives cannot incorporate. The question remains, however, how does this process of self-integration take place? In this chapter, I offer a three-step model of selfcraft and illustrate that model with an autobiographical essay by Minnie Bruce Pratt. Through Pratt's essay, I also continue to investigate the limits of self-narrative as a means to unify diverse and contradictory identities. Like the erratic but effective narrative in *Casablanca,* Pratt's autobiographical narrative is flawed in its narrative form, but it is precisely in those flaws that her essay successfully conveys the self-integration of the author.

As discussed in previous chapters, self-integration is ultimately optional. Some people never choose to take themselves up as an act of integrative kneading as described by Anzaldúa in the epigraph above. My claim in this chapter is that *if* people choose to engage in selfcraft the resources for doing so exist in the potential conflict among their multiple identities. Subjects can make choices for themselves regarding how they wish to use their multiple identity schemes and other self-constructs to shape their daily thoughts and actions. Integrative selfcraft thus presents an opportunity to balance the creative benefits of inner contradiction with the potential for agency and self-management of our otherwise unruly multiplicity. While individuals may choose to forego that opportunity, I argue that it is through the hard work of selfcraft that the potential for robust agency and *independent* critical reason are possible.

The chapter is divided into two parts. In part one, I investigate Gloria Anzaldúa's brief allegory of "the mestiza way." On the basis of

Anzaldúa's sketch, I develop a three-practice framework of selfcraft for integrating multiple identities that includes three steps: *inventory, discernment,* and *revisionary living.*[1] As mentioned above, I illustrate this framework with examples drawn from Pratt's autobiographical writings. In her writings, Pratt details her extended efforts to excavate, reconstruct, and try to bring together her multiple identities. Interestingly, she does so by adopting the same two life projects that were held by the major characters in *Casablanca,* namely love and politics—the quest for *committed love* and *political resistance* to social subordination.

In part two of the chapter, I ground this three-part model of selfcraft within the broader theory of multiple identities by relating it back to the account of personal identity offered in chapters two and four. After rearticulating the model in philosophical terms, I then explore how the process of selfcraft outlined here rejects a need for anything beyond our existing identities to achieve self-integration. More specifically, self-integration does not depend upon—and cannot be achieved solely by—self-narrative, although selfcraft may incorporate self-narrative as a means. I will contend that self-integration through integrative life projects can avoid the drawbacks and limitations of narrative unity, while still utilizing narrative's potential for bringing partial sense to the diverse and often contradictory character of the multiple and decentered subject. In closing, I describe the limitations of selfcraft in terms of our restricted ability to control the salience of our multiple identities and our own socialization. These limits, in turn, profoundly shape the political implications of multiple identities that will be discussed in the concluding chapter.

Part I: The "Mestiza Way": Toward a Framework of Self-Integration

In the epigraph above from *Borderlands: The New Mestiza,* Anzaldúa refers to herself as a project of self-integration—as a conscious meld of integrated opposites. For Anzaldúa, it is by virtue of uniting and joining her multiple identities and drawing upon their enduring contradictions that she is endowed with critical and creative abilities. She describes this process of kneading most directly in four paragraphs of *Borderlands* under the heading "the mestiza way."[2] She begins her account with a cryptic allegory. In Anzaldúa's allegory, a woman is, "Caught between the sudden contraction, the breath sucked in and the endless space, the brown woman stands still, looks at the sky." In my reading of this allegory the "sudden contraction," represents an unspecified contradiction, a space of opposites in which airless constraint meets wide-open possibility. As the allegory continues, after looking skyward in quiet reflection, the woman's response to this contradiction is to dig. She dives into the ground to examine the roots of a nearby tree. She searches the bones buried there for any marrow—the source of life—that they might contain. That finished, she sorts through the belongings she has carried in her backpack, retaining some while discarding others. Afterward she refastens her backpack and "sets out to become the complete *tolteca*."[3]

With this evocative imagery and two paragraphs that follow it, Anzaldúa merely gestures toward a practice of selfcraft. By analyzing Anzaldúa's allegory however, it is possible to further develop her gesture into a three-practice conception of selfcraft. Through this practice the raw multiplicity of a socially constructed subjectivity can be crafted into a contradictory *and* creative whole—the "I" as "an act of kneading." As stated above, I will refer to these three practices of selfcraft as the practices of inventory, discerning, and revisionary living. In the practice of inventory, the woman in Anzaldúa's image delves into answering the question "what did she inherit from her ancestors?" To answer this question, she painstakingly identifies the "baggage" given to her by the various traditions of which she happens to be a part, in this case the baggage gained from "the Indian mother," "Spanish father," and "Anglo" society. In the metaphor of self-mapping used in chapters four and five, this craft of self-inventory is equivalent to the mapping of a city of bright thoroughfares and hidden neighborhoods, taking careful stock of that city's history. It is the task of searching out and learning the history of the elements of one's subjectivity—our habits, schemes of thought, and action—with attention to the politics and forced labor, and the possible atrocities and/or beauties involved in their construction.[4]

The second practice is that of *discerning*. Anzaldúa describes this as the difficult step of differentiating among the elements within one's self that are inherited from valid and valued traditions, those that are imposed in association with forms of social subordination or exclusion, and those that have been acquired for oneself. In this, the practitioner of the mestiza way is putting "history through a sieve" by which she attempts to "winnow[ ] out the lies" and ideological falsehoods to which she has been socialized. She discerns her actual place within the various historical social forces and social groups—racial groups, the category of woman, etc.—that have shaped her.[5] Having identified the character and past influences of her own various schemes of thought and action, discernment involves rejecting for herself what she judges to be unworthy. Discernment is the act of critically forging self-endorsements, by not simply picking from among desires we have, but rather by critically assessing those desires as far as possible in terms of how and why they came to be in our psychologies. Anzaldúa asserts that this practice is not neutral with regard to social hierarchies, but rather involves "a conscious *rupture with all oppressive traditions of all cultures and religions.*"[6] Moreover, such discernment involves "communicating that rupture" in some way and documenting the struggle that discernment involves—allegorically depicted as closing (at least temporarily) one's backpack and wearing it through life. The rejection of *all* forms of social subordination is not merely ideological or an artifact of Anzaldúa's Chicana feminism. Rather, it plays a vital role in excavating and refashioning the intrapsychic intersections among different identity schemes while always keeping track of the possible effects of those elements of ourselves that we do not endorse.[7] As I shall argue below, keeping track of the ugly parts of ourselves can also play a politically significant role in selfcraft.

The third practice of *revisionary living,* involves finding ways to practice and privilege self-endorsed elements of subjectivity. Living endorsements through multiple identities thus explicitly involves a willingness to revise the self-knowledge and to put into practice meanings, values, and practices that are newly accepted over time. Having discerned and rejected one's own particular role in the subordination of marginalized peoples, a woman who accepts the mestiza way of selfcraft "adopt[s] new perspectives toward the darkskinned, women, and queer" and becomes "willing to share [of herself and], to make herself vulnerable to foreign ways of seeing and thinking" such that "she surrenders all notions of safety, of the familiar."[8] In this practice, past ways of thinking that have been critically deconstructed in the process of inventory and discerning became stepping stones to new reconstructions and "new symbols" that may give shape to new guiding principles. For Anzaldúa the critical and creative practice of revisionary living requires strengthening both "tolerance (and intolerance) for ambiguity" as part of a practical willingness to live one's endorsements in the in-between spaces between hierarchically ordered social roles and identities.[9] As I shall argue below, revisionary living also involves reshaping motivational self-constructs in ways that avoid subordination of others, thus "transforming the small 'I'" of one's multiple identities "into the total Self" that is a self-aware, self-critical, whole, and unwilling to akratically or self-deceptively damage others and fragment itself in the ways required to perform such harm.[10]

While Anzaldúa's allegorical account of the mestiza way presents self-remaking as a process that involves distinct moments (inventory, discernment, revisionary living), selfcraft also remains a fluid process of interdependent practices. As we shall see below, its three practices can overlap, take place simultaneously, and/or occur in varied sequences over extended or short periods of time.[11] Acts of revised living, for example, may generate a reinterpretation of social inheritances, which, in turn, leads to new discerning judgments about beliefs and guiding endorsements.

The autobiographical writings of poet, essayist, and activist Minnie Bruce Pratt provide a detailed and compelling example of the three practices of integrative selfcraft. A racially white woman, Pratt was born in Alabama in 1946 and raised middle-class and Christian by a segregationist father and a compliant mother. As a young adult, Pratt attended college and graduate school in the South, during which time she also became a wife and mother of two sons. As a child and as a young adult, Pratt's subjectivity was thus extensively constructed in and by the privileges of systematic racial subordination and anti-Semitism that permeated mainstream culture in the American South under both Jim Crow and de facto segregation.

In 1975, at the age of 29, however, Pratt came out as a lesbian, and on the basis of her sexual identity she was denied custody of her two children in a divorce in 1976. Thereafter Pratt began to consciously integrate her multiple identity schemes as a woman, a lesbian, a feminist, a poet, a Christian, a Southerner, an estranged mother, a civil rights activist, and eventually the life partner/wife of a Jewish transman.[12] As it happens, Pratt integrated her multiple identities around two integrative life projects similar to those of the major characters in *Casablanca,* namely political resistance to all forms of social subordination, and the quest and struggle for committed love.[13]

Pratt's process of self-integration is described in her autobiographical works—two of which in particular describe her self-integration through a juxtaposition of forceful, perceptive prose and disjointed narrative that is both compelling to read and difficult to order into a coherent narrative. The first of these pieces—the well known 1984 essay "Identity: Blood Skin Heart"—discusses the emergence of Pratt's commitment to resist racism and anti-Semitism. As autobiography, "Identity: Blood Skin Heart" is told in flashbacks and forward bending story loops, interspersed with self-critical commentary and analytical political theorizing. In it, conventional elements of autobiographical self-narrative are inexplicably absent or obscured. In a genre-inverting manner, for example, Pratt frequently presents what would conventionally be landmark life events and principal people as vague unspecified impressions. Yet she elaborates seemingly incidental characters and small incidents in vivid detail. The reader learns the names of Pratt's childhood nanny and influential strangers, for example, but does not learn the name of her husband or of the places where she attended college or graduate school.

Through this inverted pattern of rising minor details and descending great gestures, Pratt often conveys happenings without clear reference to a temporal order or to the causal connections between events and their place in the narrative whole.[14] Thus, while the essay is a richly detailed account of personal transformation, this transformation seems to have been experienced—and is certainly conveyed— with only limited narrative coherence.[15] Similarly, in her later collection of essays entitled *S/He,* Pratt dispenses almost entirely with logical and consistent narrative form. In it, Pratt offers an amalgam of disconnected and disordered short lyric essays—all episodes in her life—that together *evoke* rather than narrate the trajectory of her life story as a quest for committed love.

While the absence of coherent self-narrative in Pratt's autobiographical writings might be a function of Pratt's poetic inclinations, I read her prose instead as an illustration of the process of integrating multiple identities.[16] Just as *Casablanca* is narratively flawed, but consequently an apt reflection of the daily manifestation of multiple identities and the herky-jerky motion of self-integration, Pratt's autobiographical writings are also apt reflections of the raw effort involved in attempting to integrate our own multiple identities. Unlike *Casablanca,* in which we do not know what Rick or Ilsa thought or went through to effectively weave their contradictory identities and life projects together, however, Pratt's autobiographical works, "Identity" and *S/He,* offer insight into the thought processes that underlie integrative selfcraft in all three of its forms—inventory, discernment, and revisionary living—revealing how those three forms may operate in concert.

Based on this interpretation I would argue that Pratt also shows us how self-integration can be a long, messy, episodic, non-sequential process involving significant trial and error. Moreover, emotional pain, hardship and/or personal failure may become integral to it. Self-integrative practice may be spurred on by incidental social encounters and the emotions that arise from those encounters. It may also be motivated by widely varied factors, including painful contradictions, social subordination, romantic love, or politicized friendship. Nevertheless, Pratt's story also reveals that as with any form of skilled craftsmanship, practitioners may become more effective and efficient in their selfcraft as they practice it over time.

For the sake of theorizing selfcraft conceptually, I will attempt to impose a more linear and coherent narrative structure on Pratt's essay "Identity: Blood Skin Heart" than what her work proposes. I will draw temporal and causal connections in her story of self-integration in order to extract from her essay examples of the practice of inventory, discernment, and revisionary living. In so doing, I also trace the development of Pratt's two life projects as elements that both animate and organize Pratt's multiple identities.[17]

In "Identity," Pratt's uneven progress toward self-integration can be understood through two narrative strands that operate across her life. The first narrative strand is Pratt's own account of the events and people in her life.[18] As discussed above, this is the stream of events and turning points in Pratt's life through which she relates her personal growth and development from a girl steeped in racial privilege to a woman committed to resisting racism and anti-Semitism. As noted above, this strand is conveyed in an autobiographical narrative that is neither conventional nor linear. [19]

The second narrative strand is the *metanarrative of identity integration,* including identity formation, changing patterns of identity claims and identity significance, and the shifting intersections among Pratt's multiple identities over time. The philosophical inquiry that dominates the following discussion lies primarily at this metanarrative level, which I will describe in terms of a conventionally coherent plot line regarding how Pratt identified herself over time. Within this strand lie two subplots. *Subplot A is Pratt's project of political resistance* to systematic subordination of all kinds. *Subplot B is her quest and struggle for committed love.*

In terms of the metanarrative of identity formation, Pratt notes that as a child she identified primarily as white. As a teenager, she describes herself as belonging to a "specific class of people" who were privileged enough to escape oppression. She recalls expressing that opinion in a letter to a German pen pal, a letter her mother described as "an eloquent justification of white superiority and supremacy."[20] By early adulthood, however, Pratt had formed other identities that obscured to herself her sense of privileged white identity. She writes, "By the time I was mid-way through college, I had slipped into being unselfconscious of myself as white; this happened as I became liberal."[21] As Pratt becomes more highly identified with a liberal identity scheme, her white identity becomes less likely to be salient and thus consciously felt. Yet that white identity might nonetheless influence Pratt's unconscious thoughts and actions and how she is perceived by others. Pratt describes, for example, the night of Dr. Martin Luther

King Jr.'s assassination during what was likely her junior year in college. Pratt, her husband, and a friend drove into Birmingham that night of April 4, 1968. She writes, "we went . . . into Birmingham, curfewed after a day of violence . . . looking for I don't know what, and not finding it . . . not thinking of ourselves as white . . . because we were intellectuals, not at all like James Earl Ray or any white person who did violence."[22]

At this stage, Pratt's political project (subplot A) has taken a liberal turn away from its segregationist origins at the same time that Pratt's liberal identity obscures her recognition of her racial identity with its privilege and relationship to political conflict. Simultaneously, Pratt's project of committed love (subplot B) has apparently been completed in her marriage. In this latter project, Pratt describes her identity as a married person dominating her identity schemes, except in relatively rare instances. She writes, "I slipped from thinking of myself as white, to thinking of myself as *married,* without much regard for other categories in the meantime, except for a few startling moments."[23]

In those startling moments Pratt felt her other identity schemes when they were made unexpectedly salient by particular contexts and *in relation* to the contrasting identities of others. Pratt felt like a *gentile,* for example, when a Jewish boyfriend broke off their relationship because he did not wish to get emotionally attached enough to Pratt to consider marriage to her. Pratt recalls not knowing the word gentile at that point, and not understanding why her boyfriend would not simply convert. Pratt felt like a *Protestant* when preparing to marry her Catholic fiancé and she puzzled over "the need for an intricate resolution between *them*"—i.e. her fiancé and a priest—about *her* form of birth control.[24]

In terms of the metanarrative then, Pratt's identity as a *married* person becomes a new identity scheme through which she attempts to ignore her other identifications, particularly—and quite self-contradictorily—her identity as a woman. She states that once married, "I was relieved to be myself; a non-religious, thinking person. I tried not to think of myself as *woman,* a reality that bulged outside the safe bounds of wife, a reality that had shaken and terrified me with two unplanned pregnancies."[25] In this early stage of her adult life Pratt thus experiences her multiple identities as relatively *dis*integrated. She feels them only situationally and only momentarily *in relation* to the divergent identities or actions of others. She does not have a sense of those multiple identities together as composing a whole. In addition, newly formed identities that became significant to her—such as her liberal and married identitities—become the means not for identity integration, but rather for cordoning off her sense of her other identities, *especially* her identity as a woman.

Pratt's deliberate fragmentation and *dis*integration of her identity as a woman begins to break down unexpectedly, however, in her first year as a graduate student. Four months pregnant with her second child, Pratt was, she recalls, so eager to avoid her identity as a young woman that she "put the width of the sidewalk" between herself and a woman seated at a table of feminist literature in front of the university library. She writes, "At the other edge of the sidewalk, I tried to separate myself from the new ideas about what it meant to be a woman. *I rushed away slowly* through the humid air weighted by my unborn second child, who sat like a four month-old rock in my stomach."[26] A few months later in her pregnancy, the woman from the literature table—named Elizabeth—became a classmate of Pratt's in a course on Shakespeare's historical plays; Elizabeth openly discusses patriarchal power in the plays, a contribution that was met with derision from other students.

Elizabeth then inadvertently creates a turning point in the metanarrative plot. Pratt describes an encounter with Elizabeth one night after class when Elizabeth tells Pratt—who was carrying her "enormous heavy belly" to her car—that Pratt was "brave to stay in school, unlike so many other married women with children" and "she wished [her] well."[27] The caring comment contrasted radically with those of the men in Pratt's department who had begun to joke about her pregnancy. The incidental encounter had a significant effect on Pratt. She writes, "[t]hat night I cried the ten miles home; she had spoken to me as *a woman,* and I'd been lonely, without knowing it; her speaking to me changed how I thought of myself and my life."[28] In terms of the metanarrative, the intrapsychic fragmentation by which Pratt had kept her identity as a woman marginal among her other multiple identities—her avoidance and contradictory inattention to it—suddenly failed. In this failed fragmentation, an intersection between her female identity scheme and her principle identity as a "wife" is (re)established when she is addressed *as a woman* by another woman. This sudden reintegration is the result of an unexpected social interaction, however, and so is not yet a conscious or voluntary discernment, although it might suggest that intense emotional reaction may be part and parcel of unanticipated identity reintegration.

As Pratt's gender identity is brought to her consciousness by Elizabeth's incidental address, Pratt's gender identity brings with it a lasting affect: the emotion of loneliness. Four years later in 1974, after

Pratt has moved with her husband and sons to a "market town" in the South, the feeling of loneliness is still with her.[29] The lasting sentiment is intensified by the misogynistic, racially charged, atmosphere of the community, which is dominated by the local military base. In this new town Pratt recalls "feeling for the first time in my life, I was living in a place where I was afraid because I was a *woman*."[30] Thus overarching political and social dynamics intensify Pratt's sense of gender subordination and her feeling of gendered loneliness. While this part of the South should have felt like home to Pratt, she instead felt constricted and alone. She writes, "I wanted to go some place where I could just be; I was homesick with nowhere to go."[31]

The place Pratt wished to go—the object of her longing—only came to Pratt's consciousness as a vague intermittent memory. It "seemed like a memory of childhood, though it was not a childish place. It was a place of mutuality, companionship, creativity, sensuousness, easiness in the body, curiosity in what new things might be making in the world, hope from that curiosity, safety, and love."[32] Apparently, in this longing-induced memory, Pratt recalls that the love and safety of her childhood was owed primarily to Laura Cates, the Black woman servant who cared for and was responsible for her. She recalled a moment (during what must have been graduate school) at a feminist consciousness-raising meeting in which she discussed sexuality and felt momentarily at home. Pratt remembers feeling alienation from her father as a child because she was a girl and not a boy. Moreover, Pratt recalled these recollections in relation to how her evenings with her women friends were currently being rationed by her husband. From this handful of recollections Pratt realizes that what she longed for was a "safe place" that is made real in a life of living and love with women.[33]

Pratt thus slowly comes to understand that her lonely wish is a wish for a safe place with women. She then seeks to "make a place like the memory" through feminist activism in the market town where she now lives. The action in subplot A thus intensifies as Pratt's liberal political leanings turn into active feminist organizing. At the metanarrative level, Pratt now associates in her mind the pursuit of a loving and "safe place" with women with the work of feminist political activism. Her two life projects—politics (A) and love (B) thus become linked in her mind such that Pratt has made a new intersection between them. However, as Pratt increases the intensity of her *political* work as an indirect way to forward her project of love, that project is still defined in heterosexual terms. Those terms are ultimately unsuited to the enduring desires that Pratt feels, but that she did not yet know how to name. I would suggest that Pratt could not name her desires because they did not fit the heterosexual narrative of committed love to which she was pledged. That narrative was the only script with which she seemed as yet familiar—or perhaps willing to embrace—for describing adult romantic love.[34] I would further suggest that because Pratt's integration of her life projects is intentional but partial and takes place on the basis of limited self-understanding, it is to some degree still circumstantial, and not yet the outcome of an active practice of selfcraft.

The change in Pratt's political life project means, however, that she engages much more in feminist organizing. Eventually Pratt falls in love with a woman she has met at a consciousness-raising meeting. Falling in love seems to have completed the connection for Pratt, allowing her to understand herself not simply as *a woman who feels safe in the company of other woman,* but as a *lesbian* who might also find romantic love among women.[35] At this time, Pratt also begins to have nightmares about her marriage and violence by her husband against her and her sons.[36] Without willing herself to do so, between 1969 and spring 1975 Pratt forms a new identity as a lesbian. This identity is formed in part through a combination of happenstance and sensitivity to the meaning and sources of her loneliness. Pratt's new lesbian identity draws together her projects of political resistance and committed love, and thus forms an intersection between them.

In 1975 as Pratt begins to add specific meanings, values, and practices to her new identity scheme as a lesbian, she feels no sense of social risk in doing so, in part because of her own sense of security and privilege. When Pratt comes out as a lesbian, she is surprised at the hostility of her husband and the betrayal of her mother, who sides with her husband in denying Pratt custody of her children. Pratt's children are soon moved out of state by their father. The shock of losing her children is a cruel one for Pratt. She writes, "I had learned that I could be either a lesbian or a mother of my children, either in the wilderness or on holy ground, but not both."[37] Pratt may have been *personally* able to integrate motherhood with her lesbian identity (chapter five). Yet, prevailing homophobia denied her that option, at at time when identities as mother and lesbian were socially constructed as mutually exclusive, and the boundary between them set and policed by the state.

The realization of society's refusal to allow Pratt to integrate her multiple identities as mother and lesbian created an important transition for Pratt. That transition drives Pratt to draw an increasingly close connection between her quest and struggle for love and her political project. At this point, she now understands the latter in terms of social justice, awakened in part by the loss of her children and her past social privilege. Having described the excruciating pain of losing her children, Pratt writes, "I became obsessed with justice: the shell of my privilege was broken, the shell that had given me shape in the world. . . . I was astonished at the pain; the extent of my surprise revealed to me the degree of my protection."[38] Between 1976 and 1979 Pratt worked to build for herself a "safe place" among women through feminist activism. As she did so, however, Pratt found that her need for belonging in that feminist sphere was so great that she initially turned a blind eye to its routine exclusions. She did not consider why she was "hesitant to mention [her] lesbian identity except to a few trusted women."[39] In Pratt's urgent need to belong she did not look at what silences separated her from other women, or to ask what feminism had asked *those other women* to deny in the name of politics *for women*.[40]

By 1979, however, Pratt understood that she was not "seeking liberation as my particular, complex self"—but instead denying aspects of herself in exchange for a secure sense of group belonging and identity.[41] Rather than permit the self-fragmentation that the feminist movement enforced, however, Pratt withdrew from feminist work. While this stopped the apparent action in political subplot B, in terms of the metanarrative of self-integration it was an advance because it marked Pratt's new refusal to fragment her lately formed lesbian identity for the sake of belonging to the group of feminist women. Instead Pratt began to make a "safe place" for herself in which she pursued her poetry, teaching, independent study, and the ongoing search for committed love. Toward the end of 1979, she wrote, "I did not have my children, but I had these [three] rooms, a job, a lover, work I was making. I thought I had the beginning of a place for myself."[42]

While the three practices of inventory, discernment, and revisionary living can be retrospectively seen in Pratt's changing life, they only become clearly identifiable as consciously pursued goals for Pratt in November 1979. At a midday anti-Klan rally in Greensboro on November 5, 1979, Klansmen killed five labor organizers including four white men (two of whom were Jewish) and a Black woman. Klansmen justified that act as protecting a white Klanswoman. Nancy Matthews, a Klansman's wife, expressed bewilderment, stating, "I knew he was a Klan member, but I don't know what he did when he left home. I was surprised and shocked. . . ." Aside from its horror, Matthews's words created a sudden identity contradiction for Pratt. She writes, "I identify with the demonstrators; I am on their side: I've felt that danger. Yet in what way am I any different from this woman? Am I not surprised and shocked that this could happen? Do I have any notion, any, of what white men have been doing outside home, outside the circle of my limited white experience?"[43]

In response, Pratt does exactly what the woman in Anzaldúa's allegory of selfcraft does: she digs. Pratt excavated the buried bones of her Southern hometown and her own family. She read Black history of the area which described white lynchings and violence. She asked her mother about the past, and her mother recounted local Klan activity but denied family involvement. Yet Pratt then read family documents and letters that revealed slave ownership on both sides of her family. She returned to her home county archives and read county legal transcripts of post–Civil War proceedings in which Blacks described their torture by white men. She unearthed the connection between racial violence against Blacks and the violence perpetrated against her by the white men who denied her life with her children. She thought of the relevance of the buried bones of racial subordination to *her* current privilege of teaching at a Historically Black College with a degree from a segregated university. As Pratt conducted this inventory, she reviewed her own history, saw that she herself had suffered subordination and then sought to rebuild her life of belonging among women without seeing how that belonging rested on the subordination, past and present, of others.

Discerning the values drawn from this inventory did not lead Pratt to easy, new identifications or (initially at least) back to her abandoned political project. Rather she says, "I did not feel that my new understanding simply moved me into a place where I joined others to struggle *with* them against common injustices. . . . what my expanded understanding meant was that I felt in a struggle with myself, *against* myself." In her words, "[t]his breaking through did not feel like liberation but like destruction."[44] In this development, Pratt began differentiating between what she had been taught and what she will accept, and she discerns the personal and political significance of the overlapping social histories she has now inventoried. Because of her sexuality and her gender, white men of her own culture had subordinated Pratt. Having now inventoried her region's history, Pratt discerns from what she has unearthed a truth she will accept: that not only have white men of her culture subordinated people of color and of the Jewish faith, but in that subordination women like herself had engaged in blind complicity, accepting the privileges that white subordination of Blacks had brought them.

Based on her excavated inventories and discernments, Pratt creates in her mind an intersection between her experience of subordination as a lesbian and of the subordination of Jews and people of color. While *her* experience is not identical to theirs, she nonetheless begins to see a "deep connection" between her subordination and that of others who are *un*like her.[45] At the metanarrative level, *this intersection in Pratt's mind becomes the basis for her identification with those who are different from herself in race and religion.*

In unearthing the relationship among her different identities and the identities of others, Pratt recognizes that she is both privileged and subordinated in ways that reveal interconnections among various divided social groups. As Pratt discusses at length, it is exactly those commonalities that are obscured in discourses regarding racial, ethnic, religious, sexual, and gender subordination in white Southern culture.[46] In this sense, Pratt's practice of discernment became a method for revising intrapsychic intersections and fragmentations among her identities that she had inherited from social and political life. These linkages allow her to recognize unacknowledged similarities among divided groups upon which to cultivate a potential sense of common political cause with others despite such social divides.

Although the processes of active inventory and discernment allowed Pratt to recognize the intersecting histories and experiences between herself and other subordinated peoples, *acting* upon that recognition was often difficult. Thinking differently and *doing* differently are not the same thing, and Pratt notes that, at times, various fears prevented her from acting on her newly integrated self-understanding in what I am calling the selfcraft of revisionary living. Based on Pratt's self-description, I would suggest that there are three common obstacles to self-integration through the craft of revisionary living. These obstacles include, 1) the fear of letting go of familiar ways, 2) the fear of lost belonging, and 3) and neglect of the positive elements that exist in the flawed traditions that have shaped us.

Pratt's description of her fear-related stumbling blocks to revisionary living echo Anzaldúa's allegorical imagery of stripping away imposed baggage and letting go of all notions of the safe and familiar in order to be able to proceed in the selfcraft of revisionary living. The first fearful obstacle to selfcraft I will call *the fear of a lost positive self.* Pratt writes, "[a]s I try to strip away the layers of deceit that I have been taught, it is hard not to be afraid that these are like wrappings of a shroud" beneath which there is only "a disintegrating, rotting *nothing*: that the values that I have at my core, from my culture, will only be those of negativity, exclusion, fear, death."[47] Perhaps at the heart of the first fear is a contradiction between positive and negative images of oneself that may arise as part of self-integrative practices. If, for example, a subject's multiple identities include positions of *both* privilege and subordination, it may be painful to come to understand oneself either as a subordinated person—if one has always emphasized one's privilege—or as a member of a subordinat*ing* group that has been active or complicit in the oppression of others.

In Pratt's case, this fear of loss is associated with an identity contradiction. That contradiction involves being *at once* an oppressor and a victim of oppression, a clash that emerges from her inventory of the wrongs committed by her Southern white ethnic culture, and her simultaneous hope of holding onto something positive in that Southern culture with which she is also identified. Rather than deny this intense contradiction, Pratt grapples with it, surveying and accepting the losses and gains the contradiction entails for her revised approach to living. She states, as a woman of white and religious privilege, her search to free herself in a "complex way" is to "experience this change [of revised action and outlook] *as loss*." This is so "[b]ecause it is: the old lies, and the ways of living, habitual, familiar, comfortable, fitting us like our skin were *ours*" and as Pratt writes, the loss of that familiarity and its protections—real or illusory—is frightening in its upheaval and may inhibit some from acting upon their transformed thinking.[48]

In addition to this first fear/obstacle to the selfcraft of revisionary living is a second fear, that abandoning "old lies" and familiar ways will force us to give up the belongings upon which our identities have traditionally been based, or seem to be based. This might be called a *fear of lost belonging*. Pratt expresses this second obstacle/fear as the fear that she will be ostracized by friends, loved ones, and others for whom the "old lies" still hold sway, and who regard her rejection of those lies as a betrayal of the group and/or themselves. Pratt, for example, describes a letter from her mother in which her mother chastises her for taking part in the anniversary march on Washington, stating "[s]ome day you will understand that what you are doing is wrong."[49] The threat—real or imagined—of denied belonging can be a damaging obstacle to integrative selfcraft. The rigid adherence of loved ones or group members to outlooks rejected by selfcrafters can discourage those engaged in selfcraft, and potentially cause them to abandon their efforts at revisionary living.

In such cases, social rejection is a tool for disciplining selfcrafters to the status quo and to renewed self-fragmentation. This disciplining presents a new contradiction to the would-be self-maker: a contradiction between being oneself and retaining group belonging.

As discussed at length in chapter five, cultivating healthy forms of ambivalence toward belonging and being-in-the-moment is a way of holding the conflict between being and belonging together in creative tension. This creative tension can make space for differences of conviction and action within social groups and in interpersonal relationships. Pratt describes having gone home earlier to meet her mother. Pratt writes that her mother "welcomed me at home with the woman who, as a lesbian, as a Jew, as my lover, I feared she might treat as an enemy, but she made a place for us, fed us in the kitchen, family not company.... We talked of none of our differences that day."[50]

Here, and as discussed in chapter five, ambiguity and ambivalence in expressing differences can facilitate belonging and be instrumental in reconciling—at least momentarily—the contradictions between Pratt's sexual identity and her personal identity as her mother's daughter. While in some instances, persistence in integrative selfcraft may result in ostracism or distancing, in many other cases, the fear of rejection by beloved individuals and communities is not as significant in reality as it is a frightening prospect. Unexpected acceptance may occur when others are more open to difference than we expect them to be, or when acts of self-integration present others with a chance to rethink and revise their own beliefs and practices in a manner welcome to them.

In addition to the fears that may block integrative selfcraft, there is also a tendency to neglect the positive elements that may exist in our flawed traditions and rejected identities. In her 1984 essay, "Identity: Blood Skin Heart," Pratt attempts to overcome this neglect by completing a new inventory. She discerns that her white ethnic culture has also contributed to her chosen life projects of political resistance and committed lesbian love. In this round of selfcraft, Pratt discovers the history of Southern white *resistance* to racism and religious intolerance. She acknowledges and embraces the Pratt family's reputation for impeccable manners, and treasures her mother's tenacity in loving her family. She digs up and identifies herself with the history of masculine women and their femme lovers who found romantic love in the South against the risks of ostracism and state violence.[51] For Pratt, success in the craft of revisionary living required not only overcoming fear of the lost familiar, and the fear of lost belonging, but also making a positive effort to locate and celebrate aspects of her heritage culture that have been positive forces for love and resistance in the world.

In terms of the subplots of love and politics, Pratt's conscious engagement of self-integration reshapes both of her projects of political engagement and committed love. Pratt's political project expands beyond feminism and patriarchy to include concern with anti-Semitism and the subordination of racial and ethnic minorities. Her quest for committed love increasingly intersects with her political project as she sees the love she finds among Jewish women in the context of her resistance to anti-Semitism. Her social role identities as poet, teacher, writer, and activist are interwoven with her social identities as a white, lesbian Southerner. Perhaps most importantly, Pratt appears to have come to identify her political life with selfcraft itself. In this new interconnection, selfcraft comes to be considered a means of political resistance and intervention. Selfcraft thus becomes a way for Pratt to remake herself in the process and for the purpose of resisting subordination.[52]

In addition, selfcraft becomes a way for Pratt to regain and retain the "self-respect" that had been temporarily lost once she came to understand the harm that had been done previously by herself or in her name. Achieving self-respect through selfcraft becomes a positive motivation for revisionary living. As she puts it, it is by "find[ing] new ways to be *in* the world, [that] those very actions are a way of creating a positive self."[53] By 1983/4, the rapidity and frequency with which Pratt can and does conduct a personal inventory, engage in the craft of discernment, and integrate her findings into revised living had increased dramatically. For example, Pratt discusses quickly reexamining and modifying her understanding of local Native American cultures when her assumptions are questioned by a Native American woman. Likewise, she describes rethinking the anti-Arab postures subsumed in her over-simplified notions of anti-Semitism, when her Jewish lover brings her biases to her attention.

By the time she writes the opening pages of "Identity: Blood Skin Heart," Pratt is critically self-reflective, and constantly attuned to how her identifications are perceived and also place her in social relations of both unwanted subordination and unwanted privilege.[54] By this point, overt challenges and questioning are unnecessary for Pratt to initiate a new round of selfcraft. A month before completing her essay, Pratt encounters Korean shopkeepers who become excited by her bouquet of forsythia, seeing it as a plant from their native lands. Pratt lets the small interaction bring to her attention her Western assumptions, her stereotypical notions of Eastern cultures, of immigration and capitalism, and the narrowness of our cultural claims to the natural beauty of the earth.

I would suggest that in this mature stage of Pratt's selfcraft, she has entered an integrative mode of *continually* revised living. She has, in Anzaldúa's words, surrendered "all notions of safety and the familiar" that were once lent to her by privileged identities. For Pratt, the integration of her multiple identities has become a continual process of critique and self-remaking in which she—again in Anzaldúa's words—"makes herself vulnerable to foreign ways of seeing and thinking" and is willing to bear, and consider seriously, the criticism of those who are unlike herself, and to value the implications of the differences that others represent.[55] This continual revision does not mean the total integration of Pratt's psyche. She still feels limits to her wholeness imposed by the social denial of herself and others through enduring hierarchies and conflict. In the closing pages of *S/He* she writes, "I thought I would go mad when my children were taken. I thought they would die without me and I without them. Where was the land where they could be with me, where women, man, and children were no one's possession?"[56] Despite her extensive selfcraft, Pratt still expresses feeling torn within by social relations in which her identity as a mother and as a lesbian are not fully accepted.[57]

Part II: *The Philosophical Basis of Integrative Selfcraft; Selves that Knead, or the "Who" of Integrative Selfcraft*

If integration of multiple identities is accomplished through the practices of inventory, discernment, and revisionary living, what is the source of the motivation and agency for engaging in selfcraft? Throughout this book I have defined subjectivity as a loose configuration of identity schemes, habits, and other self-constructs. To define the self in this way is to say that there is no particular identity or other aspect of a person's subjectivity that can be named as central to the self a priori—that is prior to what is stated by that person himself or herself. There is no telling in advance which identities or partial identities will be internalized by a given individual or how significant particular identities will become in a given individual's life over time. Thus, the optional task of self-integration, *if* it is undertaken at all, is not undertaken by a presumptive central identity. Nor is selfcraft undertaken by an "Arch-Ego" or by some other element that is prelinguistic, or otherwise independent of the multiple identities within subjectivity. Rather, as discussed at length just below, self-integration is driven by the claims of some subset of multiple identities.

Yet, this point may not be immediately clear given my characterization of personal identity in chapter four in terms of William James's concept of "judging-Thought." While the concept of "judging-Thought" theorized by James and central to the theory of multiple identities that I have presented here may *seem* to constitute a substantive, overarching vantage point, it does not. Rather, judging-Thought as the locus of cognitive, affective, and motivational function is simply—but importantly—*only* the realized *capacity* for thought-in-the-moment. As such, judging-Thought has no necessary content or shape. Its *only* content is the content that is given to it moment to moment by the identity schemes and other self-constructs that become momentarily salient as frameworks for thought and action in a given instant.[58] Because human agency is commonly defined as the capacity to choose, and because that capacity to choose is rooted in judging-Thought's capacity for thought-in-the-moment, my constructivist account of multiple identities likewise presupposes that human beings have the capacity for agency. Moreover, I make this presupposition in the same manner that other poststructuralist accounts of the self—especially that in Michel Foucault's later works—have done.[59]

Thus, as Amélie Oksenberg Rorty has explained—and as was briefly noted in chapter four—subjects that undertake projects of self-integration do so only through "some *relatively* central set of his [or her] habits" and/or some subset of his or her multiple identities.[60] That subset of subjectivity—whatever collection of identity schemes and habits it ultimately happens to be—becomes only a "claimant" to centrality in the self. This claim to centrality is contestable and may give way to other claims over time. For example, consider a man who has lived as a heterosexual, married husband and father, and who in middle age comes to understand and identify himself as gay and begins to live as a single gay man. Such a man has undergone a significant shift in the identities that he recognizes as central to himself. In that adjustment, his socialized heterosexual identity scheme and his previously marginalized homosexual identity scheme shift places in their relative centrality to the self, and in their influence on his daily thoughts and actions—including their place in any self-integrative projects that he may have heretofore undertaken.

Such claims to identity centrality are—in their basic form—based on an assertion by or about a designated element or elements of the self that desire, or are desired from one identity-scheme perspective or another, to perform what Rorty calls the legitimized governing functions of the self. It is by those self-legitimized governing functions that the self intends to organize and try to shape how it lives its own multiplicity of identities. I would contend that because there is no identity-independent standpoint or a priori central aspect to the self that "chooses" which elements claim centrality of governing function, the shape that such continuity claims take, and the identity schemes from which those claims are made over time, are shaped by socialization combined with the way in which subjects grapple with their identity contradictions.

Critics may object that a socially constructed subject cannot, by definition, "choose" self-governing endorsements that are "its own" because its choices are always conditioned by language-mediated dynamics that lie beyond the subject's control. To attribute "choice" to an entirely socially constructed subjectivity, such critics might argue, would be to resurrect under a different guise the "volunteerist" notion of the self that is both centered and animated by a pre-linguistic "I." In response, I would grant that no act of agency—including an assertion of identity centrality or any establishment of guiding endorsements—could occur outside the ongoing processes of social construction. On the contrary, as the example of Minnie Bruce Pratt's self-integration and the notion of inventory itself indicate, attending to the detailed processes of social construction that form one's multiple identities is a vital part of self-integration.

However, *it does not follow* that a multiple, decentered, and constructed subject is wholly without any capacity for agency or will, however conditioned by social processes that capacity may be. With his herdsman metaphor (discussed in chapter four), William James establishes how judging-Thought-in-the-moment accounts at once for a continuing sense of personal identity, the *capacity* for cognitive, affective, and motivational function, as well as the multiplicity of the self. Yet, there is nothing for the herdsman as successive thought-in-the-moment to do in the absence of an inherited, socially constructed herd of self-constructs which comprise the necessary basis of the herdsman's activity *and being* as a herder. On this framework, agency exists as an inborn cognitive capacity, which cannot be expressed independently of the social construction of the multiplicity of the subject. Thus agency and the socially constructed quality of the subject are mutually intertwined.

Likewise, *it does not follow* that whatever the subject claims as "her own" in an act of agency may not be reasonably understood and accepted as willfully belonging to her—*even if* the source of that "owned" aspect clearly lies beyond the self. This is what William James means, I believe, with his brief reference to a distinction between herd-brand and self-brand. All herd-branded elements are part of our diverse subjectivities, but the self-brand may represent *an act of special claiming* by which subjects—or some subset of self-constructs within subjects—privilege some of the many I's within subjectivity.[61] Metaphorically, whatever calf the herdswoman claims as her own and gives her self-brand should be regarded as belonging to her *by her act of special claim,* even if the herd and calf itself come to her only as social inheritance.

Critical theorist and psychologist Joel Whitebook put this dimension of agency well in an essay on autonomy and decentered subjectivity when he wrote, "while the exegete [who comes to be and to interpret himself through language] cannot be entirely free of its effects, neither can he be completely absorbed by the illogical kingdom he charts . . . while the ego may no longer be master in its own house, it hasn't been evicted either."[62] As agents with multiple identities everyone has the capacity for selfcraft by which they can try to shape how their multiplicity influences their thoughts and action. But whether or not they will utilize that capacity is a question that individuals must answer for themselves.

The Needs of Narrativity: Narrative Self-Unity as Significant but Insufficient

While some critics may regard me as overestimating the capacity of decentered, socially constructed subjects to integrate themselves through selfcraft, others may object that something more substantive is needed to integrate a diverse subjectivity than the two elements I have proposed in this book: namely, the five-part self-system of decentered subjectivity (chapter two) and the ever-provisional results of personal selfcraft. Many scholarly works have been written since the mid-twentieth century on what may establish the unity of the subject as it is now understood after the linguistic turn in philosophy.[63] Philosophers and social theorists have advocated a variety of elements that they consider necessary for the socially constructed subject to be a coherent whole with a first person sense of continuity, including, among others, memory, commitment to future selves, a pre-linguistic central self, a sense of one's authentic self, and unifying self-narrative. Of these options, I will focus on narrative unity because it has been so widely endorsed by thinkers including Seyla Benhabib, Paul Ricouer, Anthony Giddens, Michael Sandel and (as discussed in chapter five), Charles Taylor and Alasdair MacIntyre.[64]

Despite its popularity however, narrative self-unity is at once helpful but also significantly limited in its capacity to unify a decentered and multiple subject. This is so for two reasons. First, theories of narrative unity generally privilege logical and consistent self-narratives as necessary to unify the self. For example, Alasdair MacIntyre argues that the unity of a human life is realized through all-encompassing life narratives that reach the standard of "intelligibility." In his intelligibility standard, actions in human life must make intelligible sense *against their immediate contexts.* A person with a unified life must be able to give to others an "intelligible account" of their actions whenever they are asked for one.[65] Yet, the possibility that a subject can offer a coherent self-narrative at a given time does not necessarily indicate that he or she has achieved a significant level of integration and unity.

Yet, the reading of *Casablanca* in chapter five, the discussion of akrasia and self-deception in chapter four, and the story of Pratt above all suggest, the intelligibility of self-narratives does not always reflect significant integration of the self. In *Casablanca,* for example, Renault asks Rick his reasons for coming to Casablanca. Rick famously and ironically answers, "My health. I came to Casablanca for the waters." Renault skeptically responds, "The waters? What waters? We're in the desert." To which Rick replies deadpan, "I was misinformed."[66] While MacIntyre might contend that Rick's initial answer is unintelligible given the context, Rick's follow-up makes his account of himself "intelligible" if implausible. Anyone can act on misinformation, and it might be argued that immigrants act on ungrounded expectations quite often. Despite its intelligibility, however, Rick's answer is an evasion through which he escapes revealing his motives to Renault. His self-narrative cloaks not only his actual motives, but the pain and fragmentation in his psyche produced by his real reasons for flight. This exchange indicates that intelligible self-narration need not have a basis in self-integration or unity. Rather, intelligible self-narrative may also facilitate and/or conceal ongoing fragmentation, such as that sustained by Rick in the aftermath of losing Ilsa in Paris.

Not only can "intelligible" self-narrative conceal self-fragmentation, self-narration also seems to have little capacity to heal such fragmentation. Had Rick given the more straightforward reply that he left the Paris to escape the German occupation, his answer—although intelligible self-narrative—could still be facilitating deep fragmentation, not self-integration and self-unity. Moreover, because self-fragmentation itself sometimes can be cogently narrated, even an honest and "intelligible" reply by Rick would not necessarily be enough to heal Rick's inner fragmentation. He might have simply told Renault that he lost the woman he loves in Paris, came to Casablanca to start again, and has not been the same since. Saying this would not likely change the fact. Hence, accuracy in self-narrative does not appear to give narrative alone the power to mend self-fragmentation. I have proposed, instead, that such mending can only take place when new internal intersections are built. Selfcraft is one means by which that self-(re)construction can take place.

Not only may narrative practices alone fail to integrate the self, self-narrative can also play an ambivalent role in all three integrative practices of selfcraft. Evidence that self-narrative can *produce* self-fragmentation as much as self-integration and unity, for example, can be found in Pratt's "Identity" essay. In her essay, it is clear that Pratt was able to give an intelligible account of her actions while she was still significantly fragmented. For example, asked why she came to feminist organizing around 1974, Pratt could plausibly reply that she had an interest in women's subordination. This is accurate, for Pratt's feminist organizing in 1974 is a central element in the political subplot of her life (subplot A). Yet, her engagement in politics is not solely driven by the political subplot as is suggested by her self-narrative at the time of action. Rather her politics in 1974 are also driven by vague unease and difficulties in love (subplot B). That uneasiness was triggered by an incidental event that took place years before in 1969, and the meaning of that unease will not become fully understood until later in 1975. Thus, Pratt's self-narrative regarding her motivation for increased political work in 1974, while coherent and intelligible, as a self-narration works to hide from herself and others the inner fragmentation of her nascent lesbian sexual identity from her heterosexual life.[67] In this case, self-fragmentation—involving unrecognized, unavowed, and unavowable desire in her project of finding committed love—plays out in Pratt's political project under a fragmentation-preserving but intelligible self-narrative.[68] Had Pratt not fallen in love with a fellow feminist organizer by chance, her sexual fragmentation might have gone on indefinitely, *sustained*—not corrected—by its justificatory self-narrative.

The second reason that self-narratives are potentially helpful but nonetheless inadequate for integrating a decentered and multiple subject, is that logically intelligible self-narratives generally cannot contain the sheer variety, *much less the contradictions,* among the self-constructs that are common parts of decentered and multiple subjectivity. Recall also that decentered and multiple subjectivity can include not only multiple identities, but also identity fragments, isolated beliefs, habits, and trait tendencies that can contradict and yet become salient in different contexts (chapter two). Studies show, for example, that most people have both extroverted and introverted self-constructs within their subjectivities.[69] In a research setting, it is possible to circumstantially cue one set of self-constructs (e.g. using a short reading or a suggestive questionnaire) into becoming momentarily salient as the frame of reference for thought and action (see also chapter two). Making extroverted constructs salient would also bring forward self-descriptive narratives that are related to—i.e. intersect with—the extroverted self-construct (as well as behaviors and habits of perception).[70] This response would leave the contradictory introverted self-construct(s) aside because it is not salient. Thus, the intelligible self-narrative that an individual would tell of him or herself *at that moment* would thus reflect his or her salient extroverted self-constructs.[71] But were the introverted self-constructs activated an opposite self-narrative would likely emerge. If self-narrations can vary widely based on different salient self-constructs, logically such narratives alone cannot fully integrate one's subjectivity.

In support of this point, evidence suggests that our multiple identities and self-constructs can and often do incorporate equally intelligible but potentially contradictory identity schemes and related self-narratives. For example in his research into the cultural shaping of self and identity among young adults in south Morocco, Gary Gregg encountered numerous identity contradictions that are part of the fabric of various individual's identities—so much so that Gregg defines identity as "a system of organized contradiction."[72] For example, in one set of interviews with Rachida, a Moroccan schoolteacher living in a rural village, Gregg finds that Rachida maintains two contradictory gender schemes—each is a frame of reference made salient alternately by Gregg's interview questions. He writes of Rachida, "on the one hand, she presents herself as an autonomous woman in traditional male terms and identifies with her grandfather, a noted community religious leader.... [but then] on the other hand, she presents herself as a proper/modest woman in traditional female terms, which she associates with her mother, grandmother, and . . . the Quranic *sura al ruhaman*."[73]

Describing herself as a feminist, Rachida relates stories of her own education, her increasing ambitions, her conviction about the equality of women, and her fights with male family members in which she warns, "do whatever you want, you won't rule me!" But, asked if there was "ever a time [she] thought men had the right to control women," Rachida answered, "Yes, now. It's necessary for men to have authority over women . . . because if he leaves the woman with no one to rule over her, she will do whatever she wants."[74] These are not momentary contradictions but patterns of thought and speech that repeat throughout the course of many hours of Gregg's interviews with Rachida. Such dynamics of self-narrative diversity and inconsistency may be dismissed by philosophers as personal failures of wantonness or self-misunderstanding. But they are much better explained by understanding subjectivity as a more or less integrated self-system of embodied cognitive, affective, motivational, and habitual capacities in which constituent parts of subjectivity can be independently and variably accessible to judging-Thought. Rachida exhibits two contradictory gender identity schemes, each of which has been a guiding principle in different aspects of her life.[75]

Thus, in contrast to what MacIntyre and others argued, intelligible self-narratives do not always integrate the self and may instead at times reveal, or conceal, its deep diversity and inner contradiction. While there is no doubt that self-narratives can play an important role in self-understanding and expression, including the formation and maintenance of endorsements, a logically consistent self-narrative alone is not sufficient to either explain or constitute the integration, cohesion, or wholeness of a complex, diverse, decentered, and multiple subject.[76]

These two limitations to self-narrative as a self-integrating factor are significant. In addition, however, P. E. Digeser has persuasively argued with regard to selfcraft in liberal democracy, that there are at least four major problems with insisting on the narrative unity of the self as philosophers, especially communitarians Charles Taylor and Alasdair MacIntyre, have advocated. These four problems with narrative unity stem from its intense drive and concern with constituting one's life so that it "stands as a whole" in a coherent story from birth to death.[77] Digeser argues first that this intense drive to narrative and "a well-crafted unity over time" can foster the kind of self-centeredness that communitarians deplore in contemporary societies.[78] Second, the insistence on narrative unity can "stultify growth and change . . . [and] may make us less willing to do anything that pushes against or challenges our current narrative identity. After a certain point we may become less willing to disturb the narrative we have constructed. . . . [in ways that] may ultimately stifle creativity, growth, and maturity."[79] In Minnie Bruce Pratt's case, for example, had Pratt prioritized consistency with her narrative identity as a heterosexual married woman, she may have forever foreclosed the possibility of living her life in a way that fit and satisfied her deeper desires and abilities. Narrative unity would have precluded her potential growth toward her life's work and growth toward the marriage of the heart with transman, activist, and writer Leslie Feinberg that now truly suits her.[80]

Digeser also points out a related third cost: "that the valorization of [narrative] unity may lead us to reject others who move away from or do things that fail to fit in their own life stories as we understand them."[81] This may be especially true when individuals come to depend upon the narratives of others to stabilize their own self-narrative. For example, Pratt's mother accepts her daughter Minnie and her lesbian lover one afternoon in her home, only to later send Pratt a bitter letter of rejection when her daughter's politics seem to depart too far from her own. As Digeser states, the problem with championing narrative identity is that "change becomes so much harder to accommodate and accept."[82]

The fourth danger, from Digeser's perspective, is that the insistence on coherent narrative identity "may intensify self-loathing" whenever a person cannot construct the kind of happily consistent self-narrative in which all negative elements are ultimately redeemed. While this danger is genuine when the self-loathing is unalloyed, I would argue that Digeser is mistaken in implying that such self-loathing may not be productive. Releasing the requirement for narrative unity opens the possibility for self-loathing to become a temporary stage of self-integration, or one element in a productive inner-tension from which individuals draw strength for revisionary living. For example, early in her "Identity" essay Pratt describes wishing for and achieving a degree of belonging in the predominantly Black part of Washington D.C. in which she lives. That belonging, however, is jarred and undone in various moments by the intonations of racial subordination that mark her interactions with Mr. Boone, the Black janitor in her building who hails from the Yemassee region of South Carolina.

Pratt writes, "When we meet in the hall . . . even though I may have just heard him speaking in his own voice to another man, he 'yes ma'am's' me in a sing-song: I hear my voice replying in the horrid cheerful accents of a white lady: *and I hate my white womanhood* that drags between us the long-bitter history of our region."[83] In Pratt's relation to Mr. Boone, her white womanhood, her own flesh and blood, evoke self-loathing, and the history of Southern racial conflict that cannot be redeemed. Pratt is thus caught in a contradiction produced by unfinished social change and failed social justice. To allow Mr. Boone to set the tone for their interaction is to acknowledge his humanity in a way long denied by racism. To ask him to spare *her* sensibilities by adopting a different mode of address would only be to employ and reassert the racial privileges that Pratt rejects. Thus, her best—because it is the most ambiguous—option is to bear herself the daily pain and ambivalence of this artifact of racial hierarchy and to feel a periodic self-loathing for how her own white embodiment evokes a racist reality for Mr. Boone.

Yet, Pratt's lived acknowledgment of this unredeemable self-loathing is balanced by the drive it generates in her *to reject the repetition* of the South's racist history. Pratt breaks with her culture's view by believing, "In this *world* you aren't the superior race or culture and never were, whatever you were raised to think."[84] While Pratt cannot redeem the loathsome past of racial hatred through her self-narrative, especially when she is thrust involuntarily into a position of racial privilege, she nevertheless can use that loathing by juxtaposing and binding it to its inverse—the drive for love and friendship—as ongoing motivation for taking "responsibility to struggle against injustice."[85] From the tension between her self-hateful experience and her loving hopes, Pratt works to dismantle social hierarchies produced by "blood or pain"[86] and to find methods to bring conflicting peoples together in cooperation and conversation in ways that "will lead to our friendship."[87]

In terms of narrative unity however, Pratt's conscious, routine performance of the despised racialized script with Mr. Boone is at odds with her devotion to racial equality. A logically coherent life-narrative that is intelligible in its context cannot sensibly claim resigned and reluctant performance of racial superiority *as lived resistance* to that racial superiority. Nevertheless, Pratt's capitulation to the unavoidably loathsome results of her white embodiment makes sense as different parts—and diverse ambivalence-ridden moments—of her work toward a life project of political resistance. For Pratt, such self-loathsome moments trigger and reanimate all that is loving, friendly, and self-redemptive in her subjectivity. Both love and loathing become intertwined in Pratt's integrative self-awareness and integrative selfcraft. P. E. Digeser is correct therefore, that the insistence on narrative self-unity can lead either to intensified *categorical* self-loathing or to an unjustifiable self-redemption. Either of these will diminish and fail to account for the complexity of multiple identity formation and potential for change, especially in the contexts of social and political conflict. Nonetheless, *limited* self-loathing may, as it did in Pratt's case, contribute to productive selfcraft and politics based on love and friendship.

With Digeser then, I would contend that while self-narrative may have a significant role to play in facilitating self-understanding, selfcraft, and self-integration, insistence on narrative self-unity has limitations and problems that make it both inadequate and potentially destructive as a means to integrate the self. Pratt does, after all, tell her story of self-integration *as a story*. But Pratt's self-narrative is a story that is narratively "flawed" throughout by contradictions, gaps, inconsistencies, and other flaws that nonetheless accurately reflect her arduous, but successful, work toward the self-integration of her multiple identities. I contend that conventionally and logically consistent self-narrative is generally too limited to convey the complexity of self-transformation and cohesion of multiple identities.

Moreover, Pratt's narrative stands as evidence against Alasdair MacIntyre's claim that a life narrative of an all-encompassing birth-to-death sort offers what one of MacIntyre's interpreters called "a stay of confusion"—a stay that provides the ultimate means for resisting the fragmentation of the self by societal forces.[88] For over 29 years Pratt is unable to name and honor her own interpersonal needs and desires because, I would argue, they did not fit the heterosexual and gender-binary-dominated narrative within which Pratt had attempted to understand and order her social life. Thus, the social forces and discourses that subordinate sexual minorities produced Pratt's painful sense of self-fragmentation—i.e. her lonely *dis*integration prior to 1975. Against MacIntyre's assertion that narrative can repair such socially induced fragmentation in the self, Pratt's case suggests that sometimes the attempt to live a consistent birth-to-death life narrative can reproduce internalized societal fragmentation, and thereby help to reproduce heteronormative, and transphobic social divides. Only by locating and beginning to *honor* the incongruent and unnarratable in herself does Pratt slowly become able to integrate herself, despite the enduring societal fragmentation and conflict that she experiences.

On this basis, I would agree with Digeser's general argument that insistence on narrative unity "rules out different ways of conceiving oneself in time and hence closes down other worthwhile human experiences and possibilities."[89] Given the political and personal ramifications of such a problem, it is important to find alternative *non-narrative-dependent* ways to link incongruent parts of our multiple identities—identities that may never fully fit within a single logical narrative or collection of mutually consistent narratives. Toward such an alternative, I would contend that the three practices of *selfcraft*—which incorporates processes of selective identification discussed in chapters two and five—combined with the concept of integrative *life projects* is a fluid framework of self-integration that can accommodate contradiction, ambivalence, and change to a much greater degree than narrative unity. Pratt's autobiographical writings illustrate that life projects—as cumulative non-linear movement toward valued life objectives—allows self-integration to vary in degree and in levels of intentionality over time and to proceed in fits and starts in which not every action will have a consistent, positive, or direct connection to conscious selfcraft, or one's life projects.

The Limitations on Selfcraft

While selfcraft can allow individuals to shape the intersections among their multiple identities and to manage and direct the influence of their own multiplicity of identity schemes, habits, and other self-constructs, there are limits to how far we can consciously control identity salience. In part, this is because selfcraft—when taken as a whole—is an attempt to alter the relative *accessibility* of particular identity schemes and habits within decentered subjectivity. As discussed in Social Identity Theory (chapter two), all identities and other self-constructs within subjectivity are *available* to become salient in various contexts. However, because social cues and perceiver readiness also shape salience, not all identity schemes are equally *accessible*—that is, equally easy to access—and therefore likely to become activated contextually.

Relative levels of accessibility for different identity schemes vary by three factors: 1) the subject's level of identification with a scheme, 2) how often an identity scheme is salient, and 3) how recently an identity scheme was salient (see chapter two for further discussion). Identity schemes and other self-constructs that are not often salient can become relatively inaccessible even though they remain a part of subjectivity. For example, in chapter two I discussed the example of Japanese American anthropologist Dorrine Kondo who comes to have difficulty remembering what it would be like to think and feel as an American scholar when her identities as an ethnic American and Western scholar become increasingly inaccessible compared to her Japanese ethnic identity, which is constantly salient as she lives in Japan. This shift took place gradually and without Kondo noticing until one day when catching her own reflection in a shop window somehow suddenly "re-minds" Kondo of the identities that have become inaccessible to her. By returning to the U.S. briefly, Kondo is able to increase the accessibility of her American and academic identity schemes by immersing herself in contexts in which both are frequently salient.[90]

It is difficult to say what exactly it was about seeing her own watery image in the shop window that made salient for Kondo an awareness of her little used identity schemes. One significant upshot of this example however, is that if Kondo had *intended* to assimilate into Japanese culture and relinquish all identification as an American and a Western scholar, her success in that project would have been imperfect. Moreover her failures in that project would have been unpredictable. The chance lighting of a windowpane, or the turn of phrase by a passing tourist may be enough to make salient materials that have come to lie deep into the mind's labyrinth of intersecting memories and associations. The instantaneous remembrance-interpretations that produce salience are likely to be things that we cannot ever fully anticipate or control. Social interactions are varied and nuanced in ways that can touch complex linkages within subjectivity—intersections so intricate that a word or phrase may bring to mind a feeling or outlook we feel everyday, or that we have not felt for decades. These evocations may come from the smells and sounds of daily life that trigger memories—maybe of a friend far away, or of a way of life in a distant city, or of a political speech that excited an ideological sensibility.

The potential for the sudden salience of less accessible identity schemes may be painful if it involves challenges to our selfcrafted identifications. For example, a gay Catholic man who has engaged in selfcraft to integrate his contradictory identities as a Catholic and gay may have carefully studied, considered, and rejected as unchristian the Catholic Church's rejection of homosexuality. When a respected priest's Sunday homily unexpectedly asserts that gay and lesbian life is an abomination, his self-integration may not prevent rejected identity schemes from being felt in full force as salient. But this intrapsychic barrier may not always hold, and the priest's language may suddenly bring to mind childhood religious teachings of intolerance toward homosexuality. In that instant of unexpected salience of rejected beliefs, aspects of subjectivity that may have been made relatively inaccessible through selfcraft (as distinct from unintended consequences of change as for Kondo) can become the momentary framework for interpretation, affect and motivational elements.

The sudden unexpected salience of rejected identity schemes may, in turn, generate a whole range of emotions and actions including confusion, self-hate, or anger. As stressed in chapter four, ambivalence may be a helpful tool to cope with contextually co-constructed challenges to one's self-crafted identifications. In addition, as discussed in chapter two, salience studies in Social Identity Theory also show that when a rarely activated identity scheme is made salient in an experimental context, that scheme will briefly remain salient as the framework for thought and action, but it will soon give way to identity schemes that are more frequently activated and/or with which the subject is more highly identified. Thus, given time to reflect and consider then, the gay Catholic man is likely to come back to the ways of thinking and being that he has selfcrafted and endorsed in his immediate thoughts and interpretations.

The upshot of this is that effectiveness of selfcraft as a means to help us control the influence of our multiple identities is limited in three ways. First, the effects of selfcraft are limited because although selfcraft can help us alter the relative accessibility of different identity schemes, habits, and self-constructs, it cannot be used to *eliminate* any self-construct from subjectivity once it has been internalized. What goes into subjectivity stays in subjectivity, even if it is rarely salient. As such, disavowed elements may become unexpectedly salient and may contravene other strongly endorsed aspects of ourselves. Most dangerously, the momentary salience of disavowed self-constructs may go unnoticed by us unless we are highly self-reflective.

Second, selfcraft cannot help us make accessible any self-construct or identity scheme that has not been internalized as part of subjectivity. In Pratt's case, for example, she could not make a lesbian identity scheme a central component of her life until she had internalized (and in her case learned and selectively identified with) the meanings, values, and practices of lesbian identity as it was constructed in her part of the South in the 1970s and 1980s. Coming to understand and name her same-sex (and ultimately queer) desire was the basis upon which she decided to gain a lesbian identity, but that desire alone is not the sum total of a lesbian identity scheme and the rest of the scheme could not exist in her subjectivity without socialization to it.[91]

Third, ongoing social subordination can limit the effects of reworking internal identity intersections when law and public policy, and/or conventional practices prevent or punish activities that changed intersections would sustain. For example, even though Pratt may internally reject the fragmentation of motherhood and lesbian identity, her children were still taken from her by the state on the basis of her identity. Likewise, recall from chapter two the young woman who identified herself as both ethnically Jamaican and American Black and regarded both identities as integrated parts of herself. Despite her self-integration, those who regard her identities as mutually exclusive may still deny her claims to ethnic Jamaican and Black identity—as did the white co-worker who told her not to be offended by a racial slur because she was not Black. In that case, the cross-cutting intersections of both privilege and subordination among multiple identities present the politically relevant circumstance in which a privileged white woman denies a Black woman her Black identity in a manner that assigns her upward mobility, but *at the cost* of having no critical voice against racial subordination. Thus, while selfcraft may be a tool to rework internal intersections and integrate the self, the success of this process will not automatically change conflicts and social constructions in the broader society. Others may reject those reworked intersections in social contexts in which identity claims are co-constructed.

For some readers, the discussion of selfcraft in this chapter may only beg the question of what motivates selfcraft and urges individuals to engage in the arduous, potentially painful, but potentially relieving work of self-critique, self-transformation, and self-integration. Many were exposed to the same influences of the feminist movement of the 1960s and 1970s that helped Pratt begin to rethink her internalized ways of thinking. Why did others not respond as Pratt did? My claim in this chapter, however, is only that *if* people choose to engage in selfcraft, the resources for doing so exist in the potential conflict among their multiple identities and self-constructs. As also discussed in chapter three, contradictions among identity schemes are a source of critical distance that rejects the need for identity-independent standpoints or narrative unity to render the self a coherent whole that is capable of self-critique and transformation.

However, *why* a person would be willing to engage in selfcraft is another matter, and one that cannot be fully addressed here. Like the character of integrative life projects, the nature of what drives people to self-integration is probably not open to generalization—it will be different for each person. That being said, Pratt is persuasive when she claims that the motives we have to engage in self-critique and self-remaking must be positive if they are to sustain us through the challenges of selfcraft. For Pratt, her motivation was love. She simply wished to find love, acceptance, and joy with other people. Yet, Pratt feared that those who believe that progressive thinking and action must be guided by "higher" principles would reject her motive.[92] Exploring the possibility that love may be a general motivation for selfcraft is beyond the scope of this inquiry. Yet, it is clearly the case that many secular and religious traditions offer categorical love for others as the first principle for right action.[93] In any case, whatever motivations particular people have for engaging in self-integration, those motives will likely need to be strong enough to accommodate both self-affirmation *and* self-critique if they are to sustain people through the rigorous and ongoing processes of selfcraft. This would be especially so when revisionary living requires individuals to grapple with the resistance of others to their adopted principles and chosen life projects.

Conclusions
Racial Akrasia, Selfcraft,
and the Defragmentation of Self and Society

In this concluding chapter, I explore the relevance of multiple identities for political life. The multiple identities and identity contradictions within us are constructed, in part, as a consequence of social divides and political conflicts. Thus, decentered subjectivity can be seen as a location for grappling with those conflicts. In other words, identity contradictions are frequently the manifestation of political conflicts at a personal level. Seen in this light, intrapersonal and interpersonal interactions are potential points of political engagement that are immediately and directly experienced and accessible to all members of a political community at all times. Consequently, how people understand and handle their multiple identities and any contradictions among them in daily interactions has a great deal to do with political life. Particularly significant is the way that individuals grapple with the identity contradictions associated with broad and pervasive political conflicts within a society and/or with more narrowly defined or emergent group conflicts.

The political implications of multiple identities involve at least three major elements: 1) the role of multiple identities in the social construction of social life, 2) the effects of identity contradictions on subjects as political actors, and 3) the role of selfcraft as a means for political intervention. In this concluding chapter I discuss all three of these factors in sequence. In part one of the chapter, I describe the links between multiple identities and political life. These links center on the cyclical relationship of political conflicts, often expressed in subjectivity as identity contradictions. Part two of this chapter focuses on the political implications of identity contradiction, particularly on the political implications of four common modes in which people often respond to identity contradiction. Two of these modes are likely to perpetuate existing social and political conflicts. In contrast, the other two of these modes are part of the practice of integrative selfcraft discussed in chapter six, and have important implications for political participation and for the potential for resolving ongoing political conflicts.

In part three of the chapter, I further consider the political relevance of selfcraft. I explore the political consequences of engaging in or failing to engage in selfcraft. I also sketch the special burdens and political potential of border-crossers, whose particular configurations of multiple identities equip them to cross the borders between socially and politically divided groups. While selfcraft is a potentially important political practice, there are also risks associated with it; these risks are enumerated at the close of the chapter.

Part I: Multiple Identities, Social Construction, and Political Conflict

While virtually all members of a polity have multiple identities, the configurations of multiple identities that members have may vary widely. On the whole, those configurations will generally consist of some unique combination of social and personal identity schemes, as well as other non-identity self-constructs such as identity fragments, habits, isolated beliefs, fears, traits, and concepts. A variety of contradictions and incompatibilities may exist among the multiple identity schemes and self-constructs within subjectivity. Moreover, the multiplicity of elements within subjectivity may intersect in a variety of ways. Once internalized, multiple identities and self-constructs may become salient in different contexts as various frameworks for thought and action. Those various identity schemes become alternatively salient through the workings of a five-part cognitive, affective, and motivational self-system.

The multiple identities and contradictions within subjectivity are derived from social and political life through language-mediated processes of social construction. That is, the self is endogenous to social processes—it is shaped in and through those processes, including political conflicts. In a society structured by group conflict, a decentered multiple subjectivity will be shaped not only by membership in different social groups, but also by any enduring conflicts among these groups. Thus, in conflicted societies, the multiple identities of subjects are generally an amalgam shaped by the social and political conflicts within that society.

In addition, however, the subject is not only constructed *by* social and political life, but also constructing *of* it. In other words, subjectivity and multiple identities are not only constructed in and through language-mediated social processes, including political conflict, but *subjectivity and identity are also a source of and medium for those social processes.* Thus in numerous ways every day, individuals in a polity help to construct the political life of the regime through social means. From everyday interactions among individuals to collective participation in major social movements, subjects—both individually and collectively—contribute to shaping group relations, key political discourses, and other politically significant aspects of social life on a daily basis.

If selves and political regimes are mutually constructing on an ongoing basis, then it follows that deep political conflicts will shape the subjectivities of the citizens and that in return the subjectivities of the citizens shape those conflicts in a mutually conditioning manner. For example, racial categories and the meanings, values, and practices of racial hierarchy that subordinate Blacks to whites have been a pervasive part of American social life for centuries. Today, racial group hierarchies still mark an ongoing political conflict. Thus, it should be no surprise that the constituent meanings, values, and practices of racial hierarchy that subordinate Blacks have likewise remained present throughout U.S. society and are part of the loop of mutual constitution between subjects and the political terrain.

This loop of mutual constitution appears in a recent study of the U.S. grammar school system by Amanda Lewis. Lewis demonstrates how language and practices of race appear informally but persistently in elementary school education.[1] On the one hand, the school officials Lewis studied sincerely intended to create a racially accepting educational setting. At the same time, those administrators, counselors, and others working in the school brought to their work as educators whatever socialization regarding race they had received. In the post-civil rights era that would generally include socialization to *both* racist and anti-racist meanings, values, and practices. As Lewis demonstrates, classroom teaching, student-teacher interactions, staff interactions, and racialized disciplinary practices in the school were rife with "unofficial" articulations of racial hierarchy that subordinates Blacks. Some school practices such as racialized discipline, for example, reinforced racial stereotypes that Black men are prone to criminal conduct.[2] In one instance, Lewis found that while African American boys represented a small minority of children in the school, 90 percent of the disciplinary action involved Black boys. Consequently, children in the grammar school gained firsthand knowledge of the notion that Black males are to be regarded as a criminal class.

Through the racial attitudes of the teachers, unconscious biases of counselors, and the mimicry of childhood, racial hierarchy and racial stereotypes are taught to new generations of youngsters who do not yet have the cultivated critical skills of mature adulthood with which to question that teaching. Those children then rehearse those racial teachings in various settings both inside and outside the school environment. Children who internalize beliefs in racial hierarchy not only have "gained" self-constructs of racial subordination, but also carry those meanings, values, and practices of racial subordination with them into numerous other social contexts. In those contexts, they may re-articulate outlooks of racial subordination that may, in turn, be internalized by still others. In these processes of social construction, constructs of racial privilege persist as part of identity schemes that are internalized and passed on—often inadvertently or unwittingly—from one generation to the next.

Moreover, if transferred self-constructs of racial subordination that children internalize come to intersect with motivational dimensions in their multiple identities, it is possible, if not likely, that students will not only hold racially subordinating beliefs, but will also *act* on those beliefs. When youth do so in violent or otherwise politically significant ways, the incidence of racial conflict among youth is, in turn, employed as evidence that there is continued racial conflict and hierarchy in U.S. society. That articulation of "evidence" feeds the perception of racial conflict and the internalization of that perception, and the loop of mutual constitution of racial hierarchy continues.

If Lewis's analysis can be extended to high school settings, then perspectives on race among young adults that can drive racial conflict are likely being (re)constructed in the high school setting. The school-age character of social construction does *not* make the racial hierarchies that result any less real or dangerous. But it does suggest that were students to internalize alternative self-constructs, involving racial equality, anti-racism, interracial cooperation, and group interdependence, as part of various identity schemes, other outcomes might be possible as those other identity schemes and self-constructs become salient.

Feminists and others have, at times, suggested that social constructivism is not politically useful.[3] Yet from the perspective of multiple identities, there is a clear link between multiple identities—as multiple cognitive, affective, and motivational schemes—and the reassertion of hierarchical norms that can perpetuate political conflict. Theorizing in the case explored by Lewis, some teachers who apparently had contradictory identity schemes of racial subordination were unaware of how their internalized racial biases were playing out in the classroom. Lewis found that while those teachers did not consciously endorse racism, they did not recognize that they were nonetheless rearticulating racial hierarchies in ways that shaped the subjectivities of children to include racial stereotypes and racially hierarchical norms.

At the same time, other teachers were acutely aware of racial hierarchies and sought to combat them by taking every opportunity to convey meanings, values, and practices of racial equality and intergroup recognition.[4] They were also likely shaping identities of children in ways that will influence how those children listen to, feel toward, and interact with others on the issue of racial conflict. In the racial borderlands of the schools, perhaps the only certain outcome of the circumstances studied by Lewis, is that children will at best emerge from the contemporary post-civil rights school systems and other locations of social processes having internalized both racist *and* anti-racist meanings, values, and practices that will become part of their own racial and/or ethnic identity schemes.

Based on Lewis's findings, a question emerges: Could teachers be so unaware or uncaring of the legacy of racial meanings that they were perpetuating, or were they simply disingenuous in their interest in anti-racism? One way to approach this question is to consider the kind of multiple race-related self-constructs the teachers in the schools Lewis studied were likely to have. Given that their approach to race was a function of the diverse socialization and competing discourses on race in the United States—a society that has a history of racial conflict *and* of resistance to racism, it is likely that those teachers have internalized messages of both racism and anti-racism and that those contradictory, conflict-based socialization have shaped their subjectivities to have contradictory self-constructs of racism and anti-racism configured within their subjectivity in some manner.

Such a pattern of contradictory identity socialization—a pattern also received by the children in Lewis's study—represents not only the living legacy of politicized racial conflict in the United States, but also the creation of selves—young selves and adults—with inner identity contradictions among mutually exclusive identities or self-constructs. That identity contradiction could become manifest whenever and wherever race is salient in a social context—which in the United States can be quite often.[5] As Social Identity Theory indicates, however, such an identity contradiction may go unnoticed by people because contradictory identities/self-constructs will be salient at different times. To the extent that teachers have diametrically opposed racist/anti-racist self constructs, those persons may not be aware of the extent that those contradictory aspects of themselves become salient when something in their social context brings them to mind, such as when they engage with children of color or with stereotypical accounts of people of color.[6] Given these elements of multiple identities, it is possible for grammar school teachers to justifiably believe themselves to have anti-racist beliefs, *but to also have* internalized racial biases that are, at times, the framework for their thoughts and actions. Possibly, they would not ever feel the contradictions among these two opposing aspects of themselves (chapter two).

Part II: Responses to Political Conflicts via Identity Contradictions

If the contradictions among multiple identities are often the product of political conflicts, then it follows that the ways in which people choose to grapple with conflict-induced identity contradictions can have potentially significant implications for those political conflicts. In the preceding three chapters, I have argued that there are four distinct modes in which individuals may grapple with the mutually exclusive identity contradictions that emerge from political conflicts, or politicized social conflicts. These include *akratic* and *self-deceptive* modes, and two other modes—the *resolution* of identity contradictions or the *management* of those contradictions by holding those contradictions in a productive tension through ambivalence, flexibility, and/or integrative life projects.[7] All four of these modes have different implications for political life, particularly if they are widely practiced among members of a political regime.

To some extent however, the manner in which subjects may address their deepest identity contradictions first depends in part on whether or not they *feel* those contradictions. As mentioned earlier in this chapter with regard to Amanda Lewis's study of race in grammar school classrooms, and as social identity theorists have argued, it is possible for a decentered multiple subjectivity to contain highly contradictory elements that become salient in different contexts and for subjects never to feel the contradictions between those elements because, their contradictory self-constructs do not become salient at the same time. In such cases, identity contradictions are hard to address because subjects can function socially and politically without being aware of the contradictions within them and remaining unaware of how those contradictions shape their thoughts, feelings, and actions.[8]

Based on earlier discussions of intersectionality in chapters two, five, and six of this book, however, I would contend that the conditions for unfelt identity or self-construct contradictions hold only for contradictory identity constructs that are fragmented within subjectivity. That is to say, I argue that the identity contradictions can go genuinely unfelt only when those contradictory identity schemes and constructs are not related within subjectivity via memories, associations, or via the additive, cross-cutting, or overlapping meanings that comprise identity intersectionality.

In contrast, when associations and intersections of these kinds do exist among contradictory elements within subjectivity, I would argue that intersecting contradictory identity schemes can become salient simultaneously and that in those moments of co-salience the subject can consciously feel the contradictions among them. As discussed in previous chapters, this experience of felt identity contradiction is commonly expressed among those who identify across deep, politicized social divides involving racism, colonialism, and empire, as well as other politicized social chasms such as the gender binary.[9] Expressions of felt identity contradiction can be seen throughout the work of Gloria Anzaldúa, as well as in writings by W. E. B. Du Bois.[10]

When contradictions among multiple identity schemes or multiple self-constructs arise from political conflict *and are felt,* then subjects have an opportunity to grapple more or less effectively with those identity contradictions. How successful they will be in grappling with felt contradictions will vary widely and is likely to span the four modes of response from akrasia and self-deception to selfcrafted resolution and selfcrafted management. As discussed in chapter four, those who engage in self-integration—i.e. selfcraft—hold themselves responsible for avoiding self-deception and akrasia. Those who do not hold themselves accountable in that way are thus more fragmented than those who do. In the pages that follow, I outline the four major modes of responding to identity contradiction in terms of their political consequences.

Akratic and Self-Deceptive Responses

To illustrate the political consequences of choices in these four modes of response to identity contradiction, let us turn again to race in the contemporary U.S. context. Because the color line and racial hierarchies that subordinate Blacks remain pervasive in the post-civil rights era, virtually all Americans will have both anti-racist and racist social constructs in their subjectivities. These contradictory racist and anti-racist dimensions of the self may be configured in various ways: perhaps as meanings, values, and practices within larger identity schemes, or as identity fragments, or more isolated belief constructs. In whatever way they are configured however, because racist and anti-racist constructs can negatively intersect in cross-cutting but mutually defining social meanings, regardless of specific configuration, they may also present the subject with a felt contradiction at some point or another.

Some will respond to that felt inner contradiction by *knowingly* behaving in contradictory ways with disregard for any potentially self-integrating plan or reasoning they might have adopted or established for themselves. In the context of U.S. racism, the *racial akratic* will sometimes act in ways that sustain racial hierarchies and at other times act in ways that resist those hierarchies. While she may wish to act consistently in an anti-racist manner, when it comes to daily circumstances she may not make the effort to act successfully on that wish. Racial akratics know that they are acting in ways that betray their beliefs, but they are, in philosophical terms, too weak-willed to make more consistent choices. In their struggles to face the painful inner contradictions of race as they feel them in daily life, racial akratics tend to take the easiest available option. In terms of self-integration, the racial akratic is thus engaged in mild self-fragmentation that divides her words from her deeds. In terms of collective political life and ongoing racial conflict, the racial akratic is engaged in periodical racist conduct, against the wishes of her better, non-racist self.

Others will respond to the pain of inner contradiction involving race not through akrasia, but through self-deception. Ironically, as Rorty points out and as discussed in chapter four, this approach may be more likely to be taken up by those who are highly invested in identifying themselves with one side of that conflict-based contradiction. It may be that when faced with the felt contradiction of being, for example, strongly anti-racist but also having some racist attitudes, it is preferable to avoid grappling with the contradiction directly and thereby avoid having to entertain the painful challenges to oneself as an anti-racist.[11] Whatever the case may be, self-deceivers cope with identity contradiction by using self-deception to help them to avoid recognizing the inner contradiction. In the case of the *racial self-deceiver,* this may include a whole variety of self-deceptions from the minor self-deceived "pep talk" that current racism is not so bad, to refusals to hear or accept the validity of evidence of racial subordination, to blinded self-assessments that they do not and never have acted upon self-constructs of racial hierarchy. For the racial self-deceiver, the claim to being categorically anti-racist, despite being born and raised in a deeply race-stratified society, can easily accompany racially hierarchical conduct to which they have blinded themselves. In relation to self-integration the racial self-deceiver is engaged in active self-fragmentation. Politically, like the racial akratic, the racial self-deceiver engages in race-related conduct that contradicts his avowed wishes and strong identifications.

Politically, the choice to forego integrative selfcraft in favor of racial akrasia or racial self-deception will generally result in the members of a political regime engaging in erratic conduct with regard to race in political and non-political contexts. Those erratic responses to race—i.e. speaking or acting to reinforce racial hierarchy in some instances and speaking or acting to combat racial hierarchies in others—can, in general, reinforce racial hierarchies and politicized racial conflict. The overall result is likely to be a perpetuation of those racial hierarchies and conflicts. In addition, there are politically important differences between those who act akratically toward their identity contradiction involving race, and those who are self-deceived. Racial akratics are *consciously* aware that they are inconsistent in their resistance to racism. In contrast, racial self-deceivers have engaged in self-fragmentation so as to remain *unconscious* of the discrepancies in their race-related speech and conduct. Moreover, because the racial self-deceiver is likely to have employed self-deception as a strategy to avoid the pain of contradiction involving a cherished sense of self, he is likely to vehemently *deny* he has made any contribution to racial injustice (or racial justice if he is a highly identified racist). For example, a liberal white male scholar who is highly identified with his work on racial equality may, nonetheless, vote against extending financial support to students of color. Here the fragmentation of contradictory, race-related identity schemes and self-constructs within his subjectivity shapes his thought and action in divergent ways, bringing together anti-racist speech *and* racially subordinating action in the same well-meaning person. If this inconsistency is called to his attention, as Rorty has argued, because this racial self-deceiver is highly identified with anti-racism, he is likely to be intensely defensive of his self-deception, and thus unwilling to admit that critique of his actions regarding the political allocation of resources is warranted.

Politically, therefore, the erratic race-related actions of racial self-deceivers who understand themselves to be in favor of racial justice can be particularly damaging to the cause of racial justice. Like racial akratics, their actions contribute to normalizing the contradictory combination of anti-racist sentiment with speech and action that effectively undermines efforts to dismantle racial inequality. But, unlike racial akratics who are conscious of their inconsistencies, if and when the inconsistency of racial self-deceivers is called to their attention, self-deceivers often respond defensively in an effort to preserve their own self-deception. This resistance to critique and correction among advocates of anti-racism can diffuse and contravene political efforts to identify and remedy racial subordination even when the signs of ongoing subordination are quite plain. Therefore, racial self-deception, if widespread, may do more than racial akrasia to close down dissent and chill ongoing efforts to build systematic support for antiracist policies. Furthermore, racial self-deception and racial akrasia, if widespread, can allow those who would intentionally sustain racial hierarchies to do so under the cloak of widespread discourses that celebrate racial equality, while hiding the bald statistical reality of ongoing racial subordination and unearned privilege.

The words "if widespread" however, provide an important qualification to this point. From the perspective of the *theory* of socially constructed multiple identities that I have outlined in this book, everyone in a political regime with a history of pervasive racial hierarchy and resistance to those hierarchies will have both racist and antiracist socialization whether they recognize and admit this or not. This contradictory racial socialization will generally result in virtually all members of the regime having identity contradiction broadly defined as the contradiction among diametrically opposed identity schemes and/or self-constructs. However, the question of how many people in a given regime cope with their internalized race-related contradictions via akrasia or self-deception is an empirical question.

That empirical question cannot be answered through a theoretical or philosophical perspective alone. Consequently, while potential political outcomes can be theorized and anticipated in the manner I am doing here, the actual empirical political upshot in any give regime will depend on how many members of the polity approach its most pervasive conflicts by choosing self-fragmentation over integrative selfcraft. In the case of U.S. racism, for example, much of the actual political outcome of multiple identity contradictions formed by racial conflict will depend on how the *majority* of people engage with their racial contradictions. If most Americans approach racial conflicts through self-deception, it may become hard for the United States as a political regime to acknowledge that it has a continuing problem with racism—or that racism is a problem in which many, if not most, citizens must somehow be participants. Political problems that go unrecognized are quite difficult to correct, particularly through democratic, consensual means. Alternatively, if most Americans are akratic with reference to their race-related identity contradictions, this is likely to perpetuate racial hierarchies despite the co-presence of widespread anti-racist convictions and speech. The result is that in terms of race-related socialization, if most people forego selfcraft, significant change in racial practices becomes less likely because the public tendency is toward passive or unintentional perpetuation of racially hierarchical practices *even if most members of the regime would genuinely be in favor of a shift toward racial equality.*

Selfcraft and the Resolution or Management of Identity
Contradictions

The alternative to akrasia and self-deception in addressing conflict-
derived identity contradictions is selfcraft. Rather than abdicate their
responsibility and forgo the opportunity to deal effectively with their
conflict-based identity contradictions, those members of a regime
who choose to engage in integrative selfcraft engage directly in the
inner manifestation of political conflict at the intrapersonal level. In
addition, selfcraft may also result in grappling with those conflicts
and contradictions at the interpersonal level, in daily speech, actions,
and self-presentations. As discussed in chapter six, through the practices of selfcraft, subjects can intervene both in how particular political conflicts have shaped them and also in how they will or will
not contribute to those ongoing political conflicts. To explore these
political consequences of selfcraft, we might return again to the research by Mary Waters on West Indian immigrants.

As also discussed in chapter two, Waters presents the experience
of a Black twenty-year-old, 1.5-generation Jamaican immigrant whom
I will refer to in this chapter as "Monique." Recall that Monique is
the only Black employee at her place of employment and she obtained
her job after all the Blacks previously employed at her workplace had
been fired. When Monique asked her boss why she had hired her, she
replied that it was because she was "different," because she was Jamaican. The implication is that because Monique is ethnically Jamaican,
her boss does not consider her to be a racially Black American. One
evening after work, while she is out with her co-workers, an argument
ensues between a co-worker and her boyfriend, one of whom shouts a
racial slur. Another white female co-worker suddenly urges Monique
to ignore the derogatory word that had been uttered by saying, "Oh
don't get offended, you are not black anyway."[12]

Monique is shaken by this unexpected denial of her Black identity, and the fragmentation of her Black and West Indian identities
that it declares. She states, "I was so upset. I was upset because I was
like, I'll just be caught in between. I was like, what am I? Purple,
green, yellow? Even though I don't like to be labeled just being black,
I am black. I don't know."[13] This example and Monique's response
illustrate the potential for selfcraft to become a means not only for
self-integration, but also for engaging in political conflict as it is
manifest within subjectivity and within everyday interactions. To
see the connection between politics and selfcraft, it is important to
first recognize the role that constructing social identities as mutu-

ally exclusive can play in the perpetuation of politicized conflict and group hierarchies.

In this case, ethnic West Indian and Black racial identities are constructed as mutually exclusive in ways that reflect and reproduce racial hierarchies that subordinate Blacks. For instance, Monique obtains her job because she is regarded as ethnically different and therefore "not Black." She gains acceptance and mobility within white dominated social spheres—her workplace and her evening out with white co-workers—because she is regarded by colleagues as "not Black." Thus Monique, like other West Indian immigrants in Waters's study, is in a position to claim social and economic privileges reserved for whites regardless of her Black phenotype, *but only to the extent that Black identity is regarded as mutually exclusive with West Indian ethnic identity.* In this case, construction of multiple identities as mutually exclusive sustains the system of racial hierarchy by recruiting some Black participants and securing to whites—and to those such as Monique who may function as whites in some contexts—the privileges of white racial status.

The identity contradiction that faces Monique then is that her Jamaican ethnic and Black racial identities are socially constructed and regarded by others as mutually exclusive as part of an ongoing system of racial privilege. While from her perspective her racial and immigrant ethnic identities are compatible, she cannot claim them both in many contexts without receiving challenges to those identity claims from others (see chapter five for further discussion). Thus for Monique and other West Indian immigrants in the U.S., claiming the privileges of their ethnic identities involves a disavowal of Black racial identity that can endorse and perpetuate the subordination of other Blacks. In this sense, this identity contradiction is bound up with the racial conflict and racial hierarchies as a contradiction that at once reflects and perpetuates that conflict.

If Monique chooses to respond to this identity contradiction through selfcraft, she would have at least two general courses through which to do so. Her first general course would be to *resolve* the contradiction between her mutually exclusive identifications by choosing between them. As Waters reports in her study, there are considerable numbers of West Indian immigrants who identify as *either* ethnic West Indians—and so not as American Blacks—or as Black Americans, and so not as ethnically identified West Indians. While this is a valid personal option in a social sphere in which racial stereotype persists, resolution of this kind does not necessarily ensure that others will always recognize their chosen self-identifications. Just as Monique is sometimes seen as "not Black" against her will, she may also be seen as *only* Black in others.

Monique's second option would be to retain her claim to both identities, to use selfcraft to select elements from both identity schemes to be placed into her guiding principles, and to *manage* the contradictions she faces publicly when others reject her claims to her multiple identities. In this Monique might—as Claudia does in chapter two—shift among her identities, presenting different identities from context to context as appropriate from her perspective. As discussed in chapters five and six, such an inconsistency could still be very much in keeping with any overarching, integrative life projects that she may have. Alternatively, Monique could also present herself in ways that claim *both* identities at once and prepare herself to engage in the politicized confrontations that will likely ensue as a consequence—as María Lugones does in her claims to both Latina and lesbian identity and as Christian Park does with regard to his bicultural Korean American identities (see chapter five). It is in these two broad options that the political potential of selfcraft exists. Through selfcraft, agents such as Monique may educate themselves, deliberate, and decide how they wish to respond to the kinds of mutually exclusive identity contradictions that they face and, by extension, decide how they wish to respond to the political conflicts of which those mutually exclusive constructions are a constitutive part.

From the language quoted above, Monique clearly wishes to identify as *both* Black and ethnically Jamaican. Yet, setting aside the politically offensive dimension of the encounter, the fact that a brief denial of her Black identity is enough to confuse and upset Monique suggests that her ethnic and racial identities may not be strongly self-integrated. Were those identities strongly integrated, such a challenge would be less likely to shake her self-understanding or her momentary resolve to claim her own multiple identities in a context of conflict. As it happened, however, Monique is left wondering "what am I?" and concluding "I don't know."[14] Selfcraft would offer Monique the opportunity to know who and what she is by strengthening the integrating intersections among her multiple identities and by reinforcing bonds of associated knowledge and self-knowledge between them. Were Monique to engage in the three practices of integrative selfcraft described in chapter six, for example, she could gain the meaning of the identity contradiction she faces.

Through the practice of "inventory" Monique could come to recognize that the routine construction of ethnic Jamaican American and Black American identity as mutually exclusive has little to do with the impossibility of reconciling those identities, and much to do with longstanding efforts to render Black members of society subordinate. Having grasped this connection between racial hierarchy and her personal struggles to claim both Black and Jamaican ethnic identity, she could through "discernment" decide how she will respond to the practices of racial privilege and subordination she has uncovered. Will she choose to benefit personally from endorsing a system of racial subordination that harms other Blacks? If not, how will she decline them? Alternatively—as a border-crosser who identifies with and moves between divided groups—could she accept some of the privileges offered to her on the basis of ethnicity and use them to gain opportunities to object to racial stereotyping and subordination in various "white" contexts?

Depending on her choices in the practice of discernment, Monique could regard a moment in which she is asked to ignore a racial slur as one in which to engage in "revisionary living" by putting her views into practice. Were she to have strongly integrated racial and ethnic identities, the next time a white woman tells her she is not Black and urges her to tolerate racial slurs, Monique might well react not with disturbed confusion, but with a secure refusal, correcting her companion by indicating that she is both West Indian and Black and consequently does not accept racial slurs or stereotyping. The struggle to have her claims to mutually exclusive identities accepted in contexts of conflict is thus a political struggle through which Monique, although a construct*ed* subjectivity, is also a construct*ing* agent in a position to resist the daily manifestations of racial subordination—*both* within herself and in interpersonal interactions.

These two selfcrafted approaches to politicized conflict-based identity contradictions—like akratic and self-deceiving approaches—also have implications for broad political outcomes. While the aggregate effects of widespread racial akrasia and self-deception tend toward the perpetuation of the status quo of racial hierarchies, the aggregate effects of widespread selfcraft with regard to race-related identity contradictions could be an increased potential for changes in the status quo of racial hierarchies. Those who forego the opportunities of selfcraft forego the chance to grapple with the deepest political conflicts in a regime as those conflicts shape their subjectivities, thoughts, feelings, and actions. As such, they leave in place the way in which ongoing conflicts have shaped their identity schemes—and the thoughts and actions they perform in and through those identity schemes will also likely perpetuate the conflicts that originated them. In contrast, to the extent that selfcrafters grapple with ongoing political conflicts that have shaped them, they have the potential to reweave the identity formations within them and determine which aspects of their multiple identities they would wish to have as their primary frameworks for thought and action in daily life. Consequently, selfcrafters may contribute to political life meanings, values, and practices that depart significantly from their original conflict-based socialization. Unlike those who avoid selfcraft, selfcrafters contribute to political life only that which they have received from political life that they deem of value. Those valued and considered contributions may contribute to conflict resolution and social change—especially if they become widespread.

Once again, however, the question of whether or not the practices of selfcraft are widespread is an empirical one, and cannot be answered from philosophical analysis alone. Moreover, while the tendency toward the status quo from aggregate akrasia and self-deception are fairly predictable, the *specific* political outcomes that would emerge from widespread selfcraft are much less so. If the engagement with internalized political conflict and the potential interventions of selfcrafters is more likely to contribute to variations in established patterns of social construction, then specifics of those shifts will depend on the choices that selfcrafters make in the course of their craft—i.e. the outcome of their discernments, and their specific acts of revisionary living.

Part III: Multiple Identities and the Politics of Selfcraft

Arguably one of the most important political implications of multiple identities is that they open up and draw our attention to a space of political engagement that exists at the intrapersonal and interpersonal levels. The formation of multiple identities, their system-structure as part of subjectivity, and their role as object, medium, and source of social construction in social and political life combine to make the multiple identities within a decentered subjectivity also an object, medium, and source of political thought, speech, and action. In other words, multiple identities and other self-constructs and their intersections play a triple role in the loop of mutual constitution between self and society.

In recent decades, observers of politics—including some political scientists—have come to define politics as more than simply electoral politics. Influenced in part by the post-linguistic turn philosophy and social theory, and postcolonial state transformation brought about in part by broad social movements, politics is increasingly understood to be comprised of at least three types of political engagement: electoral and other *institutional politics;* grassroots, community, and *social movement politics;* and *discursive politics* in which political ideas, norms, and group distinctions are generated through political or politicized discourses.[15] These three modes of political engagement are interrelated. At times each influences the others. Moreover, while each may sometimes be pivotal to political outcomes, at other times each may be of relatively little influence in specific political events.

In addition to these three widely accepted levels of political interaction, however, the character of multiple identities suggests that we should add a fourth level, that of *intrapersonal politics.* In this level of politics, selfcraft is central as a set of practices by which political subjects/agents can intervene in the loop of social construction between selves and political outcomes—by reworking the influence that major political socialization has had on a person's accepted beliefs, and the frames of reference that individuals would prefer to have shape their everyday thoughts and actions in political contexts. Intrapersonal politics then can be defined as the use of integrative selfcraft to integrate the self, and to respond to the ways in which political life—including political conflicts—have shaped individuals and their patterns of interaction with others. Because selfcraft involves living new or revised patterns of interaction with others, intrapersonal politics often also involves interpersonal practices that are manifest in interpersonal interactions with others in a variety of social contexts that are not overtly political, but are nonetheless politicized by association with major social cleavages such as racial divides.

Like the other three levels of political engagement, intrapersonal politics has its own set of prerequisite tools that are needed to facilitate political engagement. In electoral politics in democratic regimes, for example, while specifics vary from state to state, institutional politics requires some mechanism for holding elections and implementing the outcomes of those elections. Intrapersonal politics, I would suggest, also requires two prerequisite tools for intrapersonal political engagement: 1) diversity in the identity schemes and self-constructs within an agent's subjectivity, and 2) a willingness to engage in self-reflective thought, feeling, and action in the course of selfcraft. As I argued in chapter three in my analysis of works by Gloria Anzaldúa and Alasdair MacIntyre, inner contradiction is necessary for independent critical thought and creativity. Among multiple identity schemes, the diversity of identity schemes and their contradictions become alternative vantage points from which to reflect critically on the multiple identity schemes and other self-constructs within the self-system. This critical distance is lost, however, if the multiple identities and other self-constructs within a decentered subjectivity fall beneath a minimum level of diversity, as I argued took place in the case of the Nazi collaborator "J" whose diversity of multiple identities was minimized by the dominance of patriarchy in all of his identity schemes.

For the most part, however, while it is theoretically possible for subjects to have so little inner diversity as to have limited resources for critical analysis, in practice, an incapacitating dearth of inner diversity is likely to be relatively uncommon in complex societies. As I argued in chapter four, even in seemingly homogenous social settings and among seemingly homogenous individuals, there is often much more diversity within individuals than readily meets the eye. For a white male in the U.S., for example, the rigidity of the gender binary forces upon him certain contradictions between the form of gender expression that he might wish and what he is conventionally limited to by patriarchal norms. For most of us, the complexities of our gender and sexuality alone may be sufficient to introduce contradictions and diversity into our subjectivities. Moreover, even among those in whom inner diversity is fairly minimal, the remedy for that deficiency lies close by in additional socialization and self-education.

At the other end of the identity diversity spectrum, those subjectivities with high levels of diversity and inner contradiction are unlikely to contain all of the creatively fruitful or politically relevant identity schemes or self-constructs that world cultures have produced. Thus, even those who have high levels of inner diversity—i.e. a wide array of internalized outlooks and insights—may benefit from more of these critical resources. In addition, in most cases the diversity of self-constructs and identity schemes within the labyrinthine configurations of subjectivity are organized through internalized intersections. Some of those internalized intersections associated with racism or heterosexism, can produce inner fragmentations that close off some self-constructs from being utilized as critical vantage points by the subject. In other words, the internalization of multiple and diverse elements may not ensure us critical and political resources if—as Minnie Bruce Pratt's story discussed in chapter six suggests— the intersections and levels of fragmentation within the self are such that some of that diversity is difficult to make consciously salient as vantage points for critical thought and action. As stressed above, *feeling* identity contradiction is one indicator that identity schemes are linked enough to serve as critical vantage points on each other.

The second prerequisite to intrapersonal politics, however, is that people must be willing to participate in this level of politics by engaging in the hard work of selfcraft. To some extent, the barriers to political participation at this level are far lower than they are for any other form of political practice. Intrapersonal politics is a ground-level political intervention that anyone can do anywhere, at any time, alone or with others, with few additional resources beyond the knowledge needed to engage in the practices of inventory, discernment, and revisionary living. I would argue that intrapersonal politics requires no broad public forum in order for it to produce effective contributions to collective political life. Consequently, intrapersonal politics can be seen as a form of direct political participation in which all members of a regime may participate regardless of the size of the regime, the individual's age or citizenship status, or other characteristics of participants. Moreover, assuming an open society and a regime that does not limit broad access to the materials needed for the practice of inventory, intrapersonal politics is a form of direct political participation that does not depend on a specific set of political institutions. This is not to say, however, that there are never barriers to participation in this form of politics. While some inventories may need nothing more than a review of autobiographical memories, for example, others, such as Minnie Bruce Pratt's inventory of the racism in her history, require access to information, historical documents, or other materials as an important ingredient in successful inventory (see chapter six). Regimes that restrict access to materials needed for fully informed inventories, or that preclude actions that would be chosen by selfcrafters as part of revisionary living may be viewed as regimes that limit or undermine intrapersonal politics.

On the whole because selfcraft is optional with regard to the cohesion and basic functioning of the self, intrapersonal politics is a form of political engagement that expresses political will and volition. As such, like other forms of political engagement, when people choose not to engage in intrapersonal politics they have taken up a position of political quietude. Yet, even as a position of quietude, the refusal of selfcraft as political participation has its political effects. Those who forego the opportunities presented by selfcraft remain passive in the social constructions that shape them and decline to actively intervene in how political conflict has shaped their identities and their everyday thoughts, feelings, and actions. Yet, as both construct*ed* and construct*ing* subjects, this lack of active intervention does not mean people can opt out of the ever present and always ongoing loop of mutual constitution between the self and society. They cannot. Those who refuse to engage in the politics of selfcraft unavoidably remain conduits for the ongoing social processes that produce and reproduce the existing political terrain. Willingly or unwillingly, one's refusal of selfcraft does not constitute a refusal to contribute to political life; it is only the refusal to be thoughtful and intentional in that unavoidable contribution. In short, if to forego selfcraft is to engage in political quiescence, the effect of that quiescence is similar to inactivity in other kinds of political engagement: it leaves the political status quo in place and/or allows others who are not quiescent to advance their political agendas with greater ease.

If willingness is a prerequisite to intrapersonal politics, that willingness is not necessarily easy. As the discussion of Minnie Bruce Pratt's process of selfcraft in chapter six suggests, successful selfcraft may involve periods of intense emotion, personal pain, and uncertainty. Moreover, the potential for significant personal change in the course of selfcraft may produce challenges of reorientation and strains on existing relationships. The value of Pratt's example is that it illustrates how selfcraft can allow individuals to intervene in the loop of social construction in which subjectivity and society are created. It is this kind of selfcraft in which citizens of all political regimes may need to consider engaging if they wish to contribute to the reshaping of political life and to resolving major conflicts in their regimes at the level at which those conflicts are socially constructed and perpetuated.

For those who are willing and diverse enough, intrapersonal politics is the most proximate form of politics in that the opportunity to participate in it is immediately and always present. However, as Pratt's example also demonstrates, the political work of selfcraft can require a considerable degree of effort and stamina in the face of the substantial challenges it can involve. This is especially so for border-crossers such as Monique and other "border-dwellers" such as Christian Park and María Lugones. Such border-crossers have multiple identities constructed in the borderlands of group conflicts and thus may opt to identify with social groups that are deeply divided. As discussed below, border-crossers who can live across group divides in this way have particular assets, but they may also shoulder particular burdens as a function of their multiple identities—especially as they manage identity contradictions in conflicted spaces in everyday life. Depending on the choices that selfcrafters make in discernment and revisionary living they may opt to engage in unpopular politicized practices for which they may experience strong objections that challenge their identity claims and group memberships. Border-crossers such as Monique who dwell in and among conflicted groups may experience these challenges to a greater and/or more frequent degree than those who do not identify with conflicting groups. For individuals who are averse to the possibility of such daily confrontation as part of political engagement, the requirements of selfcraft may appear daunting.

The Special Political Assets and Burdens of Border-Crossers

Given the challenges of engaging in selfcraft as a means of political participation, border-crossers whose configurations of multiple identities include identities with conflicting groups will often have an unusually central position in ongoing political conflicts. This status as border-crossers in turn, confers special assets with which border-crossers may be able to assume special roles and responsibilities in the resolution of those political conflicts. As discussed in this chapter and in chapter two, West Indian immigrants Claudia and Monique are both border-dwellers who cross the borders between immigrant ethnic groups, Black Americans, middle and lower classes, and Euroamerican whites. As border-crossers they experience considerable pain and challenges in having to negotiate the borderlands of the conflicts among these groups. At the same time, their multiple identities allow them to effectively live in and cross back and forth among these divided groups, negotiating the contradictions of doing so in various settings.

The capacity to participate in divided social spheres on the basis of multiple identities confers on border-crossers three multiple identity-based political assets for responding to the conflicts in which they are embedded. First, border-crossers have *interpretive assets* in that their multiple identities give them a basis for incorporating the various viewpoints of the divided social groups with which they are identified into their own political judgments. Their direct knowledge of the lives and practices in various social groups allows border-dwellers to interpret the falsity of group stereotypes. Border-crossers can employ this interpretive and critical capacity to bring together divergent viewpoints in political reasoning at all four levels of political engagement from formal institutional politics to intrapersonal political selfcraft.

Second, border-crossers who identify with divided groups also have *positional assets* in that their mobility among divided groups places them in a position to carry ideas from one group to another and deliver them, not as an outsider, but as an accepted in-group member. In chapter five, for example, María Lugones expresses her political interventions as a Latina in the lesbian community by bringing interpretations and critiques from Latina cultural perspectives into lesbian communities that often exclude those perspectives, and by bringing critical interpretations and critiques from lesbian perspectives into Latina/o communities still hobbled by homophobia.

Third, border-dwellers that identify with multiple social groups that are divided by conflicts also have *motivational assets* for addressing political conflict that others who do not have their configurations of identities are less likely to have. As stressed in the examples from this and earlier chapters, those who have multiple identities that are regarded as mutually exclusive as a function of political conflict often suffer when those they encounter seek to limit and check their ability to claim *all* of their multiple identities as a cohesive whole. The burdens of frequent challenges and questioning of who they are and how they wish to be understood can be exhausting and demoralizing. Consequently, those who identify across borders between divided communities can easily become invested in conflict resolution as a means to being able to claim and live their own multiple identities in peace. This investment may give border-dwellers strong motivation to engage in political struggle to resolve the conflicts between the groups with which they identify and to build bridges between those groups that facilitate comfortable claims to identifying with both.

This asset also points again to the limits of selfcraft described at the end of chapter six. If identity claims are successful only inasmuch as others accept those claims (see chapter two), then political regimes are also in a position to reject the identity claims of members of the regime on the basis of their identifications. María de los Torres may understand herself to be Cuban American, but the U.S. government may complicate and question her claims to Cuban identity by limiting her ability to construct that identity, in part, through authorized travel to Cuba. While Torres may engage in selfcraft to better integrate her ethnic Cuban and American national identities, that effort at self-integration may still be subject to limitations by the state. Likewise, while the example of Minnie Bruce Pratt illustrates the political significance of selfcraft, Pratt's ability to integrate her multiple identities as mother and lesbian were nonetheless severely limited by the state when she was denied custody of her children based on her sexual identity. Laws and public policies that prohibit actions that aid self-integration can hobble personal selfcraft and undermine it as a means to respond to political conflict. Even in the face of these limitations, however, border-crossers who identify across various social divides and groups in political conflict bring special interpretive, positional, and motivational assets to political life. At the same time they also bear particular burdens arising from their configurations of multiple identities that others whose multiple identities do not include the capacity to cross among divided groups do not experience.

The Risks of Selfcraft

While the selfcraft of multiple identities has important political implications for grappling with ongoing political conflicts within a regime, it also brings certain political and personal risks. First, as already stressed, selfcraft is hard work. It can be arduous and involve significant turbulence in a person's life. Moreover, if successful, selfcraft may produce significant changes in a self. While those changes may benefit the subject-agent and potentially society and collective political life, it may take a toll on interpersonal relationships when the participants in those relationships are unwilling to support or accept those changes. Even in supportive contexts, selfcraft can bring challenges to the friends and family of would-be selfcrafters.

Second, selfcraft is risky at a personal level in that it can put volatile emotions into play. This is especially true when individuals have engaged in self-deception as a means to cope with particularly difficult identity contradictions such as those involved in racism or patriarchy. In potentially many cases, people "resolve" general conflict contradictions through self-deception because they are not sure how to grapple with those contradictions more directly. If subjects seek to handle those contradictions without effective strategies for doing so, it may be too much for them to handle, potentially increasing risks of violence toward oneself and others. At the same time, the same risks may be encountered when dealing with the unexpected collapse of a self-deception or the consequences of akratic behavior and/or if the subject has made no attempt to control akratic behavior. Depending on how the subject is coping with identity contradictions—e.g. ignoring them, the use of akrasia, or hostile behavior—the emotional risks of trying to grapple directly with identity contradictions may be roughly equivalent to the risks of doing nothing at all.

Third, there is a risk that subjects may employ selfcraft in ways that suppress elements of themselves that are irrepressible. The arguments I have presented in *Wealth of Selves* do not approach or seek to respond to questions of authenticity raised by scholars such as Charles Taylor.[16] If there are elements of the self that are authentic, then there may be limits to how those authentic elements may be suppressed or marginalized within subjectivity through selfcraft. If so, then selfcraft risks producing more akratic and self-fragmenting conduct as irrepressible elements of the subject become salient despite selfcraft. Alternatively, selfcraft may risk inflicting a lifetime of pain on oneself if a person succeeds in suppressing elements of themselves that are authentic, the expression of which would have made them happier.

Fourth, integrative selfcraft can be truncated to ill effect. In societies that stigmatize some resolutions or management of specific identity contradictions and/or that construct some identities as mutually exclusive, a subject may stop short of integrating their multiple identities and engage in only enough selfcraft to privilege some identity schemes over others in ways that are comforting or which protect them from ostracism in some arenas. In such cases, it is theoretically possible for the practices of selfcraft to be used, not to further integrate a decentered self, but to reorder subjectivity in ways that foster extremist identification.[17] These conclusions regarding the philosophical characteristics and political implications of multiple identities open up new questions that are beyond the scope of this book to fully explore.

In this investigation into the character of multiple identities, I have pieced together clues from a wide range of sources. Together those clues lead to this ultimate conclusion: *we are, as individuals, varied combinations of multiple identity schemes—ways of thinking and being that we inherit from social life.* We can and do function in and as those various modes of being. In our daily thoughts and actions we reflect and contribute back to social life the variety of identity schemes that we have absorbed from it. In addition, people may also actively shape themselves—and in turn what they contribute to social and political life—*if* they apply critical thought and discerning choice to their varied modes of being. To do so they must draw critical distance and perspectives from the multiplicity that exists within them. Through processes of critical discernment, people may mend the inner fragmentations that cause them pain—fragmentations that are often produced by politicized group and personal conflicts. In the process of selfcraft, people may bring greater integration to themselves and coordinate how they wish to think and act in daily life with how they in fact do. If we choose to do that work, we may depend on the wealth of selves within us for the resources we need to set about mending the conflict-based fragmentations in ourselves, and for turning that repair into speech and action that can positively transform the social and political domains to which we all contribute and belong.

Notes

1. For historical background on the first alternative, see Digeser, *Our Politics, Our Selves,* 105–108. For a philosophical argument for problem driven political philosophy see Brown, *Future of Political Theory.*

2. "The General's Daughter," *The Big Sleep,* DVD, directed by Howard Hawks (1946; Burbank, Cal.; Turner Entertainment Co. and Warner Home Video, 1999).

3. In the *Republic,* for example, Plato considers dramatic performance unsuitable for the guardians because acting in roles as women and slaves may add these multiple perspectives as "second nature" to their souls. Plato further argued that while the "double man" might be pleasing, he "doesn't harmonize" with and must be evicted from the best regime. Plato, *Republic,* lines 392c–98b.

4. In Cartesian thought, the immaterial soul is a stable and central identity that exists distinct from and prior to three elements: the physical body, conscious thought, and the effects of society on the self. Descartes thus regarded identity as a clear and unpuzzling phenomenon because he saw the soul as an unchanging basis of personal identity, separate from any other changeable parts of the self. Descartes, *Meditations.*

5. Locke rejected the Cartesian view that the immaterial soul could be known, and that personal identity exists prior to and independent of our consciousness. Rather, Locke argued that understanding the identity of a person over time calls for the concept of a "person" to be defined as the totality of its conscious thoughts and actions as distinguished from both embodied humanity, and the metaphysical self—i.e. the unknowable spirit-soul. Locke, *Human Understanding,* 439–70.

6. Kant, *Critique of Pure Reason,* 154.

7. Kant, "What is Enlightenment?," 54.

8. Hume, *Human Nature,* 251–62.

9. William James, *Principles of Psychology,* 281–82.

10. My discussion here draws upon Kirstie McClure's description of these three waves and her reading of each wave's account of subjectivity, see McClure, "Subject of Rights." James's influence on early pluralist thought can be seen, for example, in Harold Laski's work. Laski considered William James's work in *A Pluralistic Universe*—particularly James's fifth lecture on "The Compounding of Consciousness"—to be of "vital significance to political theory." See Laski, *Foundations of Sovereignty,* 169. For further examples of James's influence on pluralism, see also Barker, "Discredited State," 160–70 and Follett, *New State.*

11. Dahl, *Dilemmas of Pluralist Democracy,* 55–69. In recent decades pluralism has converged with theories of multiculturalism. For the relationship of pluralism and contemporary multiculturalism see Katkin, Landsman, and Tyree, *Beyond Pluralism.* Thank you to Peter Hall for discussing with me the significance of Dahl's account to this study.

12. McClure, "Subject of Rights," 116–20.

13. Laclau and Mouffe, *Hegemony and Socialist Strategy,* 114–48. As will be noted

in chapter three, this work reaches some conclusions similar to Laclau and Mouffe regarding the value of contradiction in critical reasoning.

14. Horkheimer and Adorno, *Dialectic of Enlightenment*, 275–76; and Adorno, *Negative Dialectics*, 9–17. For commentary by contemporary critical theorists, see Benhabib "Critical Theory and Postmodernism," 334–37; and Whitebook, *Perversion and Utopia*, 119–64.

15. While this is a fair critique of the prevailing sentiments in Enlightenment thought (see Eze, *Race and the Enlightenment*), Enlightenment discourse on subjectivity was more varied than is sometimes thought, as noted by Murray in "Western Concept of Self." Moreover, there was considerable debate and contestation during the Enlightenment regarding the violent and oppressive policies of empire building; see Muthu, *Enlightenment Against Empire*. Nonetheless, opposition to the violence of imperialism did not prevail and largely failed to prevent its oppressions. Even seemingly benign and sincere opposition by Europeans to colonial cruelty was motivated by the drive to homogenize "discovered" non-European peoples; see Castañeda, "Politics of Conquest."

16. As Whitebook put it, "Adorno . . . never fully tapped the emancipatory potential of . . . a theory of expanded subjectivity" and moreover, Adorno "never speculated about the possibility of a 'non-repressive configuration of *intraspsychic* elements,'" that could serve as the basis for such a theory (Whitebook, *Perversion and Utopia*, 161–62, emphasis in original). However, as Whitebook notes, Adorno did often refer to the multiplicity of the subject and to a "more flexible unity of an individual self" (ibid., 162). Rather than taking the path of rethinking subjectivity laid out by Adorno, Jürgen Habermas pursued "communicative rationality" as an alternative method to address the need to revise Enlightenment reason in Critical Theory. His approach led to his accounts of "discourse ethics" and his model of deliberative democracy (Habermas, *Communicative Action* and *Between Facts and Norms*). Other critical theorists later took up the project of formulating a useful model of deliberative democracy (Benhabib, "Toward a Deliberative Model," and *Claims of Culture;* Bohman, "Democratic Theory" and "Constitutional State"), which has dominated Anglo-American democratic theory for some time. Habermas, however, did consider the relationship between his communicative and a subjectivity-based approach; see Habermas, "An Alternative Way."

17. Yet the Frankfurt School regarded Freud's critique not as a departure from Kant but as an extension of Kant's project of Enlightenment. As they saw it, where Kant had advanced an abstract philosophy of autonomy and maturity, Freud had presented developmental benchmarks for attaining that maturity and foregoing one's self-imposed immaturity. For discussion see Whitebook, "Fantasy and Critique," 119–21.

18. Freud, *Basic Writings*. Later, Jacques Lacan would influentially echo and extend Freud's critique of the centered, unitary, unencumbered, autonomous Ego. Lacan stressed that the idea of a unified Ego served as a shield from reality by asserting the Ego's mastery of the world through its separation from it. This comforting shield—the fantasy of Ego—imposed a false unity and rigidity onto the self that hid the more multiple and fragmented character of subjectivity (Lacan, *Écrits*).

19. Other scholars might include other thinkers in the collection of those debating between the unitary and multiple character of the self. Some, for example, might recount the intellectual history in continental thought to include post-Husserlian phenomenology and German idealism to include Jacobi, Schelling, Heidegger, and Levinas; see Critchley and Dews, *Deconstructive*

Subjectivities, 1. In addition, Horkheimer, Adorno, and Freud may be seen in the Nietzschean tradition (*Genealogy of Morals, Thus Spoke Zarathustra*) as examining human history as the renunciation of dogma, and hence positing a self as potentially divided by its adherence to and departure from received wisdom. Moreover, other thinkers such as Rousseau who do not theorize subjectivity in as extensive a manner as Hume or Locke, nonetheless can be read as considering the self to be multiple, and as theorizing politics on that basis. See Strong, "Self and Political Order," 8. Likewise, twentieth century feminists such as Julia Kristeva and Luce Irigaray have also theorized the divided quality of the self with regard to gender; see Kristeva, *Strangers to Ourselves* and Irigaray, *This Sex Which is Not One.*

20. See, for example, Benhabib and others, *Feminist Contentions.*

21. See Cohen, *Symbolic Construction of Community;* Wittgenstein and Anscombe, *Philosophical Investigations;* Foucault, *Discipline and Punish* and *History of Sexuality;* Barth, *Ethnic Groups and Boundaries.*

22. Levine, *Constructions of the Self,* 1. In his account of the crisis-punctuated form of scientific revolutions, Thomas Kuhn argued that in the sciences "fact and theory, discovery and invention were not categorically and permanently distinct." To the extent that this blurring is also characteristic of philosophy and intellectual history in political theory, perhaps philosophical paradigm shifts—such as that ushered in by the linguistic turn—also may take crisis-driven form at times. Kuhn, *Structure of Scientific Revolutions,* 66; see also chapters 7 and 8.

23. Ibid., 3.

24. As Kirstie McClure notes in "Subject of Rights" cited above, this opposition between the poststructuralist account of the subject and agency was articulated frequently among feminist scholars in the late 1980s and early 1990s. See, for example, Benhabib, "Feminism and Postmodernism," 20–26.

25. Critchley and Dews, *Deconstructive Subjectivities;* and Cadava, Connor, and Nancy, *After the Subject.*

26. Laclau, *Emancipation(s),* 20.

27. David Laitin, for example, finds multiple identities a useful concept for analyzing politics in the former Soviet republics (Laitin, *Identity in Formation*). Others use multiple identities to explore transnational political practices in U.S.-Vincentian and Grenadian politics (Basch, Schiller, and Blanc, "Hegemony, Transnational Practices"), and for understanding the micropolitics of U.S.-Cuban relations (Torres, *Land of Mirrors*). Other scholars use multiple identities as a concept to consider political cohesion in post-Apartheid South Africa—for example Thornton, "Potentials of Boundaries," 150–52—and to understanding ethnic conflict across Africa as does Posner, *Ethnic Politics in Africa.* In addition, Alice McIntyre regards multiple identities as important to understanding the place of Irish women in the sectarian violence in Northern Ireland; see *Women in Belfast.*

28. See Walker, *Black, White, and Jewish;* Arana, *American Chica;* Davis, *My Sense of Silence;* Balka and Rose, *Twice Blessed;* Feinberg, *Transgender Warriors.*

29. Vertovec, *Migration and Social Cohesion,* xxxi.

30. Honig, "Difference, Dilemmas," 271–73; Burke, *Mestizo Democracy,* 118–21. See also, Clarke, *Deep Citizenship.*

31. Lugones, *Pilgrimages/Peregrinajes.*

32. See Meyers, *Being Yourself,* 13–48; and Sassen, "Foreword," xi–xii.

33. See Padilla, *Latino Ethnic Consciousness;* and Márquez, *Constructing Identities.*

34. Crenshaw, "Mapping the Margins."

35. See Laclau and Mouffe, *Hegemony and Socialist Strategy;* and Mouffe, *Return of the Political.*

36. See Lott, *Asian Americans;* Espiritu, *Race, Ethnicity, and Class;* Lowe, "Heterogeneity, Hybridity, Multiplicity;" Hurtado, *Voicing Chicana Feminisms;* and Romero, "Maid's Daughter," 195–209. Important discussions of multiplicity of the self can also be found in scholarship on mixed race identity; see Root, *Racially Mixed People;* Spickard, *Mixed Blood.*

37. See MacIntyre, "Threats to Moral Agency."

38. Renshon, "Dual Citizenship + Multiple Loyalties," 3–27, and 232–61.

39. Huntington, *Who Are We?*

40. Honig, "Difference, Dilemmas," 271 and 273, which nonetheless offers an insightful analysis. Likewise, Samuel Huntington devotes only four pages to describing the concept of identity, including multiple identities, and his discussion seems to be derived largely from Social Identity Theory. An exception is David Laitin, who develops a chapter-length account of multiple identities in his project on identity in the former Soviet republics. While Laitin depends heavily on Erik Erickson, the framework proposed below is constructivist and interdisciplinary, and so varies significantly from Laitin's in its detail, shape, and antecedents. See *Identity in Formation,* 3–35.

41. See Hirschmann, *Subject of Liberty.* Hirshmann's work is not the first work to address the relationship between social construction of the subject and agency. In the early 1990s, some feminists argued that the socially constructed subject could not support agency because it could not be separated from the linguistically mediated factors that forged it. This claim positioned poststructuralist thought on the self in opposition to the notion of agency and effective political resistance. A small number of feminist scholars offered compelling reasons why this opposition was both false and counterproductive for feminist theory and politics. Some, such as Nancy Fraser, called for a poststructuralist account of the subject with a focus on the capacity for critical thought—which this project attempts—to make the falsity of the opposition between poststructuralism and agency clear (see Fraser, "False Antitheses," 69). However, until Hirschmann's book a sustained feminist account of freedom had not emerged that takes poststructuralist insights as a starting point. For aspects of this debate, see Benhabib, Butler, Cornell, and Fraser, *Feminist Contentions.* For feminist critique of this opposition see McClure, "Subject of Rights;" and Flax, *Thinking Fragments.*

42. Digeser's conclusion speaks to both current pluralist and multiculturalist democratic theory after the linguistic turn. In it she seeks to understand how democratic institutions might accommodate the multiple identities of individual members of the regime without reducing that multiplicity to a unitary outlook in the moment of political choice.

43. In addition, Paul Ricoeur has also advanced an important account of narrative identity, see *Oneself as Another.*

44. "Handling Vivian," *The Big Sleep,* DVD, Directed by Howard Hawks (1946; Burbank, Cal.; Turner Entertainment Co. and Warner Home Video, 1999).

45. Brown, "Future of Political Theory."

46. On identity contradiction, for example, contrast Turner, "Social Identity and Self-Categorization," with Du Bois, *Souls of Black Folk;* and Anzaldúa, *Borderlands.* On the embodiment of consciousness, contrast Butler, *Bodies that Matter;* and Schacter, *Searching for Memory.* On the association of dissociative identity to multiple identities, contrast Giddens, *Modernity and Self-Identity,*

53, with Chu, *Rebuilding Shattered Lives*. Margo Rivera is an exception to the generalized approach often taken to dissociation. In her work she theorizes feminist concerns through an assessment of the clinical literature on dissociative disorders. See Rivera, "Psychological and Social."

47. See Bhabha, "Interrogating Identity;" Gilroy, *Black Atlantic*; Cohen, *Symbolic Construction of Community*; and Barth, *Ethnic Groups and Boundaries*. For an account of the development of the concept of hybridity in postcolonial and ethnic studies and political theory see, Moreiras, "Hybridity and Double Consciousness."

48. This is not the first application of Social Identity Theory to questions of the self in interdisciplinary Chicana/Latina Studies. For an earlier application, see Hurtado, "Understanding Multiple Group Identities."

49. Brown, "Future of Political Theory," 79.

CHAPTER ONE

1. See Tuan, *Forever Foreigners*, 18–47. This is especially so for racialized immigrants when both immigrant ethnic and non-white racial identities are associated with foreignness. Many volumes have been written on the persistent construction of U.S. national identity as racially white and the historical erasures such a construction requires. See Haney-López, *White by Law;* Omi and Winant, *Racial Formation in the United States;* and Takaki, *A Different Mirror*. As Tuan notes, immigrant responses to these stereotypical projections are complex and varied. For discussion of immigrant responses involving the negotiation of multiple ethnic and racial identities, see chapters two and five below.

2. See, for example, Gordon, *Assimilation in American Life*, 84–114. Politically, such assimilation was supposed to produce a homogenous national culture and a defined national identity that would at once unify the nation, secure the loyalty of all citizens, and provide immigrants with a path to reaping the economic and social benefits of incorporation. Little consideration was generally given to the fact that visible racial minorities could not assimilate racially. Moreover, despite descriptions of the United States as "a nation of immigrants," immigrant ethnic identities were seldom seriously thought to have significant intrinsic value, psychophysiological durability, or potential benefits for the incorporation and future success of immigrants. For history of the hostile and hierarchical approaches toward immigrants in America prior to twentieth century classic assimilationism, see King, *Making Americans*.

3. Alba and Nee, *Remaking the Mainstream*.

4. Portes and Rumbaut, *Legacies*, 44–72.

5. One indication of this can be seen in the assimilationist statements made by high-ranking political officials including Pres. George W. Bush and California governor Arnold Schwarzenegger, both of whom have made remarks stressing the need for language and cultural assimilation among Mexican immigrants in particular. See Rutenberg, "Bush Enters Anthem Fight on Language," *New York Times*, April 29, 2006, and Associated Press, "Schwarzenegger: Mexican Immigrants Should Assimilate into U.S. Culture," *International Herald Tribune*, October 6, 2006.

6. Levin and McDevitt, *Hate Crimes Revisited;* and *Korematsu v. United States*, 323 US 214 (1944).

7. The concept of "the nation" as a territorially bound unity has become problematic in the face of globalization, neo-colonialism, and other factors. I acknowledge but bracket these complexities here in order to focus on the relationship of multiple identities to prevailing understandings of nation

and national identities as both continue to operate. Because the discussion that follows illuminates how multiple and transnational identities can situate individual citizens in relation to multiple nation states simultaneously, however, this chapter also can be read as part of current reconsiderations of the concept of nation in light of global migration.

8. In 2005, U.S. Latinos numbered 41.9 million, including 25.1 million native-born and 16.8 million foreign-born residents. Of these 64 percent are of Mexican heritage, 3 percent Salvadoran, 3.5 percent Cuban, 9 percent Puerto Rican, 2.7 percent Dominican, 10.8 percent other Central or South American, and 7 percent other Latina/o (Pew Center, *Hispanics at Mid-Decade*) based on the 2005 Census Bureau American Community Survey. In addition, analysis of the March 2005 Current Population Survey estimated 11.1 million unauthorized residents in the U.S. of whom 56 percent are of Mexican origin, 22 percent other Latin American, 13 percent Asian, 6 percent European and Canadian, and 3 percent African; see Pew Center, *Unauthorized Migrant Population*, 5.

9. See de la Garza and Pachon, *Latinos and U.S. Foreign Policy*, 8–9. This is a common finding in surveys of the Latina/o population. Another recent study found that 92 percent of Latinos feel that it is very important for children of immigrants to learn English; among the foreign-born that number rises to 96 percent. At the same time, 46 percent of native-born Latinos did not feel that speaking English was absolutely necessary to consider oneself a part of U.S. society. See Pew Center, *Hispanic Attitudes Toward English*. For details regarding English language acquisition among second generation immigrants, see Portes and Rumbaut, *Legacies*, 118–46.

10. Huntington, *Who Are We?*, 221. With his phrase "demographic *reconquista*" Huntington is referring to the fact that much of the U.S. Southwest belonged to Mexico until it was annexed by force in 1848. In addition to the threat he sees in Latinos, Huntington also sees risk in how liberal political and intellectual elites, such as former U.S. president Bill Clinton, favor multiculturalism and diversity as well as bilingual education and affirmative action. Moreover, Huntington also argues that U.S. national identity is threatened by criticism from Anglo-Protestant "core culture" and scholars who question the wisdom of unbridled patriotism such as Martha Nussbaum, Amy Gutmann, and George Lipsitz (ibid., 270).

11. For the purposes of this chapter I set aside the question of whether cultural hybridity has potentially positive transformative effects for U.S. democracy. I turn to that question with regard to critical political reasoning in chapters three and five.

12. Ibid., 212.

13. Ibid., 221, emphasis added.

14. Ibid., 214. In his opposition to dual citizenship, Huntington argues that, among other things, dual citizenship provisions remove the distinctness of one's national identity and citizenship.

15. Ibid., 31.

16. While Huntington does not specify it, subjects can make these "determinations" consciously or unconsciously, as active decisions or as over-learned subconscious reactions. This is a basic tenet of self-categorization theory, a body of thought that builds upon Social Identity Theory. See chapter two for further discussion and Turner, "Social Identity and Self-Categorization."

17. Huntington, *Who Are We?*, 23.

18. Ibid., 4, 21–33.

19. Ibid., 21, emphasis added.

20. A distinction can thus be drawn between personal identities as idiosyncratic relationships to specific others and the broad social categories of which those specific relationships might also be an example. Bill's role as Sue's husband may differ in some ways but not in others from the prevailing social constructions of the category of "husband" per se. The different but sometimes close connection between personal and social identities is captured in the difference between saying to Bill, "Sue will love it if you do that for her," and saying "Wives love it when husbands do that for them."

21. For an application of a similar argument made in political science with reference to the transformation and persistence of U.S. immigrant ethnic groups, including white ethnics, see the classic Glazer and Moynihan, *Beyond the Melting Pot*, 13. See also the classic work in anthropology, Barth, *Ethnic Groups and Boundaries*.

22. Cohen, *Symbolic Construction of Community*, 11–38 and 44–46.

23. Huntington, *Who Are We?*, 30–31; Huntington also assumes that Anglo-Protestant culture is not itself an ethnicity.

24. See Geertz, *Old Societies and New States*, 109–19. Also refer to Hutchinson and Smith, *Ethnicity;* in this collection of 64 classic and/or significant essays on ethnicity excerpted and published by Oxford University Press, none of the anthologized pieces define ethnicity as Huntington does.

25. Weber, *Economy and Society*, 389; Weber specifies that for the formation of ethnic groups, "it does not matter whether or not an objective blood relationship exists" (ibid.).

26. Huntington, *Who Are We?*, 59.

27. As various political thinkers such as Charles Taylor, Bhikhu Parekh, and Jürgen Habermas have argued, binding national identity to a single cultural, ethnic, or religious identity in diverse society is unnecessary and counterproductive to democratic political cohesion. Rather, publicly emphasizing the distinction between various ethnic identities and a national identity can foster political cohesion because it welcomes all ethnic groups to develop ways of orienting their own cultures to the political principles of the nation, and allows them do so on an equal footing with all other ethnicities. Jürgen Habermas has stressed that in the history of political thought, political unity was originally thought to require a substrate of *political* ideas, values, and practices that provided the common basis upon which national political identity, political cohesion, and common purpose could be forged. Over time, he argues this political substrate has often become (con)fused with a dominant culture—thereby equating national political identity with a specific cultural, ethnic identity. Such a conflation, Habermas contends, makes it more difficult to incorporate peoples from many different ethnic, religious, and racial backgrounds into a cohesive political regime. See Habermas, "Citizenship and National Identity;" Taylor, *Politics of Recognition*, 55–61; and Parekh, *Rethinking Multiculturalism*. Taylor and Parekh have made similar arguments regarding the importance of dividing ethnic identity from national identity for the sake of democratic stability. Taylor has argued that it is possible to combine a deep societal commitment to shared political principles with respectful engagement among a wide diversity of social identity groups. He points out that while one version of liberal democracy does require a unified purpose and total neutrality toward particularity in the form of "equal treatment," a second conception of liberalism has greater flexibility. In it, the

political regime is united by a commitment to core political principles and fundamental rights that are equally present for all, but it also prioritizes the recognition and accommodation of particular identities and cultural and other differences at the level of privileges and immunities.

28. The argument that commonly shared cultural identities are a necessary basis for national political identity and political unity in a democratic regime has been common and widely accepted in Western political thought. See for example, Mill, "Considerations on Representative Government," 371–613.

29. One exception is the Children of Immigrants Longitudinal Study; for results see Portes and Rumbaut, *Legacies.*

30. Existing data on local Latina/o communities may not represent Latinos in other regions or nationwide. See García Bedolla, *Fluid Borders;* and Jones-Correa, *Between Two Nations.* Moreover, some broad survey data suggests that racial identification, particularly whiteness, is more indicative of a sense of belonging in the U.S. among second generation immigrants. See Tafoya, *Shades of Belonging.* At the time of this writing, data from a new National Latino Survey is being released that may yield some insight into the latter two questions. For unpublished data, see http://depts.washington.edu/uwiser/LNS.shtml.

31. Park, "Migration and the Marginal Man," 881–93; Stonequist, "Problem of the Marginal Man," 1–12. For this reason much research on "biculturalism" is still sometimes regarded with suspicion since it bears connotations with ideological bias toward classic assimilationism and the destruction of minority cultures. The following discussion of the research in biculturalism draws significantly from the review of the literature by LaFromboise, Colemen, and Gerton, "Psychological Impact of Biculturalism," which assesses the literature between 1929 and 1992.

32. Goldberg, "Qualification of the Marginal Man," 52–58; and Green, "Re-Examination of the Marginal Man," 167–71.

33. Portes and Rumbaut, *Legacies,* 269–86.

34. Rogler, Cortes, and Malgady, "Acculturation and Mental Health."

35. Suarez and others, "Biculturalism, Differentness, Loneliness, and Alienation;" and Szapocznik and others, "Bicultural Effectiveness Training."

36. Birman, "Biculturalism and Perceived Competence."

37. Portes and Rumbaut, *Legacies,* 274.

38. Gutierrez and Sameroff, "Determinants of Complexity."

39. Portes and Rumbaut, *Legacies,* 54; see also 166–89 on resilience to racism.

40. Both quotations Waters, *Black Identities,* 311–12. Unfortunately, in many cases the upwardly mobile aspirations associated with Americanized ethnic identification are also a way for native-born immigrants to negotiate the color line by distinguishing ethnic immigrants from American Blacks; see also Portes and Rumbaut, *Legacies,* 54.

41. While Huntington seems to assume otherwise, not all Latinos are bicultural. In addition, the ability of Latino families to preserve heritage culture and languages over several generations has been undermined in states that have eliminated bilingual education, such as in California's proposition 229. See Schmidt, *Language Policy and Identity Politics,* and Valenzuela, *Subtractive Schooling.* For counter examples of schools seeking to preserve bicultural and bilingual education, see Olsen and others, *And Still We Speak.*

42. Portes and Rumbaut, *Legacies,* 43; in their landmark study, the Children

of Immigrants Longitudinal Study, Alejandro Portes and Rúben Rumbaut have found reason to affirm the view that knowledge of family heritage can prove helpful to children of immigrants, who will often find their allegiances evolving on a different path from that of their parents. In the study they find, for example, that second generation "Children who learn the language and culture of their new country without losing those of the old have a much better understanding of their place in the world. They need not clash with their parents as often . . . because they are able to bridge the gap across generations and value their elder's traditions and goals" (ibid., 274).

43. Huntington seems to assume that all bicultural "Hispanics" are equally oriented toward Mexico or other sending states. Logically, this would be far from true when most U.S. Latinos are native-born and have never lived abroad, or have not done so for long periods. Given this lack of socialization abroad, Mexican national identity *as a political identity* is not likely to be a fully developed self-construct within the subjectivity of native-born or 1.5 generation Latinas/os.

44. Mexican immigrants were awarded more Congressional Medals of Honor than any other immigrant group during World War II. While they comprised only 10 percent of the population of wartime Los Angeles, Mexican immigrants accounted for 20 percent of the Angelenos who died in the conflict. See Acuña, *Occupied America,* 243–44.

45. Gómez-Quiñonez, *Chicano Politics,* 31–99. Innumerable examples exist, including the formation of the American GI Forum, a civil rights organization of Mexican American veterans established in 1948. The forum was given early impetus for its work when a Texas funeral home refused to provide burial rights to a Chicano veteran because of his race. The soldier, Felix Longoria, was ultimately interred at Arlington National Cemetery.

46. Public Agenda and Tomás Rivera Policy Institute Study, *Here to Stay.*

47. de la Garza and Pachon, eds., *Latinos and U.S. Foreign Policy,* 9.

48. Ibid., 10–12.

49. Levitt, *Transnational Villagers;* Basch, Glick Schiller, and Szanton Blanc, "Hegemony, Transnational Practices."

50. Vélez-Ibáñez and Sampaio, eds., *Transnational Latina/o Communities.*

51. Among the most important debates arising from transnationalism is that over how citizenship should be reconceived in the current context of globalization (see Laguerre, *Diasporic Citizenship*). In this chapter, I will not directly address this debate; however, as a background assumption I accept that prevailing legal definitions of citizenship are often inadequate to reflect contemporary political membership. In the United States, for example, over 10 million Latina/o residents are not citizens but rather unauthorized residents without legal status in the country. These undocumented immigrants and transmigrants nonetheless may be regarded as "cultural citizens" who are members of a social, economic, and political collectivity but not designated as legal citizens. For a discussion of cultural citizenship with respect to U.S. Latinos, see Flores and Benmayor, eds., *Latino Cultural Citizenship.* For the purposes of this chapter, the term "transmigrant" refers to any one—citizen or non-citizen—living a transnational life with transnational identity in the U.S., regardless of formal legal status.

52. Wolfe, "On Loyalty;" and Fletcher, *Loyalty: An Essay.*

53. Wolfe, "On Loyalty," 48.

54. Ibid., 52.

55. Among these loyalties, some loyalties are tested frequently (e.g. loyalties to our families, friends, and colleagues) while other loyalties are tested only rarely (e.g. loyalty to our country and to our fellow citizens).

56. Huntington, *Who Are We?*, 219. Huntington does not attend to the status or meaning of these commitments.

57. Peter Schuck analyzes the marriage metaphor in detail. See Schuck, "Plural Citizenships."

58. I'd like to thank Peter Spiro for his feedback on this point.

59. There is some reason not to accept it since the marriage metaphor addresses personal rather than social or collective identities. However, since national communities are constructed through processes of boundary maintenance that invite idiosyncratic interpretations of key unifying elements for the sake of cohesion (see references to work by Anthony Cohen in this chapter), this makes the analogy to idiosyncratic personal relationships not unreasonable.

60. Gonzalez, *Harvest of Empire.*

61. See Passel, *Unauthorized Migrants,* 4, 18, 19. For research on migration patterns and conditions see also Menjivar, *Fragmented Ties;* Mahler, *American Dreaming;* Hamilton and Stoltz Chinchilla, *Seeking Community.*

62. Since many U.S. Latina/o transmigrants have established families including U.S.-born children, many consider themselves settled here and would be reluctant to leave. By "integrated" I mean simply that Latina/o immigrants have become a deeply embedded part of U.S. society, not that they have adequate political voice, or economic or social equality.

63. Passel, *Unauthorized Migrants,* 30; on homeless working immigrants, see Chavez, *Shadowed Lives.*

64. Ibid., 4, 18, 19. For research on common living conditions among recent Latina/o immigrants see Mahler, *American Dreaming.*

65. Grow, "Embracing Illegals."

66. This Latina/o commitment to work persists despite disproportionately low incomes, *especially* among unauthorized residents. Latinos in California, as a whole, have generally had the highest poverty levels among all racial and ethnic groups and Latina/o *immigrant* households have been twice as likely as U.S.-born Latinos to live below the poverty line; see Hayes-Bautista, *La Nueva California,* 96–98.

67. David Hayes-Bautista cites the 1992 study in *La Nueva California,* 133; Rinku Sen, "The New Culture War." This is *not* to say that Latina/o immigrants, both authorized and unauthorized, should not benefit more from the social services to which they are, or should be, entitled.

68. Simon, "Latinos Take Root;" Millard and Chapa, *Apple Pie and Enchiladas;* and Valdés, *Barrios Norteños.*

69. Dávila, *Latinos, Inc.*

70. Grow, "Embracing Illegals," 60.

71. Passel, *Unauthorized Migrants,* 20.

72. Valenzuela, *Subtractive Schooling.*

73. At the same time, bicultural identification among the children of Latina/o immigrants has increased significantly as the waves of immigration between 1965 and 1990 have mitigated pressures for assimilation. This represents a significant departure from earlier generations that experienced significant pressure to relinquish Latina/o social identities (Ruiz, *From out of the Shadows;*

Garcia, *Mexican Americans;* Hayes-Bautista, *La Nueva California,* 101). This renewed biculturalism is exactly what Huntington opposes.

74. Inter-American Development Bank, *Remittances 2005,* 9. The total number of remittances to Latin America in 2005 was estimated at $52.6 billion.

75. Bada, "Mexican Hometown Associations."

76. Ibid.

77. These actions are part of a range of other transnational practices that are part of the emerging transnational identities among Latinos in the hemisphere (Nájera-Ramírez, "Haciendo Patria;" Vélez-Ibáñez and Sampaio, *Transnational Latina/o Communities*). For example, many Mexican and Central American populations in the U.S. retain significant social and economic ties to their homes of origin, often facilitated by hometown associations and collective living arrangements in the United States. Among these groups, the villagers of Ticuani, Mexico are divided between Brooklyn and the Ticuani village. Separated by thousands of miles, the villagers nonetheless work to retain the connection between their two locations by developing ways of having "significant lived experience" in both communities, including social practices and transnational political practices. On the political side, the self-governance of the Ticuani village is accomplished across its two locations such that "all important communal business is debated in weekly conference calls between elders in Brooklyn and Mexico" (Davis, *Magical Urbanism,* 88–99).

78. In March 2005, unauthorized residents accounted for 4.9 percent of the U.S. labor force and made up large proportions of workers in certain sectors including 24 percent of farm workers, 17 percent of janitorial laborers, 14 percent in construction and 12 percent in food preparation. Unauthorized workers comprise 27 percent of all butchers and food processors in the U.S. as well as 36 percent of insulation workers and 29 percent of all drywall and roofing installers (Passel, *Characteristics of Unauthorized Migrants,* 3). Latina/o immigrants also perform some of the dirtiest and most dangerous work in the country (Schlosser, *Fast Food Nation,* 160–66).

79. It may also be the case that the commitment felt by many Latina/o transmigrants is primarily a commitment to a particular location, often a small town or village, where their families reside. Thus, it is possible that for many transmigrants from Mexico, for example, their individual attitudes toward the Mexican government are somewhat ambivalent.

80. Hayes-Bautista, *La Nueva California,* 77.

81. Huntington, *Who Are We?,* 253–56.

82. Ibid., 253.

83. Sosa, *The Americano Dream,* 210.

84. On the decline in civic engagement among Americans see Putnam, *Bowling Alone.* The inconsistency may suggest that other motivations exist for generating this double standard, such as nativist policy agendas, hostility toward multiculturalism, or ethnocentric fears and anxieties.

85. Whether U.S. political elites actually desire the political incorporation of Latinos remains a matter of debate. The rhetoric of political inclusion rarely matches the effort or resources invested in this cause. Despite his anxiety about cultural and political bifurcation, Huntington does not strongly advocate voter registration drives in low-income Latina/o communities or other practical measures that would encourage political identification and participation among Latinos. For a case study of the disparity between the

rhetoric and reality of mainstream efforts to incorporate Latinos see Rosales, *Illusion of Inclusion.*

86. Huntington, *Who Are We?,* 28.

CHAPTER TWO

1. In addition, Anzaldúa's work can also be seen as part of a broad body of scholarly work by women of color that emphasizes the intersection of different identities within the self and the role of that intersection in achieving social justice. See also, hooks, *From Margin to Center;* Lorde, "Sister Outsider;" Collins, *Black Feminist Thought* and *Fighting Words;* Lowe, *Immigrant Acts;* Anzaldúa, ed., *Making Face, Making Soul;* Moraga and Anzaldúa, eds., *Bridge Called My Back;* Crenshaw, "Demarginalizing the Intersection;" King, "Multiple Jeopardy, Multiple Consciousness." For an account of the interconnections between Latina feminist thought and this broader body of work by women of color, see Sandoval, "Mestizaje as Method."

2. See Pérez, *Decolonial Imaginary;* Coles, *Beyond Gated Politics,* 185–212.

3. Lugones, "Playfulness, 'World'-Traveling" and *Pilgrimages/Peregrinajes;* and Meyers, "Intersectional Identity."

4. Anzaldúa, *Interviews/Entrevistas,* 267–68.

5. Contrast Dahl, *Dilemmas of Pluralist Democracy,* 63 with Anzaldúa, *Borderlands,* 79–80.

6. The term *mestiza* has been controversial at times, given its original meaning as a signifier of mixed-blood biological heritage (see Vasconcelos, *La Raza Cósmica/The Cosmic Race*). Some consider the word to have inherently essentialist underpinnings, and consequently some interpreters, such as Cristina Beltran, have justifiably criticized Anzaldúa's work on these grounds. See Beltran, "Patrolling Borders." While I agree that Anzaldúa frequently does refer to "mixed-blood" in *Borderlands,* in her later interview, she specified, albeit retrospectively, that in the preponderance of her theorizing she intended to be referring to a cultural mestizaje—not a mixture of blood, but a mixture of culturally constructed identities formed by socialization in a confluence of lifeworlds and social relations (see *Interviews/Entrevistas,* 268). The work of María Lugones and Norma Alarcón discussed below can also be interpreted as using the term *mestiza* with reference to cultural mixture. Likewise, in this work, *mestiza* refers to cultural, *not* biological, *mestizaje.* In addition, contrary to Jean-Luc Nancy who, in "Cut Throat Sun," has sought to resignify the term *mestiza* as a contemporary state of being rather than a quality of specific persons. I follow Alarcón, Anzaldúa, and Lugones in using the term *mestiza* to refer to the qualities of cultural *mestizaje* retained by specific persons. For Alarcón's response to Nancy, see Alarcón, "Conjugating Subjects."

7. Anzaldúa, *Borderlands,* 63.

8. Ibid., 78.

9. For Anzaldúa the basic condition for the formation of mestiza consciousness is the construction of the subject within a cultural "borderlands." At least two additional conditions can construct the subject so as to form multiple identities. One is the *displacement* from one culture or subculture through migration or the relocation of persons in a diaspora. Another is the *segmentation* of social life in which social domains are separated to such a degree that each social milieu has its own system of meanings, values, and practices that could construct the subject with milieu-specific identities. For analysis of the relationship between displacement and identity formation see Bammer, ed., *Displacements;* for a look at the current breadth of such displacements see

Van Hear, *New Diasporas.* For an analysis of the role of social segmentation in identity formation see Giddens, *Modernity and Self-Identity.*

10. Ryan, "Psychological Needs," 398.

11. Ibid.

12. Singer, "Seeing One's Self," 443. Psychologist Gary S. Gregg has conducted research into the life narratives of persons living in various U.S. cities and in rural Morocco. His work demonstrates that persons routinely "shift among multiple, often contradictory self-representations" not only in everyday settings but, also, even in the changing course of a research interview (Gregg, "Multiple Identities and Integration," 617). Gregg defines personality as "a system of organized contradiction" (ibid.).

13. Markus and Wurf, "Dynamic Self-Concept," 300.

14. Ibid., 301; see also Greenwald and Pratkanis, "The Self;" and Kihlstrom and Cantor, "Mental Representations of the Self."

15. Markus and Wurf, "Dynamic Self-Concept," 301.

16. Hazel Markus is among those who have developed the idea of identity schemes; see Markus, and others, "Self-Schemas and Gender;" and Markus and Kitayama, "Cultural Construction of Self."

17. The encoding of information, including identity-specific information, into memory involves the physiological production of an *engram:* an "enduring change in the nervous system" called a "memory trace" (Schacter, *Searching for Memory,* 57). The encoding of a memory trace "conserves the effects of experience across time" in memory (ibid.). If identity schemes can be seen as sets of deeply encoded episodic, semantic, and procedural memories; and each identity frame has associated sets of memories; and as the subject enters different social contexts, aspects of those contexts are recognized through cognition as fitting patterns that, in turn, serve as retrieval cues for specific memories and, potentially, the identity schemes of which those memories are a part; then via socialization, the elements that make up a given identity scheme are internalized, in part, through the encoding into memory of identity specific meanings, values, and practices. Not everything we experience is encoded in memory, however. How a person interprets, understands, or feels about an event or a piece of information has a great effect on what things are encoded in memory and exactly *how* these things are encoded, and thus how they are potentially retrieved and brought back to consciousness.

18. Singer, "Seeing One's Self." Singer has outlined a framework of personality and subjectivity that is an amalgamation of many of the most widely accepted concepts within the field of empirical psychology. The following description of subjectivity borrows significantly from his framework.

19. Ibid., 433. Affective evaluations can be distinguished from affective responses or feelings such as the feelings of fear or passion. A person might respond with fear at the prospect of entering a dark alley to look for a lost child, but they may evaluate this feeling as less important than the other elements motivating them in the task. While this distinction can be drawn, feminists have pointed out that emotional responses should not be ruled out as legitimate aspects of moral and political reasoning.

20. Ibid., 436.

21. Ibid., 442.

22. For example, affect serves three functions: a biological function (directing resources in the body in response to stimuli); a motivational function (to "focus and guide thought and behavior"); and an expressive/social function

(to communicate emotional states and preferences). For further description, see Singer, "Seeing One's Self."

23. Throughout this work I set aside the possibility that there are self-constructs, or propensities toward specific self-constructs, that are socially constructed but *also have* some biochemical or biological basis. It seems increasingly clear, however, on the basis of research in transgender identity, that at least gender identity may have psychobiological bases independent of the physical configurations of the body or an individual's dominant socialization. See Rudacille, *Riddle of Gender,* 3–20. Like other constructivist feminists and anti-racist scholars, however, I aim to resist any and all biological arguments that might be used to naturalize and sustain racial and gender subordination. In the context of ongoing anti-racist, anti-sexist struggles, therefore, I consider (re)introducing biological factors into discussions of identity as something that must be done carefully, and with an eye toward long-term political strategies.

24. Lugones, "Playfulness, 'World'-Traveling;" and Anzaldúa, *Interviews/Entrevistas.*

25. See Tajfel, *Human Groups and Social Categories;* Ellemers, Spears, and Doosje, eds., *Social Identity Context;* Turner, "Social Identity and Self-Categorization;" Hogg and Abrams, *Social Identifications;* Robinson, ed., *Legacy of Henri Tajfel;* Hogg and Terry, eds., *Social Identity Processes.* In communication, see Giles and Coupland, *Language: Contexts and Consequences.*

26. This approach is still somewhat common in personality psychology. See Turner, "Social Identity and Self-Categorization."

27. This understanding is also accepted in other domains of social and empirical psychology, and is sometimes called the "phenomenal self" or "spontaneous self-concept" (Baumeister, "The Self," 688).

28. Turner and Oakes, "Socially Structured Mind," 364.

29. As indicated above, this process of identity formation is bound up with the formation and retrieval of memory; see note 20.

30. Turner, "Social Identity and Self-Categorization," 12; Ellemers, Korktekaas and Ouwerkerk, "Commitment to the Group."

31. Specifically, Self-Categorization Theory (SCT) theorizes that salience is a function of both (a) the "fit" between a social category and (b) the "perceiver's readiness" to employ a particular identity (personal or social) as the relevant identity for a given circumstance. See Turner, "Social Identity and Self-Categorization," 12–14.

32. The process of self-categorization thus also involves categorizing others. See ibid.

33. Thanks to Reynaldo Macias for helping me to grasp the significance of contextual co-construction to the manifestation of multiple identities in everyday contexts.

34. Identification can also refer to the process in which a person internalizes some social category; for the process by which it becomes a part of the self-concept, see Turner, "Cognitive Redefinition," 17–18.

35. Waters, *Black Identities,* 287–325.

36. Ibid., 306.

37. See Portes and Rumbaut, *Legacies,* 154–61.

38. Some, such as Alasdair MacIntyre, argue that such identity shifts from context to context are indicative of moral failure on the part of individuals because moral agency requires consistency and uniformity in identification

from context to context. I address in depth MacIntyre's claim in chapters three, five, and six below.

39. Personal responses to the ascription of unwelcome or unexpected identity by others can vary as widely as people themselves. The experience can leave a strong impression or cause an intense emotional reaction that precipitates significant personal pain, self-reflection, and/or doubt. For an example involving emotions arising from unexpected racial classification and subordination see Martinez, "Identifying with America," 141–44.

40. Waters, *Black Identities,* 295, emphasis added.

41. James, *Principles of Psychology,* 314–52.

42. See Zengerle, "The Naked Guy;" and Nygard, *Trekkies.*

43. Identification across these divides is not as uncommon as many might think. See works by Yeskel, "Caught Between Two Cultures;" Abu Saba, "Heartbroken for Lebanon;" Walker, *Black, White, and Jewish;* Feinberg, *Transgender Warriors;* Ahmed, *A Border Passage;* Davis, *My Sense of Silence.*

44. My reading of Anzaldúa and my extension of her original concept of mestiza consciousness stands in contrast to those such as Jean-Luc Nancy who regard *mestizaje* as a trope for multiplicity in general as an inner diversity that "cannot be assigned to places of pure origins. . . . [as] mestizaje of identity itself, of any identity" (Nancy, "Cut Throat Sun," 121). In this work, any multiplicity of *identities* within the subject is present as a function of the specific socialization to ideas and images and their internalization and organization in memory as self-constructs. As such, a person's configurations of multiple identities can always be traced to membership in specific groups, relationships, and experiences. Not everyone—as Nancy asserts—will have the kinds of diverse memberships and experiences that will produce in them highly diverse, contradictory, or mutually exclusive identities of the kind possessed and theorized by Anzaldúa.

45. A shift in our salient identity schemes or other self-constructs may be unconscious. Priming studies demonstrate that social cues of stereotypes or trait self-concepts such as rudeness or politeness cannot make those concepts salient and influential on behavior without the conscious awareness of those studied. See Bargh, "Automaticity of Everyday Life," 17–19; and Bargh and Chartrand, "Unbearable Automaticity of Being."

46. Turner, "Social Identity and Self-Categorization," 12; Ellemers, Kortekaas, and Ouwerkerk, "Commitment to the Group."

47. Turner, "Social Identity and Self-Categorization," 12–13.

48. Crenshaw, "Demarginalizing the Intersection," 391.

49. Turner, "Social Identity and Self-Categorization;" Higgins, "Knowledge Activation."

50. The identity or identities with which the subject is most deeply identified might be any available identity scheme, a cultural identity, gender or sexual identity, a professional identity or other role-based identity (e.g. labor organizer).

51. Higgins, "Knowledge Activation."

52. For discussion of the significance of racial framing in political campaigns, see Mendleberg, *The Race Card.*

53. It is also limited by the power of salience dynamics to bring to mind frames of reference that we wish to reject. See the example of *Casablanca*'s Richard Blaine in chapter five.

54. Kondo, "Dissolution and Reconstruction." My discussion of Kondo's experi-

ence of multiple identities is informed by an essay on intersectionality by Renato Rosaldo, see *Culture and Truth,* 150–70.

55. In anthropological fieldwork jargon, this incident raises the question of whether Kondo had "gone native." Since Kondo is Japanese American, her physical resemblance to other Japanese women potentially excites the expectation among those that she encounters in Japan that she will conform to the same code of social custom observed by other Japanese women. Her immersion into the culture could therefore be virtually total.

56. Both quotations, Torres, *Land of Mirrors,* 198–99.

57. Ibid., 198.

58. For material on the political context of the development of this concept see King, "Multiple Jeopardy, Multiple Consciousness;" and Moraga and Anzaldúa eds., *Bridge Called My Back.*

59. For a history of development of the concept among a number of Black women scholars, see Collins, *Fighting Words,* 114–20.

60. Ibid., 278.

61. Crenshaw, "Mapping the Margins," and "Demarginalizing the Intersection."

62. Waters, *Black Identities,* 295.

63. Collins contends that one risk of intersectionality is to suggest equivalence between the experiences of those who suffer subordination of one kind and those who suffer multiple subordinations. My hope here is to mitigate that risk by further theorizing different dimensions of intersectionality that allow us to recognize relative variations in social burdens. The political significance of this is discussed in detail in chapter six in which the potential for recognizing social privilege is critical to self-integration of multiple identities (ibid., 210–11).

64. Crenshaw, "Demarginalizing the Intersection."

65. Waters, *Black Identities,* 295, bracketed material in original.

66. Waters, *Black Identities,* 293, bracketed material in original.

67. This point may seem to contradict a main theme in the previous chapter in which I argue that ethnic identity and national identity are distinct, and that for Latinos these two identities are, for the most part, alternately salient. There is no contradiction, however, in that in both cases, intersections are always either socially constructed or self-crafted and that many Latinos seem to regard their ethnic identities as compatible with U.S. national identity, even if others such as Huntington do not agree. Moreover, in every case, what identity scheme(s) become(s) salient is a function of how various social cues are perceived and spontaneously (sometimes unconsciously) interpreted. Thus, while it is typically the case that Latina/o ethnic identities do not intersect with national identities of other regimes (to which native-born Latinos generally have not been socialized), Latina/o ethnic identities *may* intersect with national identities, including U.S. national identity. Latina/o servicemen and -women who feel a kind of ethnic pride in serving in the U.S. military would be an example.

68. Hong and others, "Multicultural Minds," 710, emphasis added. Hong's essay suggests that this may be shifting. This and other research on bicultural identity and shifts in identity salience that utilize SIT present evidence that negative or antagonistic association is enough to link otherwise incongruent schemes to make them salient as frameworks for thought and action. Nonetheless, in contrast to Anzaldúa, these recent studies say little about the emotional experiences of those who navigate social contexts through their

inconsistent identity schemes. For brief statements that may foreshadow this shift see Hong and others, "Multicultural Minds," 718; and Benet-Martínez and others, "Negotiating Biculturalism."

69. Baumeister, "The Self," 688; see also Hogg, *Social Identifications,* 24–25; and more generally, Markus and Wurf, "Dynamic Self-Concept." Also see Turner and others, *Rediscovering the Social Group.*

CHAPTER THREE

1. MacIntyre, *Whose Justice? Which Rationality?,* 397. For a nuanced account of these communitarian critiques, see Digeser, *Our Politics, Our Selves?,* 12–23.

2. Intersectionality is defined in detail in chapter two. Briefly, it refers to overlapping or intertwined meanings or practices between two or more social spheres and their associated identities. Intersections can be manifest both in the links in understanding within subjectivity *and* in material and discursive aspects of social life. I use the term "intersectionality" to refer collectively to both social and cognitive manifestations.

3. In this chapter, I focus on multiple identities in relation to critical thought as a factor basic and significant in political life. I do not, however, investigate the broader philosophical question of how multiple identities relate to traditional conceptions of autonomy, and how such concepts might be reconceptualized to take multiple identities more fully into account. I have addressed this question elsewhere; see "Mestiza Autonomy."

4. Above quotations, MacIntyre, *After Virtue,* 32.

5. Ibid., emphasis added to quotations in this paragraph.

6. Ibid.

7. He argues that liberal democracy is itself largely to blame for the transformation in the self, see *After Virtue,* 30–31. He writes: "This democratized self which has no necessary social content and no necessary social identity can then be anything, can assume any role or take any point of view, because it *is* in and for itself nothing" (ibid., emphasis in original).

8. MacIntyre, "Threats to Moral Agency," 319.

9. Both above quotations Ibid., 318.

10. Ibid.

11. Above quotations Ibid., 315.

12. Ibid., 318.

13. Ibid.

14. Ibid., 327.

15. Ibid., 324. This separation of different social spheres is enforced by social practices of "insulation" in which the introduction of moral standards into a sphere in which they are alien is met with resistance in the form of dismissals, jokes, ridicule, or actions that simply ignore what does not fit. Moreover, insulation cannot be overcome by accountability, since for MacIntyre, there is little overlap of personnel from one context to the next in which the moral choices made in one role setting must be held accountable to witnesses from another. On all counts then, for MacIntyre it is the *diversity* of the self (and more specifically the separateness of the subject's multiple identities) that prevents the self from being able to exercise moral agency.

16. Ibid., 324–25, emphasis added.

17. Both quotations above Ibid., 317.

18. Ibid., 318.

19. Anzaldúa, *Interviews/Entrevistas,* 141. Anzaldúa considered such a transformation to be slowly taking place within feminist communities.

20. Emphasizing the identity as constructed in relation to others past and present she writes: "Identity is not just what happens to me in my present lifetime but also involves my family history, my racial history, my collective story . . ." (ibid., 240). Like MacIntyre, she too thinks a sense of one's heritage is vital to effectiveness. She states: "Kids of color growing up now don't have a sense of roots. Their identities are secondhand—derivative from the white—so they are floundering. They know they are not white, and the issues of language keep coming up" (ibid., 204).

21. For Anzaldúa's treatment of this example, see *Interviews/Entrevistas,* 168. In my reading, mestiza consciousness is a decentered subjectivity in that no internalized identity-related or identity-independent elements within subjectivity have status as hierarchically more important or are considered central to or defining of the self prior to the values assigned to those internalized elements but by the subject her self. Anzaldúa emphasizes the process of self-making in which the priority and shape of different identifications within the self are remade by the mestiza over time.

22. Ibid., 177.

23. MacIntyre, "Threats to Moral Agency," 318.

24. Anzaldúa, *Interviews/Entrevistas,* 239.

25. Ibid.

26. Ibid., 178.

27. Ibid., 239.

28. Ibid., 238.

29. Ibid., 267.

30. Ibid.

31. Ibid., 266.

32. Ibid., 239.

33. Waters, *Black Identities,* 303–304; for her data on multiple identifications among immigrants see especially 287–325.

34. Du Bois, *Souls of Black Folk,* 45.

35. Ibid.

36. Anzaldúa, *Interviews/Entrevistas,* 255.

37. Ibid., 254.

38. Waters, *Black Identities,* 300.

39. Ibid., 299–300.

40. Above quotations, MacIntyre, "Threats to Moral Agency," 323.

41. Ibid., 322.

42. In the following analysis, I focus on the ethics of deceit involving the use of scientific research and leave the cocktail party exaggeration aside. While exaggerated storytelling might be considered a shade in character and even morally blameworthy in prevailing cultural norms in the U.S., this not a serious contradiction. Rather, it is one that falls into the category of socially acceptable contradictions, which we are seldom under any pressure to resolve (see chapter four for a typology of identity contradictions).

43. Turner, "Social Identity and Self-Categorization."

44. See chapter two for further discussion and references.

45. See Cohen, *Symbolic Construction of Community.*

46. MacIntyre, "Threats to Moral Agency," 323.

47. This is at odds with a basic assumption in Social Identity Theory and discussed in chapter two. Namely, that it is widely agreed in social psychology that the self-constructs activated as the working-self at any given time *must be consistent* since two contradictory meaning systems "simply cannot simultaneously guide cognition" (Hong and others, "Multicultural Minds," 710). See also Hogg and Abrams, *Social Identifications,* 24–25.

48. The dynamics of this type of group-think are a matter of significant concern within philosophy as well as the domains of social psychology that inform this investigation. However, a deeper engagement with this in relation to critical reflection and self-critique is beyond the scope of this study.

49. Activist and writer Michael Moore, for example, makes a career out of cultivating this kind of accountability, beginning with his widely respected documentary on corporate greed *Roger and Me* to his more recent *Fahrenheit 911.* Likewise, some professions, such as investigative journalism, regard fostering such accountability as a central part of their professional mandate. The work of Moore and others underscores that cross-context accountability, while requiring effort, is not impossible to produce.

50. Shaw, *Reclaiming America,* 75–76. Most of those who took part in this movement were college students from middle class backgrounds. Their commitment to defending the rights of impoverished working women of color outside of the U.S. and the accompanying critique of corporate greed, came from those whose identities would, in MacIntyre's logic, have ruled out their critique of the capitalist system of privilege from which they had all of their lives probably benefited and still stood to gain.

51. MacIntyre, "Threats to Moral Agency," 311.

52. Ibid., 312.

53. Ibid., 325, italics in original.

54. Ibid., 326. MacIntyre does not specify how this management is to take place. As described in chapter two, it involves interpreting different contexts, assessing relationships to and among others, and enacting different identities in different contexts.

55. Ibid., 326.

56. Ibid.

57. Ibid., 327.

58. Anzaldúa, *Borderlands,* 79.

59. MacIntyre, "Threats to Moral Agency," 311.

60. Ibid. The conception of responsibility used here seems to be an empty marker left so wide open that the reader may fairly ask, "Duty to what? Responsibility to whom?" To have weight, conceptions of duty and responsibility should be related to specific factors or moral codes (e.g. Victorian responsibility tied to standards of decorum and polite society, or Chicana/o duty tied to collective responsibility for care of the family). In the analysis that follows, the omission is read as obscuring J's culturally specific "duty and responsibility" to the father and to a patriarchal model of authority.

61. Yet this group identity, like any other, will contain different and contradictory meanings and practices. Thus different individuals subscribing to it may selectively identify with it, claiming different elements as those that signify membership and group identification for them. Consequently, for many "sportsmanship" in the vernacular is associated with honesty and fair play. For others, however, sportsmanship is about obtaining victory in a contest

in which fair play is less valued. Soccer hooliganism in Europe and sporadic post-game riots in the United States are violent reminders of this latter perspective.

62. This is not to say that ideally there is *only* contradiction within subjectivity. As stressed in chapter two, there may also be significant overlap and commonality among different identities within an overall subjectivity. But in the case of J, the diversity and conflict among his various identities were so minimal as to barely count as diverse at all.

63. See Kruglanski and Webster, "Motivated Closing of the Mind." In addition, interpretive and attitudinal bias toward information that reinforces cherished self-concepts is associated with various psychological factors, some of which are relatively adaptive, such as self-esteem. See Baumeister, "The Self," 696–99.

64. Wegner and Bargh, "Control and Automaticity in Social Life," 471. As discussed in chapter two, not everything to which we are exposed on a daily basis is internalized in the form of long-term memories and self-constructs. How we feel toward certain stimuli greatly affects if and how the information to which we are exposed is internalized or integrated as part of new or existing identity schemes. See Schacter, *Searching for Memory.*

65. In her later work Anzaldúa likewise emphasized the capacity and propensity to not just hear but *listen* to unfamiliar and critical points of view beyond our own as an important dimension of mestiza consciousness and *nepantalist* thought and *conocimientos;* see for example, *Interviews/Entrevistas,* 177–78.

66. In his controversial book *Hitler's Willing Executioners,* Daniel Goldhagen argues that not only was Nazi collaboration more widespread and enjoyed among average Germans than frequently acknowledged, but that it was the product of widespread anti-Semitism that preceded Hitler's rise.

67. The tendency toward fascism and/or intense prejudice may have other sources, such as the tendency toward rigid and stereotypical patterns of thought. The sources of fascism are, of course, ongoing and now increasingly relevant topics of debate. Analysis or rigidity of thought related to this can be found in classic explanations of racism and other forms of extreme intergroup hatred such as anti-Semitism. See Allport, *The Nature of Prejudice* and Adorno and others, *The Authoritarian Personality.*

68. This point should be distinguished from cognitive dissonance. The argument is not that everyone seeks to avoid unfamiliar or cognitively unsettling ideas. Rather it is that those with minimally diverse identities are more prone to do so, *unless* seeking out new and unsettling information is a practice that is central to their relatively homogenous identities. See Pittman, "Motivation," 557–61.

69. Thanks to an anonymous reviewer for drawing my attention to this point.

70. This leaves open the question of J's moral responsibility. It may be said in reference to this that J's desire to follow orders is his only frame of reference and basis for choice because he has nothing against which to choose or reject that desire. Yet, in the act of making the desire to obey orders effective by endorsing it as his second-order preference, it becomes his will and in turn he may be morally responsible for the consequences of exercising that will. Critics might persuasively argue, however, that J would under this circumstance be unable to choose his own second-order preferences, or at least such a choice would be impossible to distinguish from having not made a choice, since there is nothing contrasting to choose from. Along this line of reasoning, J is probably not responsible (or more likely his responsibility is hopelessly obscured in the

question of whether he endorsed his one desire or simply lived it). If so, then J's moral agency is so severely weakened as to render him not fully responsible for the atrocities in which he was involved. The fact that J's responsibility for moral atrocity and weakened moral agency is not his alone, however, does not then legally vacate his responsibility. Most legal codes consider the degree of responsibility in the perpetration of any crime. J is implicated in genocide because the act of driving the train makes him an accessory. If he did not know the contents of the train, it is because of his failure to judge and critically assess the suspicious circumstances before him, a failure that renders him criminally negligent for not finding out what those boxcars held. J is morally responsible. The degree of his responsibility is lessened only in comparison with those who imagined and engineered the atrocities in which J was willingly or unwillingly complicit.

71. J's friends, family, and social groups may bear particular responsibility as those best positioned to offer diverse perspectives in ways that foster positive reception.

CHAPTER FOUR

1. A model of decentered and multiple subjectivity must therefore account not only for personal identity as having *diachronic* variation—i.e. the diversity of the self over time—but also account for its *synchronic* variation—its diversity at a given time. For works on this problem in philosophy see, for example, Parfit, *Reasons and Persons;* and Williams, *Problems of the Self.*

2. Both quotations from James, *Principles of Psychology,* 282; emphasis in original.

3. Hume, *Treatise of Human Nature,* 252.

4. James, *Principles of Psychology,* 333.

5. Ibid., 321. Both the term and the quotation may be found here.

6. Ibid., 319–22.

7. Ibid., 320. James also mentions a further distinction between *self*-brand and herd-brand. I shall return to this distinction later in this chapter and in the next.

8. Ibid.

9. Ibid., 321.

10. Ibid.

11. Ibid.

12. Ibid. James and his imagined interlocutress further agree that *logically* and *intuitively* this analogy leads to the conclusion that there is some kind of spirited sense or Arch-Ego that is the medium of personal cohesion. Fully considering this additional possibility for understanding decentered subjectivity, however, is not necessary to the project of this book and would digress from its focus. The Jamesian account of personal identity—adopted and understood in this work as one's unique and idiosyncratic relationship to one's self, has not settled the ongoing debate within the philosophy of mind as to the character of personal identity. See for example, Parfit, *Reasons and Persons,* and Rorty, ed., *The Identities of Persons.*

13. Here I am deviating for the sake of clarity from the terminology of Social Identity Theory. As stated in chapter two, SIT holds that all elements within subjectivity are *available* to become salient as the framework for thought or action at any time. At the same time, not all elements have the same degree of *accessibility,* and therefore not all are equally *likely* to become salient in a given moment. Thus in SIT terminology, thought-in-the-moment—or what social

psychologists in general call the working or phenomenological self—would be said to have a bond of *availability* to each element in subjectivity as potentially salient in conscious thought.

14. Ibid.

15. Ibid., 322.

16. Ibid., 324.

17. Ibid., 324.

18. Ibid., 319–20, emphasis added.

19. To use another metaphor, judging-Thought is like a computer's "operating system" for which identity schemes can be thought to provide the programs. This analogy is not entirely apt however, in that the complexity added to judging-Thought is embodied as part of a psychophysiological process. I shall argue below that salience permits an intrapsychic critical distance over the range of multiple identity schemes within subjectivity as a function of identity contradiction and the passively received and self-introduced intersections between identity schemes within subjectivity; see chapters five and six for detailed discussion.

20. The psychophysiological system relates to what are generally regarded as "involuntary" gestures and to what is increasingly referred to in vernacular speech as the body-mind. This concept refers to the notion that psychological processes directly and indirectly affect bodily functions and vice versa outside of conscious, intentional thought.

21. See Digeser, *Our Politics, Our Selves,* 196–213. Digeser persuasively establishes that Foucauldian postrstructuralism presupposes agency in the socially constructed subject. As Digeser concludes that " . . . examination of Foucault's position points to a general problem with seeing the self as having the capacity to act and understand [in a constructivist framework]: *it is difficult if not impossible to set out the practices that constitutes such a self. The relevant capacity. . . . is presupposed in the discussion of practices and conventions"* that are the constitutive dynamics in constructivist theory (ibid., 210). Here Digeser's analysis simultaneously turns and rebuts the longstanding view that constructivism denies the possibility of agency. I grant Digeser's point and accept the limitations in my argument that Digeser establishes. I would respond optimistically, however, that it may be still possible to "set out" the elements that constitute agency by uniting William James's account of judging-Thought with Foucauldian "technologies of the self" and with insights drawn from neurobiology and neuropsychology. While there is a gesture toward such an interdisciplinary approach in this chapter, it is beyond the scope of this project to fully address this possibility.

22. Rorty, "Self-Deception, *Akrasia,* and Irrationality," 115–16. See also McLaughlin and Rorty, eds., *Perspectives on Self-Deception.*

23. Rorty, "Self-Deception, Akrasia, and Irrationality," 116.

24. Ibid.

25. Gregg, "Multiple Identities and Integration," 621. In his qualitative research in cross-cultural personality psychology, Gary Gregg finds the overarching narrative to be the "press release," behind which many other competing narratives inevitably emerge in daily life, even in the course of a single conversation.

26. Rorty, "Self-Deception, *Akrasia,* and Irrationality," 125.

27. Ibid., 120. As she notes, and as is noted in chapter two, in terms of the behavioral subsystem of subjectivity, this is "precisely the strength and function of

habit: it is capable of being exercised relatively independently of the agent's occurent motives," (ibid., 121).

28. Ibid. emphasis added.

29. Ibid., 126.

30. Ibid., 127.

31. Omi and Winant, *Racial Formation.*

32. Waters, *Black Identities,* 295. For further discussion, see chapter two in this book.

33. Rorty, "Self-Deception, *Akrasia,* and Irrationality," 131.

34. Popular wariness of dissociative identity disorder is fueled by popular familiarity with dramatic and well-known stories of dissociated identity disorders such as novels like *Sybil* and *Three Faces of Eve,* and with various high profile criminal cases involving dissociative identity disorders. In this context, and in the context of challenges to the traditional understanding of the noncontradictory "unity" of the subject, references to a diversity or multiplicity of identities within the subject can, to some, connote the idea of dissociative identity disorder. This connotation has led at least one philosopher theorizing the implications of María Lugones's work on mestiza consciousness to avoid the language of "multiple" identity because, in her words, "its associations with the pathology of multiple personality disorder make it an unfortunate choice" (Meyers, "Intersectional Identity," 146). Concern with this connotation is not unfounded, yet having multiple identities (which virtually everyone does) is very different from having clinically dissociated identities, something that is extremely rare and quite distinct as defined below.

35. Braun, "Bask Model of Dissociation," 4.

36. This is what we mean in part in ordinary language when we refer to ourselves as having been "on autopilot." Dissociation is distinct from repression; although at times repression has been thought to subsume dissociation. The traditional emphasis on repression over dissociation in psychology is often described as a function of a disciplinary battle between Pierre Janet, *Major Symptoms of Hysteria* (the first major theorist of dissociated consciousness) and Sigmund Freud, in which Freud's idea of repression became more widely acknowledged. See Braude, *First Person Plural* and Waites, *Trauma and Survival.*

37. Task force on DSM-IV, *Manual of Mental Disorders,* 477.

38. This condition was formerly referred to as Multiple Personality Disorder. There has been extensive controversy over this condition, which has contributed to its renaming. The debate remains intensive, with some critics in various subfields denying that the disease exists and arguing that memories of child sexual abuse can be inadvertently instilled through the therapeutic process (Everest, "Multiple Self;" Chu, *Rebuilding Shattered Lives,* 41). Others provide research findings that show a high correlation between dissociative disorders and severe child sexual abuse (Chu, "Dissociative Symptomology"). Many clinicians working with DID patients contend that the disease is real and requires specific forms of treatment, the best shape for which is also a controversial topic (Chu, *Rebuilding Shattered Lives;* van der Hart, van der Kolk and Boon, "Treatment of Dissociative Disorders").

39. Margo Rivera, "Psychological and the Social," 24.

40. Braude, *First Person Plural.*

41. Rorty, "Self-Deception, *Akrasia,* and Irrationality," 121.

42. Braude, *First Person Plural.*

43. Flax, *Thinking Fragments,* 3. See also Flax, *American Dream in Black and White.*

44. *Thinking Fragments,* 220.

45. Adams, Wright, and Lohr, "Homophobia with Homosexual Arousal." Researchers note that it is also possible that physical arousal of homophobic men was rooted in intense anxiety rather than in unacknowledged homosexual desire. This possibility does not undermine the argument I have offered here, for if anxiety—rather than desire—is at the heart of the apparent identity contradiction, anxiety regarding homosexuals is likely to have been socially learned.

46. Flax, *Thinking Fragments,* 182.

47. Ibid., 212.

48. Ibid., 182.

49. Ibid., 179.

50. Ibid., 179; see also, 180–82.

51. Benhabib, *Situating the Self,* 213, emphasis added.

52. Flax, *Thinking Fragments,* 179. As Flax suggests, reluctance among some feminists to consider contradiction and multiplicity as fruitful as well as challenging preoccupied feminist scholarship for some time in the 1990s. However, the complexities of cultural contradiction are now gaining wider attention among feminists. See Benhabib, *Situating the Self* and Benhabib, *The Claims of Culture,* respectively.

53. Flax, *Thinking Fragments,* 182.

54. Rorty, "Self-Deception, *Akrasia,* and Irrationality," 121.

55. In her careful analysis of a full range of feminist discourses, Flax finds that female aggression constitutes one of the gaps in feminist theorizing of gender.

56. Flax, *Thinking Fragments,* 183.

CHAPTER FIVE

1. Their respective arguments are discussed in detail below. See Frankfurt, "Identification and Wholeheartedness," and "Freedom of the Will;" Taylor, *Sources of the Self* and *Ethics of Authenticity;* MacIntyre, "Unity of Human Life."

2. Rorty, "Self-Deception, *Akrasia,* and Irrationality;" Flax, *Thinking Fragments,* 11; Anzaldúa, *Borderlands,* 79–80, 82–83.

3. Frankfurt, "Identification and Wholeheartedness," 38.

4. Frankfurt, "Freedom of the Will," 16, emphasis added.

5. Ibid., emphasis added.

6. Frankfurt, "Identification and Wholeheartedness," 38.

7. Ibid., 39.

8. Taylor refers to similar elements, first emphasizing the ordering of goods in which hypergoods are hierarchically highest and second, that through strong evaluation the self determines not only what she values and endorses, but also, by implication, what she rejects (Taylor, *Sources of the Self,* 63).

9. Frankfurt, "Identification and Wholeheartedness," 39.

10. Anzaldúa, *Borderlands,* 79–80, 82–83.

11. Heo, *Between Two Worlds.*

12. Thanks to P. E. Digeser for assistance with this point.

13. Barth, *Ethnic Groups and Boundaries;* Cohen, *Symbolic Construction of Community;* Laitin, *Identity Formation: Russian Populations.*

14. Parekh, *Gandhi's Political Philosophy,* 20.

15. As noted in chapter one, surveys routinely find that Latinos overwhelmingly

favor the learning of English by immigrant children. A recent Pew Center survey showed that 92 percent of native-born and 96 percent of foreign-born Latinos feel that it is very important for children of immigrants to learn English. In contrast to the U.S. mainstream, however, 46 percent of native-born Latinos did not feel that speaking English was absolutely necessary to consider oneself a part of U.S. society. See Pew, *Hispanic Attitudes Toward English.*

16. For a discussion of additive intersections see chapter two.

17. Syncretic fusion can itself be seen as autonomous action. I have discussed the process of generating hybrid sets of cultural endorsements elsewhere; see Barvosa, "Mestiza Autonomy."

18. Lugones, "Hispaneando y Lesbiando." The following discussion of Lugones' Latina lesbian politics is based on her points in this essay with some departures that I will note below.

19. Ibid., 142. In New Mexico, it has been common historically for individuals of Mexican heritage to be referred as Spanish or Hispanic. This is idiosyncratic in contrast to Texas, California, and other regions of the United States in which the terms Chicana, Mexicana, and more recently Latina, have historically been more in use than Spanish or Hispana. In her essay, Lugones uses the terminology specific to New Mexico and uses the terms Chicana and Latina to refer to Latinas in other contexts.

20. Lugones, "Hispaneando y Lesbiando."

21. Ibid., 139.

22. Barth, *Ethnic Groups and Boundaries,* 14. As Fredrik Barth described in his classic work on ethnic identity, the key criteria for claiming a group identity is ascription—both self-ascription and ascription by others—by which the boundary of the identity group is established and maintained and who is inside and outside of that boundary is negotiated in an ongoing manner (ibid.). These signs and practices vary from one identity group to the next and will often vary for a single group identity over time. But as long as some elements are invoked to name the group, the group persists over time. While Barth focuses particularly on ethnic groups, his introductory essay indicates that his analysis is also applicable to other kinds of groups with the same "organizational anchoring" in which group identity is produced not through group traits, but through processes of boundary maintenance (ibid., 38). Likewise, I apply Barth's insights to other identity groups, as other readers of Barth have done. See chapter two for further discussion.

23. In practice, many inter- and intra-group boundary struggles involve contestation over what group identity markers will be accepted as indicative of group membership. Are Chicano rappers too hip-hop in style to be Chicanos? To debate such a question implicitly recognizes the daily operation of selective identification in identity group dynamics, unless that debate involves essentializing Chicano identity.

24. Waters, *Black Identities,* 239. For a relevant account of diversity in patterns of Latina self-identification, see Zavella, "Diversity Among Chicanas."

25. Cohen, *Symbolic Construction of Community.* The meanings that members of a community impute to the shared symbols of their community are "mediated by the idiosyncratic experience of the individual" (ibid., 14). Thus, a Scot "would refract 'Scottishness' through [his] personal experience—as Shetland fisherman, Kincardine farmer, Fife miner, or Clydeside shipbuilder, father, son, brother, agnostic, music lover, socialist, and so forth" (ibid., 14–15).

26. This is because the boundary is ultimately what establishes the group and ensures that it remains intact regardless of its shifting content (Cohen,

Symbolic Construction of Community, 74). To put this point in terms of Barth's conception of ethnic identity, social identity groups can persist despite changes in their cultural content and diachronic markers, despite the flow of membership across group boundaries, and despite contact with other social groups, including the exchange of information and possible mutual influence among social groups. In fact, social contact with different others is the necessary condition for the expression of group difference, since it is in reference to different others that group boundaries are established at any given time. Thus, it is logical and theoretically consistent that the greater the degree of interaction with different "others," the greater the impetus and possibility for groups to express group specificity. I believe that this explains, in part, why in an era such as ours, marked by increasing globalization and faster and more extensive communication among diverse cultures, there has been a "surprising" reassertion of group identity.

27. Lugones, "Hispaneando y Lesbiando," 141.

28. This form of self-integration contrasts with the hypothetical example of Park's self-integration via his education endorsement discussed above, in which I argued that the intersection would override in Park's mind the received cultural fragmentation on the basis of common cultural values.

29. Ellmann, *Yeats;* Foster, *W. B. Yeats: A Life.*

30. Lugones, *Pilgrimages/Peregrinajes.*

31. See Anzaldúa, *Interviews/Entrevistas,* 214–16, 156–58, 196–200; Martínez, *De Colores Means All,* 198–203.

32. Lugones, "Hispaneando y Lesbiando."

33. This situation is, of course, not unique to those with multiple identities. Anyone may experience attacks on their principled actions when those actions go against the social norms. However, those with multiple identities are more likely to experience such resistance to their chosen endorsements to the extent that they often choose their endorsements from the norms of divided groups and then practice those endorsements in social interactions across those same divided groups.

34. Given the potential trials of having multiple identities, one might reasonably ask why Park or Lugones do not simply abandon or disidentify with the identities that are the most likely to excite opposition. Given the desire for a sense of standing on firm social ground for which Christian Park seems to yearn, is it incoherent to retain social identities that cause others to question one's self understanding? The answer is that some people *do* choose to abandon one or another of their multiple identities in order to escape the conflict or forms of subordination associated with them. They may do so by "passing" as members of one group or another, or engaging in uncoerced forms of assimilation despite the fact that they could identify with two or more mutually exclusive identity groups if they chose to do so. In many cases, however, to disidentify with one of their mutually exclusive identities is not realistically available as a choice. For Park or others whose social identities are racialized and so partly defined through phenotype, disavowal of those identities is seldom possible no matter how little they identify with those identities. In other cases, people with multiple identities simply do not want to disidentify with some of their multiple identities. Coerced assimilation rejects that choice however, and it is has been a common part of ethnic group subordination. Historian Vicki Ruiz describes how in 1930s and 1940s El Paso, Texas, prenatal and pediatric health care was dispensed to low-income Chicanas by missionaries only if Chicanas were "willing" to submit themselves and their children to Ameri-

canization programs designed to have them adopt Anglo-American culture over Mexican American culture. Because healthcare was difficult to obtain in El Paso barrios, many reluctantly participated. However, many also resisted assimilation pressures by selectively identifying with aspects of Anglo culture they found useful while continuing to embrace their Mexican American identities as well. Ruiz, *From Out of the Shadows*, 33–50.

35. Flax, *Thinking Fragments*, 11.

36. Ibid.

37. Marilyn Friedman argued some time ago that a structural account of autonomy such as Frankfurt's could be amended to have endorsements ranked, not in a strict hierarchy, but in a kind of pyramid structure in which some endorsements would be on a par with one another. Friedman, "Split-Level Self."

38. This may not be true for everyone with multiple identities. Others may have endorsements according to which they will conform more readily to group norms in contexts; see Pickett, Coleman, and Bonner, "Motivated Self-Stereotyping," 545–46 and 558–59. Of course, as stated earlier, not everyone opts to develop a self-integrating set of endorsements, and some who do are weak-willed toward those endorsements.

39. See MacIntyre, *After Virtue* and Taylor, *Sources of the Self*, 47–52. In addition, there are many other philosophers that employ an account of narrative unity; see Sandel, *Liberalism;* Giddens, *Modernity and Self-Identity;* Benhabib, *Situating the Self*, 212–14; and Ricoeur, *Oneself as Another*. For Taylor's account of authentic self-fulfillment, see *Ethics of Authenticity*. A feminist account of selfhood based on authenticity can be read in Meyers, "Intersectional Identity."

40. MacIntyre, "Unity of Human Life," 255.

41. Ibid., 256.

42. Taylor, *Sources of the Self*, 29. See also chapters two and three.

43. Ibid., 30.

44. Taylor, *Ethics of Authenticity*, 47.

45. Both quotations, Taylor, *Sources of the Self*, 36, emphasis added.

46. Eco, "Casablanca," 261.

47. Ibid., 263.

48. Ibid.

49. Ibid., 264.

50. "At the Blue Parrot," *Casablanca,* DVD, directed by Michael Curtiz (1943; Burbank, Cal.; Turner Entertainment Co. and Warner Home Video, 1999).

51. The dialogue continually plays with these contradictions. For example, Rick evades Strasser's questions about his nationality by sardonically naming himself a drunkard when the audience already knows that his conservative drinking habits often give social offense. Similarly, Senor Ferrari describes himself as an influential and respected man in Casablanca because he is the local leader of the Black market.

52. "Ferrari, Yvonne and Henri," *Casablanca,* DVD, directed by Michael Curtiz (1943; Burbank, Cal.: Turner Entertainment Co. and Warner Home Video, 1999).

53. The "must" in this is a function of the field of power relations in which he must act. To give her the funds would be to openly betray Renault and reveal the bride's struggle to her husband, who certainly would wish to know the reasons for Rick's intervention. "Les Jeux Sont Faits," *Casablanca,* DVD,

directed by Michael Curtiz (1943; Burbank, Cal.: Turner Entertainment Co. and Warner Home Video, 1999).

54. Throughout the film the staff (Emile, Carl, and Sasha) and Renault present two social spheres with contradictory sets of norms and values and Rick must negotiate the contrary expectations of each. When he begins drinking heavily to cope with Ilsa's return, Louis interprets his drinking as improved sociability (ibid.).

55. "Ilsa's Plea," *Casablanca*, DVD, directed by Michael Curtiz (1943; Burbank, Cal.; Turner Entertainment Co. and Warner Home Video, 1999).

56. "'A Close One,'" *Casablanca*, DVD, directed by Michael Curtiz (1943; Burbank, Cal.; Turner Entertainment Co. and Warner Home Video, 1999).

57. "Rick and Ugarte," *Casablanca*, DVD, directed by Michael Curtiz (1943; Burbank, Cal.; Turner Entertainment Co. and Warner Home Video, 1999).

58. Rorty, "Self-Deception, *Akrasia* and Irrationality," 126.

59. "My Husband," *Casablanca*, DVD, directed by Michael Curtiz (1943; Burbank, Cal.; Turner Entertainment Co. and Warner Home Video, 1999).

60. Flax, *Thinking Fragments*, 11, emphasis added.

61. This is assuming that "what she supposed was love" was ever romantic, rather than principally respectful and admiring. She suggests the latter in her first encounter with Rick while he is drunk, after hours at the café.

62. "Here's Looking at You," *Casablanca*, DVD, directed by Michael Curtiz (1943; Burbank, Cal.: Turner Entertainment Co. and Warner Home Video, 1999).

63. He refuses to drink socially as he did routinely with Ilsa in Paris, and his social interactions are now marred by a disengaged pensiveness that makes him both rude and perverse despite his capacity to be charming and socially skilled.

64. When Rick sits down to a drink with Renault, Ilsa, and Laszlo, Renault marvels that a precedent has been broken. A second precedent goes when Rick picks up the bill.

65. In the moral borderlands of the café, the shift in Rick's drinking habits are taken by Rick's loyal staff to be dangerously negative but regarded by Renault as Rick's improved sociability.

66. Eco, "Casablanca," 262.

67. "A Beautiful Friendship," *Casablanca*, DVD, directed by Michael Curtiz (1943; Burbank, Cal.: Turner Entertainment Co. and Warner Home Video, 1999). Unfortunately, it is beyond the scope of this chapter to explore gender intersectionality in *Casablanca* and the debt that masculine efficacy owes to feminine gender expressions at various points in the film. But at least in relation to Rick's masculinity as it is expressed in his political efficacy, it is unclear whether Rick would have recovered his verve for political engagement without Ilsa's pathbreaking aid.

68. "A Beautiful Friendship," *Casablanca*, DVD, directed by Michael Curtiz (1943; Burbank, Cal.: Turner Entertainment Co. and Warner Home Video, 1999).

69. "Ilsa's Plea," *Casablanca*, DVD, directed by Michael Curtiz (1943; Burbank, Cal.: Turner Entertainment Co. and Warner Home Video, 1999).

70. "Table for Four, Eyes for One," *Casablanca*, DVD, directed by Michael Curtiz (1943; Burbank, Cal.: Turner Entertainment Co. and Warner Home Video, 1999).

71. "Les Jeux Sont Faits," *Casablanca,* DVD, directed by Michael Curtiz (1943; Burbank, Cal.: Turner Entertainment Co. and Warner Home Video, 1999).

72. Conversely, it may also be the case that such multiple self-narratives will be a function of multiple identities at varying degrees of integration, from the complete wanton to the self who successfully integrates itself using a rigid rank-order of endorsements. See Gary S. Gregg's research on multiple identities in the context of Morocco and the Middle East—"Culture, Personality, and Multiplicity."

73. Critics may fairly argue that Taylor's idea of an "authentic self" goes against the grain of the constructivist approach to the self that is foundational to this book and advocated in it. Yet, it is not outside the realm of possibility that Taylor is right that there are some things more true than others about each individual—and hence aspects of each self that are inexplicably "authentic" to them. Nor would it necessarily follow from allowing this possibility that such authentic qualities might not be as likely to arrive in subjectivity by means of social construction, as by qualities of the physical body or—as Taylor argues indirectly—by divine providence. However they get to be there, "authentic" aspects of the self could thus be seen as characterized not by their nature or source but by the limits of their malleability to internal or external forces. In this interpretation of authenticity, whatever Rick does, his political predilections and his love are so authentic to him that every effort—from self-deception to hateful rebukes from others—fails to dislodge those elements from having a relatively central place in his subjectivity.

CHAPTER SIX

1. This framework of selfcraft is partial, however, in that it draws insights only from sources that specifically address multiple identities without reference to other potentially relevant literature in psychotherapy, medicine, or contemplative spiritual practice. While traditions of thought on selfcraft could undoubtedly shed additional light on modes of self-integration and transformation, attending to them in depth is not the focus of this book. Nonetheless, methods for actively reworking the mind's thought patterns have been investigated for centuries in numerous traditions of thought, from Eastern contemplative religious practices to Western allopathic medicine and psychotherapeutic traditions. For a Buddhist account of selfcraft that has significant commonalities with the framework I develop here, see Dalai Lama and Cutler, *The Art of Happiness,* 233–45.

2. Anzaldúa, *Borderlands,* 82.

3. Ibid.

4. All quoted material in this paragraph, ibid. Paul Smith also uses the language of discernment to discuss the multiplicity of subjectivity in his 1988 book *Discerning the Subject.* The term is also used in the Roman Catholic faith tradition to refer to the process of coming to understand one's purpose in life.

5. Anzaldúa, *Borderlands,* 82.

6. Ibid.

7. This idea of resisting all forms of subordination as a recognition of the interconnectedness of all forms of social subordination is a common dimension of Chicana feminisms and work by feminists of color. See Martínez, *De Colores;* Anzaldúa, *Interviews/Entrevistas,* 156–58, 185–86; and Anzaldúa, *Borderlands,* 85–86.

8. Ibid., 82.

9. One may wonder why Anzaldúa also endorses "intolerance" for ambiguity if ambiguity is valuable. Anzaldúa's point, I would suggest, is that while in some cases ambiguity and ambivalence are fruitful, both can be put to use in cloaking or otherwise sustaining forms of subordination. Hence, there are moments when ambiguity should be refused.

10. Ibid., 82–83.

11. Anzaldúa was writing on this question of selfcraft at the time of her death in 2004. She referred to it in later works as the process of *conocimientos*. Other thoughts by her on the topic appear in her book *Interviews/Entrevistas* and also in her introductory essay in Anzaldúa and Keating, *This Bridge We Call Home.*

12. Pratt's partner Leslie Feinberg is a transgender man who combines female embodiment with masculine gender expression. Feinberg claims both masculine gender identity and her birth sex as a woman in everyday life and in her activism in transgender civil rights. The couple lives as husband and wife. At the same time, they acknowledge the complexity of their relationship as potentially at once heterosexual, lesbian, and queer. See Feinberg, *Transgender Warriors,* 92; for Feinberg's definition of her transgender identity as located *at the contradiction* between her gender expression and her anatomical sex, see *Transgender Warriors,* 101. Thanks to Bonnie Honig for first drawing my attention to Pratt's essay "Identity: Blood Skin Heart."

13. For a personal and public acknowledgement of these two life projects, see Pratt's Foreword "Family Album" to *Love Makes a Family,* in which she describes her fiftieth birthday party at which tall poster boards presented pictures that documented her "fifty years of love and struggle," ix–x.

14. We know, for example, that Pratt's African American nanny was named Laura Cates and that she first saw an influential classmate, Elizabeth, on August 11, 1969. These women changed Pratt's life and her understandings of love and loneliness in different ways. Yet we don't learn anything specific about her education, workplaces, or her former husband. Of her children the reader learns only of the cruelty of losing them and her ongoing misery, pain, and guilt of that loss. That loss is thematized again and again in Pratt's work, including the closing essay of *S/He,* 188.

15. Pratt remarks that writing the essay "Identity: Blood Skin Heart" itself aided in the integrative process. It is beyond the scope of this work to fully explore how writing, including letter writing and autobiographical writing, can be tools in selfcraft. For relevant discussion see Michel Foucault, *Technologies of the Self.*

16. See, for example, the closing essay "Stone Home" in Pratt's book *S/He* for a non-narrative expression of how Pratt integrates her various modes of committed love (for her lover, her husband, and her children), with her political work, in her thoughts and interpretation of the world around her, and in her minor actions in the world from moment to moment, 188–89.

17. My attempt to interpret another person's life story by adding linear narrative structure that they have not chosen is a potentially dubious enterprise, that risks making disrespectful presumptions I do not intend. Moreover, such a narrative enterprise is self-contradictory, in that it requires me to do my utmost to perform a task that I have just declared impossible. Thus in terms of this contradictory task my philosophical investigation depends in equal measure on *both* my success in conveying a coherent narrative of self-integration *and* my failure to fully capture the spirit and complexity of Pratt's subjectivity and self-integrative experience. The reader will judge whether the tension of these contradictions is ultimately productive. However, I apologize

in advance to Professor Pratt for any errors and omissions regarding her self-understanding and experience that this theoretical exercise entails.

18. Pratt provides few dates in her self-narrative. For instance, the only two full dates that are offered—August 1969 and November 1979—are associated with impersonal incidents that became turning points that helped her reshape her thinking. Conventional milestones such as birth of children or graduation from college or graduate school are omitted and can only be inferred from these two incidental dates and other clues in the text.

19. Pratt, "Identity: Blood Skin Heart," 20.

20. Ibid., 22.

21. Ibid.

22. Ibid., 23.

23. Ibid.

24. Ibid.

25. Ibid., emphasis in original.

26. Ibid., emphasis added. The language choice is interestingly ambiguous in this sentence given that Pratt describes this period as one of firmness of perspective. Yet, does "rushed away slowly" mean that Pratt left the table, but with (resolute) hesitation, or is slowed rushing the only type of hurried movement available to a pregnant woman? Why is the idea of ignoring one's womanhood juxtaposed with an unnecessary reference to the physical feeling of pregnancy—an exclusively female embodied experience? Does "rock in my stomach" refer to the weight of a second male child, often carried lower and with more visibility once abdominal walls have been stretched by a preceding pregnancy? Or does it refer in more vernacular terms to a "pregnant" sense of dread?

27. Ibid.

28. Ibid., 24.

29. Ibid., 25.

30. Ibid., 22.

31. Ibid., 24.

32. Ibid.

33. Whether this should be considered an active stage of inventory or the involuntary action of consciousness is unclear from the narrative. Research in a variety of fields reveals that cognitive processing can go on at a variety of unconscious levels without "voluntary" conscious effort on the part of the subject. For a widely accessible overview and analysis of the relevant scholarly literature see Gladwell, *Blink*.

34. It is also possible that Pratt is somewhat familiar with narratives of lesbian love but never made the connection to herself. In *S/He* for example, Pratt describes having lunch with a friend in which she puzzles over why her transgender lover finds her such a satisfying lover. Pratt's friend becomes frustrated with her for missing the "obvious," that Pratt is not only a lesbian but also queer in that she is drawn to a lover who is at once female and male in psyche and embodiment. Pratt then describes how this simple observation dramatically shifts her understanding of herself, her present relationship, and her past relationships with friends and lovers. She writes: "In one continuous motion, my idea of myself and who I am turns inside out, like a pond that flips upside down in the spring, when the cold winter water slides under, and the earth-warmed bottom water rises" (Pratt, *S/He*, 104).

35. Pratt, "Identity: Blood Skin Heart," 25.

36. Although theorizing the role of dreams in self-integration is beyond the scope of this project, it is often theorized that dreams are a place in which we unconsciously consider elements that we cannot or do not wish to grapple with consciously. See Freud, "Interpretation of Dreams."

37. Pratt, "Identity: Blood Skin Heart," 26. While this was a common experience among lesbian mothers for decades, gay civil rights are broadening and social acceptance increasing such that experience is now more varied. See Laird, ed., *Lesbians and Lesbian Families;* and Gillespie, ed., *Love Makes a Family.*

38. Pratt, "Identity: Blood Skin Heart," 27. Of this she writes, "I did not die, but the agony was as bitter as death . . . I had held them before they were born and almost every day of their lives, and now I could not touch them. . . . if you are helpless with grief, you do, unthinkingly, wring your hands" (ibid.).

39. Ibid., 32.

40. Ibid., 33.

41. Ibid.

42. Ibid.

43. Ibid., 34.

44. Both quotations above, ibid., 35.

45. Ibid., 38.

46. Ibid., 19.

47. Ibid., 39.

48. Ibid. This suggests that when multiple identities cross-cut each other and place individual subjects in contradictory circumstances in positions of *both* subordination and oppression, accepting responsibility for oppression, that is acknowledgement of the intersection between the identification with oppression and the other identities that we endorse and value, is difficult to accept for those who would not expressly endorse such oppression. The pain of that intersection—the unwelcome identity as complicit oppressor—can be denied through akrasia or self-deception such as the self-enforced ignorance of Klan wife Nancy Matthew. But perhaps at some level—like the lesbian desire that has no name but nonetheless affects thought and action—the self-fragmented identification with oppressive forces that is cordoned off as too painful and contradictory for positive self-narrative to embrace, nonetheless exists somewhere within the complexity of decentered subjectivity and it may become salient in unconscious ways—in the unreflective act of racism, the knowing defense of the indefensible crime. Or perhaps intersections are created such that identification with oppression is expressed in inexplicable forms of loneliness, grief, or remorse. Pratt, for example notes that for years, when she would hear Black gospel music "Always I would cry, baffled as to why I was so moved" (ibid., 41). Finally, Pratt discerned that this affective response was a product of the inner displacement of her own mourning and sorrow through Black musical expression which sorrow at her and her culture's responsibility is expressed at a comfortable intrapsychic distance through an appropriation of Black grief in song that goes unexplained to the "baffled" self. But as Pratt integrates her multiple identities as poet, lesbian, mother, white woman, and activist struggling against racism and anti-Semitism, Pratt is eventually able to rework her understanding and response to Black gospel music. As she writes, "[f]inally I understood that I could feel sorrow during their music, and yet not confuse their sorrow with mine, or use their resistance for mine. *I needed to do my own work:* express my sorrow and my responsibility myself, in my own words, by my own actions" (ibid., emphasis in original).

49. Ibid., 48.

50. Ibid.

51. Ibid., 41.

52. See chapters two, four, and five for further discussion of the connection between social conflict and identity fragmentation.

53. Pratt, "Identity: Blood Skin Heart," 42.

54. Although this explication comes late in the essay, it relates back to the fluidity of identification that she describes grappling with in the D.C. streets in the first pages of the essay.

55. Both quotations are from Anzaldúa, *Borderlands,* 82.

56. Pratt, *S/He,* 188.

57. Ibid., 188–89; see also Gillespie, *Love Makes a Family.*

58. Using a metaphor employed also in chapter four, recall that judging-Thought can be seen metaphorically as the operating system for the self-programs provided by identity schemes. The operating system of judging-Thought is, however, also embodied—i.e. it links the body and consciousness as part of a psychophysiological apparatus—and is also responsible for the sense of continuity over time through the continuing relay of thought-in-the-moment. I have argued in earlier chapters that the salience/identity shifts in judging-Thought permit a subject's critical distance over the full range of multiple identity schemes as a function of both identity contradiction and of the received or introduced intersections between identity schemes within subjectivity. See chapters three and four for detailed discussion.

59. See note 21 in chapter four above and Digeser, *Our Politics, Our Selves,* 196–213.

60. Rorty, "Self-Deception, *Akrasia,* and Irrationality," 131.

61. James, *Principles of Psychology,* 320. I would also agree that willful claims to ownership of socially constructed aspects of the self cannot be denied simply because the original source involves social relations of subordination that onlookers may reject on ideological grounds. Exploring this factor is, however, beyond the scope of this project. For a detailed and persuasive analysis of this in relation to feminist theory see Hirschmann, *Subject of Liberty.* For brief discussion in relation to autonomy and mestiza consciousness see Barvosa, "Mestiza Autonomy."

62. Whitebook, "Decentered Subject," 113. I'd like to thank Seyla Benhabib for directing me to this important essay and for our discussions on this topic.

63. These include a few in the philosophy of mind focusing on the degrees of integration that can take place even when multiple identities are highly dissociated. See Braude, *First Person Plural;* and Radden, *Divided Minds and Successive Selves.*

64. The integration of the self as a self-system and coherence of the self are not the only ways that philosophers and psychologists have sought to account for the coherence and unity of the self. Many books have been written on the subject (Parfit, *Reasons and Persons;* Searle, *Rediscovery of the Mind;* Williams, *Problems of the Self;* White, *Unity of the Self;* and Braude, *First Person Plural*) and many elements have been suggested including memory (Singer and Solvey, *Remembered Self*), commitment to future selves (Parfit, *Reasons and Persons*), a subjective sense of self, and self-narrative, to name only a few. Narrative unity has been perhaps the most widely suggested as a unifying factor in the self. It has been advocated by a wide number of philosophers and theorists (Benhabib, *Situating the Self* and "Collective Identities;" Ricouer, *Oneself*

as Another; Taylor, *Sources of the Self;* Giddens, *Modernity and Self-Identity*) and has also been advocated by scholars in various subfields of psychology (Gergen and Gergen, "Narratives of the Self;" Singer, "Seeing One's Self").

65. MacIntyre, "Unity of Human Life," 246–51.

66. "Ferrari, Yvonne and Henri," *Casablanca,* DVD, directed by Michael Curtiz (1943; Burbank, Cal.: Turner Entertainment Co. and Warner Home Video, 1999).

67. It is not clear from the essay "Identity: Blood Skin Heart" when Pratt's motivations of romantic love become clear to her, but she understands them by the time she is writing the essay and she attributes her understanding of her political motivation and her sexual identity to suddenly falling in love with a woman. Moreover, it is clear from essays in *S/He* (1995/2000) that relate to naming her queer sexual desire, that Pratt is still working to understand the character of her life project of committed love long after 1983, see *S/He,* 103–104.

68. MacIntyre acknowledges that agents may misrecognize the significance of their actions in context, but as a corrective for limited interpretations he turns to a broader comprehensive life story (i.e. embeddedness of a narrative) and narrative genre (tragedy, etc.) for better interpretations of the meanings of our actions. However, these suggestions evade the deeper question of exactly how self-fragmentation in the subject is supposed to be healed by devising and reciting an intelligible self-narrative, and why doing so may not just as easily sustain its fragmentation. MacIntyre's own work on the self-fragmenting effects of various forms of social differentiation in collective life provides a basis for this possibility. See for example "Threats to Moral Agency," in which he aptly states, "remember too that the established norms and values with which we may be invited to enter into conflict will commonly be to some large degree our norms and values, the norms and values by which we have hitherto been guided [read: our normative narratives]. So that initially at least that conflict will be within each of us," (ibid., 319). Logically, when internalized identity conflicts are derived from socially narrativized norms, the self-narratives that those internalized norms produce may also sustain fragmentation rather than produce integration within a subject's psyche.

69. Markus and Wurf, "Dynamic Self-Concept," 306–307.

70. That is unless, for some reason the subject has taken pains to integrate—i.e. build positive intersections between—their introverted and extroverted self-constructs and thus had a good sense of themselves as simultaneously shy *and* outgoing.

71. Gregg, *Identity in a Muslim Society,* 3.

72. Gregg, "Multiple Identities and Integration," 617.

73. Ibid., 622.

74. Ibid., 621.

75. Gregg also explores the interconnections between different self-constructs as well as the various sources of those intersections., see "Culture and Multiplicity of Identity," 143–44 and *Identity in a Muslim Society.* Gregg's interviews with Rachida are a good reminder that multiple identities not only exist cross-culturally, but that they may exist in many configurations.

76. Gregg's finding may suggest that there may also be limitations in narrative form itself that would prevent it from capturing the complexity of a decentered and multiple subject. In Pratt's case, for example, even a cursory examination of Minnie Bruce Pratt's original autobiographical writings in

"Identity" demonstrate that my temporally linear, logically coherent retelling of her autobiography fails to contain, much less adequately reflect, the complexity of Pratt's selfhood and the complicated quality of her self-integrative process. Instead, it is Pratt's intricate, gap-ridden narrative with levels of intersecting, but not straightforwardly compatible, multiple narratives that better conveys her multiplicity and her practices of selfcraft. It may be that the complexity of multiple identities will confound the formation of *comprehensive,* logical, coherent, and linear self-narratives of any kind. I return to this point further below; however, to fully explore the limitations of narrative form itself to convey the potentially contradictory and ambiguous characteristics of multiple identities, is beyond the scope of this study.

77. Digeser addresses the limitations of narrative unity in detail, specifically in relation to MacIntyre's argument regarding all-encompassing narratives. See Digeser, *Our Politics, Our Selves,* 61–95.

78. Digeser also specifies a fifth point of less significance here, namely that the communitarian emphasis on "well-crafted unity over time" through self-narrative may commit the kind of "self-centeredness that the communitarians attribute to modern culture," *Our Politics, Our Selves,* 94.

79. Ibid., 93–94.

80. Pratt, "Foreword" to *Love Makes a Family,* ix.

81. Digeser, *Our Politics, Our Selves,* 94.

82. Ibid.

83. Pratt, "Identity: Blood Skin Heart,"12, emphasis added.

84. Ibid., 13.

85. Ibid., 15.

86. Ibid., 13.

87. Ibid., 15.

88. The interpreter is Richard Kearney in his work on the significance of narrative. See *On Stories,* 4; see also MacIntyre, "Unity of Human Life."

89. Digeser, *Our Politics, Our Selves,* 94.

90. Kondo, "Dissolution and Reconstruction." For further discussion of Kondo's efforts to manage the accessibility of her identity schemes see chapter two.

91. Pratt, *S/He,* 103–104.

92. Pratt, "Identity: Blood Skin Heart," 19–20.

93. Patricia Hill Collins also suggests the connection between love and self-empowerment in Black feminist thought. See *Black Feminist Thought,* 196–97.

CONCLUSION

1. Lewis, *Race in the Schoolyard.*

2. Ibid., 66–79.

3. For example, see Levine, *Constructions of the Self,* 3.

4. Lewis, *Race in the Schoolyard,* 66–79.

5. This assumes the social constructions specific to the late twentieth century U.S.

6. See powell, "Beyond Whiteness and Isolation."

7. See chapter four (modes one and two) and chapter five (modes three and four).

8. See chapters two and four.

9. As social constructions, such divides can vary significantly with time and

place or remain relatively static—that is to say, reproduced without significant modification—indefinitely.

10. Du Bois, *Souls of Black Folk,* 45.

11. For a discussion of this with regard to highly identified feminists, see chapter four.

12. Waters, *Black Identities,* 293.

13. Ibid.

14. Ibid. Monique's language is strikingly similar to that of Christian Park with regard to those who question his identities as a Korean American; see chapter five.

15. See for example Foucault, *History of Sexuality;* Hirschmann, *Subject of Liberty;* and Mendelberg, *The Race Card.*

16. Taylor, *Ethics of Authenticity.*

17. As Amartya Sen has recently argued, having multiple identities may reduce tendencies toward extremism. See Sen, *Identity and Violence.* I explore exceptions to this with regard to intersectionality in a book in progress tentatively entitled *Identifying with the Extreme.* Resources for mitigating extremism and polarization may also be found in Digeser, *Political Forgiveness.*

Bibliography

Abu-Saba, Leila. "Heartbroken for Lebanon." In *Homelands: Women's Journeys Across Race, Place, and Time,* edited by Patricia Justine Tumang and Jenesha de Rivera, 185–92. Emeryville: Seal Press, 2006.

Acuña, Rodolfo. *Occupied America: A History of Chicanos,* 3rd ed. New York: Harper Collins Publishers, 1988.

Adams, Henry E., Lester W. Jr. Wright, and Bethany A. Lohr. "Is Homophobia Associated with Homosexual Arousal?" *Journal of Abnormal Psychology* 105, no. 3 (1996): 440–45.

Adorno, Theodor W. *Negative Dialectics.* Translated by E. B. Ashton. New York: The Continuum Publishing Company, 1990.

Adorno, Theodor, Daniel Levinson, R. Nevitt Sanford, and Else Frenkel-Brunswik. *The Authoritarian Personality.* Studies in Prejudice. New York: W.W. Norton & Company, 1982.

Ahmed, Leila. *A Border Passage: From Cairo to America—a Woman's Journey.* New York: Penguin Books, 1999.

Alarcón, Norma. "Conjugating Subjects: The Heteroglossia of Essence & Resistance." In *An Other Tongue: Nation and Ethnicity in the Linguistic Borderlands,* edited by Alfred Arteaga, 125–38. Durham, N.C.: Duke University Press, 1994.

Alba, Richard, and Victor Nee. *Remaking the American Mainstream: Assimilation and Contemporary Immigration.* Cambridge, Mass.: Harvard University Press, 2003.

Allport, Gordon. *The Nature of Prejudice.* New York: Addison-Wesley, 1954.

Anzaldúa, Gloria. *Borderlands/La Frontera: The New Mestiza.* San Francisco: Spinster/Aunt Lute Books, 1987.

———. *Interviews/Entrevistas.* Edited by AnaLouise Keating. New York: Routledge, 2000.

———, ed. *Making Face, Making Soul/Haciendo Caras: Creative and Critical Perspectives by Women of Color.* San Francisco: Aunt Lute Books, 1990.

Anzaldúa, Gloria, and AnaLouise Keating. *This Bridge We Call Home: Radical Visions for Transformation.* New York: Routledge, 2002.

Arana, Marie. *American Chica: Two Worlds, One Childhood.* New York: The Dial Press, Random House, 2001.

Bada, Xóchitl. "Mexican Hometown Associations." In *Citizen Action in the Americas Series.* Silver City: Americas Program, IRC, 2003.

Balka, Christie, and Andy Rose, eds. *Twice Blessed: On Being Lesbian, Gay, and Jewish.* Boston: Beacon Press, 1989.

Bammer, Angelika, ed. *Displacements: Cultural Identities in Question.* Indianapolis: Indiana University Press, 1994.

Bargh, John A. "The Automaticity of Everyday Life." In *The Automaticity of Everyday Life,* edited by Jr. Robert S. Wyer. Mahwah: Lawrence Erlbaum Associates, Publishers, 1997.

Bargh, John A. and Tanya L. Chartrand. "The Unbearable Automaticity of Being." *American Psychologist* 54, no. 7 (1999): 462–79.

Barker, Ernest. "The Discredited State." In *Church, State, and Education,* 151–70. Ann Arbor: The University of Michigan Press, 1957.

Barth, Fredrik. *Ethnic Groups and Boundaries: The Social Organization of Culture Difference.* Boston: Little, Brown and Company, 1969.

Barvosa, Edwina. "Mestiza Autonomy as Relational Autonomy." *Journal of Political Philosophy* 15, no. 1 (2007): 1–21.

Basch, Linda, Nina Glick Schiller, and Cristina Szanton Blanc. "Hegemony, Transnational Practices, and the Multiple Identities of Vincentian and Grenadian Transmigrants." In *Nations Unbound: Transnational Projects, Postcolonial Predicaments, and Deterritorialized Nation-States,* 95–144. Basel: Gordon and Breach, 1994.

Baumeister, Roy F. "The Self." In *The Handbook of Social Psychology,* edited by Daniel T. Gilbert, Susan T. Fiske, and Gardner Lindzey, 680–740. Boston: McGraw-Hill Inc., 1998.

Beltran, Cristina. "Patrolling Borders: Hybrids, Hierarchies, and the Challenge of *Mestizaje.*" *Political Research Quarterly,* 57, no. 4 (2004): 595–607.

Benet-Martínez, Verónica, JanXin Leu, Fiona Lee, and Michael W. Morris. "Negotiating Biculturalism: Cultural Frame Switching in Biculturals with Oppositional Versus Compatible Cultural Identities." *Journal of Cross-Cultural Psychology* 33, no. 5 (2002): 492–516.

Benhabib, Seyla. *The Claims of Culture: Equality and Diversity in the Global Era.* Princeton, N.J.: Princeton University Press, 2002.

———. "Critical Theory and Postmodernism: On the Interplay of Ethics, Aesthetics, and Utopia in Critical Theory." In *The Handbook of Critical Theory,* edited by David M. Rasmussen, 327–39. Cambridge, Mass: Blackwell Publishers, 1996.

———. "Feminism and Postmodernism: An Uneasy Alliance." In *Feminist Contentions: A Philosophical Exchange,* edited by Seyla Benhabib, Judith Butler, Drucilla Cornell, and Nancy Fraser, 17–34. New York: Routledge, 1995.

———. "Sexual Difference and Collective Identities: The New Global Constellation." *Signs* 24, no. 2 (1999): 335–61.

———. *Situating the Self: Gender, Community and Postmodernism in Contemporary Ethics.* New York: Routledge, 1992.

———. "Toward a Deliberative Model of Democratic Legitimacy." In *Democracy and Difference: Contesting the Boundaries of the Political,* edited by Seyla Benhabib, 67–94. Princeton, N.J.: Princeton University Press, 1996.

Benhabib, Seyla, Judith Butler, Drucilla Cornell, and Nancy Fraser. *Feminist Contentions: A Philosophical Exchange.* New York: Routledge, 1995.

Bhabha, Homi K. "Interrogating Identity." In *Identity,* edited by Lisa Appignanesi, 5–11. London: Institute of Contemporary Arts, 1987.

Birman, Dina. "Biculturalism and Perceived Competence of Latino Immigrant Adolescents." *American Journal of Community Psychology* 25, no. 3 (1998): 335–54.

Bohman, James F. "Communication, Ideology, and Democratic Theory." *The American Political Science Review* 84, no. 1 (1990): 93–109.

———. "Complexity, Pluralism, and the Constitutional State: On Habermas's Faktizitat Und Geltung." *Law and Society Review* Vol. 28, no. 4 (1994): 897–930.

Braude, Stephen E. *First Person Plural: Multiple Personality and the Philosophy of Mind*. London: Routledge, 1995.

Braun, B. G. "The Bask Model of Dissociation." *Dissociation* 1, no. 1 (1988): 4–23.

Brown, Wendy. "At the Edge: The Future of Political Theory." In *Edgework: Critical Essays on Knowledge and Politics*. Princeton, N.J.: Princeton University Press, 2005.

Burke, John Francis. *Mestizo Democracy: The Politics of Crossing Borders*. College Station: Texas A&M University Press, 2002.

Butler, Judith P. *Bodies That Matter: On the Discursive Limits Of "Sex."* New York: Routledge, 1993.

Cadava, Eduardo, Peter Connor, and Jean-Luc Nancy. *Who Comes after the Subject?* New York: Routledge, 1991.

Castañeda, Antonia. "Sexual Violence in the Politics of Conquest: Amerindian Women and the Spanish Conquest of Alta California." In *Building with Our Hands: New Directions in Chicana Studies,* edited by Adela de la Torre and Beatriz M. Pesquera, 15–33. Berkeley: University of California Press, 1993.

Chavez, Leo R. *Shadowed Lives: Undocumented Immigrants in American Society,* 2nd ed. Case Studies in Cultural Anthropology. Fort Worth: Harcourt Brace College Publishers, 1998.

Chu, James A. "Dissociative Symptomology in Adult Patients with Histories of Childhood Physical and Sexual Abuse." In *Trauma, Memory, and Dissociation,* edited by Douglas J. Bremner and Charles R. Marmar, 179–203. Washington, D.C: American Psychiatric Press, Inc., 1998.

———. *Rebuilding Shattered Lives: The Responsible Treatment of Complex Post-Traumatic and Dissociative Disorders*. New York: John Wiley and Sons, Inc., 1998.

Clarke, Paul Barry. *Deep Citizenship*. Chicago: Pluto Press, 1996.

Cohen, Anthony Paul. *The Symbolic Construction of Community*. London: Ellis Horwood/Tavistock Publications, 1985.

Coles, Raymond. *Beyond Gated Politics: Reflections for the Possibility of Democracy*. Minneapolis: University of Minnesota Press, 2005.

Collins, Patricia Hill. *Black Feminist Thought: Knowledge, Consciousness, and the Politics of Empowerment. Perspectives on Gender*. Boston: Unwin Hyman, 1990.

———. *Fighting Words: Black Women and the Search for Justice. Contradictions of Modernity*. Minneapolis: University of Minnesota Press, 1998.

Crenshaw, Kimberlé. "Demarginalizing the Intersection of Race and Sex: A Black Feminist Critique of Antidiscrimination Doctrine, Feminist Theory and Antiracist Politics." In *Feminist Legal Theory,* edited by D. Kelly Weisberg, 383–95. Philadelphia: Temple University Press, 1993.

———. "Mapping the Margins: Intersectionality, Identity Politics, and Violence against Women of Color." In *After Identity: A Reader in Law and Culture,* edited by Dan Danielsen and Karen Engle, 332–54. New York: Routledge, 1995.

Critchley, Simon, and Peter Dews, eds. *Deconstructive Subjectivities*. Albany: State University of New York Press, 1996.

Curtiz, Michael. *Casablanca,* 102 min; DVD. United States: Turner Entertainment Co. and Warner Home Video, 1999.

Dahl, Robert. *Dilemmas of Pluralist Democracy: Autonomy vs. Control.* New Haven: Yale University Press, 1982.

Dalai Lama, and Howard C. Cutler. *The Art of Happiness: A Handbook for Living.* New York: Riverhead Books, 1998.

Dávila, Arlene. *Latinos, Inc.: The Marketing and Making of a People.* Berkeley: University of California Press, 2001.

Davis, Lennard J. *My Sense of Silence: Memoirs of a Childhood with Deafness.* Chicago: University of Illinois Press, 2000.

Davis, Mike. *Magical Urbanism: Latinos Reinvent the U.S. City.* New York: Verso, 2000.

Descartes, René. *Meditations on the First Philosophy,* In *Discourse on Method and the Meditations,* 61–123. Translated by John Vietch. Buffalo, N.Y.: Prometheus Books, 1989.

Digeser, P. E. *Our Politics, Our Selves? Liberalism, Identity, and Harm.* Princeton, N.J.: Princeton University Press, 1995.

———. *Political Forgiveness.* Ithaca, N.Y.: Cornell University Press, 2001.

Du Bois, W. E. B. *The Souls of Black Folk.* New York: Signet Classic, 1995.

Eco, Umberto. "Casablanca, or, the Clichés Are Having a Ball." In *Signs of Life in the U.S.A.: Readings on Popular Culture for Writers,* edited by Sonia Maasik and Jack Solomon, 260–64. Boston: Bedford Books of St. Martin's Press, 1994.

Ellemers, Naomi, Paulien Kortekaas, and Jaap W. Ouwerkerk. "Self-Categorisation, Commitment to the Group and Group Self-Esteem as Related but Distinct Aspects of Social Identity." *European Journal of Social Psychology* 29(2–3): 371–89.

Ellemers, Naomi, Russell Spears, and Bertjan Doosje, eds. *Social Identity Context, Commitment, Content.* Cambridge, Mass.: Blackwell, 1999.

Ellmann, Richard. *Yeats: The Man and the Masks.* Oxford: Oxford University Press, 1979.

Espiritu, Yen Le. "The Intersection of Race, Ethnicity, and Class: The Multiple Identities of Second-Generation Filipinos." *Identities* 1, no. 2–3 (1994): 249–73.

Everest, Pauline. "The Multiple Self: Working with Dissociation and Trauma." *Journal of Analytical Psychology* 44, no. 4 (1999): 443–63.

Eze, Emmanuel Chukwudi, ed. *Race and the Enlightenment: A Reader.* Cambridge, Mass.: Blackwell Press, 1997.

Feinberg, Leslie. *Transgender Warriors: Making History from Joan of Arc to Dennis Rodman.* Boston: Beacon Press, 1996.

Flax, Jane. *The American Dream in Black and White: The Clarence Thomas Hearings.* Ithaca, N.Y.: Cornell University Press, 1998.

———. "Displacing Woman: Toward and Ethics of Multiplicity." In *Daring to Be Good: Essays in Feminist Ethico-Politics,* edited by Bat-Ami Bar On and Ann Ferguson, 143–55. New York: Routledge, 1998.

———. "On Encountering Incommensurability: Martha Nussbaum's Aristotelian Practice." In *Controversies in Feminism,* edited by James P Sterba, 25–45. New York: Rowman and Littlefield, 2001.

———. *Thinking Fragments: Psychoanalysis, Feminism, and Postmodernism in the Contemporary West.* Los Angeles: University of California Press, 1990.

Fletcher, George P. *Loyalty: An Essay on the Morality of Relationships.* New York: Oxford University Press, 1993.

Flores, William V., and Rina Benmayor, eds. *Latino Cultural Citizenship: Claiming Identity, Space, and Rights*. Boston: Beacon Press, 1997.

Follett, Mary P. *The New State: Group Organization the Solution of Popular Government* New York: Longmans, Green and Co., 1920.

Foster, R. F. *W. B. Yeats: A Life*. 2 vols. New York: Oxford University Press, 1997.

Foucault, Michel. *Discipline and Punish*. New York: Penguin Books, 1991.

———. *The History of Sexuality: An Introduction*. Vintage Books ed. 3 vols. Vol. 1. New York: Vintage Books, 1990.

———. "Technologies of the Self." In *Technologies of the Self: A Seminar with Michel Foucault*, edited by Luther H. Martin, Huck Gutman, and Patrick H. Hutton, 16–49. Amherst: The University of Massachusetts Press, 1988.

Frankfurt, Harry. "Freedom of the Will and the Concept of a Person." *The Journal of Philosophy* 68, no. 1 (1971): 5–28.

———. "Identification and Wholeheartedness." In *Responsibility, Character, and the Emotions: New Essays in Moral Psychology*, edited by Ferdinand Schoeman, 27–45. New York: Cambridge University Press, 1987.

Fraser, Nancy. "False Antitheses: A Response to Seyla Benhabib and Judith Butler." In *Feminist Contentions: A Philosophical Exchange*, edited by Seyla Benhabib, Judith Butler, Drucilla Cornell, and Nancy Fraser, 59–74. New York: Routledge, 1995.

Freud, Sigmund. *The Basic Writings of Sigmund Freud*. Translated by A. A. Brill. New York: The Modern Library, 1938.

———. *The Interpretation of Dreams*. New York: Basic Books, 1955.

Friedman, Marilyn A. "Autonomy and the Split-Level Self." *The Southern Journal of Philosophy* 24, no. 1 (1986): 19–35.

Garcia, Mario. *Mexican Americans: Leadership, Ideology & Identity 1930–1960*. New Haven, Conn.: Yale University Press, 1989.

García Bedolla, Lisa. *Fluid Borders: Latino Power, Identity and Politics in Los Angeles*. Los Angeles: University of California Press, 2005.

Garza, Rodolfo O. de la, and Harry P. Pachon, eds. *Latinos and U.S. Foreign Policy: Representing The "Homeland"?* New York: Rowman & Littlefield Publishers, Inc, 2000.

Geertz, Clifford, ed. *Old Societies and New States: The Quest for Modernity in Asia and Africa*. New York: The Free Press, 1963.

Gergen, Kenneth J., and Mary M. Gergen. "Narratives of the Self." In *Memory, Identity, Community: The Idea of Narrative in the Human Sciences*, edited by Lewis P. Hinchmann and Sandra Hinchmann, 161–84. Albany: State University of New York Press, 1997.

Giddens, Anthony. *Modernity and Self Identity: Self and Society in the Late Modern Age*. Cambridge: Polity Press, 1991.

Giles, Howard, and Nikolas Coupland. *Language: Contexts and Consequences*. Buckingham: Open University Press, 1991.

Gillespie, Peggy, ed. *Love Makes a Family: Portraits of Lesbian, Gay, Bisexual and Transgender Parents and Their Families*. Amherst: University of Massachusetts Press, 1999.

Gilroy, Paul. *The Black Atlantic: Modernity and Double Consciousness*. Cambridge, Mass.: Harvard University Press, 1993.

Gladwell, Malcolm. *Blink: The Power of Thinking Without Thinking*. New York: Back Bay Books, 2005.

Glazer, Nathan, and Daniel P. Moynihan. *Beyond the Melting Pot: The Negroes,*

Puerto Ricans, Jews, Italians, and Irish of New York City, 2nd ed. Cambridge, Mass.: MIT Press, 1970.

Goldberg, Milton M. "A Qualification of the Marginal Man Theory." *American Sociological Review* 6, no. 1 (1941): 52–58.

Goldhagen, Daniel J. *Hitler's Willing Executioners.* New York: Knopf, 1996.

Gómez-Quiñonez, Juan. *Chicano Politics: Reality and Promise 1940–1990.* Albuquerque: University of New Mexico Press, 1990.

Gonzalez, Juan. *Harvest of Empire: A History of Latinos in America.* New York: Penguin Books, 2000.

Gordon, Milton M. *Assimilation in American Life: The Role of Race, Religion, and National Origins.* New York: Oxford University Press, 1964.

Gregg, Gary S. *Culture and Identity in a Muslim Society.* Series in Culture, Cognition, and Behavior. New York: Oxford University Press, 2007.

———. "Culture, Personality, and the Multiplicity of Identity: Evidence from North African Life Narratives." *Ethos* 26, no. 2 (1998): 120–52.

———. "Multiple Identities and the Integration of Personality." *Journal of Personality* 63, no. 3 (1995): 617–41.

Green, Arnold. "A Re-Examination of the Marginal Man Concept." *Social Forces* 26, no. 2 (1947): 167–71.

Greenwald, Anthony, and Anthony R. Pratkanis. "The Self." In *Handbook of Social Cognition,* edited by R. S. Wyer and T. K. Srull, 129–78. Hillsdale: Erlbaum, 1984.

Grow, Brian. "Embracing Illegals: Companies Are Getting Hooked on the Buying Power of 11 Million Undocumented Immigrants." *Business Week,* July 18, 2005: 56–64.

Gutierrez, Jeannie, and Arnold Sameroff. "Determinants of Complexity in Mexican-American and Anglo-American Mothers' Conceptions of Child Development." *Child Development* 61, no. 2 (1990): 384–94.

Habermas, Jürgen. "An Alternative Way out of the Philosophy of the Subject: Communicative Versus Subject-Centered Reason." In *The Philosophical Discourse of Modernity: Twelve Lectures,* 294–326. Cambridge, Mass.: MIT Press, 1987.

———. *Between Facts and Norms: Contributions to a Discourse Theory of Law and Democracy.* Cambridge, Mass.: Polity Press, 1996.

———. "Citizenship and National Identity: Some Reflections on the Future of Europe." In *Theorizing Citizenship,* edited by Ronald Beiner, 255–81. Albany: State University of New York Press, 1995.

———. *Moral Consciousness and Communicative Action.* Cambridge, Mass.: MIT Press, 1990.

Hamilton, Nora, and Norma Stoltz Chinchilla. *Seeking Community in a Global City: Guatemalans and Salvadorans in Los Angeles.* Philadelphia: Temple University Press, 2001.

Haney-Lopez, Ian F. *White by Law: The Legal Construction of Race.* New York: New York University Press, 1988.

Hayes-Bautista, David E. *La Nueva California: Latinos in the Golden State.* Berkeley: University of California Press, 2004.

Hawks, Howard. *The Big Sleep,* 116 min; DVD. United States: Turner Entertainment Co. and Warner Home Video, 1946.

Heo, Chui. *Between Two Worlds,* 29 min; VHS. Berkeley: University of California Extension Center for Media and Independent Learning, 1998.

Herman, Barbara. *The Practice of Moral Judgment.* Cambridge, Mass.: Harvard University Press, 1993.

Higgins, E. Tory "Knowledge Activation: Accessibility, Applicability, and Salience." In *Social Psychology: Handbook of Basic Principles,* edited by E. Tory Higgins and Arie Kruglonski, 133–68. New York: Guilford Press, 1996.

Hirschmann, Nancy J. *The Subject of Liberty: Toward a Feminist Theory of Freedom.* Princeton, N.J.: Princeton University Press, 2003.

Hoagland, Sarah, and Marilyn Frye. "Feminist Philosophy." In *Philosophy of Meaning, Knowledge and Value in the Twentieth Century,* edited by John V. Canfield, 307–41. New York: Routledge, 1997.

Hogg, Michael A., and Dominic Abrams. *Social Identifications: A Social Psychology of Intergroup Relations and Group Processes.* New York: Routledge, 1988.

Hogg, Michael A., and Deborah J. Terry, eds. *Social Identity Processes in Organizational Contexts.* Philadelphia: Psychology Press, 2001.

Hong, Ying-yi, Michael W. Morris, Chie-yue Chiu, and Verónica Benet-Martínez. "Multicultural Minds: A Dynamic Constructivist Approach to Culture and Cognition." *American Psychologist* 55, no. 7 (2000): 709–20.

Honig, Bonnie. "Difference, Dilemmas, and the Politics of Home." In *Democracy and Difference: Contesting the Boundaries of the Political,* edited by Seyla Benhabib, 237–77. Princeton, N.J.: Princeton University Press, 1996.

hooks, bell. *Feminist Theory: From Margin to Center.* Boston: South End Press, 1984.

Horkheimer, Max, and Theodor W. Adorno. *Dialectic of Enlightenment.* Translated by John Cumming. New York: The Continuum Publishing Company, 1991.

Hume, David. *A Treatise of Human Nature,* 2nd ed. With textual revision and additional notes by P. H. Nidditch. Edited with an analytical index by L. A. Selby-Bigge New York: Oxford University Press, 1978.

Huntington, Samuel. *Who Are We?: The Challenges to America's National Identity.* New York: Simon & Schuster, 2004.

Hurtado, Aída. "Understanding Multiple Group Identities: Inserting Women into Cultural Transformations." *Journal of Social Issues* 53, no. 2 (1997): 229–328.

———. *Voicing Chicana Feminisms: Young Women Speak Out on Sexuality and Identity.* New York: New York University Press, 2003.

Hutchinson, John, and Anthony D. Smith. *Ethnicity.* New York: Oxford University Press, 1996.

Inter-American Development Bank. *Remittances 2005: Promoting Financial Democracy.* Washington, D.C.: Inter-American Development Bank, 2006.

Irigaray, Luce. *This Sex Which Is Not One.* Translated by Catherine Porter and Carolyn Burke. Ithaca, N.Y.: Cornell University Press, 1985.

James, William. "The Compounding of Consciousness." In *A Pluralistic Universe: Hibbert Lectures at Manchester College on the Present Situation in Philosophy.* New York: Longmans Green and Co., 1928.

———. *The Principles of Psychology.* Edited by Frederick H. Burkhardt, Fredson Bowers, and Ignas K. Skrupskelis. Vol. 1, *The Works of William James.* New York: Harvard University Press, 1981.

Janet, Pierre. *The Major Symptoms of Hysteria.* New York: MacMillan, 1907.

Jones-Correa, Michael. *Between Two Nations*. Ithaca, N.Y.: Cornell University Press, 1998.

Kant, Immanuel. *Critique of Pure Reason*. Translated by Norman Kemp-Smith. New York: St Martin's Press, 1929.

Katkin, Wendy F., Ned Landsman, and Andrea Tyree. *Beyond Pluralism: The Conception of Groups and Group Identities in America*. Chicago: University of Illinois Press, 1998.

———. "An Answer to the Question: 'What Is Enlightenment?'" In *Political Writings*, edited by Raymond Guess, Quentin Skinner, and Richard Tuck, 54–60. New York: Cambridge University Press, 1991.

Kearney, Richard. *On Stories*. Thinking in Action. New York: Routledge, 2002.

Kihlstrom, John F., and Nancy Cantor. "Mental Representations of the Self." In *Advances in Experimental Psychology*, edited by Lenoard Berkowitz, 1–47. New York: Academic Press, 1984.

King, Deborah K. "Multiple Jeopardy, Multiple Consciousness: The Context of Black Feminist Ideology." *Signs* 14, no. 1 (1988): 42–72.

King, Desmond. *Making Americans: Immigration, Race and the Origins of a Diverse Democracy*. Cambridge, Mass.: Harvard University Press, 2000.

Kondo, Dorrine K. "Dissolution and Reconstruction of the Self: Implications for Anthropological Epistemology." *Cultural Anthropology* 1 (1986): 74–88.

Korematsu v. United States, 323 U.S. 214 (1944).

Kristeva, Julia. *Strangers to Ourselves*. Translated by Leon S. Roudiez. New York: Columbia University Press, 1991.

Kruglanski, Arie W., and Donna M. Webster. "Motivated Closing of the Mind: 'Seizing' And 'Freezing.'" *Psychological Review* 103, no. 2 (1996): 263–83.

Kuhn, Thomas S. *The Structure of Scientific Revolutions*. 2nd ed. Chicago: University of Chicago Press, 1970.

Lacan, Jaçques. *Écrits*. Translated by Alan Sheridan. London: Tavistock Publications Limited, 1977.

Laclau, Ernesto. *Emancipation(s)*. Phronesis. New York: Verso, 1996.

Laclau, Ernesto, and Chantal Mouffe. *Hegemony and Socialist Strategy: Towards a Radical Democratic Politics*. Translated by Winston Moore and Paul Cammack. New York: Verso, 1985.

LaFramboise, Teresa, Hardin L. K. Coleman, and Jennifer Gerton. "Psychological Impact of Biculturalism: Evidence and Theory." *Psychological Bulletin* 114, no. 3 (1993): 395–412.

Laguerre, Michel S. *Diasporic Citizenship: Haitian Americans in Transnational America*. New York: St. Martin's Press, 1998.

Laird, Joan, ed. *Lesbians and Lesbian Families: Reflections on Theory and Practice*. New York: Columbia University Press, 1999.

Laitin, David. *Identity in Formation: The Russian Speaking Populations of the Near Abroad*. Ithaca, N.Y.: Cornell University Press, 1998.

Laski, Harold J. *The Foundations of Sovereignty and Other Essays*. New York: Harcourt, Brace and Company, 1921.

———. *Studies in the Problem of Sovereignty*. New Haven, Conn.: Yale University Press, 1917.

Levin, Jack, and Jack McDevitt. *Hate Crimes Revisited: America's War against Those Who Are Different*. Boulder, Col.: Westview Press, 2002.

Levine, George, ed. *Constuctions of the Self.* New Brunswick, N.J.: Rutgers University Press, 1992.

Levitt, Peggy. *The Transnational Villagers.* Berkeley: University of California Press, 2001.

Lewis, Amanda E. *Race in the Schoolyard: Negotiating the Color Line in Classrooms and Communities.* New Brunswick, N.J.: Rutgers University Press, 2003.

Locke, John. *An Essay Concerning Human Understanding.* New York: Dover, 1959.

Lorde, Audre. "Sister Outsider: Essays and Speeches." In *Zami, Sister Outsider: Essays and Speeches, Undersong: Chosen Poems Old and New,* edited by Audre Lorde, 7–190. New York: W. W. Norton, 1993.

Lott, Juanita Tamayo. *Asian Americans: From Racial Category to Multiple Identities.* Walnut Creek: Altamira Press, 1998.

Lowe, Lisa. "Heterogeneity, Hybridity, Multiplicity: Marking Asian American Differences." *Diaspora* 1, no. 1 (1991): 24–44.

———. *Immigrant Acts: On Asian American Cultural Politics.* Durham, N.C.: Duke University Press, 1996.

Lugones, María C. "Hispaneando y Lesbiando: On Sarah Hoagland's *Lesbian Ethics.*" *Hypatia* 5, no. 3 (1990): 139–46.

———. *Pilgrimages/Peregrinajes: Theorizing Coalition against Multiple Oppressions.* Feminist Constructions. Lanham: Rowman and Littlefield Publishers, Inc., 2003.

———. "Playfulness, 'World'-Traveling, and Loving Perception." *Hypatia* 2, no. 2 (1987): 3–19.

MacIntyre, Alasdair. *After Virtue: A Study in Moral Theory.* London: Duckworth, 1981.

———. "Social Structures and Their Threats to Moral Agency." *Philosophy* 74, no. 289 (1999): 311–29.

———. "The Virtues, the Unity of Human Life, and the Concept of a Tradition." In *Memory, Identity, Community: The Idea of Narrative in the Human Sciences,* edited by Lewis P. Hinchman and Sandra K. Hinchman, 241–63. Albany: State University of New York Press, 1997.

———. *Whose Justice? Which Rationality?* Notre Dame: University of Notre Dame Press, 1988.

Mahler, Sarah J. *American Dreaming: Immigrant Life on the Margins.* Princeton, N.J.: Princeton University Press, 1995.

Markus, Hazel, Marie Crane, Stan Bernstein, and Michael Siladi. "Self-Schemas and Gender." *Journal of Personality and Social Psychology* 42, no. 1 (1982): 38–50.

Markus, Hazel Rose, and Shinobu Kitayama. "The Cultural Construction of Self and Emotion: Implictions for Social Behavior." In *Emotion and Culture,* edited by Hazel Rose Markus and Shinobu Kitayama, 89–130. Washington, D.C: American Psychological Association, 1994.

Markus, Hazel, and Elissa Wurf. "The Dynamic Self-Concept: A Social Psychological Perspective." *Annual Review Psychology* 38 (1987): 299–337.

Márquez, Benjamin. *Constructing Identities in Mexican-American Political Organizations: Choosing Issues, Taking Sides.* Austin: University of Texas Press, 2003.

Martinez, Erika. "Identifying with America." In *Homelands: Women's Journeys across Race, Place, and Time,* edited by Patricia Justine Tumang and Jenesha de Rivera, 135–48. Emeryville: Seal Press, 2006.

Martínez, Elizabeth. *De Colores Means All of Us: Latina Views for a Multi-Colored Century.* Cambridge, Mass.: South End Press, 1998.

McClure, Kirstie. "On the Subject of Rights: Pluralism, Plurality, and Political Identity." In *Dimensions of Radical Democracy,* edited by Chantal Mouffe, 108–27. London: Verso, 1992.

McIntyre, Alice. *Women in Belfast: How Violence Shapes Identity.* Westport: Praeger, 2004.

McLaughlin, Brian P., and Amélie Rorty, eds. *Perspectives on Self-Deception.* Berkeley: University of California Press, 1988.

Mendleberg, Tali. *The Race Card: Campaign Strategy, Implicit Messages, and the Norm of Equality.* Princeton, N.J.: Princeton University Press, 2001.

Menjivar, Cecilia. *Fragmented Ties: Salvadoran Immigrant Networks in America.* Berkeley: University of California Press, 2000.

Meyers, Diana Tietjens. *Being Yourself: Essays on Identity, Action, and Social Life.* Lanham: Rowman and Littlefield Publishers, Inc., 2004.

———. "Intersectional Identity and the Authentic Self? Opposites Attract!" In *Relational Autonomy: Feminist Perspectives on Autonomy, Agency, and the Social Self,* edited by Catriona Mackenzie and Natalie Stoljar, 151–80. New York: Oxford University Press, 2000.

Mill, John Stuart. "Considerations on Representative Government." In *Collected Works of John Stuart Mill: Essays on Politics and Society,* edited by J.M. Robson, 371–613. Toronto: University of Toronto Press and Routledge & Kegan Paul, 1977.

Millard, Ann V. and Jorge Chapa. *Apple Pie & Enchiladas: Latino Newcomers in the Rural Midwest.* Austin: University of Texas Press, 2004.

Moore, Michael. Farenheit 9/11, 122 min; DVD. United States: IFC Films, 2004.

———. *Roger & Me,* 91 min; DVD. United States: Warner Home Video, 1990.

Moraga, Cherrie, and Gloria Anzaldúa, eds. *This Bridge Called My Back: Writings by Radical Women of Color.* 2nd ed. Latham: Kitchen Table, Women of Color Press, 1981.

Moreiras, Alberto. "Hybridity and Double Consciousness." *Cultural Studies* 13, no. 3 (1999): 373–407.

Mouffe, Chantal. *The Return of the Political.* Phronesis. New York: Verso, 1993.

Murray, D. W. "What Is the Western Conception of the Self? On Forgetting David Hume." *Ethos* 21, no. 1 (1993): 3–23.

Muthu, Sankar. *Enlightenment Against Empire.* Princeton, N.J.: Princeton University Press, 2003.

Nájera-Ramírez, Olga. "Haciendo Patria: The Charreada and the Formation of a Mexican Transnational Identity." In *Transnational Latina/o Communities: Politics, Processes, and Cultures,* edited by Carlos G. Vélez-Ibáñez and Anna Sampiao, 167–80. Lanham: Rowman & Littlefield, 2002.

Nancy, Jean-Luc. "Cut Throat Sun." In *An Other Tongue: Nation and Ethnicity in the Linguistic Borderlands,* edited by Alfred Arteaga, 113–23. Durham, N.C.: Duke University Press, 1994.

Nietzsche, Friedrich. *Thus Spoke Zarathustra: A Book for None and All.* Translated by Walter Kaufmann. New York: Penguin Books, 1966.

Nietzsche, Friedrich Wilhelm, Keith Ansell-Pearson, and Carol Diethe. *On* *the Genealogy of Morality.*Cambridge Texts in the History of Political Thought. New York: Cambridge University Press, 1994.

Nygard, Roger. *Trekkies,* 86 min; DVD. United States: Paramount Pictures / Neo Motion Pictures, 1999.

Olsen, Laurie, Jhumpa Bhattacharya, Mamie Chow, Ann Jaramillo, and Dora Pulido Tobiassen. Edited by Carol Dowell. *And Still We Speak.* Oakland: California Tomorrow, 2002.

Omi, Michael, and Howard Winant. *Racial Formation in the United States: From the 1960s to the 1990s.* 2nd ed. New York: Routledge, 1994.

O'Neill, Onora. *Constructions of Reason: Explorations of Kant's Political Philosophy.* Cambridge: Cambridge University Press, 1989.

Padilla, Felix M. *Latino Ethnic Consciousness: The Case of Mexican Americans and Puerto Ricans in Chicago.* Notre Dame: University of Notre Dame Press, 1985.

Parekh, Bhikhu. *Gandhi's Political Philosophy: A Critical Examination.* Notre Dame: University of Notre Dame Press, 1989.

———. *Rethinking Multiculturalism: Cultural Diversity and Political Theory.* Cambridge, Mass.: Harvard University Press, 2000.

Parfit, Derek. *Reasons and Persons.* New York: Oxford University Press, 1984.

Park, Robert E. "Human Migration and the Marginal Man." *The American Journal of Sociology* 33, no. 6 (1928): 881–93.

Passel, Jeffrey S. *The Size and Characteristics of the Unauthorized Migrant Population in the U.S.: Estimates Based on the March 2005 Current Population Survey.* Washington, D.C.: Pew Hispanic Canter, 2006.

———. *Unauthorized Migrants: Numbers and Characteristics.* Washington, D.C.: Pew Hispanic Center, 2005.

Pérez, Emma. *The Decolonial Imaginary: Writing Chicanas into History.* Bloomington: Indiana University Press, 1999.

Pew Hispanic Center. *A Statistical Portrait of Hispanics at Mid-Decade.* Washington, D.C.: Pew Hispanic Center, 2007.

———. *Hispanic Attitudes toward Learning English.* Washington, D.C.: Pew Hispanic Center, 2006.

Pickett, Cynthia L., Jill M. Coleman, and Bryan L. Bonner. "Motivated Self-Stereotyping: Heightened Assimilation and Differentiation Needs Result in Increased Levels of Positive and Negative Self-Stereotyping." *Journal of Personality and Social Psychology* 82, no. 4 (2002): 543–62.

Pittman, Thane S. "Motivation." In *The Handbook of Social Psychology,* edited by Daniel T. Gilbert, Susan T. Fiske, and Gardner Linzey, 549–90. Boston: McGraw-Hill Companies, Inc., 1998.

Plato. *The Republic of Plato.* Translated by Allan Bloom. 2nd ed. New York: Basic Books, 1968.

Portes, Alejandro, and Rubén G. Rumbaut. *Legacies: The Story of the Immigrant Second Generation.* New York: Russell Sage Foundation, 2001.

Posner, Daniel N. *Institutions and Ethnic Politics in Africa.* Political Economy of Institutions and Decisions. New York: Cambridge University Press, 2005.

powell, john a. "Dreaming of a Self Beyond Whiteness and Isolation." *Journal of Law & Policy* 18, no. 13 (2005): 13–45.

Pratt, Minnie Bruce. "Foreword, Family Album." In *Love Makes a Family,* edited by Peggy Gillespie, ix-x. Amherst: University of Massachusetts Press, 1999.

———. "Identity: Blood Skin Heart." In *Yours in Struggle: Three Feminist Perspectives on Anti-Semitism and Racism,* edited by Elly Balkin, Minnie Bruce Pratt, and Barbara Smith, 9–63. Brooklyn: Long Haul Press, 1984.

———. *S/He.* Ithaca, N.Y.: Firebrand Books, 1995.

Putnam, Robert D. *Bowling Alone: The Collapse and Revival of American Community.* New York: Touchstone, 2000.

Public Agenda and the Tomás Rivera Policy Institute. *Here to Stay: The Priorities of Latino Leaders.* New York: Public Agenda, 1998.

Radden, Jennifer. *Divided Minds and Successive Selves: Ethical Issues in Disorders of Identity and Personality.* Cambridge, Mass.: MIT Press, 1996.

Renshon, Stanley A. "Dual Citizenship + Multiple Loyalties = One America?" In *One America?,* edited by Stanley A. Renshon, 232–82. Washington, D.C: Georgetown University Press, 2001.

Ricoeur, Paul. *Oneself as Another.* Translated by Kathleen Blamey. Chicago: University of Chicago Press, 1992.

Rivera, Margo. "Linking the Psychological and the Social: Feminism, Poststructuralism, and Multiple Personality." *Dissociation* 2, no. 1 (1989): 24–31.

Robinson, W. Peter, ed. *Social Groups and Identities: Developing the Legacy of Henri Tajfel.* Boston: Butterworth/Heinemann, 1996.

Rogler, Lloyd H., Dharma E. Cortes, and Robert G. Malgady. "Acculturation and Mental Health Status among Hispanics: Convergence and New Directions for Research." *American Psychologist* 46, no. 6 (1991).

Romero, Mary. "Life as the Maid's Daughter: An Exploration of the Everyday Boundaries of Race, Class, and Gender." In *Challenging Fronteras: Structuring Latina and Latino Lives in the U.S.,* edited by Mary Romero, Pierrette Hondagneu-Sotelo, and Vilma Ortiz, 195–209. New York: Routledge, 1997.

Root, Maria P. P. *Racially Mixed People in America.* Newbury Park: Sage Publications, 1992.

Rorty, Amélie Oksenberg, ed. *The Identities of Persons.* Berkeley: University of California Press, 1976.

———. "Self-Deception, *Akrasia* and Irrationality." In *The Multiple Self,* edited by Jon Elster, 115–31. New York: Cambridge University Press, 1986.

Rosaldo, Renato. *Culture and Truth: The Remaking of Social Analysis.* Boston: Beacon Press, 1989.

Rosales, Rodolfo. *The Illusion of Inclusion: The Untold Political Story of San Antonio.* Austin: University of Texas Press, 2000.

Rudacille, Deborah. *The Riddle of Gender: Science, Activism, and Transgender Rights.* New York: Anchor Books, 2006.

Ruiz, Vicki L. *From Out the Shadows: Mexican Women in Twentieth-Century America.* New York: Oxford University Press, 1998.

Ryan, Richard M. "Psychological Needs and the Facilitation of Integrative Processes." *Journal of Personality* 63, no. 3 (1995): 396–427.

Sandel, Michael. *Liberalism and the Limits of Justice.* Cambridge and London: Cambridge University Press, 1982.

Sandoval, Chela. "Mestizaje as Method: Feminists-of-Color Challenge the Canon." In *Living Chicana Theory,* edited by Carla Trujillo, 352–70. Berkeley, Cal.: Third Woman Press, 1998.

Sassen, Saskia. "Foreword." In *Latino Metropolis,* edited by Rodolfo Torres and Victor Valle, *ix–xiii.* Minneapolis: University of Minnesota Press, 2000.

Schacter, Daniel L. *Searching for Memory: The Brain, the Mind and the Past.* New York: Basic Books, 1996.

Schlosser, Eric. *Fast Food Nation: The Dark Side of the All-American Meal.* 1st ed. New York: Perennial, 2002.

Schmidt, Ronald. *Language Policy and Identity Politics in the United States.* Philadelphia: Temple University Press, 2000.

Schuck, Peter H. "Plural Citizenships." In *Dual Nationality, Social Rights and Federal Citizenship in the U.S. and Europe,* edited by Randall Hansen and Patrick Weil, 61–99. New York: Berghahn Books, 2002.

Searle, John R. *The Rediscovery of the Mind.* Cambridge, Mass.: MIT Press, 1992.

Sen, Amartya. *Identity and Violence: The Illusion of Destiny.* Issues of Our Time. New York: W. W. Norton & Company, 2006.

Sen, Rinku. "The New Culture War." *Applied Research Center.* http://www.arc .org/content/view/469 (accessed February 3, 2008).

Shaw, Randy. *Reclaiming America: Nike, Clean Air, and the New National Activism.* Berkeley: University of California Press, 1999.

Simon, Stephanie. "Latinos Take Root in Midwest" *Los Angeles Times,* October 24 2002, A1, A22.

Singer, Jefferson A. "Seeing One's Self: Locating Narrative Memory in a Framework of Personality." *Journal of Personality* 63, no. 3 (1995): 429–57.

Singer, Jefferson A., and Peter Salovey. *The Remembered Self: Emotion and Memory in Personality.* New York: The Free Press, 1993.

Smith, Paul. *Discerning the Subject.* Vol. 55, *Theory and History of Literature.* Minneapolis: University of Minnesota Press, 1988.

Sosa, Lionel. *The Americano Dream: How Latinos Can Achieve Success in Business and in Life.* New York: Dutton Books, 1998.

Spickard, Paul R. *Mixed Blood: Intermarriage and Ethnic Identity in Twentieth-Century America.* Madison: University of Wisconsin Press, 1989.

Suarez, Shirley A., Blaine J. Fowers, Carolyn S. Garwood, and Jose Szapocznik. "Biculturalism, Differentness, Loneliness, and Alienation in Hispanic College Students." *Hispanic Journal of Behavioral Sciences* 19, no. 4 (1997): 489–505.

Stonequist, Everett V. "The Problem of the Marginal Man." *The American Journal of Sociology* 41, no. 1 (1935): 1–12.

Strong, Tracy B. "Introduction: The Self and the Political Order." In *The Self and the Political Order,* edited by Tracy B. Strong, 1–21. Cambridge, Mass.: Blackwell, 1992.

Szapocznik, José, Arturo Rio, Angel Perez-Vidal, William Kurtines, Olga Hervis, and David Santisteban. "Bicultural Effectiveness Training (BET): An Experimental Test of an Intervention Modality for Families Experiencng Intergenerational/Intercultural Conflict." *Hispanic Journal of Behavioral Sciences* 8, no. 4 (1986): 303–30.

Tafoya, Sonya. *Shades of Belonging.* Washington, D.C.: Pew Hispanic Center, 2004.

Tajfel, Henri. *Human Groups and Social Categories.* New York: Cambridge University Press, 1981.

Takaki, Ronald. *A Different Mirror: A History of Multicultural America.* New York: Little, Brown, & Company, 1993.

Task Force on the DSM-IV. *Diagnostic and Statistical Manual of Mental Disorders.* 4th ed. Washington, D.C: American Psychiatric Association, 1994.

Taylor, Charles. *The Ethics of Authenticity.* Cambridge, Mass.: Harvard University Press, 1991.

———. *Multiculturalism and the Politics of Recognition.* Princeton, N.J.: Princeton University Press, 1992.

———. *Sources of the Self: The Making of the Modern Identity.* Cambridge, Mass.: Harvard University Press, 1989.

Thornton, Robert. "The Potentials of Boundaries in South Africa: Steps toward a Theory of the Social Edge." In *Postcolonial Identities in Africa,* edited by Richard Werbner and Terence Ranger, 136–61. London: Zed Books, 1996.

Torres, María de los Angeles. *In the Land of Mirrors: Cuban Exile Politics in the United States.* Ann Arbor: University of Michigan Press, 1999.

Tuan, Mia. *Forever Foreigners or Honorary Whites?: The Asian Ethnic Experience Today.* New Brunswick, N.J.: Rutgers, 1998.

Turner, John C. "Some Current Issues in Research on Social Identity and Self-Categorization Theories." In *Social Identity,* edited by Naomi Ellemers, Russell Spears, and Bertjan Doosje, 6–34. New York: Blackwell, 1999.

———. "Towards a Cognitive Redefinition of the Social Group." In *Social Identity and Intergroup Relations,* edited by Henri Tajfel, 15–40. New York: Cambridge University Press, 1982.

Turner, John C., Michael A. Hogg, Penelope J. Oakes, Stephen D. Reicher, and Margaret S. Wetherell. *Rediscovering the Social Group: A Self-Categorization Theory.* New York: Basil Blackwell, 1987.

Turner, John C., and Penelope Oakes. "The Socially Structured Mind." In *The Message of Social Psychology: Perspectives on Mind in Society,* edited by Craig McGarty and S. Alexander Haslam, 355–73. Cambridge: Blackwell, 1997.

Valdés, Dionicio Nodín. *Barrios Norteños: St. Paul and Midwestern Mexican Communities in the Twentieth Century.* Austin: University of Texas Press, 2000.

Valenzuela, Angela. *Subtractive Schooling: U.S.-Mexican Youth and the Politics of Caring.* Albany: State University of New York Press, 1999.

van der Hart, Onno, Bessel van der Kolk, and Suzette Boon. "Treatment of Dissociative Disorders." In *Trauma, Memory, and Dissociation,* edited by Douglas J. Bremner and Charles R. Marmar, 253–83. Washington, D.C: American Psychiatric Press, Inc., 1998.

Van Hear, Nicholas. *New Diasporas: The Mass Exodus, Dispersal and Regrouping of Migrant Communities.* Seattle: University of Washington Press, 1998.

Vasconcelos, José. *La Raza Cósmica/The Cosmic Race: A Bilingual Edition.* Translated by Didier T. Jaén. London: The Johns Hopkins University Press, 1979.

Vélez-Ibáñez, Carlos G., and Anna Sampiao, eds. *Transnational Latina/o Communities: Politics, Processes, and Cultures.* Latin America Perspectives in the Classroom. Lanham: Rowman & Littlefield, 2002.

Vertovec, Steven, ed. *Migration and Social Cohesion.* Northampton, Mass.: Edward Elgar Publishing, 1999.

Waites, Elizabeth A. *Trauma and Survival: Post-Traumatic and Dissociative Disorders in Women.* New York: W. W. Norton & Company, 1993.

Walker, Rebecca. *Black, White, and Jewish: Autobiography of a Shifting Self.* New York: Riverhead Books, 2001.

Waters, Mary C. *Black Identities: West Indian Immigrant Dreams and American Realities*. New York: Russell Sage Foundation, 1999.

Weber, Max. *Economy and Society,* Vol. 1. Los Angeles: University of California Press, 1978.

Wegner, Daniel M., and John A. Bargh. "Control and Automaticity in Social Life." In *The Handbook of Social Psychology,* edited by Daniel T. Gilbert, Susan T. Fiske, and Gardner Lindzey, 446–96. Boston: McGraw-Hill Company, Inc., 1998.

White, Stephen L. *The Unity of the Self.* Cambridge, Mass.: MIT Press, 1991.

Whitebook, Joel. "Fantasy and Critique: Some Thoughts on Freud and the Frankfurt School." In *The Handbook of Critical Theory,* edited by David M. Rassmussen, 287–304. Cambridge, Mass.: Blackwell Publishers, 1996.

———. *Perversion and Utopia a Study in Psychoanalysis and Critical Theory.* Cambridge, Mass.: MIT Press, 1995.

———. "Reflections on the Autonomous Individual and the Decentered Subject." *American Imago* 49, no. 1 (1992): 97–116.

Williams, Bernard. *Problems of the Self.* Cambridge: Cambridge University Press, 1973.

Wittgenstein, Ludwig, and G. E. M. Anscombe. *Philosophical Investigations: The German Text, with a Revised English Translation*. 3rd ed. Malden: Blackwell, 2001.

Wolfe, Alan. "On Loyalty." *Wilson Quarterly: Survey of the World of Ideas,* Autumn (1997): 46–56.

Yeskel, Felice. "Caught Between Two Cultures." *Journal of Women and Religion* 12, Winter (1993): 16–19.

Zavella, Patricia. "Reflections on Diversity among Chicanas." In *Challenging Frontera: Structuring Latina and Latino Lives in the U.S.,* edited by Mary Romero, Pierrette Hondagneu-Sotelo, and Vilma Ortiz. New York: Routledge, 1997.

Zengerle, Jason. "The Naked Guy." *The New York Times Magazine,* Dec. 31 2006, 57–58.

Index

The letter *f* following a page number denotes a figure.

ISBN-13: 978-1-60344-069-1
ISBN-10: 1-60344-069-0

53500

9 781603 440691